GENDERED FORTUNES

GENDERED FORTUNES

DIVINATION, PRECARITY, AND AFFECT

IN POSTSECULAR TURKEY

Zeynep K. Korkman

Duke University Press   *Durham and London*   2023

© 2023 Duke University Press
This work is licensed under a Creative Commons Attribution-
NonCommercial 4.0 International License, available at
https://creativecommons.org/licenses/by-nc/4.0/.
Project editor: Bird Williams
Typeset in Garamond Premier Pro and Knockout
by Westchester Publishing Services

Library of Congress Cataloging-in-Publication Data
Names: Korkman, Zeynep K., [date] author.
Title: Gendered fortunes : divination, precarity, and affect in
postsecular Turkey / Zeynep K. Korkman.
Description: Durham : Duke University Press, 2023. | Includes
bibliographical references and index.
Identifiers: LCCN 2022040017 (print)
LCCN 2022040018 (ebook)
ISBN 9781478019541 (paperback)
ISBN 9781478016908 (hardcover)
ISBN 9781478024163 (ebook)
ISBN 9781478093558 (ebook other)
Subjects: LCSH: Muslim women—Turkey—Social conditions—
21st century. | Sexual minorities—Turkey—Social conditions— 21st
century. | Fortune-tellers—Social conditions—21st century. |
Fortune-telling—Economic aspects—Turkey. | Postsecularism—
Turkey. | Islam and social problems—Turkey. | BISAC: SOCIAL
SCIENCE / Gender Studies | SOCIAL SCIENCE / Anthropology /
Cultural & Social
Classification: LCC HQ1726.7 .K67 2023 (print) |
LCC HQ1726.7 (ebook)
DDC 305.48/6970905—dc23/eng/20221107
LC record available at https://lccn.loc.gov/2022040017
LC ebook record available at https://lccn.loc.gov/2022040018

OA ISBN 9781478093558

Cover art: Hayal Pozanti, *Swinging and Rippling* (1916—MULNA),
2021. Oil and oil stick on linen. 40 × 30 inches / 101.6 × 76.2 cm.
Courtesy of the artist and Jessica Silverman, San Francisco.

This book is freely available in an open access edition thanks to
TOME (Toward an Open Monograph Ecosystem)—a collaboration
of the Association of American Universities, the Association
of Uni-versity Presses, and the Association of Research Libraries—
and the generous support of Arcadia, a charitable fund of Lisbet
Rausing and Peter Baldwin, and the UCLA Library. Learn more at
the TOME website, available at: openmonographs.org.

TO MY MOTHER,
FATMA MEFKURE BUDAK

Contents

PART III.
FEELING LABOR, PRECARITY,
AND ENTREPRENEURIALISM

Acknowledgments

I am deeply grateful to the people who generously allowed me into their lives throughout this research. I hope that this work reflects my appreciation of them and their work.

As a first book, this work owes much to the substantial investment and engagement of a number of people who nourished me over the past few decades at various academic institutions. I get to thank some of them here. I developed an early taste for research and gendered analysis as an undergraduate and later as an MA student in the Department of Sociology at Bosphorus University in Istanbul, Turkey. For this, I am particularly grateful to the late Dicle Koğacıoğlu, as well as to Nükhet Sirman, Belgin Tekçe, and Nazan Üstündağ. Many thanks to Berk Balçık, Özgür Ergüney, and Elif Özkılıç for having given me the gift of friendships that last.

This project was conceived while I was a PhD student in the Department of Sociology at the University of California, Santa Barbara. I am grateful to my chair, John Cruz, for mentoring me with a trusting wisdom, and to my PhD committee members John Foran and Denise Segura for supporting this project. Thanks especially to Jennifer Rogers Brown, Krista Bywater, Debra Guckenheimer, Tonya Lindsey, and Amandeep Sandhu for companionship through the highs and lows of life lived running toward a PhD. Outside the department, I thank Grace Chang for having introduced me to academic feminism in the classroom. I was fortunate to have been in close proximity to the Department of Anthropology at the University of Texas at Austin, my second home during my PhD work, together with Ufuk Soyöz, Ruken Şengül, Hişyar Özsoy, and Halide Velioğlu.

At the College of William and Mary, I am thankful to Jennifer Bickham Mendez, Sibel Zandi Sayek, and especially Gül Özyeğin, whose generous engagement and mentoring have been ongoing. At the University of Arizona, I am especially grateful to Sapana Doshi, Erin Durban, Adam Geary, Miranda Joseph, Emrah Karakuş, Jamie Lee, Adela Licona, Eithne Luibhéid, Patricia MacCorquodale, Tracey Osbourne, Özlem Ayşe Özgür, Tatiana Rabinovich, Brian Silverstein, and Susan Stryker for remaining interlocutors and friends after my departure.

I am grateful to all the brilliant students, faculty, and staff in the Department of Gender Studies at the University of California, Los Angeles, for their ongoing support in all aspects of academic life, including this book project. I am especially grateful to Grace Chang, Aisha Finch, Joshua Guzman, Ju Hui Judy Han, Beth Marchant, and Juliet Williams. Special thanks to Sherene Razack for close mentoring and enlivening collaboration. Outside the department, my thanks go out to Hannah Appel, Aslı Bali, Melissa Bilal, Aomar Boum, Philippe Bourgois, Genevieve Carpio, Sondra Hale, Laurie Hart, Jocelyn Ho, Purnima Mankekar, Norma Mendoza-Denton, Ruken Şengül, Michael Rothberg, Abigail Saguy, Umut Yıldırım, and Yasemin Yıldız for collegiality, mentoring, friendship, and comradeship.

I am grateful to all the many folk who listened and responded generously as I circulated this work in various venues over the past fifteen years. Special thanks to Zeynep Gürsel for the invitation to accompany the screenings of her smart documentary, *Coffee Fortunes*, with my work on several occasions. I am thankful to Laura Briggs, Mounira Maya Charrad, Ann Cvetkovich, Lizel Hint, Minoo Moallem, Sandy Soto, Kathleen Weston, and Jenny White for providing feedback on presentations from this work at various conferences and workshops. I am also grateful to Kaya Şahin for his valuable suggestions on one of the chapters of this book. Thanks to the members of the Reproductive Health Working Group, and the Religion, Secularism, and Political Belonging Research Group. Special thanks to the members of the Rethinking Transnational Feminisms Group, including Maylei Blackwell, Rachel Fabian, Monisha Das Gupta, Grace Hong, Rana Jaleel, Karen Leong, Jessica Millward, and Judy Wu, who read several chapter drafts and offered direction and encouragement.

At Duke University Press, many thanks go to Elizabeth Ault for seeing this project through and to my reviewers Attiya Ahmad and Banu Gökarıksel, who helped the book to become a better version of itself. Special thanks to Theresa Truax-Gischler for helping me fine-tune my authorial voice and develop the book's arc.

I am grateful for the support awarded to this project by numerous fellowships, including the American Association of University Women's Postdoctoral Research Leave Fellowship, the Hellman Fellows Award at UCLA, the Faculty Career Development Award from the Office of Equity, Diversity, and Inclusion at UCLA, a research fellowship from the National Endowment for the Humanities and the American Research Institute in Turkey, and a research professorship from the Social and Behavioral Sciences Research Institute at the University of Arizona.

Heartfelt thanks to my family for their unwavering love and support. Thanks to my aunt Emel Budak and my uncle Ulvi Budak, and to my late grandparents Ferit and Vacide Budak, for being there for me through thick and thin. Thanks to Ayla Ant for becoming family. Thanks to my cousin-cum-sister Güneş Cansız for enthusiastically sharing the joys and ordeals of femininity, popular culture, and more.

My deepest thanks go to Salih Can Açıksöz, my love, my fire, my rock. Not only did you dedicate countless hours of listening, talking, thinking, reading, writing, editing, cooking, cleaning, coaching, and parenting to make this book possible. It is in your mirror that I found the courage to write it. Mavi Açıksöz-Korkman, my son, my ocean, my sky. I am so thankful that you have arrived. It is in your invitation to be present and playful that I have found the will to let go of this book. Finally, Fatma Mefkure Budak, my mother, my anchor, my wind. Your courageous love and feminist wisdom sustain and inspire me. I dedicate this book to you.

Introduction
GENDERED FORTUNES

"You'll achieve your goals in two years' time. It's incredible." I listen intently to my fortune being read by an articulate middle-aged woman whom I have met only moments ago but who now engages me in a private conversation about all the hopes and disappointments of love, marriage, parenthood, work, family, and health that can make or break the gendered promises of life.

> Are you married yet? Well, I do see a boy. Do you have a son? You will have a son. Your partner, is he a Capricorn or a Virgo? Okay, a Virgo. I did sense an earth sign. Well, I see he's troubled. Why is that? He's a fighter and puts a lot of effort into his work, but his love for you is pure, I can see that. He's a sensitive person and can sometimes become rather pessimistic. He's also fond of his freedom, almost like a child. I do see a balanced relationship with mutual understanding, like soul mates. Are you in the same industry? Is he abroad? Well, I ask because I see that you'll be traveling soon. And who is this older woman with health issues? Your mother or your mother-in-law?

She is interpreting the shapes the coffee grounds have dried into inside my recently consumed cup of Turkish coffee to divine my past, my present, and, importantly, my future. Giving voice to the many worries and hopes she feels I must be quietly harboring as a newly married, secular middle-class woman, the coffee cup reader is still talking energetically, adding a few more comments on health and family. As I observe her blow-dried hair starting to frizz and her makeup beginning to run in the beads of sweat on her face, I imagine the long workday ahead of her on this already hot and humid summer morning in a downtown Istanbul café. She is preparing to end our session, making a final inquiry to see if I have any last lingering questions. She needs to move the queue along, I suppose.

I return to my seat in the next room of the café, surrounded by less than a dozen women. Most have arrived in small groups; only a few are sitting alone. Some are waiting for their turn for a reading; others stay to think or commune after their session. There is only one young man, seated with a woman. I wonder if he will be getting a reading, too. In the air, the quiet pace of the ordinary mingles with a sense of anticipation that is at once evoked and eased by the intimacy of this feminized community gathered around divination. We are, after all, in no ordinary café. This is a fortune-telling café (*falkafe*), one among hundreds of similar establishments that have since the turn of the twenty-first century become a regular feature of secular middle-class neighborhoods in Turkey.

THIS BOOK APPROACHES the proliferating fortune-telling economy of millennial Turkey as an affective window onto the gendered contradictions of (post) secularism, Islamist authoritarianism, and neoliberalism. It demonstrates how secular Muslim women and lesbian, gay, bisexual, transgender, intersex, and queer (LGBTIQ) individuals navigate the anxieties of the postsecular condition, the vulnerabilities of gendered marginalization, and the precarities of neoliberalization through the medium of divination in twenty-first-century Turkey. As such, the book forwards attention to feeling as a way into the disregarded realms of the minoritized, both as a feminist analytics and as a methodological strategy for bringing into relief how gender and sexual minorities traverse broader social formations.

Criminalized by the early twentieth-century laws of an ambitious secularist state and disdained by the reinvented religious puritanism of today's Turkish Islamist government, commercial fortune-telling has, despite these obstacles, boomed in millennial Turkey. This postsecular divination economy provides its largely secular Muslim, cisgender, heterosexual women participants, as well as its LGBTIQ participants, with an opportunity to make a living amid precarious labor conditions intensified by neoliberalization. In this context, fortune-telling provides its practitioners with a form of affective labor through which gender and sexual minorities attune to their gendered vulnerabilities and to each other. Fortune-tellers are lay sociologists, so to speak, who have a feel for social types marked by habitual tones of voice, gesture, clothing, and body language, as well as common life experiences, aspirations, and frustrations. Well attuned to the intimately harbored yet collectively formed wishes and worries of diverse classes of strangers, fortune-tellers successfully ventriloquize the gendered desires and troubles of their clients. It is in this way that fortune-tellers' labors of divination conjure up safer publics in which to articulate gendered hopes and fears that are otherwise disciplined in a larger public sphere dominated by a religiously inflected gender conservatism that aggressively pushes back against a vibrant feminist and queer movement. In a transnational milieu where women (imagined as pious) and LGBTIQ people of the Muslim Middle East have been the favorite subjects of Islamophobic discourses that dress themselves up in the guise of a (colonial, pseudofeminist) concern to "save" them, this book shines a spotlight on how secular women and non-heteronormative men acclimate to and survive a global tide of religiously accented gender conservatism, secular hegemonic decline, political authoritarianism, and economic neoliberalism through gendered practices of divination.

Drawing on extended ethnographic research in the flourishing niche of commodified divination in Istanbul, this study asks how and why women and LGBTIQ minorities who identify as secular Muslims seek their gendered fortunes in divination. The key setting is fortune-telling cafés, innovative business arrangements where readings are provided as a free or promotional service upon the purchase of an overpriced beverage in order to sidestep a ban on the sale of divination services. Given the practicalities of attaching a reading to the sale of a legally permissible commodity, reading coffee grounds for divination (*kahve falı*) is the most convenient form of fortune-telling provided here. Soon after the opening in 2001 of the very first fortune-telling café in Beyoğlu, Istanbul, other cafés began mushrooming; first in the same street, but very soon throughout the neighborhood, the city, and eventually across the entire country. Over the next two decades, this divination economy would expand to include a variety of fortune-telling and supplementary services (Reiki, lead-pouring sessions, life coaching, and others) and a range of locations (fortune-telling houses, cafés, offices, and online platforms). Today the Turkey-based divination economy is increasingly globalized and digitalized, recruiting tourists from the Arab Gulf who get readings at stylish cafés, Syrian refugees and returned migrant workers who translate for them, labor migrants from post-Soviet republics who read fortunes in their native languages, and, the most significant development, a plethora of online fortune-tellers and clients from around the globe who meet in a flourishing sector of digital divination platforms.

Thanks to an early twentieth-century law passed in the service of an ambitious secularist project, commercial fortune-telling is a criminal offense in Turkey. In the early period of the Turkish Republic, fortune-tellers, along with a host of other religious and divination practitioners, from the heads of religious orders to amulet writers, were judged too traditional, too religious, and too irrational to

FIGURE I.I. Customers waiting for a reading at Angels Café (Melekler Kahvesi), the first fortune-telling café in Turkey.

suit the secular Western modernity the country aspired to. Externalized from the new Turkish nation-in-the-making as the products of an Arabic influence that had been corrupting Turkish culture for centuries, fortune-tellers and other practitioners associated with religious orders were banned beginning in 1925, first in Turkey's Kurdish region and later throughout the country. They were otherized in accordance with ethnoracial hierarchies; refracted through the prism of civilizational differences that in the Turkish case were articulated as a doubled Western/Eastern and secular/religious axis. Through criminalization, they were pushed out of a public sphere now reorganized according to the imperatives of Turkish nationalist secularism.[1]

After the ban, fortune-telling was funneled through the gendered politics of secularism and religion into a criminalized underground economy of male practitioners and a tolerated domestic economy of housewives. Peopled mostly by male hodjas, this underground economy circulated divining and healing modalities that drew liberally upon Islamic imagery and symbolism, such as praying and the conjuring of jinn. These hodjas were painted in the popular secularist literature and media as ignorant, malicious, and perverted men who sexually and financially took advantage of susceptible women. A mirror to their vice, their female victims were depicted as in need of rescue by heroic secular men, often a policeman or a journalist who would ceremonially un-mask the hodja as a charlatan in a news story, novel, film, or, later, a televised show. These narratives reasserted the secularist project and a secular mascu-line subject. In contrast, women engaging in popular practices such as reading coffee grounds or wearing evil eye charms were perceived as practicing little more than mundane elements of heteronormative domesticity. Unlike hodjas, superstitious housewives were insignificant, not threatening enough to require intervention yet different enough to mark ordinary men as secular and ratio-nal by comparison. While hodjas' divinations and cures became the persistent subject of scandal and criminalization, parallel feminized practices were de-meaned, disregarded, and ultimately tolerated as a marker of feminine irratio-nality.[2] The continued presence of superstitious housewives and the incessant persecution of hodjas served to demarcate (urban, educated, and ethnoracially Turkish) masculinity as secular, with irrational femininity and overreligious masculinity set as its others.

Today, fortune-telling is still looked down upon within Turkey's dominant discourses: within secularist critique; within the body of knowledge pro-duced by the Turkish Republic's official religious institution, the Diyanet İşleri Başkanlığı (Presidency of Religious Affairs, hereafter Diyanet); and within the reinvented religious puritanism of contemporary Islamism. In all these discourses, fortune-telling figures as a superstition incompatible with being a secular citizen and/or a proper Muslim. Yet this is not to say that the Turkish politics of secularism and Islam has stood still. Indeed, it has shifted signifi-cantly in the many decades since the early twentieth-century criminalization of fortune-tellers, posing here in the twenty-first century a postsecular condition wherein secularism has proven institutionally and ideologically durable but no longer hegemonic, given Islamism's increasingly authoritative dominance. In an irony of history, the secular and even secularist citizens of Turkey flock in the early 2000s to fortune-telling cafés to find relief whenever their personal fortunes seem limited by, among other things, the waning prospects of the very secularist political project that criminalized fortune-tellers in the first place.[3] In this context, more and more working- and middle-class women and a minority of young and gay men are drawn into the postsecular economy of divination, only to insistently claim secular Muslim identities, not despite but through their engagement with fortune-telling.[4] Fortune-tellers take advantage of the gendered line separating tolerable from intolerable divination practices and concentrate their services around the feminized practice of coffee divination. This focus on feminized divination forms highlights the centrality of gendered logics to the politics of secularism and in the negotiation of the increasingly volatile distinctions between the secular and the religious in contemporary Turkey.

Informed by the gendered contradictions of secularism and religion, coffee fortune-telling emerges as the most popular form of fortune-telling in Turkey's millennial divination economy. Coffee fortune-telling refers to the reading of residues left at the bottom of a ground-rich cup of Turkish coffee. After the coffee is served and consumed, the drinker places the saucer on top of the coffee cup, thereby closing (*kapatmak*) the cup in the lingo of divination, shakes the cup and saucer together, and turns the whole thing upside down in one quick motion. This allows the coffee grounds that have sunk to the bottom to stick to and dry on the cup's inner surfaces, while the remaining liquid drips into the saucer. When the cup has cooled, the grounds can be safely assumed to have dried into idiosyncratic shapes for interpretation. The cup is then "opened" (*açmak*) and turned upright, providing an inside view of the intimate fortunes of the person who has just drunk the coffee. The residues are read so as to offer comments about the recipient's mood and character and about the past, present, and future, including matters of the heart, family, health, education, work, and money.

Coffee readings foretell gendered fortunes, providing an affective genre of femininity through which those disadvantaged in the heteropatriarchal hierarchies of age, gender, and sexuality attune to their intimate feelings. As coffee cups are filled with boyfriends who have not called but are still thinking of their partners, husbands who have been distracted by their deteriorating businesses or by other women only to return to the embrace of their wives with improved prospects, and pregnancies long awaited and soon to happen, coffee fortune-telling predominantly tracks women's tenacious yearnings as cultivated within the heteroromantic fantasy. But if, as evidenced by the almost universal inclusion of predictions about marriage and parenthood, divinations routinely place the recipient in normative scenarios prescribed by heteropatriarchal imperatives, they also regularly address the fragilities and distresses of

FIGURE 1.2. Stenciled ads for the online divination website Binnaz Abla on an apartment building wall in Moda, Kadıköy district, a few blocks away from the many fortune-telling cafés populating the neighborhood: "It is true my child, if Binnaz says so" and "Binnaz Abla: Real Fortune-Tellers." Binnaz Abla's ads blend in with political stenciling and graffiti urging the public to get out the vote in the coming 2019 Istanbul municipal election for a secularist mayor after over two decades of Islamist party municipal rule, which began with the 1994 mayoral election of Turkey's current president, Recep Tayyip Erdoğan.

such gender conformity—as well as the diversions and departures from it. Lesbian women, gay men, and, less often, transgender women taking part in divination as readers and clients often make room for the non-heteronormative desires that have limited visibility in the larger public sphere. Whether they avoid naming the gender of a prospective suitor, point to a tarot card with the client's own sex category as a potential love interest, or more explicitly acknowledge the gender-nonconforming feelings of their clients, divinations provide ways to chart both heteronormative and queer desires through veiled metaphors, generic truisms, and clichéd but alluring scenarios. Fortune-telling sessions traverse competing scripts of femininity (and to a lesser extent, of masculinity) as fortune-tellers invite clients into gender normativity and track its escape routes.

Providing a genre in which to process the feelings of precariousness that attend the gendered vulnerabilities of the feminized, coffee reading has long served as an everyday mode of care.[5] Cup readers describe divination as a way of "spending good time with" (*güzel vakit geçirmek*) someone as well as "relaxing" (*rahatlatmak*), "entertaining" (*eğlendirmek*), "improving the morale" (*moral vermek*), and "pleasing the heart" (*gönlünü yapmak*).[6] Echoing the readers, recipients explain that they value the chance to share their troubles and to be comforted in the gendered intimacy of fortune-telling. In the domestic economy of feminized divination, this specific form of caring is provided overwhelmingly by women for women as they read each other's fortunes in family gatherings, neighborhood visits, and friendly get-togethers. This domestic and neighborhood practice has now been thoroughly commercialized in a new divination economy of cafés, businesses, and even online platforms, where the readings are displaced from embedded social relations and locations.

The commercialization of coffee cup readings allows urban poor women and young and gay men to make a living amid a labor precarity that has been intensified and generalized to include secular working and middle classes under neoliberalization executed by an Islamist government in the twenty-first century.[7] Channeled into an informal economy of fortune-telling where high unemployment and informal and insecure work are normalized for youth and women, readers are rendered precarious workers via a threefold process: a secularist ban criminalizing divination; an Islamist stigmatization of unorthodox religious practices; and a neoliberal restructuring of the Turkish economy. This new niche of fortune-telling draws mostly racially and ethnically unmarked workers, leaving Roma women, who have long read fortunes on the streets, excluded from the marketplace, only to have their names and clothing be stereotypically appropriated for online fortune-telling avatars. At divination cafés and online platforms, readers work flexible hours without any guarantee of income or job security as they perform the presumably unskilled and devalued work of fortune-telling.

The gendered practices of divination constitute a labor of "feeling" (*hisset-mek*), as readers describe it. Feeling the client and making the client feel depends on the conjuring of an enchanted intersubjective space in which the client can explore, experience, and engage with a range of affective intensities and emotions. This allows the client to affectively inhabit the gendered scenes of bliss and desolation fortune-tellers conjure and to explore, experience, and articulate their personal wishes and apprehensions in the idiom of divination. The feeling labors of divination thus provide a medium through which to process the affective demands of the compounded conditions of anxiety and precariousness secular Muslim women and LGBTIQ individuals must contend with, from the anxieties of an increasingly Islamist postsecular terrain, to the mundane and intersectional layers of gendered vulnerability, to the neoliberally exacerbated depths of labor precarity.[8]

Drawn more and more deeply into a therapeutically inflected neoliberal terrain, divinations join energy healings, evil eye treatments, and a host of therapeutic new age modalities designed to help their anxious secular Muslim subjects attune to precariousness and invest in themselves, thereby replenishing their capacities for (affective) labor. Fortune-telling here becomes a vehicle for a self-entrepreneurial mode of working and living, providing an alchemy that turns the struggle to survive labor precarity, gendered vulnerability, and postsecular uncertainty into a quest for personal meaning and a refueling of care and hope for workers and clients alike. A new generation of divination business owners and workers reframes fortune-telling as a spiritual venture in which economic and personal goals magically overlap, even touting it as an enchanted remedy for the wounds neoliberalism inflicts at both the individual and societal levels. Increasingly provided at online fortune-telling platforms that recruit workers and clients from around the world, the feeling labors of divination are transformed under the pressure of performance and pay scales derived from customer reviews, inciting readers to continuously self-monitor and self-improve and to direct their feeling labors toward themselves in order to manage the ensuing anxiety. In this context, self-entrepreneurship is deployed as an economic, moral, and affective response to precaritization under neoliberalism at the same time that it reproduces the precarity of the now digitalized and transnationalized work of fortune-telling.

While fortune-telling labors are devalued through precaritization, secular disavowal, Islamist condemnation, and feminization, only to be increasingly funneled toward capitalist circuits of value, their productivity and potentiality cannot be fully captured or accounted for by the economic, political, and gendered formations organizing them as a form of commodified labor. Feeling labors produce more than profits; they conjure the social. In the case of divination labors, they generate the social relations and spaces through which gender and sexual minorities craft lifeworlds that are shaped under but are irreducible to the logics of neoliberal capitalism, secularist and Islamist authoritarianisms, and heteropatriarchy.

The feeling labors of divination not only render labor precarity habitable, propelling neoliberal subjects, they also summon hospitable publics in which anxious secular Muslim gender and sexual minorities can feel intimate and comfortable in one another's presence under the shadow of a broader public sphere that is increasingly dominated by Islamist authoritarianism. Made up of a majority of women and a minority of young and gay men and exclusive of heterosexual adult men, divination publics are populated by those disadvantaged and feminized in heteropatriarchal relations of domination and subordination.[9] In these publics, secular Muslim gender and sexual minorities mobilize feeling labors as a way to articulate ordinary yet deeply felt gendered desires and anxieties like losing a romantic partner or finding a job.

In millennial Turkey, gendered norms and expectations have been thoroughly destabilized. In the first decade of the twenty-first century, an increasingly vibrant feminist and queer social movement presence was accompanied by a host of gender equality policies and discourses that were undertaken, if surprisingly, by none other than the Islamically accented Justice and Development Party (Adalet ve Kalkınma Partisi, hereafter AKP) government, which in the early 2000s challenged the formulaic equation of Islamism with gender conservatism and authoritarianism. But by the 2010s, the AKP government had stepped back from gender equality policies, launching violent attacks on the country's strong feminist and LGBTIQ movements and harnessing the power of the state apparatus alongside a growing network of progovernment NGOs to promote its reinvented "Turkish family values" (Kocamaner 2019; Korkman 2016; Mutluer 2019; Savcı 2020). Today, at the start of the third decade of the twenty-first century, the government still encourages youths to avoid flirting, marry early, have more children, avoid divorce, and closely follow the prescribed life script of a reinvented traditional family life. Such prescriptions are to little avail, however, as women (and men) become more and more likely to remain unmarried, get married later in life, get divorced (slightly) more often, and have fewer children (Engin, Hürman, and Harvey 2020). The neoliberal ideals of individual self-fashioning through choice in romantic love and sexual desire pull young men and women potently toward, as well as away from and beyond, such heteronormative scenarios of the good life (Özyeğin 2015). In this milieu, secular Muslim women and young and gay men have instead been divining their frustrated gendered aspirations in fortune-telling publics.

In conjuring the social, the feminized practices of divination disrupt the dominant conceptions of gendered space and sociability set by the fault lines of secularism and religion in Turkey. Historically, the Turkish secular public sphere was constructed by the production and display of mixed-gender socializing against a background where practices of gender segregation had come to stand for the harmful excesses of tradition and religion. At the same time, segregated spheres and intimacies continued to shape the social fabric, albeit with a self-conscious sense of their incompatibility with the femininities and masculinities prescribed by Turkish secularism. Indeed, the skirmishes between Islamism and secularism have been and are still played out most spiritedly around the issues of women's public presence and mixing with men. In this context, postsecular fortune-telling publics destabilize the given terms of the dually conceived formulas of gender and publicness: they are neither exactly gender-mixed, as proposed by secularist recipes, nor are they strictly gender-segregated, per reinvented religious precepts; rather, they remain tightly nestled in Islamicate notions of gendered intimacy (*mahremiyet*) and secularist notions of publicness (*kamusallık*) that are layered together to constitute the heteronormative order in the country.

Divination publics provide a novel sociospatial arrangement that combines the joys of feminized intimacy with the benefits of public anonymity. In commercial fortune-telling businesses, mostly women and some men exchange coffee readings in an intimate encounter among strangers who are partaking in a transient commercial transaction. This is a particularly valuable recipe for those whose personal lives are otherwise disciplined in the context of familial and communal relations, as well as in the larger public sphere, where the intimate is more thoroughly debated and prescribed than ever. Despite the growing impetus to subject the intimate to public discourse, for gender and sexual minorities, revelations of nonnormative intimate behaviors can be highly costly. Commercial readings are refreshingly unbound from the otherwise attendant social controls of familial and neighborly relations because of the anonymous and disembedded nature of social relations in the cafés and online platforms. They also exist at some distance from the pressures of the political public sphere. As such, they provide the feminized with a safer space in which to manage their intimate feelings. This is particularly significant in a context where gendered aspirations are simultaneously incited and marginalized by the neoliberal promises of abundance contradicted by ever-deepening precarity, the threat posed by an authoritarian Islamist government to individuals' enduring attachments to the gendered promises of secularism, the vocal choir of feminist and queer voices provoked and quelled by a religiously accented gender conservatism, and the eruption of juxtapolitical and counterpublics in proximity to a public sphere stifled by political authoritarianism.

The research set out in this book is situated against the backdrop of the downwardly mobile secular Turkish working and middle classes' tenacious hopes and persistent anxieties over their economic precaritization and cultural and political marginalization because of rapid economic restructuring and an increasingly religiously inflected and gender-conservative political and cultural landscape. Anxieties over ever more precarious futures are felt most acutely by youths and gender and sexual minorities, whose chances of economic mobility and personal autonomy are stifled in a country whose president chastises college students for feeling entitled to land a job upon graduation but urges citizens to marry early, have many children, and simply trust that God will bless and provide for them and their families if they are pious. The political uprisings of 2013 in Turkey to which feminist and queer movements centrally contributed their critiques of masculinist state power exercised through aggressively intimate controls over the lives of the feminized provided a highly visible but fleeting chance for these populations to voice their discontents and collectively reclaim their futures through an oppositional political language. But the political developments, especially of the late 2010s, including the crushing waves of state violence and mass persecution that followed the 2013 uprisings and the 2016 coup attempt, thoroughly suppressed dissident voices, the persistent resistance of feminist, queer, and other oppositional groups notwithstanding. In such a milieu, *Gendered Fortunes* attests to how those disempowered along the heteropatriarchal hierarchies of age, gender, and sexuality come together, outside the political spotlight and away from oppositional political languages, to express their anxieties about and hopes for their futures in the language of divination.

Taking as its object of inquiry a seemingly minor practice that is looked down upon as a feminine foible at best, this research asserts that feminized and marginalized ways of relating to the self, others, and the world provide an important window on understanding macrolevel social, economic, and political processes from the perspective of the minoritized. Indeed, it is through the feminization and devaluation of these individuals, feelings, spheres, and labors that these formations enact their power even as it is through the same disregarded affects, realms, and practices that gender and sexual minorities make sense of and

FIGURE I.3. Stenciling by the youth organization Öğrenci Faaliyeti on a wall in Moda, Kadıköy district, on a main street that houses fortune-telling cafés: "We can't make a living. We demand a future!" The slogan sits below another that reads, "Hope is everywhere," in support of secularist mayoral candidate Ekrem İmamoğlu in the 2019 municipal election in Istanbul. Someone casually scrawled "Burn, baby, burn" (*yan cehennem yan*) to index the affective tone of the political and economic issues the slogans addressed.

make their way through these formations. Despite and ironically through its energetic disavowal, fortune-telling remains central to the gendered politics of secularism and religion in that it has come to stand for a feminized irrationality and superstition that marks masculine secular reason and enlightened religion. Similarly, while they are criminalized and jettisoned outside the secular public sphere, divinatory practices also sustain the very femininities and intimacies that the secularist project and its heteronormative gender regime depend upon. Moreover, although thoroughly dismissed, devalued, and irregularized, divination also plays a central role as a feminized affective labor that reproduces the depleted precarious and anxious subjects of neoliberalism, guiding them in the business of reinventing their labor and their selves. Taking gendered practices of divination seriously therefore offers a feminist window not only on the affects and sociabilities that surface feminized subjects but also the gendered logics of neoliberalism, (post)secularism, and the public sphere under and in excess of which these practices and subjects emerge.

Focusing on gendered divinatory practices further poses an opportunity to reckon with feeling as a mode of relating to the self, others, and the world. Long held at a distance from the modernist secularist project as a way of knowing the world and displaced as irrationality onto gendered and racialized others, orienting toward feeling holds feminist methodological and epistemological potential. Inspired by my research participants' insistent descriptions of their divination process as "feeling" (*hissetmek*), this book takes up feeling as part of the academic and feminist endeavor. In this book, *feeling* narrowly refers to the subterranean deployment of divinatory practices as a way to register and navigate at the affective level otherwise distanced and occulted social processes.[10] As a broader analytic, feeling highlights a way to attune to macrolevel processes and formations in all their (in)tangibility as they are felt diffusely yet strongly in everyday life by gendered subjects. Feeling as a conceptual lens magnifies how ordinary people navigate terrains inflected by large-scale formations like neoliberalism, secularism, Islamism, and gender conservatism, feeling their way into, through, and away from them. Alongside the questions of how gendered precariousness, secular identities, and public spheres are shaped by accumulated and systemic influences, this book asks how it feels for women and LGBTIQ individuals to be secular Muslims navigating a postsecular condition, how it feels to find feminized intimacy in an increasingly stifled public, and how it feels to perform precarious labor under neoliberalism. Here, the emphasis on feeling, in particular on the structures of feeling that ethnographic and cultural inquiry track, enjoins the kind of holistic understandings that complement structural analysis.

The book is composed of three parts that together build toward the main substantive argument that gender and sexual minorities of millennial Turkey navigate their secular anxieties, gendered vulnerabilities, and economic precarities through divination. The analyses in these parts forward the book's theoretical and methodological arguments that the otherwise elided and trivialized because feminized individuals, feelings, spheres, and labors are central to the many heteronormative formations and transformations of secularism, the public sphere, and the capitalist economy and that a focus on affect renders that centrality visible. In part I, "The Religious, the Superstitious, and the Postsecular," chapter 1 situates divination in a historical context and tracks its consignment during the making of the Turkish secular to the sphere of superstition, highlighting how the disavowal of superstition in the figure of fortune-tellers was vital to the making of the secular. Chapter 2 places secular Muslim fortune-tellers in an ethnographic present animated by the ongoing negotiations of the gendered dynamics of Turkish secularism to illustrate how heteropatriarchal secularist economies of desire and contempt fix femininity to irrationality. Chapter 3 characterizes the emergent postsecular condition in which secular Muslims paradoxically negotiate their persistent attachments to secularism through their engagements with divination. In part II, "Femininity, Intimacy, and Publics," chapter 4 situates divination publics in the context of the historical emergence and gendered transformations of the public sphere to demonstrate how a novel, sociospatial, intimate public is conjured in fortune-telling cafés through the negotiation of Islamicate logics of intimacy, secularist logics of publicness, and neoliberal incitements to public intimacy. Chapter 5 argues that contemporary divination businesses broker a new type of public intimacy that is distinguished by anonymity and relative safety in the context of an increasingly intimate public sphere that proves risky for the feminized. In part III, "Feeling Labor, Precarity, and Entrepreneurialism," chapter 6 analyzes the affectivity and commodification of feminized labors of divination and details how feeling labors help secular Muslim readers and their clients manage the compounded gendered anxieties, vulnerabilities, and precariousness of the present historical juncture, albeit at the expense of precarious divination workers. Chapter 7 examines the newly digitalized and transnational incarnations of feeling labors as they are reconceived as a spiritual/economic self-entrepreneurial endeavor for healing the impossibility of postsecular neoliberal selfhood. These three parts build upon each other to reveal how the minoritized practices and feelings produced through feminized divination are key to the coconstitution of a heteronormative gender order in which secularity is premised upon a disavowal of feminine irrationality, the public sphere is built upon the dismissal of the sociabilities of women and LGBTIQ peoples, and neoliberal capitalism depends upon the devaluing of feminized labor.

Mixed Feelings

I came into this research with mixed feelings. I first visited a fortune-telling café in 2002, on my way back from taking the Graduate Record Exam in support of my application to doctoral programs in the United States. After the test, all I could do was wait to hear back, my future prospects now bound to tests, forms, letters, and a host of unknown dynamics outside my knowledge or control. Standing still on the threshold of what might or might not turn out to be a great change in my life, I was filled with anticipation and a mix of joyous expectation and fear of both outcomes. The testing office was on Nişantaşı Avenue of Istanbul, host to upscale boutiques, stores, restaurants, and cafés. As I walked away from the testing station, I noticed a café advertising free cup readings with the purchase of Turkish coffee and free tarot readings with the purchase of a cappuccino. I would later learn that this was one of a growing number of fortune-telling cafés that had started mushrooming around the city over the previous year.

Curious and agitated, I entered, ordered, and drank a cup of Turkish coffee. After a short wait, a server walked me over to the table of a middle-aged female reader in a separate room. I cannot remember much of what she told me that day. What I do remember distinctly, however, is my mixed feelings. I felt affirmed when she recognized me for who I was with accurate descriptions of the challenges I then faced, but I was also unnerved that she painted my future in such picture-perfect gender-conformity colors with marriage and children. While I treasured the way the reader moved me from feeling uneasy and nervous to feeling supported and encouraged, I was disturbed that this intense and personal interaction was commercial and nonreciprocal. On the one hand, I enjoyed the communication between two women who were complete strangers yet able to share a moment of closeness. On the other hand, I felt guilty for having indulged in this intimacy for a temporary moment by purchasing it from a meagerly compensated, poorer woman. If as a secular feminist woman I felt self-conscious about having paid to have my fortune read and having listened to the reading with great interest, I could not deny the enjoyment I felt while getting my cup read, a feeling evoked by other, seemingly insignificant practices deemed superstitious, such as wearing evil eye charms or reading my horoscope in the newspaper or other, supposedly petty practices deemed feminine, such as watching soap operas or indulging in gossip. This was a refreshingly engaging and comfortingly familiar experience that nevertheless left me with nagging doubts. My investments in femininity and feminism left me confused. The sense of inner conflict and subsequent curiosity I had following this first encounter motivated the research this book is based on.

The research subject matter and the analytical focus on affect demanded multiple research and writing strategies. For the book's ethnographic research, I explored the proliferating gendered practices of divination by following coffee cups as they circulated among friends, relatives, neighbors, and increasingly among strangers, both in the privacy of homes and in the emergent public spaces of fortune-telling cafés. The location was Istanbul, the cultural capital of Turkey and the birthplace and capital of fortune-telling cafés. After my initial visit, I returned to the fortune-telling cafés, now the focal venues of my ethnographic fieldwork, first in 2005, spending two years at over twenty of the hundreds of fortune-telling cafés Istanbul then hosted. I updated this extended fieldwork with annual summer visits between 2008 and 2015, and again in 2019. During this time, I talked to amateurs who read cups and anyone who had had their cup read. I accompanied friends of friends to get readings from fortune-tellers working from their homes. I attended fortune-telling parties at peoples' homes, where readers had been invited to perform their services. I systematically observed and took ethnographic field notes on daily life at fortune-telling cafés, interviewed fortune-telling café owners and workers, witnessed fortune-telling sessions, and had my fortune told countless times.[11]

To be able to parse the various temporalities and spaces in which the structures of feeling I was studying become palpable and to track feelings through their internalizing, individuating, and, importantly, publicly circulating forms and forces, I drew upon an extensive ethnographic and autoethnographic fieldwork augmented by archival research and deployed a variety of analytical and representational strategies. Given the anonymous nature of readings at cafés, most fortune-telling sessions I could directly and closely observe were my own. The research thus took an autoethnographic turn, as my own experiences and feelings became a significant source of data. Over time, this autoethnographic quality, initially a result of issues of access and convenience necessitated by the nature of my research topic, grew into a conscious methodological and analytical strategy. I came to appreciate autoethnographic attunement as an invaluable opportunity to attend to the affective processes that gave fortune-telling and the relationalities around it their force. Furthermore, while my field research took me to various intimate publics conjured in fortune-telling locales, from private homes to divination businesses, I also found myself taking research notes during my time away from my designated field sites. Leisurely watching television or reading the news become another scene of immersion into intimate publics, blurring the boundaries between ethnography, autoethnography, and cultural analysis.

Cultural analysis was more than a mere supplement to the ethnographic scenes I sought to affectively conjure; it was a substantive component of research that allowed me to trace the broader circulation of public feelings around and beyond the divination sites I frequented. To this end, I built upon various registers of public culture, including social media, where people collectively interpreted personal and political divinations; television series in which the right and wrong kinds of fortune-telling were construed and segregated; and legal dramas/sex scandals in the media, where the gendered and sexualized tensions of secular Muslim identity were negotiated time and again. The diverse array of materials I pulled together did not cohere into a complete or representative picture of a singular cultural universe in which my interlocutors operated; instead, they constituted a fragmented yet evocative affective archive in which to trace the public feelings that thickened around the unfolding social worlds in which divinations were exchanged.

I complemented these modes of inquiry with qualitative research into the historical, religious, governmental, and juridical contexts shaping and regulating divination. I drew upon secondary historical sources and very limited primary data so as to place the millennial café fortune-tellers of Turkey within the genealogy of fortune-telling men and women and then situate them within the historical coimbrications of religion, secularism, and the public space that preceded and produced them. I surveyed the various by-products of state efforts to contain and control divination, including articles of law, higher court decisions criminalizing fortune-tellers, and Diyanet press releases and sermons condemning divination. I also explored the ideological foundations of the criminalization of divination through a discourse analysis of select texts of state ideology. Together, this data allowed me to further place the voices and feelings of practitioners of divination today within their larger historical, political, and legal contexts.

In an ethnographic context where respondents lived with the risk of criminalization and the cloud of stigma, trust was an ongoing negotiation complicated by privilege and vulnerability. My urban, secular, middle-class status, amplified by my ongoing studies at an American university and my international mobility; my identity as a straight, cisgender femme; my white-looking body; and my Istanbul accent worked to differential advantage, at times widening and at other times narrowing the social distance between me and my differently located research participants. As I introduced myself to prospective research participants, often shaky with anxiety and caffeine in my body, and weighed them up in an attempt to determine the best way to frame who I was and why I was there, they returned my observational gaze in search of answers to the same questions, reading my fortune first and deciding what to do with me only once I had properly introduced myself as a researcher. The threat of persecution of my interlocutors by competing businesses, disgruntled customers, state prosecutors, and the police was uncommon but ever-present. Television shows and newspaper articles regularly featured fortune-telling cafés with interest, but the on-screen busting of similar practitioners working from their homes, and occasionally from their offices or fortune-telling cafés, was still a popular media genre. Quite a few informants could not help but inquire if I might be an undercover spy or police officer. Social scientific research into fortune-telling was hard to make sense of, not only for my research participants but also for many academics. My institutional relationship to an American university and research procedures designed to protect subjects, such as the use of pseudonyms and the omission of identifying information, sounded rather suspicious. Some readers remarked that they did not use their legal name anyway, having taken a chosen name in their fortune-telling persona and/or as queer folk. Others, hoping to gain publicity from my research, were disappointed that their names would be changed. In the field, risk and benefit were calculated in ways too complex to fit nicely into the discrete categories of human subject protocols; building research rapport required attuning to those complexities.

Reflexivity in this research involved not only recognizing how my positionality shaped the ways I navigated the world; reflexivity also entailed a growing (dis)comfort with the self-reflexivity demanded by how centrally and explicitly my own intimate gendered hopes and qualms became part of my data and analysis. The data I collected included the life narratives and work histories of readers and intimate if transient pictures of their clients' lives, as well as the divination readings I was offered about my own life. These readings were filled with volatile promises bundled into reader-concocted scenarios of starting a career while navigating the vulnerabilities of the marriage market, searching for relationship stability while striving for meaningful intimacy, marrying timely enough to have children, and giving birth to twins, understood by most fortune-tellers and customers to mean undergoing fertility treatment likely because of older maternal age. As the broad array of fraught desires possibly attending a middle-class straight woman in her thirties not wearing a wedding ring filled my field notebook, there was no avoiding my identity as a constitutive part of the research process and data analysis.

Native status in the field did not come readily by sheer dint of being a woman born and raised in Turkey. At first glance, I did look like I belonged in a fortune-telling café. As a thirtysomething woman embodying a Turkish, secular, middle-class habitus, I was remarkably similar to the majority of the customers in age, gender, race/ethnicity, religion, and class. But I was in fact not as familiar with cup reading as others assumed me to be. I was raised by a devotedly secularist grandfather who looked down upon the world of feminized superstitions and a feminist mother who did not immerse herself in the social world of normative femininity, where relatives, neighbors, and friends exchanged cup readings. Growing up, my encounters with coffee divinations were sporadic. Once in the field, however, I was often upgraded from the status of stranger to being included in the social relations of the café as a regular, a guest, a friend, a niece, a daughter, or a pseudo-worker. I was given ample opportunity to become proficient in properly preparing and serving Turkish coffee and getting my cup read.

Ethnographic conversions came in many shades and temporalities. I became more open and playful about matters of faith and practice, learning to be a secular Muslim who "doesn't believe in fortune-telling but doesn't do without it either," as the popular saying goes. I grew more comfortable in the feminized intimacies of divination publics, coming to terms with the strong pulls, claustrophobic closures, and scattered escape routes of heteronormativity as a straight cisgender feminist woman. I gradually learned to see, hear, and feel the labor involved in fortune-telling. It is within this larger habitus that my feelings grew, so to speak, and I started reading cups, albeit not commercially.

My many conversions notwithstanding, my mixed feelings stayed with me.[12] My idealization of feminized subterranean practices as resistant or subversive of heteropatriarchy was brought down to earth by the persistence of heteronormative dreams revealed in and gender conformity espoused by the readings. My desire to approach fortune-telling and related popular religious practices as feminized forms of relating to the world was dampened, even as I grew suspicious of both the secularist critique of believers' fatalism and the postsecular romanticization of the oppressed's spirituality. My excitement about the feminized publics readers conjured for gender and sexual minorities was stifled by the ways neoliberalism and neoconservatism inflected publics by putting the intimate thoroughly to work in the service of neoliberal accumulation and masculinist restoration. My appreciation for the strength and initiative with which urban poor women and young and gay men repurposed a feminized domestic activity as an opportunity for paid work was in conflict with the deep precarity and criminalization of their labor. My romantic investment in a vision of women and LGBTIQ individuals supporting each other competed with the presence of grave inequalities that situated them unevenly in their most intimate encounters. In the end, these dilemmas were not resolved but instead inhabited as tensions that animate this book.

Gendered Negotiations of the Postsecular

As a Muslim-majority country well known for its past radical secularization and present Islamization, both of which have been articulated in gendered terms and have been fought over in the public lives of (un/veiled) women, Turkey provides the perfect context in which to analyze the gendered discontents of secularism and religion. Part I, "The Religious, the Superstitious, and the Postsecular," explores the gendered negotiations of the secular and the postsecular in Turkey. It situates the secular in historical analysis and ethnographic observation to ask what the secular signifies across time and place, as well as what the secular feels like when it is no longer normative, as when the nagging anxieties and insistent hopes of today's secular Muslims are refracted through the gendered practices of divination. Inspired by Connolly's (1999) critique of the secularist idolization of reason at the expense of the visceral, I highlight the affective in my inquiry into the postsecular.

The conundrum of secularists who mobilize a medium otherwise associated with superstition and irrationality in order to coagulate secularist feelings and secular identities provides an opportunity to explore how secular(ist)s affectively attune to the postsecular condition in which the category of the secular is neither normative nor stable. It is in this context that those secular(ist) citizens of Turkey who feel threatened by the ruling party turn toward coffee readings in divination cafés and virtual spaces. In these spaces, through feeling labors of divination, they find breathing room away from worry and hopelessness, feelings that often characterize their relationship to their personal and national futures. The affective conjuring powers of divination give shape to secularist feelings and subjects by providing a productive medium in which secularist hope and faith, as well as pessimism and doubt, can circulate. This secular foray into divination and the affects it thickens illustrates how feeling secular has been structured through the contingency, instability, and contradictions (not to mention the versatility and persistence) of the category of the secular itself.

The postsecular is a suggestive term that may help destabilize conventional ways of understanding a country whose future has long been fought over and analyzed (locally and globally, politically and academically) in terms of a secular/religious dichotomy. Whether described as an age of return to religion, an increasing presence of religion in the public sphere, or a new acknowledgment of the religious in what has come to be presumed as secular modern life, the concept *postsecular* communicates the pervasive sense that secularism no longer holds its unquestioned position in social and critical theory, nor indeed in the public sphere (Bradiotti 2008; Gorski et al. 2012; Habermas 2008; McLennan 2007). The term *postsecular* has been used in explanations of the Turkey of the early 2000s to point out the interpenetrations of the secular and the religious (Göle 2012; Rosati 2016) and to highlight how the category of the secular has been denaturalized and its normative position destabilized (Parmaksız 2018).

Islamic values and practices articulated at the level of Turkish state and popular ideology grew powerful in the 2010s, but were not yet securely hegemonic. While secularism as the foundational state ideology and a popular basis of identity and mobilization remained alive and well in the same period, it was increasingly on the defense. In an irony of history, to lift their spirits, disheartened secular and even secularist citizens now flock to divination businesses under the threat of a secularist law dating as far back as 1925 that outlaws commercial fortune-telling. On their end, the fortune-tellers negotiate for themselves secular Muslim identities as they mix and match a range of divination and other therapeutic modalities with Islamic and new age resonances to craft fortune-telling profiles that will be attractive to their clients but still not attract criminal complaints. Recruiting a secular(ist) worker and clientele profile around a practice that is seemingly at odds with the secular values of reason and skepticism, fortune-tellers and their customers blend secular and secularist identities, Islamic beliefs and rituals, and new age ideas and practices around divinatory practices. In the process, they produce novel constellations of the secular and the religious that disrupt their previously taken-for-granted distinctions in an atmosphere where these categories are increasingly mobilized and fused together by various actors to render even their presumed separateness futile (Göle 2012; Kandiyoti 2012).

As an analytic, the postsecular thus prompts an epistemological stance from which to critically scrutinize the concept of the secular, especially in its assumed difference from the religious. This complements genealogical approaches to the emergence and attempted closures of the concepts of the secular and the religious (Asad 1993, 2003; Mahmood 2005; Scott and Hirschkind 2006). Chapter 1, "Crimes of Divination," addresses the complexities of the secular by tracing the historical construction and gendered afterlives of divination in relation to the constitutive outsides of the secular, namely, religion, tradition, and superstition. The chapter reveals how the disavowal of fortune-tellers was central to the making of the secular through a civilizational project premised upon gendered, classed, ethnoreligious, and racialized exclusions. Turkey is well known for its unique brand of active, authoritative, and militant secularism (Keddie 2003; Kuru 2007; Özyürek 2006). Turkish secularism has depended upon the construction of a masculinized reason that paternalistically protected the people by disciplining those who are feminized via their proximity to superstition, including the female, illiterate, non-Muslim, Arab/Black, "ignorant," and "corrupt" practitioners of divination. The historical detour in this chapter explores the processes by which fortune-tellers were pushed outside the secular national and came to function as a node through which feelings of dismissal, disgust, and abhorrence could be circulated to affectively cement the secular itself. This gendered affective politics of secularism prepared the grounds on which fortune-tellers were criminalized in the early twentieth century, only to be bifurcated into an Islamic underground economy of outlawed and heavily persecuted male hodjas and a domestic economy of trivialized and tolerated housewives.

Showcasing in genealogical fashion a feminized group of secular Muslim fortune-tellers and clients negotiating a postsecular condition in a Muslim-majority Middle Eastern country with a secularist history and a religiously accented government in the present, this research both provincializes dominant conceptions of the secular and makes legible their gendered characterizations. Studies examining the secular beyond its taken-for-granted location in Western Europe have demonstrated that secularism is appropriated and remade in relation to other projects of social transformation: postcolonialism, nationalism, modernization (Asad 1993; Cady and Hurd 2010; Dressler and Mandair 2011; Warner, VanAntwerpen, and Calhoun 2010). Particularly in contexts of (almost postcolonial) nationalist modernization such as Turkey, the politics of secularism and religion are closely tied to an uneasy relationship between the remaking of gender relations and the remaking of the nation, where a specific brand of femininity gets tasked to carry and resolve the paradoxical goals of becoming modern and secular while remaining distinctly Muslim and national (Chatterjee 1993; Kadıoğlu 1996). Under the weight of this paradox, contestations over the ideal shape of gender relations serve as a central arena for articulating secular and religious identities (Çınar 2005; Kandiyoti 1991; White 2014).

While feminist scholars of Turkey and the larger Middle East have pondered the relationships between religion, secularism, and gender (Çınar 2005; Deeb 2006; Göle 1996; Mahmood 2005; Saktanber 2002), the focus has been primarily on pious Muslim women and politically engaged pious Muslim subjects. This book focuses instead on the multiple ways nonpious Muslim women relate to the supernatural in everyday life, identify with various positions along the spectrum of the secular and the religious, engage with the gendered logics of secularism and Islamism, and craft nonpious and secular Muslim identities. It also broadens previous research's focus on women with a more inclusive understanding of gendered marginalization that includes sexual minorities.

Moving the postsecular debate beyond its initial focus on national and international politics and into other social and cultural realms, I join recent interrogations into the gendered and quotidian discourses and experiences of the postsecular (Gökarıksel and Secor 2015) with an eye for affective constellations that contour secular subjects. I ask how the postsecular condition feels in the textures of everyday life as I explore the exertion of feeling labors of divination as a way to soothe the anxious subjects of a postsecular condition. In the process, I shift the focus from the recently emphasized aberrant pious subject of feminism to the largely taken-for-granted normative secular(ist) subject and engage with the postsecular turn in feminist studies and its critiques (Abbas 2013; Bradiotti 2008; Jamal 2015; Vasilaki 2016).

Chapter 2, "The Gendered Politics of Secularism," continues the critical inquiry into the category of the secular by turning to the gendered subjects that traverse secularist attachments and postsecular negotiations. Tracing hodja-bashing narratives in the media and in everyday accounts both past and present, this chapter explores how secularist economies of desire and contempt animate gendered conceptions of tradition, religion, superstition, and secularity. The chapter demonstrates that, throughout the shifting and volatile parameters of the secular and religious, the effort to fix femininity to irrationality and superstition persists as an amalgam against which masculine authority is constituted. The persecution of hodjas and the tolerated presence of housewives bestows legitimate authority upon secular men and the secularizing state in their patriarchal rule over women, non-heteronormative men, and the people, constructed as objects of rescue from traditional and superstitious influences of religion. From conventional stories in which secular men save victimized women from malicious hodjas to their postsecular remixes where fortune-tellers themselves become the heroes, this chapter highlights how cup readers and their clients subvert normative categories by mimicking the gendered conventions of secularism.[13] As contemporary secular Muslim fortune-tellers redirect the feelings of disdain and contempt attending the generic figure of the fortune-teller away from themselves and reclaim the deference and admiration once securely commanded by secular masculine figures for themselves, they gesture affectively and figuratively toward the postsecular.

Chapter 3, "Feeling Postsecular," provides a fresh perspective on a well-trodden debate by introducing secular Muslim women who confess to an individualized belief system defined less by orthodox Sunni ritual and dogma and more by a flexible and eclectic set of feelings and sensibilities. These women pray but also insist on wearing short skirts. They drink alcohol but not during Ramadan. They engage in popular religious practices such as fortune-telling but with a grain of rational salt. This chapter demonstrates novel postsecular brokerings of the supernatural that sit alongside nonpious articulations of secular Muslimness, such as may be seen in coffee divination, in which the silhouette of Atatürk can appear in a coffee cup to reassure concerned secularists about the continued political future of Turkish secularism. Situating coffee divinations in the context of ongoing contestations over the legality and legitimacy of fortune-telling, chapter 3 sketches those emergent assemblages of the secular and the religious that destabilize the long-established terms of the gendered politics of secularism, affectively and discursively surfacing in the process the secular Muslim subjects of a postsecular condition. This section of the book takes particular issue with the dichotomy of secular versus pious Muslims that so often subtends studies of gender and Islam, contributing instead a nuanced account to analyses of the persistent centrality of various politics of gender and sexuality within ongoing contestations over secularism and religion around the world (Abu-Lughod 2002; Puar 2007; Razack 2008).

Gendering Publics and Intimacies

This book focuses on divination publics constructed for and by gender and sexual minorities as a way of challenging dominant perspectives on the nature of the modern public sphere (Habermas [1962] 1991) in favor of a pluralized, gendered, and queered reconceptualization of publics. As such, it contributes to feminist and queer scholarship that brings gender and sexuality to the center of analyses of the public sphere by counterbalancing the emphasis on the political public sphere with a curiosity for a multiplicity of unequally situated publics (Berlant 2008; Fraser 1990; Warner 2005). With this twofold aim in mind, part II, "Femininity, Intimacy, and Publics," probes how the gendered practices of fortune-telling conjure feminized publics in which women and LGBTIQ individuals find care and recognition in each other's intimate company.

Chapter 4, "Feeling Publics of Femininity," explores how divination publics are summoned through the circulation of a genre of femininity that uses an affective vocabulary to express and negotiate feminized pleasures and discontents.

My conceptualization of divination publics here is in dialogue with works that emphasize the mutual productivity of affects, subjects, and publics (Ahmed 2004, 2014; Mankekar 2015; Papacharissi 2015). It pushes models of cultural analysis inspired by literature, linguistics, and communications beyond their original scope in order to scrutinize genres and publics that differ radically in their mediums and styles of expression (Warner 2005), stressing the affective performativity of an irrational, nontextual medium. As such, this study foregrounds the fact that publics are tucked into and constitutive of social relations and places. Like other genres of femininity embedded within the sociospatial arrangements of their production, circulation, and consumption—the shooting of a daytime women's show in the television studio or the meeting of a book club's members to discuss a chick-lit best seller—divinations are embedded in women's domestic gatherings in the living room and in their visits to the fortune-telling café. Feeling publics of divination thus conjure an intimate affective terrain of femininity through the spatialized sociabilities they operate in.

In Muslim Middle Eastern contexts, the gendered relationship between genres, affects, and publics is brokered through a specific spatialized social formation of gendered intimacy. This formation has often been conceptualized as sex or gender segregation or seclusion (in reference to the separation of males/men and females/women as an organizing logic of social space and relationships) and interpreted as a religious, repressive, and unbending structure. For the secularizing elites of early twentieth-century Turkey, this formation signified a harmful religious tradition that would come to serve as a counterpoint against which they envisioned modern public life. In this context, similar to neighboring modernization processes across the Muslim Middle East (Thompson 2003), the modern public sphere in Turkey emerged as the product of an authoritarian reformist state marked as secular by the presence of unveiled women and mixed-gender socializing (Göle 1997). Importantly for this research, at the heart of a modern domesticity constructed to complement this secular public sphere lies the publicly denigrated social practices of same-sex intimacies and fortune-telling. These remain constitutive of normative femininities, attesting to the fact that an Islamicate model of gendered intimacy is neither external nor antithetical to but coconstitutive of modern gender formations in Turkey.

This book takes feminized publics of divination as existing nestled inside the complex constellations of gender, space, and sociability. As such, it approaches what has been commonly conceived of as gender "segregation" as instead an "institution of intimacy" (Sehlikoglu 2016, 144) that maps gendered affinity in spatial, embodied, and relational terms; an adaptable formation that is subject to historical change and is self-reflexively engaged with. Chapter 4 thus establishes the novelty of feminized publics of divination, in which a majority of women alongside a minority of young and gay men gather around coffee cups in a social terrain long reduced to a binary schema of gender-segregated versus mixed-gender sociabilities. This chapter traces the gendered and spatialized historical trajectory of coffee sociabilities in which a bifurcation between male-only coffeehouses and mixed-gender cafés emerged and tracks the ways different actors from secularist nationalists to feminists have politically engaged with these sociospatial arrangements. It further explains how fortune-telling cafés are preferred locations for secular, but often not pious, Muslim women, who also engage in (coffee) fortune-telling but mostly in other venues.

Gendered Fortunes thus controverts the ways feminized social worlds have been over- and misrepresented in Orientalist imaginaries and self-Orientalizing modernist representations of "the harem," not least as a reified space/place one can(not) enter or leave. These representations are accompanied by colonialist (feminist) assumptions of women's exceptionally severe oppression in Muslim-majority societies, assumed to be self-evident in their bodies covered under veils and their lives constrained behind latticed windows (Ahmed 1982; Mernissi 2001). To sidestep this overdetermination of gendered space and lack of (liberal) agency, I shift the terms of analysis from gender segregation, exclusion, and oppression to the relationships between femininity, intimacy, and publics.

Chapter 5, "The Joys and Perils of Intimacy," highlights the significance of divination publics as spaces where the feminized can explore their lives at some distance from the disciplining imperatives of an increasingly intimate public sphere. Here, feminized publics of fortune-telling are set against a larger public sphere, where the intimate is increasingly incited to public discourse and where public intimacies abound, from a political public sphere in which government and feminist and queer discourses on gender and sexuality explode to popular culture with television shows in which ordinary women continuously display and dispute their homes, marriages, and relationships. In this milieu, commercial divination brings together secular Muslim women and young and gay men to share intimately in the relative safety of the urban anonymity afforded by fortune-telling businesses. Exploring a mother-daughter cup-reading episode, a café divination session, and an online fortune-telling interaction, where revelations of the intimate create differential results, ranging from betrayal and violence to trust and protection, this chapter enumerates the circumstances under which the anonymous intimacies of commodified fortune-telling provide safer spaces in which to air and work through intimate issues for those whose personal and especially sexual lives are closely regulated by their family, community, and government through public policy, shaming, gossip, and violence. Inspired by inquiries into the gendered genres and affective blueprints that mediate both national and minoritarian publics, I highlight divination publics that are oriented away from the political public sphere, but which nevertheless hold feminist potentiality.

Together, these two chapters situate contemporary divination publics of femininity within a number of contending sociopolitical formations: Islamicate formations of intimacy (Göle 1996; Sehlikoglu 2016, 2021), predominantly conceived as a principle of gender segregation that prevents women's entry into the public sphere; the secularist politics of the public sphere (Göle 1997; Kandiyoti 1991), often regarded as a significant if limited inclusion of women in public life; and the recently cemented postsecular neoconservative politics of intimacy that dominates contemporary Turkey's political public sphere (Acar and Altunok 2013; Korkman 2016), often viewed as a threat to the secularist politics of the public sphere and a return to Islamicate formations of intimacy. Against this background, this study moves beyond a discussion of gendered publics narrowly clustered around questions of exclusion and segregation to examine the productivity and potentiality of feminized publics.

The book thus provincializes the Western-centric feminist insight that the modern public sphere was and is primarily constituted by the gendered exclusion of women and femininity (Fraser 1990). It reveals this feminist analysis not as a universal, but as a particular critique requiring realignment in Muslim-majority and/or postcolonial contexts of modernization, where women's public visibility, if not inclusion per se, is central to the formation of the modern public sphere and to the gendered projects of nation building. As such, it puts the US-based feminist and queer theories of publics in conversation with Middle East feminist scholarship on the public sphere to invite an exploration of the multiple genealogies of the secular public sphere. By attending through ethnographic research to the minoritarian publics, sociospatiality, and everyday practices that arise within these multiple genealogies, it calls for a nuanced inquiry into the variability of gendered intimacies and sociabilities around which different types of publics are organized, with an eye for their differential political stakes and potentials.

Gender, Feeling Labor, and Neoliberalism

Gendered Futures engages with feminist debates on how formations of capitalism and heteropatriarchy coconstitute gendered lives and livelihoods. The book explores the central role feminized affective labors play in the global economy under neoliberalization (Boris and Parenas 2010; Dedeoğlu and Elveren

2012; Ehrenreich and Hochschild 2002) by investigating the contexts, terms, and costs involved in recruiting gender and sexual minorities into the thoroughly commercialized and increasingly digital and transnational divination economy. More specifically, it joins inquiries that situate feminized, embodied, and affective engagements with the supernatural at the very heart of an analysis of gendered labor: for example, Silvia Federici's (2004) historical analysis of how the persecution of witches accompanied the relegation of women to unpaid housework during the emergence of capitalism in early-modern Europe, Aihwa Ong's (2010) ethnographic study of the spirit possession–induced seizures through which female Malay factory workers experienced and negotiated their enlistment into the ranks of the late modern proletariat, or Attiya Ahmad's (2017) inquiry into South Asian migrant women's conversions to Islam that mediate their domestic labors in the Kuwaiti households where they take work.

Part III, "Feeling Labor, Precarity, and Entrepreneurialism," explores the gendered feeling labors of fortune-telling. While attention to gendered labor is long-standing in Turkish studies, with the issues of women's low labor force participation and their high concentration in the informal sector at the forefront (Dayıoğlu and Kırdar 2010; Ecevit 2003; İlkkaracan 2012; Tunalı, Kırdar, and Dayıoğlu 2017), the account here is informed by ethnographic explorations of the gendered processes of labor (Akalın 2007; Dedeoğlu 2010; Isik 2008; Ozyegin 2000; Sarıoğlu 2016; White 2004). In a field often focused exclusively on women's labor at the expense of a more inclusive understanding of gendered labor that includes sexual minorities, this book also joins research that turns to LGBTIQ subjects (Yılmaz and Göçmen 2016) and, in ethnographic settings, to transgender sex workers (Güler 2020; Özbay 2010, 2017; Zengin 2020).

In the tradition of earlier Marxist feminist analyses of reproductive labors (Dalla Costa and James 1972; Federici 1975) and housewifization (Mies 1998), and in dialogue with more recent studies of emotional and affective labors, chapter 6, "Feeling Labors of Divination," explores fortune-telling as a form of feminized labor. It demonstrates how fortune-tellers conjure an affective space in which clients can explore their gendered hopes and disappointments (Korkman 2015b). While divination requires work at various levels, the dominant mode of labor is affective/emotional. Here the emotional dimension refers to the socially constructed processes of identifying, managing, and displaying emotions, while the affective dimension refers to the unstructured, precognitive, and embodied intensities underlying emotional experience itself (Massumi 2002). I coin the term *feeling labor* to denote this dual work of inciting, identifying, and expressing cognitively articulated, culturally meaningful emotions and at the same time attuning interpersonally to the underlying affective intensities in all their amorphousness, fluidity, and contagiousness. The term *feeling* is grounded in the language fortune-tellers themselves use to describe their labor process: readers frequently use the word *feeling* as a verb (*hissetmek*), a pertinent reminder of the manner of labor involved in reading fortunes. The concept of feeling labor synthesizes the insights of feminist and critical scholarship on emotional and affective labors (Ducey 2007; Freeman 2011, 2015; Hall 1993; Hardt 1999, 2007; Hochschild 1983; Kang 2003; Lively 2000; Negri and Hardt 1999; Paules 1991; Pierce 1999; Weeks 2007; Wissinger 2007) while emphasizing what has not been adequately engaged by theorists of affective labor: the gendering of affective labor (Freeman 2011; Shultz 2006) and the rich genealogy of feminist thinking on reproductive and emotional labors (Federici 2008; Weeks 2007).

Approaching divination as a medium through which to feel precariousness and its attendant anxieties, *Gendered Fortunes* provides a window onto the central role feminized affective labors play in containing the contradictions of neoliberal capitalism. Chapter 6 details how the feeling labors of divination render precarity inhabitable not only by providing much-needed work, but also by affording a type of labor designed to process the affective experience of precarity. Readers find in divination a precious opportunity for paid work amid labor insecurity exacerbated by the intersectional inequalities that render their lives precarious. Feeling precarious under the neoliberal impetus for becoming a self-making and ever-anticipatory subject paradoxically fuels divination economies on both ends. Secular middle-class clients are also often precarious economic subjects who either fear or suffer through cycles of insecure employment, unemployment, and underemployment and who feel anxious in the face of the postsecular condition they find themselves in. This labor precarity and secular anxiety are further compounded by the gendered feelings of precariousness as the intimate attachments to femininity stir up emotions of vulnerability, directing gender and sexual minorities into the postsecular neoliberal divination economy as workers and clients. *Gendered Fortunes* thus contributes to scholarly inquiries of the affective imprint of neoliberal capitalism (Beer 2016; Berg, Huijbens, and Larsen 2016; Berlant 2007, 2011; Cossman 2013; Isin 2004; Molé 2010; Muehlebach 2011; Neilson 2015; Pettit 2019; Scharff 2016) with an ethnographically situated analysis of the processes that allow gender and sexual minorities to attune to precarity by working (on) their feelings.

As neoliberal economic transformations encounter local contexts around the world, the therapeutic spirit of neoliberalism travels transnationally with it, only to be variably translated and appropriated (Freeman 2015; Kanna 2010;

Ong 2006; Takeyama 2010). In this context, cup readings are sucked into a larger postsecular neoliberal terrain of therapeutic modalities that alternately feed into and on the anxieties of precariousness (Foster 2016, 2017; Peck 2016; Rose 1990). The millennial allure of fortune-telling is thus informed by the multivalent, local, and gendered experiences and idioms of precarity and possibility in Turkey; by secularity, religion, and tradition; by intimacy and publicness. It is only through these multilayered and overlapping vectors that people are able to navigate their gendered fortunes in dynamic relation to the global ascendency of neoliberalization and its selective affinity with occult ways of understanding and responding to socioeconomic marginalization (Comaroff and Comaroff 1999, 2000a, 2000b).

Chapter 7, "Entrepreneurial Fortunes," considers close-up how feeling labors become increasingly self-entrepreneurial as they are mobilized to craft and heal the impossibility of postsecular neoliberal selves that are subjectified into an ideal of individual mastery of their own fate under conditions that render personal fortunes thoroughly unstable. Selectively harvesting new age discourses alongside Islamic ones, the feminized practitioners of divination enchant the self-entrepreneurial and thoroughly integrated processes of making a living and a self. The expansion of transnational and online divination economies further entrenches the precarious labor conditions of and self-entrepreneurial demands on cup readers. At the same time, the owners of this booming industry are paraded as the poster children of a happy union between neoliberal and new age economic/spiritual understandings of work as an enchanted activity of self-realization. *Gendered Fortunes* thus adds to inquiries of self-entrepreneurialism (Foucault 2008; Rose 1992), particularly of the feminized kind (McRobbie 2009; Ringrose and Walkerdine 2008; Scharff 2016; Weber 2009), with an emphasis on the role of gendered affective labors in crafting self-entrepreneurial responses to precariousness (Freeman 2015; Ouellette and Wilson 2011).

While the transformation of feminized divination practices into a form of precarious labor directs (re)productive capacities toward capitalist circuits of value, the productivity of affective labors is not exhausted by these circuits. Feeling labors of divination produce more than profits. They produce a variety of social relations among the feminized, from supportive ties workers cultivate as they read each other's fortunes noncommercially to the broader gendered intimacies and feminized publics fortune-telling fosters for secular Muslim women and LGBTIQ individuals. In conversation with the autonomous Marxist emphasis on the potentiality of the social factory, with a dose of feminist criticism of its romanticization of affective labor (Gill and Pratt 2008), I provide a gendered account of the ways in which affective capacities are put to work, but without reducing the feelings, subjectivities, and sociabilities produced to a mere function of capitalist, secularist and Islamist, and heteropatriarchal domination.

Feeling Femininity

Animating this book's multifaceted inquiry into the gendered practices of divination is an abiding interest in feeling femininity. The project thus joins longstanding inquiries in feminist cultural studies to ask how femininities take shape via genres and practices that are devalued as petty and insignificant, for example romance novels and gossip, yet are invested with strong feelings and partialities. Feminist and queer cultural studies draw attention to the many ubiquitous genres through which femininity is felt, produced, consumed, and subverted (Berlant 2008; Cvetkovich 1992; de Lauretis 1999; Radway 1983), analyzing subjectification beyond identitarian gender and sexuality categories and examining the processes of identification (Muñoz 1999) with the aim of troubling conventional analyses of the relationship between representation and identification. These interventions deconstruct gender categories as fixed social roles or identity sets and recast them as the effects of the discursive and performative process of subjectification, a process that is re/destabilized via active reiteration (Butler 2011). Informed by this theoretical legacy, I conceptualize fortune-telling as a genre that provides affective surfaces and discursive spaces through which the desires and trials of heteropatriarchal subordination are felt and articulated. Approaching femininity as a node of affective coagulation and subjectification, I do not take women as a self-evident category. Instead I focus on those who are summoned as feminized subjects through the affective intensities generated by the circulation of divinatory scenes of femininity.

In Istanbul, the affective genre of cup reading coagulates feminized subjects. Participants in the divination economy are neither passive consumers of a hegemonic culture industry nor romantic subversive figures of a resistant subculture, but are produced through and in excess of the larger formations of power and inequality shaping the terrain of their subjectification. Building upon a rich cultural studies legacy that explores the social and material production, circulation, and consumption of culture in general and of popular culture and subcultures in particular as terrains of meaning making and subjectification (Fiske 2011; Hall 1997, 2001; Hebdige 1995), *Gendered Fortunes* complements textual analyses of mediatized cultural products in British and American contexts that have long constituted the bulk of the research in the field by looking at a recently commodified nontextual practice though ethnographic analysis conducted in an understudied context.

Informed by the feminist insight that the devaluation and marginalization of those practices deemed feminine is key to understanding how gendered power operates, I insist on the significance of feminized divinations that are disdained but that reveal on closer analysis the centrality of quotidian realms and labors of the feminized to larger formations. Joining Middle East feminist scholarship in its inquiry into how processes of nationalist modernization, secularization, and Islamization operate in gendered ways, particularly at the level of everyday culture (Kandiyoti and Saktanber 2002), *Gendered Fortunes* explores femininity at the junctures of state projects writ large, from nationalist modernist secularism to neoliberal Islamist conservatism, that shape the terrain in which gendered lives and livelihoods are made. Positioned centrally in this way, the gendered practices of divination recounted here provide a window through which to explore the transformation of three related world historical processes: secular modernity, the modern public sphere, and capitalism. When taken in such a frame, the feminized practices of fortune-telling are revealed as multiply imbricated in larger formations. They are criminalized praxes excluded by the secularist project, only to emerge later as central to feeling the postsecular condition. They are mediums through which to feel intimate in feminized publics embedded in a larger public sphere that is constituted via the disavowal of the very gendered intimacies that sustain heteronormativity. They are devalued and irregularized labors of feeling that are nevertheless key to reproducing the neoliberal economy. Such a feminist analysis lays bare the discontents of larger formations that are sewn together and pulled apart daily though the feeling labors of the feminized.

Feeling comes to the fore as an analytic that informs each of the multiple strands of analysis in this book. In conversation with feminist and queer scholarship on public feelings (Ahmed 2014; Berlant 2011, 2008; Cvetkovich 2012, 2003; Stewart 2007, 2011), *Gendered Fortunes* deploys feeling as an analytic with which to attune to the gendered affects and sociabilities of divination. This book takes up the term *feeling* for its very ambiguity, which simultaneously conjures the social and embodied life of emotion/affect (Cvetkovich 2003). In so doing, it inherits the attention by earlier Marxist cultural studies theorists to "structures of feeling" (Steedman 1987; Williams 1977), which emphasizes the merely felt and emergent and yet deeply social and structuring/structured nature of emotion/affect.[14] With an eye to provincializing the affective turn in the social sciences and humanities (Clough and Halley 2007) by turning to non-Western sources to think affect with (Navaro 2017), including earlier thinking on gendered emotions in Middle Eastern studies (Abu-Lughod 1986), and in dialogue with the more recent turn toward affect in Turkish studies (Açıksöz 2019; Bilal 2019; Biner 2019; Gill 2017; Korkman 2015b; Navaro-Yashin 2012; Parla 2019; Stokes 2010; Yıldırım 2019), the book probes how femininities that take shape at the intersections of secularization, Islamization, and neoliberalization are felt affectively on the surfaces of everyday life.

Fortune-tellers overwhelmingly describe divination as a process of feeling, understood as an affective, intuitive way of attuning and knowing. Feeling also constitutes an otherized form of knowledge that has been excluded from secular Western modernity and consigned to its ethnoracial and gendered others and their traditional and superstitious ways of (not) knowing (Lloyd 2004). While affectivity is ideologically excluded, it remains central to heteropatriarchal colonial capitalist domination and exploitation of feminized bodies and labors. Devalued in the secular public sphere, in the formal capitalist economy, and in the modern gender regime, feelings are nevertheless mobilized to rally, comfort, and care for citizens, workers, and family members. Indeed, the very presence and othering of feelings remains key to the project of constructing the differences between secular rational (masculine) and superstitious emotional (feminine) citizens, public (masculine) and private (feminine) spheres, paid and valued (male) and unpaid and devalued (female) workers, and, more broadly, masculine and feminine subjects and sociabilities. Centralizing feeling within our understandings and analyses of these formations in a thoroughgoing fashion provides our analyses with a feminist impetus with which we may destabilize the metanarratives that frame the heteronormative gender order, the secular public sphere, and the capitalist economy. And as a feminist endeavor of revaluation, it takes its cue from the very ways of attunement that the feminized themselves use to navigate these formations.

PART I

THE RELIGIOUS,

THE SUPERSTITIOUS,

AND THE POSTSECULAR

1

CRIMES OF DIVINATION

"The Ankara Chief Prosecutor's Office has opened a criminal court case against fortune-telling café [*fal kafe*] owners in Kızılay District and their coffee-, tarot-, and water-reading employees. In accordance with the law banning dervish lodges and cloisters, the prosecutor is demanding a punishment of up to twenty years' imprisonment."[1] This excerpt is from a news story published in 2005, when, after five years of mushrooming across urban Turkey, fortune-telling cafés were suddenly placed under legal scrutiny, and the legality of their circumvention of the prohibition against profit-oriented fortune-telling through the provision of divination services as a promotional giveaway with the purchase of a drink was thrown into question. "The owners of cafés and patisseries who converted their businesses into fortune-telling centers with the slogan 'Coffee on you, fortune-telling on us' are being criminally charged," the report continued. "Psychologists point out that personality weaknesses can explain the appeal of divination and magic. They add that their appeal is also a sign of underdevelopment."[2]

Long hailed as a paradigmatic example of secularization in the Muslim Middle East, modern Turkey has been structured by its own brand of secularism and by the peculiar discontents it unleashed. The persecution of fortune-tellers in early twenty-first-century Turkey on the basis of an eighty-year-old secularist law hints at the complexities of a secularist project that energetically seeks to control, with nothing less than imprisonment, a category of religious practitioners as ostensibly trivial as fortune-tellers. Taking its cue from this rather curious case of secularist criminalization, this chapter explores the making of the Turkish secular in all its particularity through the incessant affective, discursive, and institutional production of its traditional, religious, and superstitious others—in this case, the figure of fortune-tellers.

It was the extraordinary, at times absurd, fervor of the Turkish brand of secularism that rendered fortune-telling cafés significant enough to make the news on December 7 and 8, 2005. It was circulated promptly and uniformly across national time and space, with almost every major Turkish newspaper and online news portal reporting on the criminal investigation of the owners and employees of fortune-telling cafés.[3] The depth and tone of the coverage varied. Most news articles were dry and monotonous, reproducing the official narrative by parroting a selective but verbatim version of the prosecutor's written accusation that had launched the criminal procedure. Some supported the story with additional context and analysis. By pathologizing divination as a symptom of personality weakness and deficient national development, the news article quoted above framed criminalization as a benevolent act on the part of the prosecutor, who was seen as regulating the public per secularist laws, protecting citizens from their own weaknesses, and prompting the nation along a linear line of modernization and secularization. The article echoed the paternalistic tone of a modernist secularist project that mobilizes its avowed mission to guard and uplift the people in order to justify its disciplinary and repressive operations.

The prosecutor, Nadi Türkaslan, whose last name fittingly translates into English as "the Turkish lion," was a secularist nationalist who took to his duty of protecting the public with great zeal, initiating case after case against Kurdish and human rights activists for alleged crimes of "insulting Turkishness." Determining that many cafés in the capital city of Ankara offered fortune-telling as a promotional giveaway, Türkaslan used the pamphlets and signs promoting them as evidence to conclude that café employees had turned fortune-telling into an occupation and that the café owners were profiting from fortune-telling.[4]

Türkaslan charged café employees who told fortunes with the criminal offense of being fortune-tellers, as defined in Law No. 677, which abolished religious orders and criminalized related religious titles in 1925, two years after the declaration of the Turkish Republic. Legally considered to be the perpetrators of this criminal act by proxy, café owners were charged with the same offense. If convicted, the defendants would face a minimum sentence of three months' imprisonment and an astonishing maximum sentence of twenty years, according to Article 49/1 of the new Turkish Criminal Code, passed in 2005 as part of legal reforms undertaken for Turkey's accession to the European Union as a member state. The first sentence of the minimum of three months' imprisonment was issued to a café owner after a year of legal proceedings and was later converted to a monetary fine. Neither this case nor the ensuing sporadic criminal trials would halt the flourishing of fortune-telling cafés in urban Turkey. They would, however, provide a recurrent pretext for reasserting the boundaries of the secular.

The politics of secularism depend both on the construction of the secular and, in particular, given the almost postcolonial context of Turkish nationalist secularism, on the production of the traditional, the religious, and the superstitious as constitutive outsides of the modern secular.[5] By anchoring the 2005 persecution of fortune-telling cafés and its eighty-year-old 1925 precedent of decisively outlawing fortune-tellers in the larger historical processes through which fortune-tellers came to be criminalized subjects of state secularism, this chapter pursues a genealogical understanding of the secular and its others. The ideological and institutional shifts accompanying the modernizing reforms of the late Ottoman and early Turkish Republican eras, which sought to redraw the empire's social organization and gendered distribution of religious authority and divinatory practices, served to carve out the secular vis-à-vis the traditional, the religious, and the superstitious. These shifts were summarily negotiated over, among others, the figure of the fortune-teller. Importantly, in the making of the secular national, the proper sphere of religion was designated and delimited in contradistinction to the so-called traditional and superstitious, which were set aside as realms of gendered, ethnoracial, and socioeconomic alterity. Fortune-tellers were effectively pushed outside the secular national, functioning as a node through which feelings of dismissal, disgust, and abhorrence could be circulated to affectively cement the secular itself.

Together with the remaining chapters in part I, which extend the historical analysis of the secular into the ethnographic present, this chapter reveals how the seemingly minor figures of fortune-tellers have been and remain central to the making of the secular through their incessant repudiation. The three chapters in part I further reveal the production of the secular as a gendered process in which a masculinized claim to reason provides a benevolent excuse to subordinate a feminized class of overly or improperly traditional, religious, and superstitious subjects, reinforcing gendered, racial, ethnic, religious, and socioeconomic inequalities through the prism of the secular.

Genealogies of the Secular and the Religious

[In the Ottoman Empire of the nineteenth century,] the word "religious" acquired a new meaning and connotation. . . . The static or traditional was perceived as being "religious," irrespective of its sources of inspiration, while the "changing" and the "new" were understood to be "worldly" or "non-religious" even though the sources may have been partially or wholly religious in nature.

—Niyazi Berkes, *The Development of Secularism in Turkey*

In contending that the secular and the religious are neither essential nor universal domains of human life or experience, but are rather socially constructed categories hatched at the specific historical juncture of early-modern Europe, within which we have subsequently come to live and act upon the world, the inquiry below takes its cue from Talal Asad's trio of questions: "How, when, and by whom are the categories of religion and the secular defined?" (2003, 201). Following Asad's (1993) methodological imperative in favor of a historically and culturally specific study of the development of the categories of the secular and the religious in relation to the growth of secularism as a political project outside the West, this chapter traces the shifting fortunes of divinatory practitioners in relation to the emergence of the categories of the secular and the religious during the Ottoman and Turkish modernizations.

Such a genealogy of the secular and the religious requires that we forgo the assumption that these worldly and heavenly powers proceed from two discrete, separate, and competing orders. This bifurcated idea lies at the heart of the modern concepts of secularization (the separation of church and state) and laicization (the separation of the lay and the clergy), but is itself a modern projection into the past (Asad 2003). Indeed, in classical Ottoman thought and political organization, religion and the state, these worldly and heavenly powers, were not perceived nor did they function as distinct and competing spheres. Rather, "the state was conceived as the embodiment of religion, and religion as the essence of the state" (Berkes [1964] 1998, 7). The project of secularization therefore required not the delinking of two preexisting yet comingling realms, but rather a two-step process: the (re)making of those realms as distinct (religion and the state) and, once this had been accomplished, the synchronized expansion of this worldly state authority and restriction of religious authority. Unlike Asad, however, Niyazi Berkes, a positivist and modernist writing in the 1960s, is not critically distanced and disenchanted from the historical process that made the secular he describes. The modernist epistemological stance visible in his approach notwithstanding, his canonical work on the late Ottoman and early Republican contexts suggests, too, that the emergence of secularism needs to be studied in terms of the making of religion as a separate domain and the delimiting of its sphere of authority so as to make, in effect, the sphere of the secular.

When informed by this genealogical method, historical inquiry becomes an exploration both of how religion was socially organized in the Ottoman Empire when no realm of social life was designated as nonreligious and of where fortune-tellers fit into this social order. Rather than being a competing sphere of authority outside the state, religious authority was a constitutive part of the Ottoman state and its legitimacy. Institutionalized religious orthodoxy, represented by an exclusively male class of religious-scholarly-judicial officials (ulema), was an integral part of the state apparatus. The ulema produced and protected the orthodox tradition of Sunni Islamic thought and jurisprudence and were overseers of education and justice for Muslim subjects of the empire. The ulema "constituted an official and temporal body" (Berkes [1964] 1998, 16) that "belonged to the ruling elite" (Zürcher 2004, 11) and was not autonomous from the state.[6]

Importantly, religious orders, whose criminalization in the twentieth century would serve as grounds for the criminalization of fortune-tellers in the twenty-first century, were perhaps the only "specifically religious institutions" (Berkes [1964] 1998, 16) of the Ottoman Empire. They were relatively autonomous from the centralized state and its official religious-scholarly-judicial apparatus. In contrast to their exclusion from the male ulema class, women were welcomed in certain Sufi orders such as the Bektaşi, but by the sixteenth century they, too, excluded women from positions of authority (Kafadar 1993). In contrast to the more centralized social structure and homogenized Sunni orthodoxy produced by the ulema, multiple detached religious orders represented varieties of Sunni Islam and Sufism, some of which approached Shi'ism too closely for the ulema's taste. Members of religious orders gathered to perform religious rituals in spaces ranging from the simple house of a sheikh to a comprehensive dervish lodge, comprising classrooms, tombs, prayer rooms, kitchens, and accommodation for disciples. Religious orders performed various community functions and, especially in the periphery of the empire, even staffed mosques and courts. Against the grain of the all-encompassing common denominator of Islam, which subjected all Muslims of the empire hierarchically to the ulema and ultimately to the sultan, membership in religious orders situated individual Muslims in a tangible, local, relatively lateral web of social, economic, and political relationships. While mosques around the empire honored the sultan and pledged allegiance to him during the Friday prayers, religious orders "provided many women and men with a set of vital, personal, and intimate religious experiences that alternately combined with or transcended those of the mosque" (Quataert 2005, 162–63).

With their literacy and command of Sunni orthodoxy, the ulema were the official brokers of high culture and the gatekeepers of official religious culture; in contrast, the religious orders constituted a "link between the elite civilization and popular culture" (Zürcher 2004, 12), informing the popular religiosity of the illiterate masses, who constituted the majority of the empire's population. Accompanying the multifaceted relations between ulema, religious orders, and the people was a hierarchical yet complex and fluid relationship between the official culture of the empire's center and the differentiated (counter)cultures of its periphery. These power-laden, unstable, and contested lines of distinction between the high and popular (religious) cultures of the empire would later come to inform the politics of secularism during Ottoman and later Turkish modernization efforts (Bakiner 2018; Mardin 1973).

The disparities between the ulema and the religious orders, official and popular religious cultures, and the center and the periphery of the empire reflected the central axes of differentiation that animated the empire's organization of political power and religious authority. Nevertheless, these axes of social stratification were neither static nor exclusive binary dichotomies but were rather crosscut by multiple and at times contradictory axes of inequality—ruling/subject, educated/ignorant, wealthy/poor, male/female, and urban/rural (Quataert 2005)—that were themselves subject to change over time. Members of the ulema and the religious orders did not therefore fall into two distinct, internally homogenous, timeless social groups that enjoyed similarly differentiated economic, political, and cultural capital. Class, regional, and cultural differences could just as well place a member of the ulema closer to the popular classes or a member of a religious order closer to the ruling elites. Prestigious ulema posts in central cities were relatively monopolized by an established group of elite families, while lower-ranking posts across poor urban neighborhoods and the empire's rural hinterland were populated by the less well-educated ulema, who were recruited from the lower classes and who held limited local power. This group of ulema "had more in common socially, culturally, and economically with their artisan and peasant neighbors than the lofty ulema grandees" (Quataert 2005, 143). Similarly, a sheikh could command great power and prestige not only over a peripheral population but also in the center of the empire through his followers holding state offices. Some religious orders, like the Mevlevi and the Bektaşi, gained proximity to the religious orthodoxy of the state, were incorporated into the center, and penetrated the ruling elites of the empire, including the ulema and even the sultan. Others were harshly criticized by the ulema elites, and the more popular and rebellious of them were accused of heresy and targeted as political enemies of the state.

Despite being categorically barred from positions of religious authority in the official religious orthodoxy and being gradually excluded within the religious orders, Ottoman Muslim women had some access to religious knowledge and authority. Depending on their status, women received religious education ranging from the local mosque school to private tutoring. Some became respected tutors themselves (Peirce 1993), while others possessed books on mystic literature (Kafadar 1993). Sufi teachings influenced not only the men and women of letters but also "the world of illiterate village women" (Schimmel 1992, 120). In addition to public performances of female piety in the form of making pilgrimages and establishing pious foundations, Ottoman Muslim women consulted the religious men of mosques and dervish lodges and visited popular Sufi saints' tombs, churches, and synagogues as part of their public religiosity. Despite criticism, such eclectic practices were generally tolerated by the men of religious authority (Peirce 1993). Women also participated in an intricate web of everyday and momentous ceremonial religious activities, from protections against the evil eye (*nazar*) to Koran recitals. The ulema, whose struggle to control popular religious culture was always incomplete, was suspicious of popular religiosity, among other reasons for its syncretism and the room it provided for women's religious authority (Berkey 2003).

While the Ottoman Empire was never formally colonized, it began to lose power in the seventeenth century because of the rise of European imperialism and was gradually pushed to the periphery of the changing world system. At this conjuncture of unequal confrontation with the West, Ottoman elites reflexively constructed an idea of tradition in an effort to strengthen the empire with an eye to its future (Deringil 1993). They initially sought to restore the proverbial golden age of tradition but, by the eighteenth century, the idea of restoring the old order was gradually abandoned in favor of emulating the power of the West. Moving from a desire to restore the traditional order of the past to a modernist orientation toward the future and novelty, Ottoman reformists began adopting Western techniques and technologies. This state-led modernization project would gradually change both the meaning and social organization of religion in the empire (Berkes [1964] 1998).

The driving cadres of this transformation, a new class of Westernized/Westernizing cultural elites with a novel version of high culture, emerged in the eighteenth century during the period of Ottoman modernization. Trained for military and administrative posts in new institutions modeled after their Western counterparts and traveling to Europe in newly created diplomatic posts, their main cultural capital was their familiarity with European languages, thought, and societies. This new generation found a voice in the emerging political public sphere of the empire, organizing itself in the nineteenth century into flourishing associations and publications. There, they discussed the European states and societies they observed so as to identify the reasons for the increasing power of the West and to propose reforms at home. Overshadowed by these new elites were the ulema, who were losing both their prestige and their power. As their monopoly over the production of high culture, the training of scholarly elites, and the administration of justice waned, they were gradually pushed into what would come to be perceived as the realm of religion.

As this emergent elite culture became distanced from the official religious culture of the ulema and the popular cultures of the periphery, the distancing was negotiated in the political sphere in the language of religion. According to Mardin, "embracing Islam and its cultural heritage was the response of the periphery to a center that had failed to integrate the periphery into the new cultural framework" (1990, 45). When the role of the state itself evolved from being the guardian of the traditional order and the official religion to becoming the agent of sociopolitical reform, the legitimacy of the state and its higher-ranking ulema as the protectors of traditional religious orthodoxy began to erode. In this vacuum, religious orders and lower-ranking ulema emerged as new political actors who increasingly expressed their opposition to the reformist state in the language of religion. The changing relations between the state, the ulema, and the religious orders of the nineteenth century resulted in a new understanding of religion such that the religious was increasingly associated with the traditional, while the new and changing took on the connotation of nonreligious (Berkes [1964] 1998, 109). The challenge for the coming generations of Westernist cultural elites who would become the designers, cadres, and supporters of later modernizing and secularizing reforms in both the late Ottoman Empire and the early Turkish Republic was to negotiate and reclaim the meanings of the traditional and the religious. These elites' shifting and complex understandings of, feelings toward, and efforts to control different classes of fortune-tellers in their society would constitute a seemingly inconsequential but in fact deeply felt and contested flashpoint of their macrolevel endeavors to delineate a secular national.

Fortune-Tellers of the Empire

Zati was a famous male poet of modest means who practiced geomancy in early sixteenth-century Istanbul. One day, while gazing at the sea in contemplation, Zati is teased by a man who remarks, "Zati, I see now that you have quit geomancy and have started reading water instead!" Zati teases him back, saying that he might certainly earn more reading water or even throwing beans than the few coins he earns by straining his eyes with geomancy.

—Cited in Sennur Sezer, *Osmanlı'da Fal ve Falnameler*

As the joke implies, Ottoman society hosted a varied landscape of divinatory practices. When Zati complained that his trade of geomancy, an occult science of historical divination involving the interpretation of dots and markings on sand (Aydın 1995), brought him less income than reading water or throwing beans might, the humor in his remarks depended upon his audience's familiarity with the presumed hierarchy of divination methods of his era.[7] Some (learned, masculine, and Muslim) fortune-telling forms like geomancy held more authority and commanded respect, while others like reading water or throwing beans were less valued in price and prestige. Such undervalued forms of divination have for the most part been ignored by historical chroniclers and researchers. In her nonacademic but highly attentive survey of secondary sources regarding fortune-telling in the Ottoman Empire, author Sennur Sezer remarked, "Fortune-telling from coffee, beans, and playing cards most certainly existed. But because these were read either by non-Muslims or by amateurs, they have not been widely documented" (1998, 143). Historian Cemal Kafadar similarly notes that there were reports of "faith healers, ignorant women who relied on incantations, superstitious practices such as pouring molten lead into water, charms, and prayers to cure their patients," with the observation that "witchcraft and fortune-telling were also a female domain" (1993, 204). We thus know little of the informal and gendered margins of fortune-telling in the empire. While the literary, institutionalized, male, public, and Muslim sectors of divination such as astrology and geomancy have been more closely studied, historians have barely begun to document the lower-ranked economy of fortune-telling practiced in nonliterate, non-Muslim, and/or feminized modalities.

Divination was widely practiced at all levels of the diverse landscape of Ottoman society, among the courtly elites and the unlearned and uninitiated alike. While ostensibly at odds with Sunni orthodoxy, divination was integral to Ottoman courtly culture and political life, particularly during the empire's consolidation in the fifteenth and sixteenth centuries (Fleischer 2010; Şen 2017). At the pinnacle of the hierarchy of diviners of that era, astrologers (*münec-cim*) were an institutionalized part of the elite ulema, producing astronomical and astrological knowledge for the courtly elites. They prepared imperial calendars, timetables for fasting hours during the month of Ramadan, and astrological tables and horoscopes, and calculated the most auspicious times for all kinds of courtly events, from marriages to war declarations (Aydüz 2006). They influenced and officially marked the timing of all significant events in the life of the sultan and his family and in the political life of the empire. Ottoman sultans and courtly elites also consulted various other scholars of esoteric sciences who populated the Ottoman courtly circles; some even became the sultan's intimates. Divinatory sciences, especially the science of letters and names, were a "deeply embedded part of the mystical, philosophical, and political environment of even the most self-consciously Sunni environments of the period" (Fleischer 2010, 235). In the fifteenth and early sixteenth centuries, prognostication, particularly of the apocalyptic and messianic type, played a key role in legitimizing not only individual sultans and their particular policies but also the Ottoman imperial identity and the nature of Ottoman sovereignty itself. Following the decline of public interest in apocalyptic prognostication in the second half of the sixteenth century, "neither prognostication nor its sources disappeared. Rather, they were absorbed into the fabric of private life at the Ottoman palace" (Fleischer 2010, 243).

Fortune-telling in its various forms permeated multiple social classes of the empire across the divisions of ruler/subject, wealthy/poor, learned/unlearned, Muslim/non-Muslim, and male/female. In the second half of the seventeenth century, the famous traveler Evliya Çelebi noted that parading artisans of the empire included seventy astrologers and three hundred geomancers (*remmal*) from fifteen different shops. In contrast with the sober attitude of the astrologers, a testament to their higher courtly ranking, geomancers shouted at the crowd, "Show us your fortunes and misfortunes" (cited in Sezer 1998, 10). While astrologers' tasks required highly specialized and literary knowledge acquired in imperial colleges that was rewarded by a prestigious ulema post, geomancers were organized as an artisan's guild and learned the art by apprenticeship. In addition to astrology and geomancy, many other divination techniques were used in the court and beyond. For example, both Sultan Murat III (r. 1574–95; see Fleischer 2010) and Asiye Hatun, a Muslim Ottoman woman living in Macedonia in the seventeenth century (Kafadar 1994), recorded their dreams for interpretation (*tabir*). Whereas the sultan summoned his chronographer/ astrologer (*saati*) to interpret his dreams, Asiye Hatun wrote letters to a sheikh of her choice. Although Sultan Murat III and Asiye Hatun both recorded their dreams in writing, as a nonliterary method accessible to the illiterate, dream interpretation was probably one of the most common forms of divination. Another widespread method was book fortune-telling (*kitap falı*), which required consulting a book, usually the Koran or a collection of religious or mystic poetry. A randomly selected verse, letter, or combination of letters was then interpreted, sometimes by consulting a *falname*, a fortune-telling book prepared for this purpose (Şenödeyici and Koşik 2015). Given that some Koran copies came with a *falname* booklet attached, book fortune-telling seems to have been a popular divination method that did not always necessitate consulting a specialist (Sezer 1998). Distinctions of status were no less pronounced in book fortune-telling. While sultans possessed personalized horoscopes and *falname* signed by court astrologers, their subjects consulted public astrological calendars and turned to diviners of lower status, who read their fortunes from a *yıldızname*, a horoscope book prepared and read according to the occult science of letters and numbers. When consulted on what should be done about such fortune-telling from the Koran, the sixteenth-century head of the empire's ulema, Sheikh-ul-Islam Ebu Suud, reportedly answered, "Nothing" (cited in Sezer 1998, 13). Popular divination, while not condoned by Sunni religious orthodoxy, was tolerated.

Once integral parts of social and political life, fortune-tellers would be expelled from the public sphere through criminalization in the twentieth century. The reasons for this exile lay in the changing meaning of religion during the long-drawn-out process of Ottoman and Turkish modernization. Brokered by a new class of (proto)nationalist elites, a nonreligious/secular realm of knowledge and authority would come to know and order the religious as an increasingly separate and gradually restricted realm. In the constitution of a secular national vis-à-vis the (re)invented categories of tradition, religion, and superstition, the disciplining of divinatory practitioners would serve as a productive venue in which to summon feelings ranging from familiarity, admiration, and tolerance to distance, repulsion, and fury. The public circulation of these feelings would help demarcate the boundaries of the secular in alignment with gendered, ethnoreligious, racial, and socioeconomic hierarchies that shaped the fault lines of the nation in the making.

The Traditional and the National

The various classes of fortune-tellers of the late Ottoman Empire were documented by a protoethnographer, Abdülaziz Bey (1850–1918). Born to an elite family in Istanbul, Abdülaziz Bey learned Arabic and French from his tutors and spent his career as an administrative official in various prestigious posts. A man of letters, he wrote poetry and published widely, compiling an extraordinary chronicle of Ottoman traditions, ceremonies, and expressions, including divinatory practices (Abdülaziz Bey 1995).

Abdülaziz Bey recognized astrologers at the service of the palace and courtly elites as a respected professional class, but assumed a didactic stance toward his readers when describing geomancers. He observed that when geomancers read fortunes, "naturally, since part of all the interpretation and words would agree with what the person had in mind and heart, people would say 'it hit the mark' and immediately believe" (Abdülaziz Bey 1995, 2:368). Dreaming and dream interpretation were also common methods of prognostication, he noted, and famous dream interpreters (*muabbir*) included sheikhs and imams. Drifting from his characteristically distanced and rationalist prose, Abdülaziz Bey remarked, "From experience, it has been seen many times that interpretations of such dreams by famous *muabbirs* have hit the mark" (2:366). According to Abdülaziz Bey, fortune-telling from the Koran (*tefeül*) was also widespread, and a women's version consisted of counting the beads of a *tespih* (prayer beads).

In contrast to his respect for and admitted familiarity with these forms of divination, Abdülaziz Bey described the informal, nonliterary, feminized, ethnicized, and non-Muslim strata of fortune-telling quite disparagingly:

> Another bizarre way used to "discover" the unknown was this: people called fortune-tellers [*bakıcı*] would sit down, usually in their own houses but sometimes here and there on an empty street, with a piece of cloth upon which they would place a handful of blue beads, seashells, and beans, throw them, and then "interpret" their placement. They would use pleasant bromides, and, if these were not understood, they would say, "You interpret it," and leave it at that. Famous fortune-tellers read the fortunes of women and sometimes of men, consulting them in their houses. . . . Fortune-tellers of this kind were often Rum [Ottoman Greek Orthodox]. Some were Muslim Roma women. . . . At the end of the fortune-telling,

she would ask for bread or a dress, then take the opportunity when the man answering the door entered the house [to fetch the things she had requested], break in, grab what she could, and run away with it. And this is how it would end. (1995, 2:368)

Practiced in the privacy of homes or on street corners, particularly by non-Muslim and Roma women who also worked in public as petty traders and visited their customers in their homes, this type of divination was a marginalized female niche that Abdülaziz Bey readily equated with petty crime and dismissed as having no legitimate claim to authority.

His distaste for and dismissal of feminized divination notwithstanding, Abdülaziz Bey had even stronger resentment toward and serious concern about another class of fortune-tellers who claimed to be able to command the jinn (*cin*) to heal, cast and undo spells, and predict the future. According to Abdülaziz Bey, this racialized niche of divination was populated by liberated Black slave women and male occultists from Sudan and the Maghreb, who not only practiced out of their houses but even opened shops in Istanbul. Abdülaziz Bey considered their trade as one of manipulation and moneygrubbing, declaring it to be the source of grave crimes, including murder, and complaining in feigned surprise that distinguished men frequented them regularly. This most offensive group of fortune-tellers was described as Arab and Black, as these two ethnic/racial markers tend to collapse together in Turkish. Marking this group as representative of the worst kind of fortune-teller allowed Abdülaziz Bey to retrospectively rehabilitate the other kinds of fortune-tellers as relatively benign, setting them aside to be potentially tolerated at the margins of the secularist project and possibly to be revived for reinvented traditions of the nation in the making. These Arab/Black commanders of the jinn were such a dangerous source of public vice feeding on the ignorance of ordinary people that Abdülaziz Bey kept to a brief description and dramatically declared, "It has been decided not to further explain them here" (1995, 2:370).

ABDÜLAZIZ BEY'S ACCOUNT of Ottoman fortune-tellers reflects not only the stratified and widespread economy of prognostication in the late nineteenth and early twentieth centuries but also the perspective of a proto–Turkist Ottoman intellectual on divination and, more broadly, on religion and tradition. Motivated by his stated fear that Ottoman traditions might be lost to subsequent generations, given the Ottoman elites' superficial imitation of the European way of life (*alafrangalık*), Abdülaziz Bey felt compelled to meticulously document what he perceived to be his society's traditions. Importantly, Abdülaziz Bey was not an old man clinging to the past. Rather, his reflexivity about tradition was informed by a modernist orientation toward governing the future. In his foreword, dated around 1910, Abdülaziz Bey explicitly expressed his sympathy toward the emergent Turkist political movement, to whom his cataloging of Ottoman traditions was addressed. Negotiating (self-)Orientalizing discourses that pathologized tradition and religion (Islam) together with nationalist discourses that (selectively) reappraised tradition and rehabilitated religion, Abdülaziz Bey hoped his book would guide the next generation of Turkist political elites in choosing the traditions they could be proud of and would want to revive as part of a national culture fit for Western civilization.

His complex classifications of and strong feelings against the various groups of fortune-tellers he describes attests to the classed, gendered, and racialized complexity of the task of recalibrating the traditional, the religious, and the national. Abdülaziz Bey matter-of-factly notes the presence of a highly educated Muslim male stratum of astrologers, while describing the literate Muslim male class of geomancers from the composed perspective of a distanced observer who interjects rational explanation and doubt into their scene of reading. In describing the educated Muslim male class of dream interpreters, Abdülaziz Bey even allows himself a moment of reverent and credulous participation, unmarred by the disenchanting and distanced cross-examination that is the hallmark of the masculine secular reason he otherwise speaks through, and joins other fortune-telling clients to admit that the reader does sometimes hit the mark.

On the subject of female, illiterate, non-Muslim, ethnicized, and racialized forms of fortune-telling, however, Abdülaziz Bey retreats to his position of an external observer. This time, he is neither calm in attitude nor brief in description. He quickly dismisses the practices via rational explanation accompanied by a liberal dose of scorn. In a display of unabashed gendered, classed, and ethnoreligious anxieties, he criminalizes Greek Orthodox Christian and Muslim Roma female practitioners by alleging theft.

Ultimately, though, it is the racialized group of Arab/Black practitioners who conjure jinn that Abdülaziz Bey deems most dangerous and detestable. Fueled with ethnoracial hatred, Abdülaziz Bey attributes to this group the worst of intentions and the most serious of crimes and declares them manipulators, party to grave crimes, possibly even murderers. His attitude takes shape in the larger context of the nineteenth-century criminalization of Arab/Black (freed) slave women of the Ottoman Empire for offenses like theft, arson, and murder, with court proceedings suggesting that magical practices facilitated communal relations and (criminalized) acts of agency among this population (Erdem 2010). For Abdülaziz Bey, part of the sense of danger posed by this group comes from their alleged ability to place educated, respectable Muslim men under their influence, threatening the very distinctions required to construct and uphold a secular national masculine ideal. Indeed, having included them in his ethnographic inventory of fortune-tellers, Abdülaziz Bey then refuses in declarative tones to further document this group of practitioners in the hopes that such a public act of deliberate literary erasure might help eradicate them from the future, if not the memory, of the new nation. He warns that these types exist only to suggest that we should not allow them to. Such othering is on par with Ottoman Orientalism and the emergent Turkist project of delineating Turkishness and its compatibility with modern civilization through the construction and ousting of internal ethnicized/racialized others as traditional, irrational, and foreign to the nation (Makdisi 2002).

Abdülaziz Bey's affective mapping of the gendered, classed, ethnoreligious, and racial fault lines of the divination economies of the late Ottoman period leading up to World War I foreshadows the complex feelings that would later attend the making of the secular national during the formation of the Turkish Republic in the early 1920s. Reverent if at times also disenchanting vis-à-vis the educated Muslim male forms of divination; trivializing and even criminalizing vis-à-vis the illiterate, non-Muslim, and ethnically and racially otherized female forms; ethnoracially hateful and expunging vis-à-vis the Arab/Black forms: Abdülaziz Bey's collection of Ottoman traditions provides a prescriptive account of divinatory practices designed to inform the Turkist political agenda of reviving a national culture compatible with Western secular modernity. Cataloging the first class of elite divinatory practices as traditions to be treated with a mixture of the doubtful curiosity of secularizing reason and the respectful interest of nationalist appreciation, the second as trivialities to be disregarded or petty criminals to be avoided, and the third as treacherous alien elements to be known only to be prohibited, Abdülaziz Bey successfully predicts the fate of this complex divination economy in the secularist nationalist project of modern Turkey.

The Superstitious and the Secular

Gentlemen, the aim of the revolutions we have been and still are undertaking is to transport the people of the Turkish Republic into a social form that is both wholly modern and civilized in every sense and appearance. This is the fundamental principle of our revolutions. It is necessary to smash those mindsets that cannot accept this reality. Even now, those who have corroded and dulled the nation's minds have this mentality. The superstitions that exist in such minds will of course be banished. Without expelling them, it is not possible to bring the light of truth into the mind.

—Mustafa Kemal Atatürk, *Atatürk'ün Söylev ve Demeçleri*, vol. 2

The founder of the Turkish Republic, Mustafa Kemal (later Atatürk), delivered the speech above in 1925, just months before the criminalization of fortune-tellers, who, together with a range of religious actors, would be expelled from the nation. Mustafa Kemal's discourse is in dialogue with the colonialist metanarrative of a civilizing mission set on replacing the darkness of superstition with the light of reason and translates the mission into the local contestations over the nation in the making. Verbs like *corroding* and *dulling* describe the alleged effects of superstition on the individual's and the nation's (collective) consciousness and associate superstition with decline and ignorance. Such language in effect paints the promised secular modernity as a bright and exciting horizon and colors it with feelings of hope and enthusiasm. Terms like *banishing* and *smashing* evoke jagged feelings of anger and the attendant promise or threat of aggression directed rightfully and correctively, in the name of secularization and modernization, at the nation's designated enemies. The forceful tone of the speech hints at Turkish secularism's authoritarianism, described by numerous authors as having been assertive (Kuru 2007), didactic (Gellner 1981), and pedagogical (Kaplan 2006). Marked by its forcible expulsion from the public sphere of what had by then been constructed as superstitious, the revolutionary force of the speech was meant to make room for a modern, secular national future.

The making and remaking of the categories of tradition, religion, and superstition reflected and sought to contain the powerful contradictions of the Turkish nationalist project, in which the exact contours of the sphere of religion remained the subject of intense political debate in relation to questions of national identity and difference from the West. If those sectors of the elite that felt threatened by the Westernizing reforms of Ottoman modernization and later Republican secularism translated their grievances into the language of religion, the modernizing elites driving the reforms were themselves in disagreement over the question of which areas of state and society should be subjected to modernizing reforms and which should be circumvented and left under the authority of religion. While the Ottoman reformers were neither postcolonial nor (yet) nationalist, they and their intellectual heirs, the Turkish nationalists, shared an almost postcolonial consciousness and a contradictory desire to become like, yet remain distinct from, the West, a contradiction characteristic of postcolonial nationalist discourses (Chatterjee 1986; Kadioğlu 1996). To contain this contradiction, Turkish nationalists would reformulate the meanings of and relations between the traditional, the religious, and the superstitious and subordinate them to the national by articulating a particular form of nationalist secularism.

By the turn of the twentieth century, the increasingly powerful ideological current of Turkism identified the problem of the empire as the decline of Turkish national culture, proposing paradoxically that the restoration of national culture should be accomplished through Westernization and secularization. Insisting that "a backward nation could 'modernize' itself while retaining its cultural identity" (Chatterjee 1999, 30), the main ideologue of Turkism, Ziya Gökalp, distinguished between national "culture" (*hars*) and international "civilization" (*medeniyet*). Gökalp proposed emulating the internationalized civilization of the West, including its material civilization and its political and cultural organization into nation-states, while at the same time fostering a pure Turkish national culture. His argument was that while religion formed a part of every national culture, including modern Western ones, in the Ottoman Empire, Arab civilizational influences had been mistaken for Islamic ideals and had contaminated Turkish national culture. According to Gökalp, although Islam was compatible with both Turkish national culture and Western civilization, the Arab civilizational influences mistaken as Islamic were simply not. It was under these Arab influences, he argued, that religion had become a dysfunctional social institution that had not only failed to perform its proper role of promoting and guiding piety but had also impeded the proper functioning of society. Gökalp maintained that while what Westernists argued was true—that the religious beliefs and practices of the Ottomans seemed "absurd, superstitious and contrary to reason" (Berkes [1964] 1998, 293)—this was not because they were Islamic but because they were distorted by ignorant popular beliefs and corrupt religious institutions that were shaped under the influence of Arab civilization. Expanded to the point where it had come to regulate most aspects of social life at the expense of national culture, religion had now to be relegated once and for all to its proper domain of faith and worship, in Gökalp's words, the domain of religion/piety (*diyanet*). *Diyanet*, the proper realm of religion pertaining to dutiful devotion to religious faith and worship, Gökalp asserted, was the only legitimate arena for religious men and institutions.

In the name of nationalization, religious institutions had therefore to be restricted in their authority and scope, and superstitious religious traditions had to be disciplined via rational secular reasoning and rule.

Identifying the roots of the relative weakness of the Ottoman Empire vis-à-vis the West in its corrupt and superstitious traditions, the founder of the new republic, Mustafa Kemal, and the official ideology of the new state, Kemalism, closely echoed Gökalp's Turkism.

> Given the place they inhabited and the area they lived in, the Turks were in contact with Persia to one side and the Arab and Byzantine nations to the other. Contacts clearly have an effect on nations. The civilizations of the nations the Turks were in contact with had begun to decay. The Turks could not help but be influenced by the flawed traditions and bad qualities of these nations. This state of affairs generated mixed-up, unscientific, and inhuman mentalities in them. This is one of the most important causes of our decay. (Atatürk 1989, 143)

These traditions and mindsets were seen to cause decay, not only because their alien origins rendered them harmful to the purity of the national culture in the making, but also because their superstitious qualities rendered them incompatible with the Kemalist vision of a modern, enlightened country that would be allowed into the fold of Western civilization. Secularist interventions into religious beliefs, practices, and institutions seeking to discipline and restrict religion to its proper shape and sphere were defined as prerequisites to the full development of a national culture fit for Western civilization.

This epistemic closure around the paradox of a Westernizing nationalist project would structure the Turkist, and later Turkish Republican, brand of secularism and its contradictions. Shaped by the way Turkism contained the primary contradiction of postcolonial nationalism wherein the nation-to-be's relation to the West was complicated by the attempt to become alike through modernization and assert difference through nationalization, Turkists' "reform program would consist, not of secularization via Westernization, but secularization via Turkification" (Berkes [1964] 1998, 366). Destabilizing this elegant, if fragile, closure was the fact that the resolution of the postcolonial nationalist paradox, in Chatterjee's words, "necessarily implies an elitist program, for the act of cultural synthesis can only be performed by the supremely refined intellect. Popular consciousness, steeped in centuries of superstition and irrational folk religion, can hardly be expected to adopt this ideal: it would have to be transformed from without" (1999, 51). Following the declaration of the Turkish Republic as a nation-state in 1923, this cultural synthesis would be undertaken by the Republican elites, who would define and intervene in the sphere of tradition and religion from within the interpretative framework of a nationalist secularist project (Kadıoğlu 1996).

Recognizing themselves as the leaders of an undifferentiated mass of people, the nation, Republican elites were resolved to accomplish a social revolution (Ahmad 1993) and refine the popular (religious) culture of the people before it could be reappropriated as national. One of the major endeavors of these Republican elites was to dismantle the Ottoman moral order in favor of an epistemologically positivist and nationalist cosmology. The proper subject of the new republic was to be a secular, rational, and enlightened citizen constructed in opposition to the pious, superstitious, and ignorant Ottoman subject. This meant that the new republic was to be tasked with a domesticized version of the colonialist civilizational and racial burden of protecting and disciplining those under its rule who were feminized by their alleged superstitiousness and irrationality.

Turkish Republican elites preferred secularist social engineering to simply waiting for economic and social modernization to gradually diminish the authority of tradition, religion, and superstition over the people, influences they held responsible for the backwardness and resultant fragility of the country's national sovereignty. In the imaginary of Kemalist secularism (called laicism, *laiklik* in Turkish), superstitious and corrupt religious beliefs, actors, and institutions were conceived not just as obstacles to Westernization but as dangerous enemies of the nation. From the Sheikh-ul-Islam to the last sultan/caliph of the Ottoman Empire, Mustafa Kemal argued, the corrupt men of religion used their religiopolitical authority to betray the nation and had therefore to be eliminated. Preparing to announce a set of secularist reforms targeting all existing religious institutions, from the ulema to the religious orders, Mustafa Kemal categorized the ulema of his day into two classes: one composed of genuine ulema who were scientifically trained "as though they had been educated in Europe" and one composed of corrupt ulema who were "ignoramuses dressed like hodjas" (Atatürk 1989, 148). In this dichotomy of modern versus traditional religious actors, those sorted into the first class were designated as model religious scholars of the new republic who would be assigned to regulate a limited terrain of piety. Those sorted into the second class were deemed traitorous corrupters who did not belong to the nation in the making. But even for the first class of praiseworthy men of religion, their only legitimate realm of authority was that of piety (*diyanet*), which was to be organized under the Presidency of Religious Affairs (Diyanet İşleri Başkanlığı), a state apparatus designed to produce and disseminate a nationalized and rationalized Islam cleansed of obscurantism and superstitions.[8] For the rest, repressive Kemalist reforms came to police and punish any transgression of the proscribed boundaries of the privatized realm of piety and the secularist public sphere. Among the suspected transgressors of these prescriptive boundaries were fortune-tellers, especially those of the wrong kind, who would soon be designated as one among many superstitious influences endangering the secular nation.

Remains of the Secular Nation

What is the purpose of the existing religious orders if not to render their followers happy in worldly and spiritual life? In the civilized society of Turkey, I cannot accept the existence of people primitive enough to seek material and spiritual happiness in the advice of this or that sheikh, today, when confronted by science, technology, and the whole scope of civilization. . . . Gentlemen and the nation, understand well that the Republic of Turkey cannot be a land of sheikhs, disciples, and followers. The most righteous, the truest order is the order of civilization. To be a human being, it is enough to do as civilization commands and demands.

—Mustafa Kemal Atatürk, *Atatürk'ün Söylev ve Demeçleri*, vol. 2

Set in a hierarchical scheme of the evolution of humanity, Turkish nationalism represented religious orders as a primitive social form that was incompatible with the more advanced (Western) civilization. In this sense, Turkish nationalism echoed closely the Orientalist template that juxtaposed rationality with obscurantism, modernity with primitiveness, humanity with savagery, and the West with the East. The sheer existence of the second qualities in each binary was simply unacceptable, as expressed in the quotation above from Mustafa Kemal, as they barred the individual from civilized humanity and disqualified the nation from secular modernity. Informed by this template, the first decade of the Turkish Republic was characterized by the outlawing of a wide range of religious actors who had been classified as ignorant hodjas and deemed to be potential enemies of the Kemalist revolution. Early secularizing reforms included the dismantling of institutions that had explicitly granted religious legitimacy to the political authority of the state, such as the caliphate and the office of Sheikh-ul-Islam. All extrareligious functions of the ulema, from legal to educational services, were outlawed, centralized, and nationalized.

In a bid to justify the violence that accompanied its civilizing mission, the Turkish state's cleansing of undesired religious elements would operate through ethnoracial othering. The disbanding of religious orders and the criminalization of associated practitioners, including fortune-tellers, was initially executed through the brutal suppression of a religiously accented Kurdish revolt under the leadership of Sheikh Said in 1925. With the rebellion as pretext, the violent disbanding of religious elements in the name of civilizational enlightenment and the purging of ignorance and superstitions was thus first practiced in the southeast Kurdish region of Turkey as part of efforts to subjugate Kurdish political agency to Turkish national sovereignty. This move would solidify the marking of the Kurdish region by an excess of religion and tradition. Months after the banning of religious orders in this area, the violent civilizing mission of taming an ethnoracial other was replicated upon the rest of the citizens, and the ban on religious orders was extended across Turkey. The construction and subjugation of an internal Orientalized other thus enabled the Turkish nation to proclaim itself as modern/modernizing by recourse to a set of civilizational/ethnoracial hierarchies (Zeydanlıoğlu 2008), thus justifying state violence in the name of secularist nationalism. Significantly, the mark of civilizational/ethnoracial difference deployed at the turn of the twentieth century by Abdülaziz Bey for Arab/Black people and in the pre- and early Republican eras by Ziya Gökalp for Arab/misguidedly Muslim people was now transferred to Kurdish/superstitiously Muslim people. This transfer of the mark of difference from one population to the next points out the floating, but central, role that civilizational and ethnoracial othering played in the localized reassertion of the hierarchies of Western/Eastern, secular/religious, and Turkish/non-Turkish.

Constituted as Oriental others, politically suspect actors, corrupt influences on Turkish national culture, and traditional and superstitious obstacles to the desired modernization and secularization of society, religious orders were outlawed with the enactment of Law No. 677, titled "The Abolition of Dervish Lodges [*tekke*], Cloisters [*zaviye*], Shrines [*türbe*], and Related Titles." The law annulled the legal status of religious orders, enabling the state to confiscate their estates and sources of income, and criminalized the use of a variety of titles, the performance of that title's services, and the wearing of that title's clothes.[9] Titles specified in the law included, in the following order, *şeyh* (sheikh), *derviş* (dervish), *mürid* (disciple), *dede* (senior dervish), *seyit* (sayyid, a descendent of the Prophet), *çelebi* (leader of a Mevlevi order), *baba* (Bektaşi sheikh), emir, *nakip* (oldest dervish), *halife* (caliph or ordained successor of a sheikh), *falcı* (fortune-teller), *büyücü* (sorcerer), *üfürükçü* (healer), *muskacı* (amulet writer), and those who seek to "give information about the unknown" (*gaipten haber vermek*) and to help realize wishes (*murada kavuşturmak*). While many of these titles denoted membership and status in a religious order (*şeyh, derviş, mürid,* and the like), fortune-telling, like other services specified in the law, was not restricted to the religious orders but was instead integral to the ulema class, Sunni orthodoxy, and the empire's elite culture. The law nevertheless collapsed all kinds of religious practitioners together as corrupt, superstitious, and ignorant in the Kemalist vocabulary of "'true' acceptable Islam and 'bad' dangerous Islam" (Shively 2008, 707).

Fortune-tellers were officially exiled from the new nation in 1925. When the last Ottoman chief astrologer died in 1924, he was never replaced, in effect abolishing the astrologer class of the ulema. In its place, the office of chief timekeeper (*başmuvakkitlik*) was founded in 1927 to oversee the calculation of prayer and fasting hours. During this time, the secularizing state succeeded in unmaking the established structures in which Muslim, male, public fortune-tellers once operated legitimately by completely dissolving institutionalized forms of divination such as the official astrologer class and the geomancers' guild. On the other hand, the diverse and multilayered strata of feminized and informal fortune-tellers that had been categorically criminalized by Law No. 677 were diffused into an underground economy of divination away from public scrutiny and proved more resilient. The ongoing persecution of these fortune-tellers remained uneven and, as foretold in Abdülaziz Bey's chronicles, was shaped by the ways in which gender, ethnicity, race, religion, literacy, and socioeconomic status rendered certain fortune-tellers less tolerable than others.

Tracing the history of fortune-tellers from their legitimate, if stratified, social existence during the Ottoman Empire to their criminalization in early-modern Turkey, this chapter has explored how, informed by the gendered and ethnoracial hierarchies of a (self-)civilizing mission, fortune-tellers emerged as superstitious and dangerous figures to be forcefully expelled outside the secular nation. Recasting the gendered, ethnoracial, religious, and socioeconomic differences that characterized the landscape of divination in the Ottoman Empire through the ideological prism of nationalist secularism, the Republican-era criminalization of fortune-tellers would affect different kinds of practitioners unequally, extending leniency to some while harshly persecuting others. Tracking the multiple appropriations and postsecular subversions of the secularist narratives that demonize hodjas who command jinn and excuse housewives who read cups, chapter 2 continues the inquiry begun here as to how the secular depends on the continued presence, and spirited disavowal, of its constitutive outsider figures. To this end, chapter 2 turns to those cultural and ethnographic scenes in which the gendered affects of secularism coalesce.

2

THE GENDERED POLITICS OF SECULARISM

Sıdıka (Ergun 1997) is a 1990s televised comedy focusing on a young misfit girl whose aspirations conflict with the gender-conformist expectations of her poor, undereducated family. In one episode, Sıdıka's mother, worried about her daughter's lack of appropriate female demeanor and consequent inability and unwillingness to get married, consults a neighborhood *cinci hoca*, a popular male religious practitioner called hodja who treats those afflicted by jinn and deploys jinn for divination and magic. The hodja prays and breathes upon a piece of Turkish sausage and promises the mother that, upon eating it, Sıdıka will become a proper girl, thus improving her chances of marriage.

When Sıdıka finds out about her mother's plans, she decides to deceive her. She eats the sausage and commences a grotesquely exaggerated performance of domesticity, cooking, cleaning, sewing, knitting frenziedly, and eagerly awaiting a suitor to marry. At the climax of her immersion into normative femininity, Sıdıka serves Turkish coffee and offers to read the cups. Her brother, doubtful of the genuineness of her sudden transformation, asks Sıdıka when she had learned to read cups. Sıdıka responds, "I just tell whatever I see in the cup. But it does sometimes turn out to be true." To this, her mother exclaims with pleasure, "You have even mastered the vocabulary of a housewife!"

Initially pleased, her family become increasingly annoyed as Sıdıka's sessions with a noisy sewing machine extend into the wee hours of the night and disrupt the rhythms of family life. Their annoyance turns to alarm, however, when Sıdıka dresses up and goes out with female friends in search of a candidate husband. Worried about Sıdıka's lack of modesty in seeking a suitor and chastised by her own angry husband, Sıdıka's mother makes another visit to the hodja for a cure that will cancel the effects of the sausage. She finds the hodja's house deserted, with a police seal on the door. Returning home, she admits to her already-disapproving husband that the hodja is in fact a charlatan and that she regrets all the extra sausages she gifted to the hodja in exchange for his services.

AS THIS EPISODE from the popular television show *Sıdıka* humorously demonstrates, in the interpretive framework of Turkish secularism, the realm of divination is divided by gender into tolerable feminine and dangerous masculine domains. On the one hand, as the busting of the hodja in the story attests, hodjas, Islamic male practitioners who perform services such as healing and divination, serve as the abject figures of secularism to be continually ousted and criminalized. On the other hand, as the reactions of her brother and mother to Sıdıka's newfound cup-reading skills indicate, the cup-reading woman figure constitutes the epitome of proper if irrational femininity. Within this formula, the once explicitly racialized civilizational line that was drawn between reason and superstition to distinguish tolerable from intolerable fortune-tellers gets domesticated and condensed into the modern idiom of heteronormative difference. Barred from proper documentation and wished out of existence by Abdülaziz Bey, targeted as "ignoramuses dressed as hodjas" by Atatürk, parodied in popular television shows like *Sıdıka*, repeatedly unmasked as charlatans in reality and news shows, and insistently referred to by café fortune-tellers as a counterpoint from which they might draw legitimacy for their own fortune-telling practices, the hodja figure serves as a constitutive outsider whose continuing persecution cements the secular (Dole 2006). The figure of the hodja and his ousting remains crucial in a postsecular terrain where the secular is no longer normative. Complementarily, the figure of the cup-reading woman stands as a proxy for the feminine difference from masculine reason that is set apart (but not too far) from the secular, attesting to the mutual constitution of heteronormativity and secularity. Tracking the persistent yet unstable deployments of hodja-bashing narratives in cultural and ethnographic scenes, this chapter explores the affective and gendered makings and remakings of the Turkish secular and the effort to fix femininity to irrationality and superstition, against which masculine authority is constituted.

Expelled from the secularist public sphere into both the privacy of the criminalized and scandalized underground economy of hodjas and the feminized and trivialized domesticity of housewives, divination became tangled up in Turkish secularism's gendered operations. For modern masculine reason to (purport to) preside over the modern secularist public sphere, a hypermasculinized predatory figure of misguided religiosity has to be both othered and outlawed and a feminized private realm of superstition both tamed and tolerated. It is in this way that, almost a century of superstition fighting and hodja bashing notwithstanding, a variety of seemingly non-Islamic "superstitions" such as fortune-telling from coffee residues or taking precautions against the evil eye have flourished as hallmarks of normative femininity within the spaces of domesticity, the gendered habitus enabled and sustained by the nationalist secularist project. Whereas male and religiously accented superstitions mark a criminalized and othered masculinity, feminine and domestic superstitions signify a normative(ly irrational) femininity.

Consulting hodjas, wearing evil eye charms, and reading coffee cups, the housewife, the prime figure of domestic femininity, appears not only as a potential victim to be saved from hodjas but also as a vessel for the gendered difference of reason and superstition. Her engagements with the supernatural are perceived as a sign of female irrationality rather than religiosity, and her mundane, nonthreatening, feminized superstitions mark a heteronormative difference from the masculinized rationalism of her husband. By staging the rescue of women from hodjas in the public sphere and the toleration of feminine superstition in the private sphere, secularist narratives of hodjas and housewives masculinize and bestow authority upon those men who subscribe to the secular.

The sexual economy of desire and contempt that coagulates around the cunning male hodjas and their gullible feminine victims has long informed popular culture. In the late Ottoman and early Republican periods, the Turkist politician, journalist, and parliamentarian Hüseyin Rahmi Gürpınar (1864–1944) wrote numerous popular novels depicting superstitious beliefs and practices as harmful and offering their demystification by way of rational explanation remedial (Gürpınar [1913] 2015, [1924] 2018, [1964] 2010). Gürpınar's critique of superstitious meddling in familial and romantic relations provided a major foil for his larger agenda of criticizing what he deemed to be either overly Westernized or too-traditional femininities and masculinities. Secular masculinity and the masculine as secular were thus reasserted not only vis-à-vis women but also vis-à-vis the juxtaposing of overly Westernized, too-modern, effeminate men with too-traditional, too-religious, hypermasculine men. The characters he introduced included ignorant women who believed in superstitions and engaged in the rituals surrounding them, the male hodjas they consulted, and educated, urban, effeminate men who irrationally held onto their belief in the supernatural. His novels thus staged a tension between a masculine reason and a feminine irrationality that was resolved in favor of secular men of reason triumphing over the irrationality of the female and the feminized (Koşar 2008).

The hodja figure is often stereotyped as a sexually predatory man who abuses his naive female clients, inducing them to reveal their intimate personal troubles and otherwise inaccessible bodies to him and who abuses his gullible male clients who are feminized through their superstitiousness, inducing them to bestow authority and wealth on him. A 1953 historical fantasy movie set in the Ottoman era titled *Cinci Hoca* (Tedü 1953) richly plays upon this stereotype thematically and visually. The movie is an adaptation of the novel *Osmanlı Rasputin'i Cinci Hoca* (Tan [1938] 1990), which is loosely based upon the real historical characters of Ottoman Sultan "Deli (Crazy)" İbrahim (1615–48) and Cinci Hodja, the seventeenth-century healer Karabaşzade Hüseyin Efendi, who was initially summoned to help cure the sultan's ailments, gained his confidence, and rose in rank to become a chief judge, becoming a controversial figure whose influence over the sultan was cited to attest to the sultan's irrationality and incompetence and, more broadly, the superstitiousness and ineptness of the political elites of the Ottoman Empire. In typical historical fantasy style and reminiscent of other films excoriating the Russian mystic Rasputin, the film depicts in fanciful brushstrokes the controversy surrounding Cinci Hodja and Sultan İbrahim. In the movie poster, the hodja is depicted as a bearded man dressed in religious attire. He is shown writing a charm on the exposed chest of a woman whose face is turned away from view, her hands lowering her dress down her shoulders. By inciting desire for the damsel in distress, the scene voyeuristically hails the viewer as a secular, rational man to rebuke the hodja and drive him out. The secularist contempt for the hodja sets up a fantasy scene in which the secularist new man may triumph over traditional masculinity, refract his masculine desire for women through the secularizing act of lifting women up out of their backward victimhood, and gain

FIGURE 2.1. Poster for the 1953 historical fantasy movie *Cinci Hoca*, about the seventeenth-century healer and controversial political figure Karabaşzade Hüseyin Efendi.

access to the woman he has just rescued. The hodja's hypermasculinity, othered as sexually transgressive and aggressive, is disciplined by a secularist desire for (rescuing) his feminized victim, thus frustrating the hodja's desire for women. Through the deviant masculinity of the hodja figure and the rescue of women and feminized men, including Ottoman sultans who in their irrationality fall prey to them, secularist state elites can be constituted as embodying masculine reason and as rationally male.

Reflecting the spatialized and ethnoracial contours of the nationalist secularist project, the hodja figure is conveniently displaced onto the past and/ or the periphery of the nation. In addition to the court hodja exemplified in the novel and the movie depicted above, the figure of the village hodja appears in the progressive literature of the Republican era as a symbol of the obscurantism, fatalism, and ignorance that hindered the desired modernization of the country's rural periphery (Karpat 1960). Religious village hodjas compete with secularist village teachers, the Republican civil servants tasked with lifting villagers up out of their backwardness through a secular education in modernity and nationhood.[1] In this context, the subdued ethnoracial markers of civilizational inferiority are displaced onto the distinctions of urban/rural and educated/ignorant.

If the hodja and his superstitious victims are at times pushed back within the linear time and space of modernization—into the Ottoman past or out to the country's rural and ethnic hinterland—their continued presence and disciplining here and now serve to reassert the gendered logics of Turkish secularism (Dole 2006, 2012). In the 1990s, secularist anxieties over the rise of political Islam, neoliberal economic restructuring, rural-to-urban migration, and the increasing visibility of ethnoracial minorities fueled a renewed interest in hodja scandals. In these stories, hodjas were viewed as having plagued the allegedly ignorant urban poor. They became popular figures in televised media exposé stories, providing the public with timely and familiar scapegoats whose criminalization served to censure political Islam, legitimize secularist state authority, and assuage secularists' economic, racialized, and gendered anxieties.

Hodja bashing continues to be a prominent genre in contemporary popular culture. From mundanely scandalous third-page stories to televised scenes, hodja persecution stories, especially those of the titillating kind involving sexual harassment, regularly appear in the media. The characters of this genre include male hodjas, female (and less often male) victims who are economically and sexually taken advantage of, and the journalist or the policeman who baits and busts the hodja. Hodjas are depicted as deceitful predators operating under the guise of piety and traditionalism, often promising to guide their clients along the traditional paths of heteronormativity. Their clients in turn are depicted as ignorant victims whose superstitions place them in a situation of economic and sexual vulnerability and impropriety. The captioned image accompanying an ordinary news story succinctly expresses this dominant theme: "The 'cinci hoca' who harassed the women whose marriages he promised to save is busted."

Together, the sexual economy of desire and contempt that fuels the repetition of hodja-bashing scenarios and the accompanying tolerance of feminized superstitions demonstrate how central the politics of gender and sexuality are to Turkish secularism. The assembly of the Turkish secular has been closely tied to the construction of new national femininities and masculinities. While the national public sphere was produced through top-down secularist reforms as "a site for the implementation of a secular and progressive way of life" (Göle 2002, 176) and marked as secular by the presence of mixed-gender sociabili-

Kadınları taciz eden 'Cinci Hoca' yakalandı

İstanbul Esenler'de kadınları taciz eden cinci hoca, yakayı ele verdi.

FIGURE 2.2. News article featuring photos of a *cinci hoca*, on the left "treating/harassing" a female client, and on the right escorted by a police officer into custody. The bold headline overlaid across the image reads, "'Cinci hoca' who harassed women whose marriages he promised to save is busted" ("Kadınları taciz eden 'Cinci Hoca' yakalandı," *Haber46*, September 14, 2020, https://www.haber46.com.tr/asayis/kadinlari-taciz-eden-cinci-hoca-yakalandi-h368076.html).

ties, a complementary familial/domestic sphere was coconstituted as a site for the production of modern heteronormativity and marked as secular by the conjugal intimacy of husband and wife. The gendered project of producing a secular(ist) public sphere required a cyclical purging of "misguided religious traditions" and "superstitions," for which the hodja served as the perfect embodied target: a male antihero placeholder whose expulsion opened up legitimate space for the secularist authority of the state and its secularizing men. Parallel to this, women's weakness for hodjas and their engagement in various superstitious practices in the domestic sphere marked their gendered difference, allowing for the secularist superiority and authority of ordinary men over women. Superstition and its gendered embodiments had to remain in order for the hierarchy to be imposed.[2]

If secular masculinity is constructed vis-à-vis both religious hypermasculinity and superstitious femininity, feminized subjects are invited to approximate the modern secular, especially as a way to find relief from the traditional demands of femininity. This is evident in the *Sıdıka* show, which is built on the dynamic tension between Sıdıka's modern, secular, gender-progressive aspirations and the more conventional, gender-conservative expectations of her family, indexed onto the family's lower socioeconomic status. Her mother, an undereducated housewife from a lower-class urban neighborhood, turns to a hodja only in an effort to bring Sıdıka back into the fold of heteronormative femininity. Sıdıka's mother's trust in the hodja's authority is thus a function not only of her superstition but also of her attachment to gender conservatism. Eating the sausage, Sıdıka pretends to fall under the influence of both her mother's superstitious, conservative brand of femininity and the hodja's ignorantly religious, improperly sexual masculinity. The absurd humor of a hodja praying over a sausage, which upon being eaten renders Sıdıka a submissive woman, depends partly upon the sexual connotations of the sausage as a phallic appendage of the hodja and partly upon the recognition of the Turkish sausage (*sucuk*) as a traditional food item that is too spicy and smelly for the refined tastes of secular urban elites. After consuming the sausage, Sıdıka overperforms domestic femininity as a proper *ev kızı* (literally, "house girl," a young unmarried woman who does not work outside the home) to such an extent that her submission becomes a parody that threatens to destabilize the patriarchal controls over her. In the end, Sıdıka's mother is saved from her superstitions by the police who bust the hodja, apologizes to her husband whose better judgment she now admits to, and releases her daughter from her hodja-powered efforts to bring her into gender conformity, if only until the next episode. The story's coda reaffirms Turkish secularism's gendered promise to aspiring young women like Sıdıka that secularism can deliver them from those patriarchal controls deemed excessive, traditional, and irrational. Sıdıka is able to maneuver the realms of religion and superstition inhabited by the housewife and the hodja successfully, not only because she is clever and witty but also because both of these realms are held in check by the rational if patriarchal rule of the father and the police. The story thus not only circulates disdain for the hodja and dismissal of the housewife; it also cultivates attachment to secular reason, in both its familial and public guises. In this way, the masculinized claim to secularity brokered via the figures of hodjas and housewives is rendered inviting to and inhabitable by feminized subjects. The story thus sutures the gendered hopes of relief from feminized subordination onto the secular itself.[3]

In the same vein, many fortune-telling women and young and gay men—all comembers of *mahrem*—insistently distance themselves from hodjas and distinguish themselves from housewives in order to situate themselves as secular(ly

Adana'da 'falcı' operasyonu

Adana'da tarot ve kahve falı bakıldığı iddiasıyla kafeteryalara düzenlenen operasyonda 6'sı yeri sahibi 12 kişi gözaltına alındı.

24.05.2017

ADANA

Adana'da **tarot** ve **kahve falı** bakıldığı iddiasıyla kafeteryalara düzenlenen operasyonda 6'sı iş yeri sahibi 12 kişi gözaltına alındı.

Emniyet Müdürlüğü Güvenlik Şubesi ekipleri, şikayet üzerine merkez Seyhan ve Çukurova ilçelerinde 6 kafeteryaya eş zamanlı operasyon düzenledi.

Operasyonda fal baktığı ileri sürülen A.U (33) ile Gürcistan uyruklu kadın E.V. (41) ve R.Ç. (39), T.I. (35), D.K. (46) ve N.B. (61) ile 6 iş yeri sahibi gözaltına alındı. İş yerlerinde yapılan aramada tarot kartları ele geçirildi.

İş yeri sahipleri "677 sayılı Tekke ve Zaviyeler Kanunu"na muhalefetten Kabahatler Kanunu'na göre idari para cezası uygulanarak serbest bırakıldı. Fal baktığı iddia edilen 6 şüpheli ise emniyetteki işlemlerin ardından Adana Adli Tıp Biriminde sağlık kontrolünden geçirildi.

Adliyeye sevk edilen şüpheliler cumhuriyet savcısının talimatıyla serbest bırakıldı.

Muhabir: Eren Bozkurt

FIGURE 2.3. News article reporting a police raid targeting fortune-telling cafés in Adana in 2017. Several owners and readers were taken into custody, and tarot cards were confiscated (Bozkurt 2017).

gendered) subjects.[4] Not incidentally, this endeavor also helps to keep their businesses safe from prosecution. Fortune-telling cafés' legal status remains ambiguous in practice and ranges from toleration to lenient persecution: a formal complaint from a client or a highly publicized conviction case may trigger sporadic criminalization.

In this context, as they bargain for legitimacy, café readers continuously reiterate and remix familiar hodja and housewife narratives by flexing the gendered dynamics of Turkish secularism. In this way, they destabilize, if only by reinscribing, the binaries and hierarchies between masculine reason and feminine irrationality that congeal in contemporary remakings of the secular.

Postsecular Remix: "We Are Not Like Hodjas"

There is a very rich woman who lives here in Kadıköy. She's separated from her husband. She is fifty-five and he is seventy. But they're separated. Believe me, she was going from one fortune-teller to the other. She was traveling all over the country running after sorcerers, hodjas, and the like. She comes to me one day begging. She wants her husband to fall back in love with her; she wants him back. She doesn't care about anything else. She loves him so much. She means well. And she's a great person. I mean, she's a retired teacher. She lost her husband of thirty-three years. He left. I don't know why. She says that he fell in love with another woman. . . . The other day, she points to an exquisite apartment in the neighborhood. "Do something. Bring my husband back, and this apartment is yours," she says. I tell her, "*Ablam*, let it go, now. Don't believe in these things anymore."[5] I worked with her for six months. Finally, I convinced her to quit. "You will not consult hodjas anymore. Your fortune says that if you visit hodjas again, terrible things will happen, and your husband will never return. Stop it. Don't waste your money. Give that money to the needy and Allah will recognize your good intentions and your husband will return." She left crying. She told me that she believed only in me now. People would send her from this hodja to that sorcerer. She admitted to me that she had spent fifty billion liras on these people, and still they could do nothing to help her. I said to her, "Think about it! You're educated. You're a teacher! None of these people can help you. Why are you still trying?"

—Sinan

Sinan, an unmarried man in his thirties who reads cups part-time at a café in exchange for treating himself and his friends to occasional drinks and snacks, told me this story in the café he worked at while waiting for a customer to arrive. In his retelling of the events, Sinan saves an educated woman (more precisely, a teacher) from her superstitious beliefs and her desperate attachment to gender conservatism, both of which make her fall prey to hodjas. Most intriguing for this discussion, Sinan accomplishes this mission with the help of pedagogically crafted fortune-telling sessions. This rather curious anecdote told in miraculous tones echoes many such stories I have heard from male and female café fortune-tellers alike. The details vary, but characters, plot, conflict, and the moral of the narrative remain constant: a female client who is very naive and open to manipulation seeks help from all manner of occult practitioners, blindly following their every advice despite receiving only economic and psychological abuse in return. One day, she comes to a fortune-telling café and meets a fortune-teller who proceeds to fervently and long-sufferingly advise her over the *longue durée* until ultimately rescuing her both from her own folly and from the ever-abusive hodjas. And so the story goes: an innocent and vulnerable victim (the client) who is abused by evil and cunning antagonists (hodjas) is saved by a good and wise protagonist (the café fortune-teller). The irony here is that this is but repetition with a difference, an inversion of the hodja-bashing narratives used to censure and criminalize fortune-tellers. In this postsecular version of the secularist narrative, however, the usual villain, the fortune-teller, has become the hero.

The postsecular remix of hodja-bashing narratives simultaneously mimics and disrupts the logic of secularist pedagogy. In Sinan's hodja narrative, the double continuity/inversion of the hodja-bashing narrative convention is particularly explicit. The figures of the sheepish believer (the client) and the omnipotent manipulator (the hodja) remain the same in this version, but the paternalist savior figure has been transformed from a journalist or policeman into a(nother) fortune-teller. The narrative invokes the themes of education and superstition as typical of the promises of secularist salvation, but with an important twist: in Sinan's version, the teacher, the preferred didactic agent of the top-down modernist project who saves the public from their own ignorance, becomes herself the victim. In his retelling, Sinan emphasizes the promise of education as an antidote to superstition but reveals it in this case as a failed promise he seeks to restore. Invoking a postsecular moment when the secularist project has failed to deliver but is not disavowed, the fortune-teller inserts himself as the hero who saves the victim-teacher from villains who are both hodjas and other fortune-tellers. Importantly, Sinan educates and enlightens his client by reading her fortune. The reading here becomes a pedagogical gesture that advises the client not to consult hodjas anymore or more troubles will ensue. Like Sinan, many café readers emphasize that, contrary to the hodjas, who seek to scare or manipulate their clients, fortune-tellers operate from within an enlightened and compassionate pedagogy through which they seek to empower clients who often arrive vulnerable to suggestion and abuse. In their revision of the hodja-bashing narrative structure, female, queer, and young male café fortune-tellers not only distance themselves from the hodja stereotype that haunts them; they also subvert the metanarrative of Turkish secularism and, often, the gendered relationship between reason and superstition it posits. Such subversion is possible in (and contributes to) the postsecular condition in which fortune-tellers operate where the hegemonic hold of secularism has already been challenged but its promises have not yet been abandoned.

In a country where secular education has long served as a key marker of social distinction and has been offered as the solution to every social ill associated with tradition, religion, and superstition (Kaplan 2006), education still holds sway. As part of their quest to differentiate themselves from "ignorant" hodjas, many café fortune-tellers like to stress the elevated educational level and social status of their clients. In response to a secularist discourse that deems fortune-telling a pursuit for the backward, the ignorant, and the urban poor, café workers describe their clients as coming from all walks of life and a range of educational, occupational, and cultural backgrounds: they are teachers, university students, faculty members, doctors, nurses, lawyers, judges. Öznur, a college-educated, thirtysomething divorcée who took work at a fortune-telling café after a long period of unemployment, offers her observations.

> When you look at it, most of them are students. There are so many students. . . . A lot of them are university students. Of the clients who work, most are highly educated with prestigious jobs. I mean, generally speaking, this is what I see. In terms of housewives . . . a significant percentage [of the women] are certainly housewives. But women who work and have economic independence are more common. And when you look at the housewives, most of them are actually educated, isolated housewives. I mean, uneducated housewives are rare. It's really a very interesting picture—educated people are more interested [in fortune-telling].

Öznur's observation that café fortune-telling draws a different clientele than the underground economy of hodjas is accurate. In part, this appeal reflects the virtues of fortune-telling's setting in cafés: the clientele is more likely to be younger, urban, middle-class, and highly educated. Still, the emphasis on the elevated educational status of their clients is strategic for fortune-tellers operating under the shadow of the secular figure of the fortune-teller-as-charlatan who benefits from the ignorance of ordinary people.

Café fortune-tellers further profess allegiance to modern secular epistemologies by expressing their respect for medical authority, differentiating themselves from hodjas who perform healing services such as praying over an object, food, or the body of the patient (*okuyup üflemek*), amulet writing (*muska yazmak*), and other cures for various afflictions that might be caused by the evil eye (*nazar*), jinn (*cin*), spells (*büyü*), or other misfortunes. In a defensive gesture, most emphasize that, unlike hodjas, they neither diagnose nor cure, volunteering without being prompted that they "are not doctors." Nermin, a married café fortune-teller in her late forties, complained about the mismatch between client expectations and fortune-teller limitations.

> The kinds of questions they ask! Only a doctor can answer those questions. I can't. What's the use of my answering? The answer to that sort of question is biological. My clients object. "But another fortune-teller answered it." I positively lose it when they say this! [*Laughing.*] A fortune-teller cannot answer that. I certainly can't provide that kind of answer. If you ask a doctor, even they may not be able to answer it. I mean, if you have a women's health problem [*kadınsal rahatsızlık*], you have to see a doctor, and a doctor has to see you. Another fortune-teller might answer the way a doctor would, but she probably made it up. I mean, not probably—she most certainly made it up. I can't do that. I tell them to go to a doctor.

Once again, the naive and duped female client and the abusive and dangerous practitioner of the secularist imaginary are used as a foil for café fortune-tellers' self-presentation as enlightened and ethical subjects. Complaining of clients seeking health-related diagnoses from unethical readers, Nermin insists that she advises that clients visit a doctor with their health problems. Other fortune-tellers are more willing to voice their hunches or issue warnings about possible health issues during a reading than is Nermin, but will often temper their prognostications with the recommendation to "have it checked out by a doctor." Café fortune-tellers thus attest to their congruence with modernist regimes of authority and expertise that secularist laws criminalizing fortune-telling sought to make room for.

While hodja-bashing narratives abound among most café fortune-tellers, readers are not universally distanced from hodjas. The nonmedical healing and care provided by hodjas is both precious and central to the identity of a minority of café readers. A few fortune-tellers told me that they had audio or visual hallucinations that were resistant to medical treatment but which, after they became fortune-tellers, became meaningful and manageable as occult experiences. Growing up, Hasan, a young queer man who read coffee cups, tarot cards, and water at a restaurant full-time, had mental health issues that were exacerbated by the conflict with his family, who could not come to terms with his increasingly apparent queerness and repeatedly admitted him to a psychiatric hospital. He recounted these medical encounters as troubling episodes that brought neither relief nor healing. During this time, Hasan found his way to a hodja, who performed healing sessions and taught him how to distinguish his hallucinations from real people and recognize them as jinn who took human form. Hasan felt that he had been given new ways to relate and respond to his hallucinations and grew more confident as he learned to read fortunes with the help of the jinn. When I met him, Hasan referred to his jinn straightforwardly, explaining how they disturb and keep him up many nights, especially those both male and female who are in love. In Hasan's case, healing and relief did not mean an eradication of symptoms, but rather an improved ability to cope with and accept his hallucinations and, possibly, his queerness as meaningful. Transformed under the hodja's care from being a patient into being an expert, Hasan eventually became a café fortune-teller. This newfound career offered him a way to manage his mental states and his nonnormative gender identity outside the pathologizing frames of biomedical and gendered normality.

The care provided by hodjas has at times also afforded respite from other kinds of gendered marginalization. Ayşe, a married woman in her early forties, was a café reader who became a fortune-teller only after receiving healing sessions with a female hodja.[6] Ayşe recounted to me how one day she poured out leftover pasta water under a tree in her backyard. Looking out her kitchen window a bit later, she saw a horse under the tree. In surprise, she went out to take a closer look. The horse whipped its tail against her face, leaving a red mark on her cheek. When her mother visited her later that day with some women from the neighborhood, they inquired about the mark. But when Ayşe told them her story, she was met with disbelief. She was particularly hurt when her mother, with whom she did not feel emotionally close, suggested in front of her guests that her husband must have hit her.[7] Some time after, Ayşe formed a deeper relationship with an older neighborhood woman who heard her story and believed it, offering her an explanation of how she must have unintentionally disturbed a jinn by pouring water over it. The jinn must have then taken the shape of a horse. The mark, the old woman suggested, was the proof of the encounter. Over the coming weeks and months, they held many sessions with the aim of helping Ayşe to prevent such occurrences and to prepare her should they happen again. During her work with the old woman, Ayşe found the female intimacy she had not been able to build with her own mother and her neighbors. She also learned to read fortunes. While neither Hasan nor Ayşe offered services other than fortune-telling in the cafés where they worked, their fortune-teller identities and their gendered sense of self remained closely anchored to these nonmedical modalities of healing, which provided them with valuable nonfamilial space for recovery and empowerment in the face of gendered and sexual marginalization they felt in their families and communities.

For a majority of café fortune-tellers, however, the range of healing and other services hodjas provide signifies their participation in a corrupt moral economy that stands in contradistinction to the secularist universe of legitimacy they seek to align themselves with. For this reason, they discredit services beyond divination in an attempt to distance themselves from the aura of depravity and criminality that the hodja-bashing genre conjures. Semra explains: "Why was fortune-telling forbidden? [Because hodjas say things like,] 'You are under a spell and only I can undo it,' or 'I will take this much of your money, that much of your property.' There are laws against this. But just going somewhere to have your fortune told . . . because we're only selling the coffee here, fortune-telling is a freebie. There's no law against this. There's no law on this subject whatsoever. By doing it this way, what we're doing is legal." According to Semra, in the informal economy of hodjas, fortune-telling is the bait, and the additional treatments offered as cures for the conditions diagnosed during divination are the payoff. Many café workers similarly insist that fortune-telling cafés should not be confused with the underground divination and healing sector of hodjas, since they do not use fortune-telling as a gateway to convince their clients that they need additional services such as the dispelling of the evil eye or a malicious spell. In their narratives, they make sure to clarify that fortune-telling cafés help move divination out of the underground economy of hodjas, thereby freeing it up for circulation in the market and attaching it to the legal commodity of coffee as a promotional gift. They thus position themselves as being in sync with the very modernist spirit that seeks to do away with hodjas.

Like cup readers, café managers also seek to draw and maintain the boundaries between their businesses and the larger informal economy of divination and healing. They actively work to control and curtail the provision of services other than the designated fortune-telling sessions, both in order to have full control over the labor of their employees and to safeguard the precarious legality of their businesses. Owners often forbid fortune-tellers from providing services other than divination or from providing services outside the café, advising them against suggesting to their clients that they need additional services or treatments. Owners habitually complain about and are cautious of those fortune-tellers who "work at various cafés to build up a portfolio of clients," as Ekrem, a divorced café owner in his sixties, put it. To prevent this, owners forbid readers from exchanging personal information such as phone numbers with clients and even recruit clients as informants by gently questioning them to make sure no disallowed contact is established.

Drawing a contrast between the aboveboard transparency of fortune-telling cafés and the hidden and unregulated informal economy of hodjas that is open to abuse, café readers and owners emphasize that, having moved divination out of the unsafe and illegal context it had previously been confined to and into the formal and public business sector, fortune-telling cafés provide a safe space for divination practices in which economic and psychological abuse is less likely. Although their labor remains mostly informal and under the threat of criminalization, by disassociating themselves from the hodjas and the range of healing and other services offered by them, café fortune-tellers mobilize claims associated with the capitalist market such as transparency and regulation in order to increase legitimacy for their work.

Subverting the secularist hodja-bashing narrative through repetition with a difference, café fortune-tellers ingeniously insert themselves in the role of the secularist savior. By pledging allegiance to the pedagogical and epistemological premises of secularism represented by secular education and biomedicine and by drawing upon the legitimacy of the capitalist market to bolster their legal and moral status, café fortune-tellers exploit the dominant tropes of the secularist hodja-bashing narrative while simultaneously bending it to make space for themselves. At times, however, such avowed distancing from hodjas comes at the expense of discounting the treasured support some café readers have found from hodjas in their quest to survive gendered marginalization. Nonetheless, café readers' reiterations of hodja-bashing stories with a difference provide a legible template with which to assert their own secularity, a fragile but essential endeavor, given their perceived proximity to the realms of religion and superstition, the ongoing criminalization of their labor, and the increasing denormativization of the secularist political project.

They Read with the Jinn; We Read with Our Feelings

How do I know? I don't know. I don't know how I know. Do I have jinn? Do I have fairies? No. I don't have anything like that. You know, some very good fortune-tellers have told me that I have jinn. But no. I don't have jinn. I would know if I did! They would speak to me or disturb me. I don't know—something would happen! I don't believe those who say that jinn even exist or that they have them. Jinn and fairies existed in the old days. People were very pure, very clean then. Jinn and who knows what would come and go. Today, people have become the jinn themselves! [The second meaning of *cin* in Turkish: a clever person.] What would the jinn come for? They would be driven away paralyzed/swindled [*çarpılıp giderler*]! There are no jinn, no fairies, nothing like that. No, I don't believe in such things. Nor do I believe in those who say they exist.

—Semra

The most important line of distinction fortune-tellers draw between themselves and hodjas lies in their methods of divination. Like most secular Muslim fortune-tellers, Semra, a café cup reader in her forties, distrusts those hodjas who claim to have contact with jinn, going so far as to question the very existence of jinn. Punning on the double meaning of the word *cin* in Turkish, which denotes both a jinn and a clever person, and on the double meaning of *çarpılmak*, which means both to be paralyzed, a common affliction that results from jinn hauntings, and to be swindled, Semra drives home her point that practitioners who claim to have contact with jinn are inauthentic liars motivated by self-interest. Deserted by jinn and fairies, the dispirited world described by Semra is nonetheless animated by cunning human beings. Semra distances herself from jinn, and by extension from morally corrupt hodjas and fortune-tellers, through a romantic critique of modernity wherein the world gets disenchanted. Jinn may have existed once, she contends in nostalgic tones that land almost as a time-worn adage—in a purer, cleaner past of innocence—but they do not belong to the modern world.

In their bid to designate themselves as secular, like Semra, most café fortune-tellers explicitly deny and disparage the claims of traditional and popular Islamic authorities to have command of the jinn. Comparatively downplayed, but acknowledged as part of Islamic cosmology in the Diyanet's modernized piety, jinn are supernatural beings who inhabit a parallel universe alongside that of humans. Subject to the human world of distinctions such as believer and nonbeliever, male and female, and good and evil, the jinn are shape-shifters who sometimes interact with humans, appearing to them as loved ones or animals. As some of my informants relate, jinn interact with humans when people unintentionally disturb or annoy them by doing the wrong thing at the wrong time or place, such as, in Ayşe's story, pouring leftover pasta water under a tree that was frequented by jinn. Jinn may also haunt people to whom they are attracted, such as in Hasan's story, or those they dislike. Some individuals are known to have the extraordinary gift/curse of being able to perceive and speak to jinn. Jinn hauntings may be the cause of many and various troubles that require healing sessions by a hodja. With competence in managing such hauntings, attained as a result of having been haunted and subsequently healed and trained by a hodja, some individuals may communicate with and command jinn to their advantage so as to learn about the unknown (*gaip*). Diyanet-branded religious knowledge asserts that jinn may indeed know things that humans cannot by the virtue of their longer life spans and their proximity to heavenly conversations, but they do not have proper access to the unknown and thus cannot be trusted for acquiring reliable knowledge (Kılavuz 1993). Nevertheless, jinn remain central figures in popular religious culture, especially present in the practice of hodjas, whose divination capacities may depend upon communicating with them.

While the majority of café fortune-tellers seek to provide a form of fortune-telling relatively sanitized of the traditional pedagogies, tools, and contexts of divination forms associated with hodjas commanding jinn, a few (mostly male) fortune-tellers—like Hasan, who frames his predictions with the phrase "they say" (*diyorlar*) in reference to his communion with jinn during his sessions—claim authority on the basis of their command over the "three-lettered," a common euphemism for jinn, spelled *cin* in modern Turkish. They may even offer healing services associated with hodjas, advertising safer forms of divination such as coffee cup reading and tarot fortune-telling explicitly while offering other services verbally and selectively, providing them in a more secluded part of the business space. Outside the cafés, readers are freer to offer a wider range of services without the supervision of café owners. There, they enjoy the relative security of working in a private apartment and selectively admitting clients who can only find them via personal reference and can only visit after making an appointment via phone interview.

Given the risk of criminalization and their claims to secular identities, café readers are often too cautious to lay claim to most conventional Islamic forms of religious authority. In addition to avoiding claims to knowledge of the unknown via jinn, many café readers disclaim the forms of divinatory authority nestled in familiar Islamicate idioms and volunteer that they are neither the recipients of supernatural ordainment nor have they been handed down the authority to practice (*el almadım*). This is in contrast to a smaller number of readers who spoke in more traditional idioms about the acquisition of divinatory authority, sharing a dream in which a saintly figure bestowed upon them divinatory powers or relating that a practitioner in their immediate or extended family or close social circle had passed the practice on to them. In the same vein, most café readers avoid explicit Islamic associations or guardedly include them only as limited pieces of an eclectic postmodern patchwork informing their identities at work. This is in contrast to the more liberal use of religious signs used by several fortune-telling women I met at their home-based offices, including consultation of the Koran, praying, religiously conservative attire and head covering, and spaces decorated with photos of the Kaaba or calligraphic paintings of the suras.

As they distinguish themselves from the criminalized figure of hodjas, café readers stand to benefit from approximating the stereotype of the coffee cup–reading housewife, allowing them to share in the tolerance she enjoys. But because they must also differentiate themselves from the housewife figure, who, unlike the hodja, has no authority or expertise and thus cannot make a legitimate demand for compensation, they walk a fine line. Many female café readers note that they began reading cups "just like any housewife" or even "just like any woman." But they are also quick to add that they do "know" better than others, certainly more than the average cup-reading housewife, and offer anecdotes attesting to the accuracy of their reading. Given the double bind of hodja versus housewife stereotypes and the pressures of criminalization on the one side and not being considered skilled enough to warrant payment on the other, café workers navigate a difficult terrain, where their claims to authority are always fraught.

As part of their challenges in claiming just the right kind of authority, many cup readers are informed by but also explicitly seek to distance themselves from the well-established cup-reading schema of interpretation (*tabir*).[8] In this framework, specific shapes and scenes identified in coffee residues carry particular meanings, which are deciphered by the reader in relation to the recipient's individual circumstances. Öznur, a college-educated, single café cup reader, explained the process to me during our conversation after she read my cup.

> Actually, I'm not really bound by the shapes. As an example, a horse has two, maybe three interpretations: *kısmet* [destiny] and *murat* [wish/ desire/goal]. Let me make a very crude *tabir* of that. Think of a person atop that horse. The client is female, and so is the person you see [in the residues]. "Look, your wish is coming true—you're riding a horse." This is a very classic, very generic, and, usually, the only interpretation. That's how it's typically interpreted. But to me, it's also about the shapes I see around the horse. Those shapes, too, are binding only to an extent. My interpretation changes dramatically depending on what I feel. So a horse does not simply mean a wish to me. I can't rehearse all of its different meanings for you. It is about the energy I receive when I open the cup, when I'm looking.

Öznur refers to the traditional key concepts of divination, such as kismet/destiny (*kısmet*) and wishes/desires/goals (*murat*), and conventional symbols that carry an established meaning, such as a horse, commonly interpreted as *murat*. While demonstrating her familiarity with this traditional divinatory framework, however, Öznur seeks not to establish herself squarely within it so much as over it. In diverging from the standard interpretation, she distinguishes herself both from the Islamic authority of hodjas and the amateurishness of housewives, thereby placing herself on a higher terrain of skill and originality.

Combining an eclectic variety of fortune-telling methods into one cup-reading session is another strategy café readers use to separate themselves from those vocabularies and techniques of divination that might be readily stereotyped as hodja or housewife readings. Many cup readers combine tarot cards with coffee readings. While some tarot readers readily admit their unfamiliarity with tarot cards' conventional meanings and claim simply to be inspired by them, others claim knowledge of the cards' established meanings and the methods for ordering them. They favorably compare what they characterize as a learned skill, usually developed through the independent study of instructional books, to the allegedly unlearned method of cup reading, which requires the exercise of oral and visual but often not reading skills.[9] Other café readers incorporate astrological methods, such as asking for a client's birthday and responding with their astrological sign and comments on how it affects the client. Less common but present are water readings, which are sometimes offered on the side, given their association with jinn and hodjas. Whatever it is they are interpreting, fortune-tellers often incorporate ritualized or special gestures or objects into their sessions: a piece of cloth to cover the table, a candle to be lit during the session, an uncommon fortune-telling deck, a piece of paper to scribble on while reading, or another personal signature. All these measures ensure that the service fortune-tellers offer is perceived as a form of divination that is neither so amateurish as a housewife's cup readings nor so religious as a hodja's jinn possessions.

Given the lack of formal regulation, education, and certification of the sector, the suspect status of hodjas, the low status of cup reading as a feminized practice, and cup readers' fragile claims to secularity, fortune-tellers are left to attempt to anchor themselves in an amalgam of loosely defined fields of authority that are informed by an eclectic mix of claims. Some café readers express their unique abilities without resorting to religious languages of authority, only stressing that they have been different from others since childhood or that they were born with a special gift. Similarly, others contend that everyone has what it takes to read fortunes, but note that only a few ever develop their innate skills. When I ask what it takes to read fortunes, many cup readers insist that it is difficult if not impossible to capture in language. They may use words like feeling (*hissetmek*), sensing (*duymak*), intuition (*sezgi*), premonition (*önsezi*), sixth sense (*altıncı his*), telepathy (*telepati*), emotional IQ (*duygusal zeka*), receiving electricity (*elektrik almak*), and energy transfer (*enerji alıp vermek*). I have also heard them cite popular Sufi concepts like "feeling (something) from the heart before it happens" (*hissi kalbel vuku*) or "the heart's eye" (*kalp gözü*).

A secularized but enchanted discourse of feeling (*hissetmek*) is the most common framework café readers offer for their practice.[10] Çiğdem, a single middle-aged woman who has worked as a fortune-teller for over a decade at various venues, including an independent fortune-telling business, a fortune-telling café, and out of her own house, dismisses traditional fortune-telling frameworks and their claims to access occult knowledge through communion with jinn or by interpreting the shapes in coffee residues. "There is no such thing as fortune-telling. It depends entirely on the feel for it." Echoing Çiğdem's succinct assertion, fortune-teller after fortune-teller described to me how they simply "feel" their way into a reading. They concur that the medium they read—residues, cards, what have you—is almost a pretext. It is their feeling during the fortune-telling interaction that guides them into offering up interpretations for their clients. Many readers describe such attuned feeling as distinct from reflexive reasoning. In contrast, feeling allows readers to articulate a feminized way of knowing that is as elusive as it is familiar. After all, everyone feels, but some feel more, or more skillfully, or more intently, or more intensely, than the ordinary person.

The multivarious set of meanings invoked by the concept of feeling allows readers to conjure up various forms of authority and draw upon various fields of knowledge. The discourse of feelings is widespread, and it resonates and hybridizes with many different discourses such as new ageism, psychology, and Sufism.[11] Some café workers borrow from new age vocabulary extensively, read new age literature regularly, and have studied various new age spiritual and self-help techniques, from Reiki to neurolinguistic programming. Some are literate in pop psychology and even draw eclectically on other fields of knowledge such as mythology, philosophy, literature, or performance to inform their practice. Others are more familiar with Islamicate idioms of divination and draw upon them to give substance to their practices. The glocalized and eclectic realm of divinatory authority fortune-tellers create through the discourse of feeling is at once enchanted and secularized; it is this doubled quality that makes feeling well suited to their larger self-fashioning as secular Muslims navigating a postsecular country.

Through a syncretic combination of Sufism, pop psychology, and new ageism, achieved under the overarching discourse of feeling, café fortune-tellers work to distance themselves from the prevailing secularist allocation of their practices into the categories of misguidedly religious hodjas or naively superstitious housewives. Navigating the double bind of masculine dangerous and feminine trivial fortune-teller stereotypes, café readers advance their claims to the secular by attempting to reassert (but in practice thoroughly destabilizing) the very distinction of the secular from its constitutive others. In advancing such claims, they hope to conjure up for themselves a postsecular field of authority where they may be relatively unbound by the established gendered hierarchies that structure the dualisms between the traditional/religious/superstitious and the secular.

Hodja Bashing in a Postsecular Landscape

Famous yoga instructor Prof. Dr. Akif Manaf was taken into custody under charges of fraud. The well-known yoga teacher Akif Manaf was discovered to have sexually assaulted female members, saying [to them], "I will cleanse your bioenergy field" and "I will purify the energy centers in your body." Manaf was released under parole. Manaf hypnotized and sexually abused his clients under the pretense of yoga training and "inner peace." According to the petitions of some complainants, Manaf brainwashed clients into divorcing their husbands. . . . Prof. Dr. Akif Manaf was taken into custody under charges of sexual assault and was released after testifying at the prosecutor's office. . . . Some of the victims, who had been trained by Manaf and had later become instructors, said the following in their testimony at the police station: "I can reveal that students who participate in his trainings and come under his influence follow his every word. Some fight other [students] to be the one to help him put on his shoes or to eat his leftovers. They eat whatever he eats on the assumption that he does so wisely. But there's more, and it's worse. I can also testify that he accepts payment from people who are under his influence. In 2011, in my hotel room at a [yoga] camp I participated in without my mother, I felt that he was hugging me in a different way. I was deeply disturbed. These acts of sexual harassment continued. One day, he started fondling my waist, saying, 'Having (sexual) relations with the master is a privilege. It will make you special in the universe. It doesn't hurt.' I refused him and pulled away, saying, 'I see you as a father. I don't feel that way.' It was then that he began to exclude me. He pressured me, saying, 'You have a hormonal problem. No one can refuse the master.' Under this pressure, sometimes I couldn't say no, and he would continue to molest me. I grew cold toward him and stopped attending his classes. I can state that there are many other victims who are too afraid to complain. He accepts money under the pretense of donations. I too gave him money indirectly and helped others to do so. I want to press charges."

—*Hürriyet*, July 14, 2014

This news of a sexual predator-cum-yoga teacher, reported in feverish detail in the Turkish daily papers in 2014,[12] in effect helped to craft a new age edition of the familiar hodja-bashing narrative. The old trope about a cunning male religious practitioner who sexually and economically abuses his gullible female clients had found a new host in Manaf, a prominent yoga teacher against whom multiple women pressed charges of sexual assault and fraud. Speculating that Manaf may have pocketed the hefty sum of one million new Turkish liras, news stories provided titillating details. Their pages reported verbatim from survivor testimonies, which depicted the extent of Manaf's economic and sexual conquests in both number and kind. Painting Manaf as immorally, aggressively, and excessively greedy and sexual, the story reinvested in the sexual economy that propels savior narratives. A photograph of Manaf under arrest in handcuffs surrounded by policemen provided a sense of secularist mastery and closure. Diverging from the hodja-bashing genre, however, the news story simultaneously included photographs of Manaf posing half-naked, clad only in white yoga pants, doing yoga poses against scenic views of mountaintops and waterfronts. Placed together with Manaf's defense testimony and a verbatim copy of his self-glorifying bio taken from his personal website, these last images stood in an uneasy contrast to the hodja narrative that shaped the larger news piece. As part of a competing register of representation, the yoga images, defense testimony, and bio presented Manaf not as the usual personification of secularist disgust—stereotypically envisioned as a conservatively dressed, bearded hodja—but as a competitor for secular modern female desire.

Manaf's transgression was in crossing the conventional lines of difference that distinguish hodjas from the secular men who rescue women from them. Although like hodjas he claims to have special spiritual abilities and promises healing through his teachings and practices, his cures and prescriptions mark neither him nor his clients as Islamic or traditional. Rather, he fashions himself at the crossroads of secular and religious regimes of authority, using the title "Grand Master" to indicate his emanation from a respectable line of Indian yogis and the title "Prof. Dr." in reference to his doctoral degree in philosophy from the Moscow Institute of Economy. Like many café fortune-tellers who eclectically mix regimes of authority—the secular with the religious, the contemporary with the traditional—Manaf is a typical male new age practitioner who defies the distinction between modern secular and traditional religious men that has long animated the secularist economy of desire fueling hodja narratives.

Emblematic of the transnational flows of new age beliefs, practices, practitioners, and business models in millennial Turkey, Manaf is perhaps the highest-profile yoga entrepreneur operating in Turkey. A dual citizen of Turkey and Azerbaijan, Manaf is the author of dozens of yoga-themed books and DVDs and the founder of an international yoga-training franchise, Yoga Academy. Seeking to "provide yoga techniques, improve people's physical, mental, and psychological health, and further their spiritual evolution," the academy opened its first center in Turkey in 2001 and expanded to seventeen locations in Istanbul, sixteen in Izmir, and dozens more in other cities.[13] As yoga studios, retreats, festivals, teachers, teachings, and accessories became abundantly and commercially available in Turkey in the twenty-first century, yoga began to attract mainly secular, and a smaller group of pious, Muslim women and, to a lesser extent, men. Appealing to the new age taste for seemingly nonreligious spiritualities and self-improvement techniques, yoga triggered both secularist and Islamist masculine anxieties. Manaf's legal prosecution and its enthusiastic coverage in the secularist newspapers was followed by the pronouncement of several unofficial opinions by men of religion and, finally, an official fatwa from the Diyanet on yoga. Occasioned by an inquiry from the Ministry of the Interior concerning yoga businesses, the fatwa stated that "yoga can be performed as an exercise, but it is not permissible to attribute religious functions to it."[14] Suspiciously spiritual but not recognizable as a conventional form of piety, yoga was deemed not necessarily but potentially illegitimately religious by the Diyanet. Suspiciously hodja-like but preaching a recently popularized, non-Islamic spiritual practice, Manaf was framed in the hodja-bashing genre as a fraud and abuser, but was eventually acquitted of the charges and continued his career.

While Manaf's relatively non-Islamic version of new ageism attracts a mostly secular(ist) clientele, other practitioners, such as the self-styled spiritual counselor Uğur Koşar, craft millennial new age identities with an unabashedly Islamic accent, attracting a pious Muslim clientele. Featured on his website with a long, full facial beard and clad in the collarless white shirt that is fashionable in pious circles, Koşar assumes the modest posture of hands brought together over the belly while posing in front of Süleymaniye, the prominent Ottoman imperial mosque in Istanbul. Next to Koşar's image is his brand logo: his signature written in calligraphy.[15] In addition to his hodja-like self-presentation, which draws generously on Islamic aesthetics, Koşar also claims to descend from the lineage of the Prophet, which would make him a seyyid, a legally prohibited title. Indeed, Koşar styles himself as a spiritual counselor, not a seyyid or a hodja. In addition to claiming to be a scholar of Islamic fields of knowledge such as *fiqh* (Islamic jurisprudence), *tefsir* (interpretation of the Koran), and the *hadis* (reports of the Prophet's utterances, actions, and tacit approval on various matters) as well as of Sufism, Koşar also claims mastery of the "science of the mind."[16]

Client testimonies on Koşar's website attest that the fluidity Koşar enjoys across secular and religious healing schemas resonates with his (mostly female) clients, one of whom readily expresses that she has "visited every other doctor *and* hodja over the years to address her obsessions" before finding relief with Koşar.[17] While clients often emphasize that they had previously sought but could not find respite from doctors and drugs, Koşar interjects a warning into one such testimony: "Let us not ignore the work of psychiatrists and [the fact] that drugs do work temporarily for neurotic states."[18] Wary of dismissing or replacing biomedical authority and of advertising conventional hodja healing modalities powered by the mastery of jinn, Koşar instead offers relief using therapeutic models of his own invention. Calling himself a theatrical therapist and a divine light therapist (*nur terapisti*), Koşar promises relief in a single session. Those who have found respite from psychological afflictions attest that they have also grown more pious. One client succinctly described how she had "regained both her health and her [belief in] God."[19]

Combining popular Islamic concepts like submission (*tevekkül*) and contemplation (*tefekkür*), references to Koranic verses and the Prophet's sayings, religious stories, and concepts from new age, Buddhist, self-help, and pop psychology discourses such as energy (*enerji*), loving one's self (*kendini sevmek*), knowing one's self (*kendini bilmek*), and self-realization (*kendini gerçekleştirmek*), Koşar has authored over twenty books that have sold hundreds of thousands of copies.[20] His books are read in the larger context of the burgeoning new age/spiritual/self-help book business in Turkey, which sports volumes by Akif Manaf and other local authors alongside globally acclaimed ones. According to Birol Gündoğdu, the Turkish publisher of the international and local best seller *The Secret* (Byrne 2007), "seventy-five percent of the readers are women" and "sixty percent belong to the highest education and income bracket."[21] In the 2010s, the market niche for Sufism-tinged works grew substantially, attesting to the localization of transnational new age discourses. One of the biggest best sellers was Koşar's (2013) eclectically titled tome *Praise Allah and Let Go of the Rest*.

Like Manaf, Koşar became the subject of scandalous media exposés that sought to reveal him as a fake. Only two years after being reported by *Forbes* as the highest-paid Turkish author of 2014, Koşar was accused, but not in a criminal proceeding, by some duped and seduced female client: this time, the plaintiff was none other than Koşar's wife, and the juridical process was a civil divorce case. Koşar's wife accused him of adultery and released unflattering information about her husband to the media, who reported it enthusiastically. Revealed as a self-taught computer repairman who had only managed to finish primary school, Koşar was exposed as an "ignoramus." And, in line with the hodja-bashing genre, Koşar was branded as sexually immoral. To prove Koşar's adultery, his wife presented photos of Koşar and his extramarital partner vacationing at the seaside wearing shorts and sunglasses and visiting Mecca robed and veiled, implying that the contrasting images provided proof not only of his adultery but also of the inauthenticity of his piety. His wife further claimed that after finding fame and wealth, "he would give compliments to each young woman he encountered. His adultery and psychological assault left me wounded beyond repair. Over the past five years, he regularly and repeatedly cheated on me. . . . My psychological balance was disturbed, so I started therapy. . . . He had our son erase his (father's) electronic messages and images with sexual content. Our child had serious emotional crises."[22]

According to his wife's testimony, Koşar's sexual impropriety was evident not only in his disregard for their marital bond and his predatory interest in young women, but also in his failure to protect his child from exposure to sexual content. She attested that Koşar was not a healer but a cause of psychological distress. In his defense, Koşar charged that his wife was the real adulterer and that while he did have a romantic relationship with the woman in the photos, this relationship had begun only after his marital separation, and that it would lead to marriage after his impending divorce. Already a popular figure of the Turkish daytime shows, Koşar would repeat his defensive claims in a paparazzi show, responding live on air to his wife, who called into the program.[23] Like Manaf, Koşar was, for a time, placed in the familiar hodja-bashing narrative and depicted in a court scene as an ignorant charlatan motivated by deviant sexuality preying upon a female victim. He, too, was ultimately able to move on without having incurred much damage to his reputation or profitability and continues to practice as a spiritual counselor, authoring ever new spiritual/self-help best sellers.

The popularity and insistent if ultimately inconsequential media exposés of figures such as Manaf and Koşar attest both to the persistence of the secularist hodja-bashing genre and to its new incarnations in a thoroughly postsecular public culture. Manaf and Koşar's predecessors emerged in the 1990s, a time when the public acceptance of hodjas was beginning to outstrip their persecution as villains. The most famous hodja figure of this earlier era was Medyum Memiş, who performed healing and other services associated with male hodjas. Memiş reached the peak of his rating value in 1994 when he physically attacked his rival, Medyum Keto, on-screen, for stating that people were saying that Memiş was gay (Kado 2016). Within months, both mediums were framed and arrested by policemen posing as clients. Memiş denied the accusations and was released on bail. He would nevertheless serve nine months in prison in 1997–98 for providing services through a pay-per-minute phone service. His troubles with the law notwithstanding, Memiş's public persona developed well beyond the realm of scandal and crime: he became the subject of news as an aid to the police in a famous murder case, a consultant to businessmen in times of economic crisis, and the author of several books. In 2009, Memiş was a guest on a talk show, where he explained that he had met with the Iraqi Kurdish political leader Masoud Barzani in Iraq, and then proceeded to comment on political developments in Turkey. In the same year that Memiş spoke on television as a respectable political commentator, another hodja was invited to a live daytime women's show, only to be taken into custody in the studio. The police called the program and ordered it to schedule a commercial break so that they could enter the studio and arrest the guest offscreen. Thereafter, one of the female hosts admonished her audience for having consulted the hodja, whom the host now claimed had been invited onto the show for the sole purpose of exposing him as a charlatan.[24] This incident marked the shifting and unstable parameters of the postsecular public sphere in which hodjas like Manaf, Koşar, and Memiş circulated. They were figures to be simultaneously consulted with interest and persecuted with fervor.

For over a century, hodja bashing has proved to be a tenacious genre. Its economy of desire continues to fuel titillating exposés and cement the secularist and masculinizing fantasy of saving women both from the sexual transgressions of hodjas and from their own ignorance. The continued appeal and repetition of hodja bashing in fortune-tellers' accounts and in the media owes as much to the persistence of the gendered politics of secularism as it does to the genre's novel articulations within the cracks and fissures of Turkey's formative secularist history and its ongoing postsecular present. Liberally remixed with postsecular beats, hodja-bashing narratives are repeated with a difference that unsettles the conventional lines of distinction that separated secular savior men, villain hodjas, and their feminized victims. New practitioners complicate the rational/superstitious, Western/Eastern, and masculine/feminine distinctions the genre depends upon. Secular Muslim cup-reading women and men position themselves as saviors of impressionable hodja victims. Yogi/therapist/hodjas are represented as potentially abominable yet ultimately desirable men attracting secular and pious women. Instead of constraining the meaning and moral value of the practitioners they seek to discipline and the clients they purport to save, hodja-bashing narratives increasingly bring to life novel postsecular ways of engaging with religious belief and practice and conjuring gendered subject positions.

Even as postsecular remixes of hodja-bashing narratives traffic in the familiar affects put into circulation by secularism, they recycle and redirect those feelings onto the new figures of the millennial divination economy. Operating within the affective terrain of disgust and anger, emotions typically directed at hodjas, such postsecular narratives transfer the desire and respect typically reserved for secularist savior figures onto new kinds of fortune-tellers and allied practitioners. These new versions of the hodja-bashing narrative find their momentum in the postsecular structure of feeling explored closely in chapter 3. Situated in this postsecular terrain of feeling in which the binaries and boundaries that have long structured the secular are in flux, secular Muslims feel threatened into a reactionary defensiveness and beyond, leading them to articulate through their engagements with divination emergent postsecular ways of being both secular and Muslim.

3

FEELING POSTSECULAR

"What do you see in this coffee cup? Please comment. Am I the only one seeing it?" This online comment was posted in 2015 above a close-up of coffee residues sitting inside a cup by a Facebook user who had adopted the profile picture and name of Atatürk, Turkey's secularist founding father, and who commanded almost a million and a half followers.[1]

"I'm getting goose bumps. It's him!" confirmed a commenter. So many users recognized Atatürk's silhouette in the coffee residues that the photograph garnered over ten thousand likes and a thousand shares in a single day. Some commenters simply confirmed "Atatürk," which literally means the father of the Turks, a surname bestowed upon Turkey's first president, Mustafa Kemal, in 1934 by the Turkish parliament. Others reacted with the more intimate address *Atam*, my (fore)father, a term used respectfully and affectionately by Kemalist

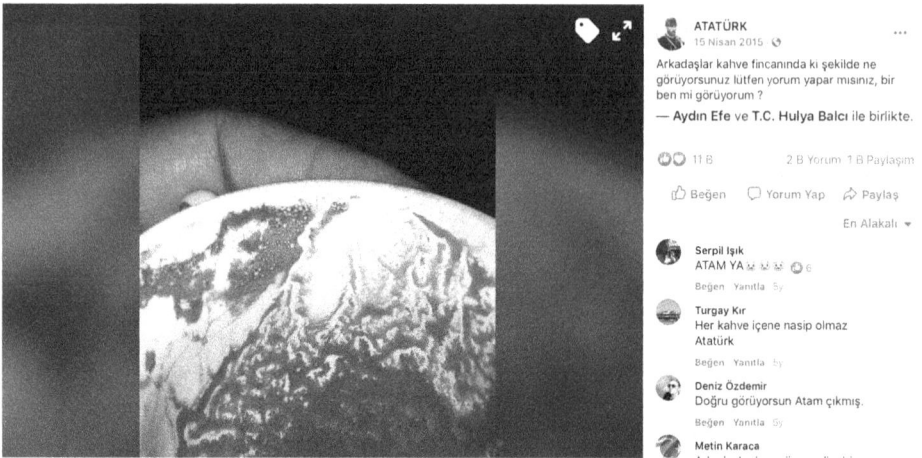

FIGURE 3.1. Online photo of the silhouette of Atatürk in coffee residues.

nationalists. Others added words of affection and admiration. "Seeing him gives one such happiness, even if it's only in coffee residues. Never wash them away!" someone demanded, and the users all spread the joy by sharing the post to their network. "Atatürk, the nation is applauding," said another user, as if to conjure the national community of Kemalist secularists. Many took this sign as a confirmation of their commitment. "Atatürk!" one of the commenters cheered. "In our cup, in our consciousness, in our resoluteness. Our strength, our faith, our fortune."

The reading was widely interpreted as a political omen: a commentary on the current political situation and a foreshadowing of events to come. "Atatürk is watching over us from on high. He's upset about the condition of the country," lamented one user in pessimistic tones, hinting at the larger context subtending the many comments emphasizing perseverance in the face of adverse political circumstances. "He feels sorry for us. That's why he's showing up in readings," someone offered sadly. "Beautiful, beloved Atam—better days are ahead of us," another wrote, offering hope. "Atatürk appeared in the light against the enemies of secularism who are in the dark," noted someone, confidently deploying a light/dark symbolism that is characteristic both of the coffee fortune-telling idiom and the modernist paradigm. "His enemies are kneeling before him," declared one. "Atatürk and his children will defeat the darkness," wrote another. "Atatürk is calling on the nation to make the right choice to save your motherland and yourselves," urged one user, framing the reading as a political message to the entire nation. "Atatürk ... meaning that the Kemalists are coming to power, God willing!" said a user, optimistically interpreting the residues as a sign of victory in the upcoming 2015 electoral cycle for the secularist Republican People's Party, Turkey's founding political party, whose electoral losses in the first two decades of the 2000s were matched by the persistent victories of the Islamist AKP. "Atatürk and the rise of Republican women," declared a user, taking the opportunity to reaffirm secularism's gendered promises. "What a beautiful fortune. May it be auspicious [*hayırlı*]," she continued, using the fortune-telling vocabulary commonly deployed to bless a favorable reading.

These secularist divinations were welcomed by most but not all. For some online posters, the familiarity, comfort, and enthusiasm for fortune-telling demonstrated by their fellow secularists was a source of unease. The skeptics expressed difficulty seeing the image as intended: "I don't see it," they calmly dissented. Others suggested that the residues had been manicured to look like Atatürk, conducting an alternative way of looking at the image so as to dissect it and gather evidence for a reasonable explanation with which to dispel the magic: "An adhesive figure of Atatürk was attached inside the cup, and the residues naturally gathered over it in the shape of Atatürk. It's visible on the upper side." To disengage others from the collective reading and lighten the affective intensity that had built around the image, some resorted to playfulness: "If you love Atatürk, if you don't claim to be a fortune-teller, if you didn't see the light [*hidayete ermediysen*], if you didn't draw it with a spoon, then you are truly blessed!" Secularists reading residues and offering interpretations in the traditional vocabulary of fortune-telling prompted the need to redraw the boundaries between the secularist self and the Islamist other. One user objected: "I'm a dedicated Atatürkçü [Atatürk follower], but this [coffee cup divination] diminishes his meaning and significance in the same way that those [Islamists] now governing us are [diminishing] religion. It's not acceptable to use a computer-enhanced image to mess with people's feelings." Another warned that the post made secularists look "just like those we ridiculed for seeing the word 'Allah' in a potato." "Do we really need this?" someone asked.

ON SOCIAL MEDIA, in online divination platforms, and in fortune-telling cafés, the secular and secularist citizens of twenty-first-century Turkey are turning to coffee cups to divine their individual and collective futures. As the scale and range of social media responses to the photo of Atatürk divined in a coffee cup attests, secular(ist)s engage in coffee divinations with a generous and comfortable intimacy. The hesitant distance and lingering skepticism of some notwithstanding, many locate an abundant source of hope and faith at the bottom of their coffee cups. This chapter follows secular Muslims as they read cups to divine their personal and political fortunes, but with a measure of doubt; as they articulate for themselves Muslim standards of religious belief, practice, and decorum, but with a dose of moderation; as they take advantage of the recent registration and taxation of divination business to seek livelihoods from it, but with a wariness of ongoing criminalization. As such, it suggests that a new type of postsecular brokering of the supernatural has emerged alongside nonpious articulations of secular Muslimness. In this postsecular formation, the central but ambiguous role played by divination in the making of secular/secularist ways of attuning to the world contributes to the political and analytical destabilization of the secular as a hegemonic construct that is confidently distinct from its disavowed traditional, religious, and superstitious others.

The complex allure of coffee divination highlights the discontents of the secular in Turkey in a postsecular time and place. Secular Muslims of Turkey deploy coffee divinations to affectively negotiate their persistent attachments to secularism and to craft secular identities in a context where secularism is no longer dominant but is revitalized in defense, and where Islamism is increasingly entrenched in power but is still contested. The political denormativization of secularism advanced in the broader context of the neoliberalization of both the public sphere and the market, and the concomitant reclamation and commodification of fortune-telling practices that were once discarded in the name of secularization. In this socioeconomic climate, the increasing popularity and visibility of coffee divination has kept pace with the growing discontent of the secular and secularist citizens of Turkey.

The conjuring trick of circulating a photo of coffee residues resembling the silhouette of Atatürk on Facebook accumulates and dissipates contrasting sets of secularist affects: from happiness, hope, faith, and belonging to sadness, pessimism, doubt, and ridicule. It also puts bodily intensities into motion to create goose bumps and coagulates a range of collective feelings to summon a community of secularists. In a country where secularism has long been sacralized, in this moment of secularism's uncertainty, secularists have testified to phantom appearances of Atatürk silhouettes in such unexpected places as hilltop shadows (Navaro-Yashin 2002). In the hopes of asserting a divinatory hold over the future just when the political fortunes of secularism seem most grim, secularists have even claimed that Atatürk himself had a supernatural ability to predict the future (Özyürek 2006). If secularism was thoroughly sacralized from the very beginning and we have never been fully secular so to speak, then secularism is being further enchanted at the exact moment when its fortunes in this world do not bode well.

At a time when secularist politics cannot deliver, divinations provide a space in which to process the angst of the present and procure hope for the future. The first two decades of twentieth-century Turkey have been marked by the political victories of an Islamist party, the AKP, which has troubled the secularist political and cultural status quo by branding itself as pro-Western, liberal, and pious.[2] Successfully combining Islamic discourses and gestures with a neoliberal agenda, the AKP consistently defeated secularist political rivals, growing more confident and authoritarian in the 2010s. The less proficient Turkey's conventional mediums of the wider political public sphere (the media, political parties, nationalist celebrations and ceremonies) became at cultivating the affective flows that sustain the secularist community, the more urgently alternative publics and mediums were mobilized to generate and process the anxious feelings shaping secularist subjects forced to manage this new postsecular condition.

While the denormativization of secularism that fueled increased public circulation of coffee divination and religious and spiritual practices was felt most acutely in the twenty-first century, the postsecular landscape was in fact prepared earlier by Turkey's post-1980s political and economic liberalization, which loosened (secularist) state controls over the political sphere, public culture, and the market. In the decades following neoliberalization, divination practitioners took advantage of new commercial and public avenues such as private radio and television channels, pay-per-minute phone lines, and malls to advertise and provide their services. Şengül was one of several middle-aged women who hosted the dream interpretation show *Rüyanız Hayrolsun* (May Your Dreams Be Auspicious), which ran on a national television channel during the early morning hours of 2009. Here, Şengül interpreted callers' dreams and answered their questions about their lives and futures. After being replaced by another dream interpreter who also doubled as a fortune-telling café reader during the day, Şengül began reading coffee cups on a new radio channel, *Radyo Astroloji* (Astrology radio), which began broadcasting in 2010. Şengül was featured in a daily two-hour slot in which clients sitting outside the studio who had already drunk their coffee and had turned over their cups called into a pay-per-minute phone number to reach Şengül, who would then read their cups via live broadcast webcam.[3] Despite their continuing persecution and representation in the media as exposed criminals, since the 1990s, fortune-tellers like Şengül have appeared increasingly as service providers, talk show guests, and even the hosts of their own shows.

If neoliberalization provided new impetus and spaces for the provision of commercial divination services, the postsecular culturalization of what in the secularist project was judged to be deficient, backward, and in need of re-form or outright abolishment added to the growing demand for commercial fortune-telling. Once the secularist state lost its grip over the terrain of cultural politics, a "mutual 'culturalization' of politics and 'politicization' of culture" (Kandiyoti 2002, 5) meant that particularistic identities and their accompany-ing cultural and increasingly commercialized objects and practices saturated the public (Özyürek 2006). In this climate, a new taste for "culture on the [religious and ethnoracial] margins" (Cruz 1999) fueled the reinvention and commercialization of traditions ranging from belly dancing to coffee fortune-telling (Korkman 2015c; Potuoğlu-Cook 2006).

The postsecular rediscovery and popularity of coffee cup readings is thus squarely situated within the emergent culturalizing and consumptive sensibilities of neoliberal Turkey. These sensibilities culminated in the "Ot-tomania" of the early 2000s, a popular taste for the Ottoman era and an ac-companying appetite for consuming its associated reinvented traditions (Ergin and Karakaya 2017). Through practices of representation and consumption, some commodities acquired the mark of civilizational difference and became affectively loaded with desire and value (McClintock 1995; Moallem 2018). Spanning pious and secular habitus alike, Ottomania fueled a desire for spe-cific culturalized commodities: marbling and calligraphy courses taught in re-stored shrines, imperial gowns donned in themed photo studios for placement in extravagant family albums, television serials glorifying the empire, confer-ences on traditional healing methods like cupping, and Turkish coffee and all its associated traditions, from cooking coffee over coal and serving in *zarflı fincan* (a demitasse cup in an ornamental holder) to cup reading.[4] The neo-Ottomanist culturalization of Turkish coffee produced novel commodities. For example, when a fortune-telling café created an overpriced Turkish cof-fee tray sold with a promotion of fortune-telling, the gold-colored, elaborately decorated tray sported a fancy Turkish delight (*lokum*) holder and a handleless coffee cup with an ornamental holder (*zarflı fincan*) to match neo-Ottomanist sensibilities. In keeping with its functional use as part of a fortune-telling pro-motion, however, the *lokum* holder contained packaged chocolate and chew-ing gum instead of Turkish delight, and a spare saucer, never used with a *zarflı fincan*, was provided for turning the cup over for a reading.

These new appropriations of coffee consumption thus form part of a larger millennial process of reclaiming the traditional, religious, and superstitious for a new brand of Turkishness. The reading of Turkish coffee residues is repeatedly described by the inhabitants of fortune-telling cafés as traditional (*geleneksel*), local (*yerel*), authentic (*hakiki*), and "ours" (*bize ait*), but not as religious or

FIGURE 3.2. An ornamental Turkish coffee tray that comes with promotional fortune-telling at Angels Café.

Islamic per se. The consumption of coffee-reading services provides a perfect occasion for secular Muslims to claim and integrate a dimension of their national identity that was publicly disowned during the formation of the Turkish secular. They do so, however, with lingering ambiguity, given their fragile secular Muslim identities and alarmed secularist sensibilities. The culturalized commodity of coffee readings assists these secular and secularist subjects in navigating the postsecular condition, even as the cup readings themselves constitute a symptom of the very condition from which they offer relief.[5]

Muslims from Turkey who identify as secular, secularist, and/or nonpious and who take up divinatory practices provide a suggestive window onto how subjects reflect and respond in the oft-overlooked grain of everyday life to the denormativization of the political project of secularism and the category of the secular. Coffee readings are a productive terrain in which secular Muslims can play out their complex feelings toward and attempts to fix (if only temporarily and ambiguously) the destabilized categories of the secular and the religious. As nonpious secular Muslims read coffee cups to find secularist hope, they also craft their new identities through careful negotiation of the norms of religious belief, observance, and gendered modesty, distinguishing themselves from those they deem to believe and practice too much, and managing the contradictory terrain of simultaneous regularization and criminalization of commercial fortune-telling. In doing so, they bring forth new ways of being secular Muslims in a context where the secular and the religious still signify political fault lines and nodes of affective coagulation despite becoming increasingly fluid and futile categories. Attending to the contingent, performative, and strategic ways in which feminized subjects negotiate these gendered categories of the secular and the religious on the ground helps dislodge the dichotomous and stable ordering of these concepts (Gökarıksel 2012; Gökarıksel and Secor 2015; Göle 2012; Kandiyoti 2012) at the same time that it points to those emergent affective constellations of the secular, where renegotiating the gendered logics of Turkish secularism remains central.

Secular Muslims of a Postsecular Condition

I try doing as much [worship] as I can. So, you ask, do I pray [*namaz kılıyor muyum*]? Do I fast? No, I do not. But I do believe. I mean, I feel that it's more virtuous to make someone happy here in this world than to pray and beseech Allah. That's how I try to make up for my deficit. I don't know how much of this Allah will accept, but this feels like more of a good deed to me.... I try reading as much of the Yasin [a Koranic sura] as possible, for example. For our dead, for those who have passed away, for those who are gone. I take a bath, perform my ablutions, sit down, and read [the Koran]. That comforts me. I can't fast because I'm a smoker. I can't resist cigarettes. I mean I just couldn't. I tried, but it didn't work out. I was breaking everyone's hearts. My kids were avoiding me. Then I said, "No, I won't do it." It's no good if you hurt ten people on a day of fasting. That's more of a sin than a good deed. But I do believe. And I try to make my children believe. They should believe too. Because there is an entity [*varlık*]—call it God [*tanrı*], call it Allah, call it whatever you like—but there's something. Can you create this [pointing to a rose bush in the garden]? I call anyone who does not believe in this ungrateful.

—Semra

Semra, a café cup reader who is married with two children, identifies herself as a Muslim believer but is quick to admit that she is not pious by any orthodox standard of observance, such as fasting and daily prayer. If Semra's religiosity is not bound by Sunni ritual observance, neither is it based on its refusal. To demonstrate her religiosity, Semra occasionally recites the popular Yasin sura, for which she observes ritual cleansing. Having reached the extent of her practice, however, she excuses herself from regular ritual observance (prayer and fasting) by way of a personal justification (her smoking habit) and a substantive argument that favors good deeds in this world over ritualized obedience to God. Her moral universe is populated by common Islamic ideas such as gratitude (şükür), which she applies to a range of situations: from being thankful for her modest circumstances to appreciating the beauty of a rose. The latter example is far from incidental, as the beauty of the rose is a prominent metaphor in Sufism. Nonetheless, Semra offers a flexible framing for her moral and religious sensibilities, even suggesting an equivalence between God, Allah, and other names that might be given to a sacred entity. In her account, religion is circumscribed within a privatized frame of morality, and pious observance is moderated by way of personal limitation and ethical consideration.

Semra does not defy the value of religion and piety: "I care about religion a lot. I mean, most people don't believe much nowadays, but I do." If Semra insists on her sense of self as a Muslim believer, she clearly operates with an individualized, internalized, and accommodating definition of religion that does not compete with her secularist sensibilities. She will now and then cite religion as a moral guide, as when she reproaches her college student daughter for going to a bar and drinking alcohol during Ramadan. But religion does not constitute an explicit frame of reference that regularly informs her everyday behavior and discourse. Whether in her extended family, workplace, or lower-middle-class neighborhood, Semra is mostly in the company of other nonpious Muslims. From the newspaper she reads to her daily commentary on political issues, Semra assertively situates herself close to secularists and at a critical and condescending distance from Islamists.

The eclectic and syncretic nature of everyday religiosity, especially that of women, is to be expected. However, in a context where Kemalist secularism is increasingly self-aware and on the defense, Islamic piety and its particular appropriation by the ruling party are more and more present in political and public life, and identities are polarized around an oppositional axis of secularist versus Islamist, the negotiation of nonpious Muslim position by women like Semra is a tricky affair. Yeşim, a thirtysomething married woman who runs a small fortune-telling café where she is the only reader, similarly defines her religiosity by constructing for herself a nonpious secular Muslim identity that gives rise to discord with the social world she inhabits:

> To be honest, I am not a very pious Muslim. As I said, I grew up in a very modern family. About performing my religious obligations, well . . . I don't pray daily or fast. But when my older son was in primary school, a mosque school [Kuran kursu] opened up in the neighborhood. I sent my

son there to learn a few suras and prayers. He went there and came home only to ask—a seven-year-old child!—what "infidel" [*kafir*] means. They had told him that Atatürk was an infidel. Of course I didn't send him back. They weren't even providing religious education. They weren't doing a decent job there. I sent my son to learn prayers. I did not send him to learn that!

Admitting to not being pious as a consequence of having been raised in a "modern family" and excusing herself from Sunni ritual observance, Yeşim nonetheless maintains that she was interested in giving her child a basic religious education. Like some other Muslim families, she found the limited religious instruction in secular public schools insufficient. It is for this reason that she had decided to send her son to the mosque school. But her secular Muslim commitments clashed rudely with the Koran school's lesson that Turkey's secularist founder was in fact an infidel and that secularism and Muslimness were incompatible. While the Koran school teacher defines proper Muslim identity in contrast to secularism, Yeşim defines proper Muslim identity in contrast to Islamism. She qualifies her religious identity carefully by saying, "About being a Muslim . . . I mean, okay, I'm a Muslim too, but extremism in anything is harmful." Faced with a postsecular condition where secularism cannot be taken for granted, crafting a secular Muslim identity is achieved by the regular distancing of its constitutive other, the overly and misguidedly religious subject.

When talking on the subject of religion, the imagined audience of fortune-tellers' utterances habitually switches to a national public. As my informants speak through me about and to Islamists, they congeal their own political and religious affiliations as secular. While they overwhelmingly identify as Muslims, they are "secular Muslims" (Öncü 2005), who qualify their Muslim identities and the nature and extent of their religiosity in contrast to "those fundamentalists" who place religion at the center of their own personal and the nation's political life. Even those few fortune-tellers who identify with a religion other than Islam or who do not identify with (an organized) religion at all situate themselves politically as secularists vis-à-vis the Islamists. By giving voice to the dominant secularist discourse about Islamism, fortune-tellers position themselves as secular Muslim subjects, thereby carving out a space for themselves within the very secularist discourse that otherizes and criminalizes fortune-tellers.

In a context where both secularist and Islamist political mobilization depend upon regulating women's bodies and sexualities, gender norms serve as an important medium for articulating secular Muslim identities. This conjuncture of secularist and Islamist politics with gender is felt deeply and alarmingly by secular and secularist women, whose political fortunes seem increasingly grim and whose gendered identities seem increasingly in crisis. From the 2010s, the second decade of the AKP's rule, the party turned increasingly away from the gender equality policies and discourses it had previously adopted as part of its European Union harmonization efforts and coalitional politics and turned increasingly toward religiously accented neoconservative policies and discourses, such as emphasizing women's God-given motherly nature and expanding gender-segregated religious secondary education. In this context, gender norms and, in particular, modesty expressed in terms of veiling—both the covering of hair and (in the larger sense) hiding of different parts of the body from the gaze of others—becomes an important marker by which secular Muslims distinguish themselves. Not all secular Muslim fortune-tellers are as outspoken as Çiğdem, a single middle-aged female fortune-teller who declares in an assertive joke, "I am a believer, but I show my ass too!" Nor do all wear to work the sleeveless T-shirts and tight capri pants Çiğdem prefers. But then again, none of the café fortune-telling women I met covered their hair. Indeed, not wearing the veil operates as a key signifier of a secular Muslim brand of religiosity and spirituality, not only for café fortune-tellers but also for female Sufi and new age leaders like Cemalnur Sargut (Burak Adli 2020) and Vedia Bülent Çorak Önsü (Korkman 2021), who command a distinctly secular, middle-class, and female following. The same style of modesty largely holds true for their clientele, among whom veiled women are a rarer sight than male customers.[6]

It is not that veiled women do not read coffee cups to divine their precarious gendered fortunes. They just do not tend to do so in fortune-telling cafés, given the social significance of cafés as secular, mixed-gender places.[7] One of the few veiled customers I encountered in the cafés I visited in Kadıköy and Beyoğlu, both of which are known as secularist neighborhoods, was one of Semra's clients, a teenager who had recently graduated from high school and was just starting to wear a headscarf. She was getting her fortune told with the hope of gaining insight into her fate in the central placement exams and her chances of being accepted to a university. The customer was quizzed and lectured at length by Semra about her veiling and how it might limit her from being able to fulfill her aspirations, given, among other reasons, the then ongoing ban against veiling in public institutions, including universities. This was in 2007, and Semra could draw upon secularist state regulations and the then well-established practice of trying to "convince" (*ikna*) veiled students to unveil as she attempted to cultivate secular Muslim sensibilities in what she saw as a naive young Muslim woman in danger of being recruited into Islamism.

Yeşim was facing a different landscape in 2014 when the AKP government began expanding single-sex religious education in secondary public schools, thereby decreasing the number of seats available in secular public schools and leaving the religious public schools (*imam hatip lisesi*) the only choice for those who could not afford private secular schools. In the first decade of the 2000s, Yeşim had sent her then primary school-aged son to a mosque school, only to immediately withdraw him when the religious education he received turned out to be incompatible with her nationalist secularist sensibilities. She was now anxiously awaiting, alongside millions of other Turkish parents, to hear the results of the national middle school exams that would determine where her now teenage son would be placed. When the phone rang, Yeşim was initially distraught to hear that her son had earned a meager score. This would place him in the only public school available in their neighborhood, an *imam hatip* school. Unable to afford a private secular school, Yeşim soon made peace with the situation. Outspoken and upbeat, she quickly gathered up her courage and reassured her son over the phone that he would be just fine. "Besides other things, you'll learn about your religion," she offered calmly, if not enthusiastically. She later turned to me to say, "My son is so handsome and such a charmer that when he becomes an imam, he'll steal all the girls in the mosque." Navigating a landscape of Islamization shaping her and her family's life as secular Muslims, Yeşim remained optimistic that her son would subvert the religious disciplining the school might seek to inculcate, if only by means of seduction, a sign of sexual immodesty. Yeşim herself embodied a secular femininity with chic clothes that emphasized her body contours, long brown hair with blonde highlights that she would tie quickly in a high pony tail at work, and a confident, lively laugh that has become the recent target of masculinist religious commentors seeking to discipline women into Islamist modesty.[8] Indeed, for the providers and consumers of café fortune-telling who are secular Muslims of the postsecular era, gendered nonconformity to pious norms of modesty is a key strategy with which to reassert and reaffirm a(nother) version of being Muslim.

Semra and Yeşim are quite typical of other secular Muslim woman readers I talked to who are relaxed about orthodox ritual observance and doctrine, drawing loosely and liberally from Sunnism, Sufism, and other forms of Islam to explicate their version of religious belief and practice and centering their gender presentation in their constructions of a secular identity. All the while, they insistently identify themselves as Muslims and believers over and against pious and particularly Islamist individuals. For these women, secular identity is not exclusive of religion but depends on a negotiated excusing of oneself from conventional Sunni piety, a confident insistence on nonpious standards of gendered (im)modesty, and a highlighting of those aspects of inner feeling and outward behavior that together signify one as a moral and religious person, but in a measured manner that is not too much like that of a pious or Islamist Muslim.

"Don't Believe in Fortune-Telling, but Don't Do Without It Either"

You know the saying, "Don't believe in fortune-telling, but don't do without it either"? Actually, some [clients] come in believing too much. That's wrong. I say this even though I read fortunes. I have my own cup read when I need to, too. But . . . that woman you saw yesterday, she comes to me and tells me, "Everything you predicted came true! Not just this one thing. Everything you told me. So after experiencing all you said, I've returned." I told her, "All the same, don't believe in it too much." I mean, she shouldn't believe so much and go along with it word for word. Okay. She can believe, read, listen. But she shouldn't blindly attribute everything to it. Everybody likes fortune-telling. Everybody has a weakness [*zaaf*] for it.

—Semra

In addition to insistently distancing themselves from the norms of pious practice and gendered modesty while avoiding outright objection, secular Muslims mark themselves with a modicum of secular faith in fortune-telling that nevertheless stops at suggesting its full-out rejection. According to Semra, belief in fortune-telling is a human shortcoming to be indulged—within limits. Repeating the stereotype of the gullible client while reversing the stereotype of the cunning practitioner that animates popular hodja-bashing narratives, fortune-tellers like Semra assert themselves as moral and pedagogical agents who caution their impressionable clients. Believing in fortune-telling is fine, Semra insists, but blindly adhering to its predictions and allowing them to guide one's life travels too far across the continuum that stretches between doubt and belief. This formula is highly resonant for secular Muslims, for whom faith qualified by a measure of distance is the preferred way of relating to fortune-telling in particular and religion in general.

Far from being an idiosyncrasy of café fortune-tellers, the secular Muslim attitude of "believe, but not too much" is codified in the widely used axiom, "Don't believe in fortune-telling, but don't do without it either." The dialectic of belief and doubt expressed in this common saying, quoted time and again in fortune-telling cafés and beyond, also reflects the commonsense awareness that, despite modernist claims to the contrary, faith and skepticism are not exclusive but rather constitutive of each other (Taussig 2003). The axiom further cultivates a space for engaging with fortune-telling through an array of simultaneously held seemingly contradictory feelings, from hesitation to trust.

Belief and skepticism can work both ways in this contextual game of flexible postsecular responding. If believing in fortune-telling in general does not exclude the possibility of remaining skeptical of this particular fortune-teller or that particular session, then being skeptical of fortune-telling in general does not exclude the possibility of believing in this particular fortune-teller or that particular session. It is the premise that many fortune-tellers are probably shams and a few are possibly the real deal that enables faith and doubt to function simultaneously and reproduce each other. For this reason, time after time, upon finding out that I am a researcher interested in fortune-telling, people have approached me to assert that they "do not believe in fortune-telling but have a story they must share." Derya, a married secular Muslim woman in her thirties, had just such a story:

> I don't believe in fortune-telling, but I remember this from my childhood: I was in middle school. We had just moved to a new town. All the neighbors were visiting to extend their welcome. People were meeting and greeting, drinking coffee and tea, chatting. One of them, a woman in late middle age—I remember her well. The neighbors said she read cups, that she was good at it. She read my mother's cup. And we were all shocked. The things she said: about our past, about our relative who was in trouble, a fugitive back then. It was nerve-racking because we had just arrived, and nobody knew these details.

Like Derya's childhood memory, such stories are testimonial narratives, as unique in each iteration as they are generic. The narrative reaches its climactic turning point when the narrator encounters a fortune-teller who demonstrates accurate intimate knowledge or makes predictions that cannot otherwise be explained by rational means. There is no trick the fortune-teller has hidden up her sleeve that can be exposed. The story conjures awe and wonder through its insistence on continued disbelief. The key element is that these narratives are told as exceptional stories. They do not suspend doubt: neither the narrator nor the listener is converted to an unconditional faith in fortune-telling. Quite the opposite; these stories produce curiosity and skepticism, leaving open the possibility of encountering an accurate reading even after numerous disappointing ones. This active concurrent engagement with belief and doubt allows fortune-telling to work its magic. It is precisely the exceptional and ever-elusive promise of encountering a really "good" (*iyi*) fortune-teller that makes visiting fortune-tellers a worthwhile experience for clients who believe, but not too much.

Importantly, having faith in a particular fortune-teller or a particular session is neither a monolithic nor a passive process. Faith is actively developed, contested, and reaffirmed throughout each fortune-telling session and works in tandem with skepticism. Accurate predictions about the past and present build in reliability for prophecies about the future, which clearly cannot be judged as accurate or inaccurate in the present. Even if uncommon or concerning insignificant events, a prediction that hits the mark precisely can earn a fortune-teller enough credit to make up for several inaccurate ones. The balance is delicate: loose, open-ended predictions or an overabundance of advice may turn a client off; focusing on something too closely may risk wild inaccuracy and loss of the client completely. Crucially, clients who refuse to cooperate actively in the session or who fail to offer comments, ask questions, or give answers are the ones most likely to get disappointed. Those who are too involved, too exacting, or have expectations that are too ambitious may prove the hardest to please. Still, the particular mode of consuming fortune-telling captured in the phrase "don't believe in fortune-telling, but don't do without it either" allows clients to simultaneously and strategically believe in and doubt fortune-telling. Here, doubt does not preclude practice, and practice does not require suspension of doubt.

The pedagogical insistence on the right combination of faith, skepticism, and practice reflects how secular Muslims relate to fortune-telling and, by extension, to religious belief and identity. This stance comes in particularly handy in postsecular times. Through ongoing engagements in what has been ousted from the secular that emphasize ambiguity and moderation, cup readers integrate practices and beliefs deemed religious and superstitious with the kind of reasoning and orientation that has been associated with secular doubt and secularist politics, crafting for themselves a secular Muslim position fit for a postsecular landscape.

Boundaries in Flux

Ada is a fortysomething divorcée whose decisively secular middle-class habitus is evident in all aspects of her fortune-telling persona, which includes everything but conventional signs of Sunni female piety such as the veil. She sports business casual dresses and short dyed-blonde hair and combines tarot readings, Reiki, and life coaching together with cup readings and lead pouring.

Ada emphasizes that she is a believer and that she is firmly convinced that there is a "creator"(*yaratıcı*). She practices (irregularly, she says) the Sufi recitation ritual of dhikr (*zikir*) and prays (*namaz*). However, she notes that she does not buy into the "hard-core rules" that she observes her pious friends abiding by, such as animal sacrifice. Informed by familiar Sufi teachings, Ada defines her belief as springing from love and insists on a secular and mystical understanding of the otherworldly in which "heaven and hell are in this world and within us." Ada explains that she picked up her love of the Sufi master Rumi from her mother and combined it with a hunger for any and all books and trainings related to new age self-development, spirituality, and healing. Her adopted name, Ada, is what Rumi called her in a dream from which she "never woke up."

Alongside her many certificates of course completion in new age modalities, Ada draws upon the authority of having been ordained in a dream by a Sufi master—an allusion to traditional modes of spiritual authority—to assert her capacity to feel people and read their fortunes. She cites the various and disparate authorities of a wide array of discourses and symbols liberally, as visually

FIGURE 3.3. The waiting room of a formally registered fortune-telling office that also offers Reiki and various other services, eclectically decorated with evil eye charms, Rumi figures, and paintings of Chinese characters.

represented in the decoration of her office where evil eye charms and dervish figures are accompanied by paintings of Chinese letters and angel figurines, attesting to the glocalization of an already unabashedly eclectic set of new age discourses and practices.

When I visited her office in Kadıköy in 2014, Ada proudly presented her framed tax registration certificate (*vergi levhası*) to me.[9] The certificate read "fortune-telling, astrology, and spiritualist services" and proved that her business was part of the formal economy and subject to taxation. Ada was one of the small but increasing number of fortune-tellers who were taking advantage of new regularization opportunities to register their businesses despite, or perhaps as a strategic defense against, the ongoing criminalization of commercial fortune-telling.

FORTUNE-TELLERS LIKE Ada who formulate a secular Muslim femininity through their measured and eclectic engagements in religion and divination operate today in a peculiar setting of ongoing criminalization and emergent legalization, testimony to the fluctuating boundaries of the secular in relation to the traditional, religious, and superstitious.[10] Ada and other fortune-tellers benefited from regulations passed during the AKP-led but later abandoned European Union harmonization processes, which provided them with opportunities to legalize their fortune-telling businesses. Despite the standing secularist legal clauses rendering commercial fortune-telling a criminal offense and the disciplinary reflexes of parts of the state apparatus that target divinatory practices, businesses like Ada's that have blossomed in the postsecular culturalization and commodification of divination are now finding opportunities for formalization. Secular Muslim readers like Ada operate in this postsecular landscape, where their identities and livelihoods are tightly bound to the complex transformations of the secular as a political and everyday category.

In keeping with the European Union's legal compatibility efforts, in 2002 the Turkish Ministry of Industry and Trade adopted the 1957 Nice Agreement Concerning the International Classification of Goods and Services for the Purposes of Registration of Marks (Nice Classification). In conflict with the then seventy-seven-year-old Law No. 677, the Nice Classification casually listed astrology as part of the legitimate service economy. In this context, the ministry issued a communique that classified "reading fortunes from stars" (*yıldız falı bakma*) as one of "the services performed on behalf of third parties."[11] Another part of the harmonization process involved the adoption of the NACE codes, the industry standard classification system used by the European Union. In 2008, the Union of Chambers and Commodity Exchanges of Turkey (Türkiye Oda-lar ve Borsalar Birliği) adopted the NACE codes, and in the following years local chambers of commerce and state agencies, including the Ministry of Treasury and Finance, began using a Turkish list of NACE codes. These codes provided economic activity categories for registration and taxation purposes and included the category of "fortune-telling, astrology, and spiritualist ser-vices" (*fal, astroloji, ve spiritualist hizmetleri*) with the code number 96.09.03 as a service class under which businesses could register and report income. It is these codes that Ada and others are now taking advantage of in order to regu-larize their businesses.

The recent legalization trend is part of a longer decriminalization process that can be traced not incidentally to the 1950s and the end of the Republi-can People's Party's single-party rule, which allowed for some changes to the secularist laws and the increased presence of religion in political and public life. In this period, Law No. 677 was modified to include a more specific and narrow definition of the criminal offenses the law stipulated.[12] In 1955, the Su-preme Court ruled that in order for someone to be judged guilty of such crimes as being a healer or amulet writer, as specified in Law No. 677, they must be known to others with these titles, benefit from these activities, and be engaged in the specified activities as an occupation, and that occasional noncommer-cial practice of the activities did not align with the mandate of the law to pro-tect the people from superstitions and related abuses.[13] This ruling specified that fortune-telling constitutes a criminal offense punishable by Law No. 677 only when it is a habitual occupation engaged in for one's own benefit (*men-faat amaçlı mutat iştigal*). Despite these offenses not requiring a complaining party, in practice, fortune-tellers and hodjas seem to have been criminalized almost exclusively upon the complaint of disgruntled clients and only rarely on the basis of Law No. 677. The majority of cases have been tried instead on the basis of the criminal offense of "fraud by the abuse of religious beliefs and feelings" (*dini inanç ve duygularının istismarı suretiyle dolandırıcılık*), as defined by Article 158 of the Turkish Penal Code (TCK 158).[14] Although the criminalization of fortune-tellers has continued, the 1925 Law No. 677 has been moderated over the years, not only through formal changes to its word-ing but also by changes to the de facto legal practices. The new administrative routes for legalization that emerged in the first two decades of the twenty-first century represent a continuation of this trajectory.

That there are opportunities for legalization does not invalidate the ongo-ing threat criminalization poses to fortune-tellers. On the one hand, the Turkish secularist project has been criminalizing fortune-telling since the early twentieth century, its guardians zealously persecuting Islamic forms of divination performed by hodjas while tolerating domestic and feminized fortune-telling. On the other hand, secularist hegemony is currently being uprooted by an increasingly authoritative ruling party that secularists fear is determined to fold secular Turks into its own brand of Muslimness through sociopolitical pressure on women's piety and public presence. It is seemingly paradoxical, then, that under the rule of this same government and its (former) aspirations to join the European Union, (secular Muslim) readers are finding opportunities for legalization of commercial fortune-telling. In a context where registration and taxation seem to offer a promising if fragile path toward decriminalization for some practitioners (individuals and companies), most fortune-telling businesses that pay taxes on the other goods and services they sell (cafés, restaurants, bars, beauty salons, and offices) still avoid explicit charges for fortune-telling services, offering them instead for free.

That the secularist project is no longer hegemonic in its mandate to sanitize the public sphere of undesired religious and superstitious elements does not imply that the state in its many incarnations and faces has abandoned its multifaceted ambitions of control. Alongside the repressive hand of Turkey's criminal justice system, which continues to forcefully intervene to cleanse the public sphere of fortune-tellers (particularly those of the wrong kind), and the newly mobilized hand of the financial system, which catalogs and taxes them, is the hand of those disciplining forces seeking to manage their presence in public culture. Two state organs whose aim it is to determine the boundaries of popular and religious culture—the Radio and Television Supreme Council (Radyo ve Televizyon Üst Kurulu, hereafter RTÜK) and the Diyanet—continuously issue warnings that frame fortune-telling and other questionable popular religious practices from yoga to magic as superstitions (*batıl inanç*).

In its eagerness to delineate the bounds of popular religious culture, the Diyanet issues opinions and sermons that declare over and over again the superstitious nature of fortune-telling and endorsing state controls over it. In the 1995 edition of the *Encyclopedia of Islam* published by Türkiye Diyanet Vakfı, a foundation closely affiliated with the state's official religious body, the Diyanet, the entry titled "Fortune-Telling in Islam" stated that the religion of Islam forbids fortune-telling and deems it superstitious (*batıl*), complained about astrology columns in the print media and the then novel phone lines that provided fortune-telling services, and emphasized the need for taking precautions against the spread of such legally banned activities (Çelebi 1995). In 2002, the Diyanet prepared a sermon to be delivered during Friday prayer in mosques throughout the country declaring fortune-telling to be incompatible with both reason and Islam. Coming on the heels of the fortune-telling café fad, the sermon specifically cited fortune-telling from coffee grounds, reading cards and beans, summoning jinn, and pouring lead as irrational and un-Islamic superstitions that had survived into the contemporary era.[15] In a parallel effort to exercise control over popular culture, this time via regulating the media, RTÜK has over the last decades repeatedly issued reminders that the media must abide both by Law No. 677's criminalization of fortune-telling and with broadcasting Law No. 6112, which states that "broadcasting cannot abuse people with fortune-telling or other superstitions." Further, RTÜK has issued numerous warnings and temporary closures of local and national channels for hosting mediums and hodjas or for broadcasting cup-reading programs.

For all their active engagement, the regulatory efforts of state agencies in the criminal, economic, cultural, and religious spheres seeking to govern fortune-tellers are neither concerted nor total. These efforts are not even particularly effective at curtailing or controlling popular commercial and noncommercial forms of divination in Turkey, as evidenced by the continuous and repetitive nature of the pronouncements and other punitive measures. They do, however, function as a way for the state to mark the contours of national identity by way of the meticulous cataloging of what is deviant. Such pronouncements and punishments delineate which religious beliefs and practices can be legitimately reinvented and incorporated into the contemporary version of Turkishness.

Responding to a complex and moving political, cultural, and legal landscape of Turkey's postsecular condition, fortune-tellers lay claim to both secular and Muslim modes of belonging through their ambiguous yet insistent engagements in religion and divination. They turn to coffee cups to cultivate hope in their personal and collective futures, carefully gauging the exact combination of belief and doubt that is to accompany the right way of reading fortunes and their preferred way of being a Muslim. It is by tempering their belief and observing the specific secular standards of gendered modesty that they are able to distance themselves from the pious observance of their superstitious and religious others. But in reasserting the secular as distinct from the superstitious and religious in the postsecular Turkey of today, they must also labor meticulously to distinguish themselves from the wrong kind of fortune-tellers, personified in the figure of Islamic hodjas, and the wrong kind of believers, personified in the figure of pious and Islamist Muslims. They do this by taking advantage of the recent European Union–sparked regularization and culturalization of divination to craft legitimate practices for themselves and their clients. Such secular Muslim adaptations to the neoliberal postsecular landscape via the medium of coffee divinations reveal the messy intractability of the secular, which cannot be easily disciplined or simply and clearly separated from its constitutive outsides: traditional, religious, and superstitious.

Part I has explored the adventures of the Turkish secular from Turkey's early secularist era to its postsecular present, featuring fortune-tellers as central and yet abject figures, and increasingly as active brokers in the makings and unmakings of the secular. By tracing the racialized and gendered contempt cultivated against fortune-tellers as the antitheses of a secular nation (chapter 1), the sexual economy of fear and desire animating the energetic public attacks on masculinized hodjas and the tolerant dismissal of feminized housewives (chapter 2), and contemporary cup readers' laborious and complex investments in a secular Muslim way of attuning to their postsecular world (chapter 3), this part presents a nuanced account of the persistent centrality of the politics of gender and sexuality within the affective lives and afterlives of the secular in Turkey. The next part turns to the affective and sociospatial formations of femininity, intimacy, and publicness in which coffee readings circulate as a window into the gendered ways of feeling and inhabiting the postsecular public sphere in Turkey.

PART II

FEMININITY, INTIMACY, AND PUBLICS

4

FEELING PUBLICS OF FEMININITY

"You're a sensitive person. Your heart has been broken. You've been trusting, but were disappointed. You wonder if you'll ever get it right." She pauses briefly. "You will marry. Two years. In two years, you'll be wed."

Listening to the middle-aged woman reading my cup, I ask myself, "Is this my future?" It could be any woman's. It could be mine. I can make it mine. I rehearse the disillusionment of loss and the anticipation of promised happiness. The sorrow conjured up by the possibility of a romance gone awry draws me in. I reach out tentatively for the reassurance promised by the age-old remedy for any and all feminine troubles—marriage—and am summoned to a scene of femininity at once so personal and private, so generic and shared, that there is no way around it but to be hailed by the reading. I am a woman in the intimate company of another woman. It is uncannily suffocating and yet reassuringly familiar. It feels like femininity.

I am not the only one who is summoned to this scene of femininity. On this weekday afternoon, one reader will serve several waiting customers in this small fortune-telling café. My reading is quickly over. Processing the reader's many remarks on life in all its predictable unpredictability—health, career, friendship, family, and, of course, love, I return to the little wooden table in the foyer where I had earlier sipped my coffee, waiting among the others. I watch the reader as she approaches a table where two young women are seated, covered coffee cups drained and ready in front of them. The reader picks up one of the cups and walks back to her reading table tucked away in the back corner of the café. Her new customer follows. I can see but not hear them. I watch the client as she listens, nods, and talks, as she moves from expectant and worried to relaxed and pleased, as the reader moves her through the various mundane and extraordinary scenarios that a younger woman is better primed for than I. I notice how she lingers a bit longer after the reader has set her cup aside, savoring the intense conversation that follows on a good reading.

I look around the café, my eyes meeting those of the twentysomething woman sitting at the table across from mine. She asks if the reader who has just read my cup is any good. She's waiting for her friend to finish her reading with the same fortune-teller. She's been here before. "That one was good," she confirms of another woman who had read her cup that day. She hasn't tried this fortune-teller before. She'll have to wait and see. I ask what brings her here today. She tells me she just wants to relax and have a good time. She goes to fortune-telling cafés occasionally, but today hopes to find out about her situation with her boyfriend, which is complicated. She's single now—in fact, recently separated from her boyfriend—but is wondering if there's any chance of a reunion or if it might be better for her to leave him behind altogether. She's also recently graduated from college and could use some clues as to what her employment prospects are. She's not desperate yet. She has some leads, but nothing has yet materialized.

After her reading, she and her friend stay to enjoy a deep conversation. Incomplete pieces of their dialogue drift into my ear: "She said he will . . . I would never . . . My mom thinks so . . . I wonder if . . ." I watch the two women talk about the predictions and the reader's comments. And about other things: strategizing, guessing, despairing, hoping, and simply relaxing in the intimacy of the same-sex friendship of young single women.

THIS CHAPTER DETAILS the affectivity of fortune-telling as a window onto the coimbrications of femininity, intimacy, sociability, and space. In particular, it highlights the affectivity of fortune-telling as a venue to track the production of and transformations in gendered publics. Circulating scenes of femininity in which gendered hopes and anxieties are generated, divination conjures femininity as an affective terrain, contouring it as a felt condition. The troubles and joys of femininity parade in divination as a way of mapping feminine realms that are normatively deemed petty and banal, terrains invested with great affective intensity. The affective flows of divination are structured and habitual, channeled by the riverbed of gendered scripts and conventions that characterize the genre of fortune-telling. As the reader and the client interpret and reinterpret the coffee grounds and the predictions, these flows, ever fluid and ephemeral, are bent, stretched, and fleetingly inhabited.

Divination surfaces femininity as both a subjective and subjectifying affective terrain. It simultaneously assumes and opens up the subject position of femininity as a universally shared yet uniquely personalized condition, inviting the cup reader to recognize the client and the client to recognize herself as a particular type of person. Being hailed and interpellated as the subject of divinatory scenes of femininity presumes and produces feminized subjects. This feminized personhood is (usually but not exclusively) recognized as a woman, one among many women, one particular woman. But if such affective investment in femininity is not an automatic function of sex/gender categories, then neither is divination simply an activity for an already existing category of woman. More accurately, womanhood emerges at the nexus of divinatory scenes as a node of identification.

Coffee divination is thus a genre of femininity. Reading coffee grounds is a ubiquitous and ordinary practice that is both symbolic and constitutive of an unmarked normative femininity. In providing an affective genre within which to express the intimate yet ordinary desires and aversions associated with femininity and through which to process the feelings of hope and disappointment that accompany femininity's (usually but not necessarily) heteronormative scenes, coffee cup readings facilitate homosocial intimacies. The symbolic relationships between coffee, femininity, and domesticity extend beyond the cup reading. The brewing and serving of coffee serve as a rite of passage for adult femininity. Brides serve coffee to their suitor's family when they come for the ceremonial visit to ask for her hand. Young girls are taught how to make and serve coffee, and their proficiency is a marker of proper socialization into adult womanhood, signaling their readiness for marriage. Reading cups is such a naturalized part of normative femininity that many women who read cups as amateurs or café workers reiterate that they "tell fortunes just like any other housewife would."

Divination thus functions as part of a larger terrain of femininity generated through the circulation of many genres, which may be oral or written, textual or performative, collegial or commercial. From women's talk to the daytime talk show, these genres both assume a common experience of and circulate a common knowledge of femininity. Like a book, a song, or a movie that is put into circulation to be read, listened to, or watched by an audience of anonymous strangers, divination summons the audience it supposes and addresses it from its outset. This specific group of strangers it addresses share something in common—in this case, their affective investments in femininity. Like other genres mediating publics of femininity, divination assumes a public whose members are summoned as an audience to the extent that they find echoed in the genre their sense of gendered commonality. This commonality is not merely reflected in the genre; it is rallied by it. In simulating feminized subjects, divinations conjure up a public of femininity by and for those who are interpellated into feeling the intimacy of a shared affective terrain as femininity.

Divinations deal in the currency of feminized intimacy. People do not get cup readings to divine the results of coming elections or the best stocks to invest in. They get readings to hear about prospective suitors, unfaithful spouses, controlling parents, and misbehaving children. The scheming enemies and faithful supporters that are to be found among one's relatives and friends. The lost jobs, failed family businesses, and new prospects one may encounter. The personal debts to be paid or collected, houses or cars to be bought or sold, exams to be passed or failed. The routine and grave illnesses to be suffered. Those yet to be born and to die. In this parade of private joys and troubles, the shameful and the scandalizing appear alongside the proper and the ordinary. The hidden affair is revealed after the heralding of a respectable marriage, the secretive abortion follows the coveted birth of a son. At their heart, divinations are about the intimate in all its banality and scandal. Divinatory scenes and the affects they elicit foster a feeling of intimacy between the reader, the one whose cup is being read, the patrons of fortune-telling cafés, and the imagined community that divination summons into being as an intimate public of similar strangers.

Coffee divinations are appropriated by young and gay men as well as lesbian and transgender women as a medium with which to navigate gendered and sexualized marginalization. In effect, they provide a subaltern vernacular for those disadvantaged along the multiple axes of heteropatriarchal hierarchies. At each iteration, coffee divination opens the feminine wisdoms of managing and surviving the gendered banalities of life to appropriation. In this sense, coffee divination may be compared to Lubunca, the queer slang of Istanbul (Kontovas 2012) that articulates in its alternative vocabulary how it feels to be queer. Like

Lubunca, which conjures up through the queer intimacy of speaking Lubunca together its own intimate public, a community with which outsiders would rather not be affiliated, coffee divination summons an intimate public for the feminized. While queer publics are not identical to feeling publics of femininity, they may and do overlap, particularly in contexts where those who fall outside the heteronormative social order are stigmatized as feminine.

Thus, coffee divinations also conjure an intimate public of those (who are or who dare to be) marked by femininity. They do this not only through the feelings of intimacy that are evoked when divinatory scenes circulate but also through the intimacy of partaking in the activity of coffee divination. Whether during house visits or at cafés, reading cups is something women do among themselves, something others would either not care for or be ashamed to partake in. Like gossip or witchcraft, divination is considered either ridiculously pointless or cunningly sinister. It is a feminine propensity that (heteronormative) men, as well as women who do not indulge in the minor domestic pleasures of normative femininity (because they "know better" or have "better" things to do), look down upon or look away from. Femininity is of course not equivalent to womanhood as a social position and a gender identity. As relations of power and subjectification, heteropatriarchal hierarchies of age, gender, and sexuality feminize youths and nonheteronormative men who socialize around coffee cups alongside women, especially in the booming café scene of urban Turkey. Here, the feminized cultivate intimate publics in each other's familiar, comforting company.

This conceptualization of divination is informed by Laurent Berlant's (2008) formulation of women's intimate publics, where she analyzes the relationship between the literary genre of "female complaint" and its audience as an active affective process through which femininity circulates to produce women as a public. Cataloging and circulating the disappointments of the heteroromantic fantasy and women's emotional labors of persistence and reinvestment in the face of these disappointments, the feeling-centric epistemology of the sentimentalist style of "female complaint" constitutes an "archive of feeling" (Cvetkovich 2003). More specifically, this sentimentalist style of female complaint is an archive of feeling feminine. In this formulation, a public appears as a terrain of affective expectations in which individuals can recognize themselves and each other as generic subjects (here, of femininity) in the intimate assurance of belonging to a community (here, of women). By focusing on the circulation of affects as constitutive of publics, divination practices become visible as the conjuring of intimate publics of femininity. In divination publics, the social spaces in which affects circulate and publics coagulate do not constitute an empty category to be disregarded. To the contrary, spatiality lies at the heart of the conjuring of gendered intimacy.

In Turkey, the gendered relationship between genres, affects, intimacies, and publics is brokered via a thoroughly spatialized gender formation. This sociospatial formation and its many intimate publics of femininity are informed by the reciprocally interacting layers of an Islamicate formation of gendered intimacy (*mahrem*), a secularist remaking of the public sphere, and a neoliberal intimization of the public sphere. Building on the genealogy of the secular and postsecular presented in part I, part II explores the productive mutuality and fissuring of these layers by drawing upon an (auto)ethnographic analysis of fortune-telling cafés where women, alongside young and gay men, gather in each other's intimate company. Chapter 4 situates this ethnographic present in the histories of the feminized postsecular publics that have emerged for the first time around coffee sociabilities, while chapter 5 places the gendered intimacies of divination businesses into a broader politics of intimacy brokered in a postsecular public culture and political public sphere by examining the novel forms and differential costs of public intimacies in scenes ranging from fortune-telling cafés to daytime television shows. Together, these chapters approach divination as a window onto the gendered and gendering productivity of the specific sociospatial arrangements of affect, affinity, and intimacy in today's postsecular, neoliberal Turkey. Part II thus emphasizes affectivity and femininity as a gendered lens into the dynamic coconstitution of publicness and intimacy.

Intimate (*Mahrem*) Publics of Divination

"Zeynep." As he leans in toward me from the other side of the table, the man I just met addresses me by my first name in a warm, affectionate voice that demands my full attention. He takes a quick look at the overturned coffee cup he has just opened and scans the residues revealed inside. "You've encountered deceptive, devilish people in the past. You've had many troubles. You've not been lucky. Your private life was a mess. You broke off a relationship. Breaking off was painful and distressing. Secrets were revealed." He pauses briefly and looks directly into my eyes. I feel his gaze. Focused and intensified by this gaze, I feel his words. He is saying that he knows. That he knows me. He knows me inside out. He knows my past. He knows what secrets were revealed. He is the one now revealing secrets. I nod my head up and down under his probing gaze. Leaning back in his chair, he confidently points to one of the tarot cards he placed on the table next to my coffee cup. I follow to where his finger is, but the card does not divulge its meaning to me. I look back at him to hear his interpretation. As our gaze meets, he declares decisively, "This is the past. These things are over." I feel relieved. I'm ready to hear more things, better things. "It will get better in two months," he announces. "You know how?" I don't know. I wait eagerly for him to tell me how. "Good luck is at your door, my dear," he addresses me with the presumptuous sincerity of a diva speaking to a fan. "Inside a box waits the delayed paperwork you have been expecting." He continues to read my fortune, revealing more secrets from my past and opening more doors and boxes, inside which lies my future.

My intimate hopes and regrets are uncovered through these openings and revelations. They are revealed to me via stock stand-ins that mask as much as they lay bare, refracted into shapes the coffee residue has dried into while my cup sat closed upside down, waiting for the reader who is in the business of opening what is closed and revealing what is hidden. The magic of closing and opening. Inside out. I feel exposed, disclosed by and to a complete stranger. Yet I feel comfortably safe, as though I am with a close confidant. How is this possible? It takes me a while to figure it out; then I know. I am reading him as a queer man. Is it his tone of voice, his choice of words of endearment, how he called me "my dear"? "My dears" was Zeki Müren's preferred address to his audience, the lone queer public persona of the Turkey of my childhood, whose unruly gender performance was as much an unspoken public secret as a flamboyant spectacle. I feel comfortable sharing the details of my private life with this male fortune-teller because his queer gender presentation allows him to share in the feminine intimacy that the exchange of divination demands and creates. I assume that, despite this relaxation of the gendered boundaries of what would otherwise remain concealed between a man and a woman who did not know one another, he will not make an unwelcome sexual advance such as could be encouraged in such an intimate space. Had he performed a heteronormative adult masculinity, it might have felt improper and intrusive to have this kind of talk and this level of intimacy with an unfamiliar man.

This fortune-telling café is no place for male strangers (*yabancı erkekler*). We are in a space marked by feminine intimacy. It's not just that most visitors are women. The sights, sounds, and smells of this place are those of domestic femininity. In the background of my divination session is a playing toddler watched over by her grandmother, the woman who runs the café and reads fortunes herself. The grandchild is on a pink plastic tricycle. There's not enough space to ride in the crowded little café, but the toddler seems to enjoy the high-pitched melodies she can produce by pushing the brightly colored buttons spicing up the handlebars. The room is decorated with several American diner-style seats, not arranged in seating groups but lining the walls of the café, facing inward toward the center of the room, each with a tiny table in front of it. While individuals and small groups may hold semiprivate conversations thanks to the ongoing background noise of the music, traffic, clients, workers, and today the tricycle melodies, the place feels domestic, almost like a large living room. At the innermost part of the café there is a seating circle arranged around the main desk and the cash register where the owner is enjoying some tea over a leisurely conversation with a middle-aged woman. This guest is no stranger. She is a neighbor, the owner of the small women's boutique next door, who often steps inside to casually kill time during slow business hours. She has brought over some sweet snacks, the way a proper guest would, and is feeding them to the child, who could use some fattening up, she says, the way a good auntie would. Although I'm seated at the café's outermost table next to the sidewalk where I can see and be seen by the busy traffic of pedestrians and smell the fumes from passing cars, I'm also feeling the spontaneous joy of the toddler as she sings along with her noisy toys, the casual tone of the women's conversations, and the homely smell of freshly brewed tea. I'm outside, out in a café, just by the street, and I am inside, in the familiar safety of feminine intimacy, in the easy comfort of feminine domesticity.

THE FELT INTIMACY of femininity has sociospatial effects. As a heteropatriarchal compass, this felt intimacy orients individuals toward or away from gendered others in social space, congregating them into intimate publics. These intimate publics of divination situate gendered subjects within a broader matrix of social proximity and distance that is sensed through affective intimacy and navigated through relational and spatial arrangements. Divination's intimacy is thus derived from and feels right within this larger sociospatial schema of gendered intimacy that makes it sensible for women and young and gay men to come together and share intimate issues in domestic spaces and fortune-telling cafés.

Animating this formation of intimacy is the concept of *mahrem*, derived from the Arabic root *hrm*, meaning forbidden/sacred/inner (Schick 2010). Although mahrem corresponds to the range of meanings captured by the English words *intimate, familiar, private, confidential,* and *concealed,* such one-to-one translations gloss over the gendered logic of affinity that permeates the concept. According to the Turkish Language Institute's online dictionary (Türk Dil Kurumu 2019), *mahrem* (adverb and noun) means (1) "unmarriageable close kin," (2) "something hidden that is not to be told to others," and (3) "confidant," one to whom secrets are entrusted. The condition of being *mahrem*, *mahremiyet* (noun), is glossed as meaning "secrecy/privacy" (*gizlilik*). The combination of these multiple and layered definitions captures the constitutive relations between hidden/forbidden and intimate/familiar that together make up the concept's sense. A measure of intimacy, *mahrem* denotes those who are intimate with each other (those who are closely related and thus forbidden to marry each other) and shapes what can be revealed to whom (one becomes an intimate by dint of someone sharing what is hidden from others).

Mahrem and its spatial corollary *harem* (*mahrem* spaces) are often viewed through the lens of the Western-centric dichotomies of male/female and public/private, which are inadequate to explain how femininity and intimacy are mapped onto space and sociability in Turkey and the Middle East (Ozbay 1999; Thompson 2003).[1] In the narrow sense, *mahrem* is a religious legal category denoting those who are forbidden to marry one another because of close kinship status. As such, conventional modern formations of *mahrem* reflect heteropatriarchal imperatives demarcating (il)legitimate objects of masculine sexual desire and (il)legitimate sexual and reproductive intimacies by denoting which pairs are (in)eligible to marry. Based upon a heteropatriarchal gender schema, an adult woman's *mahrem* includes adult men she is not eligible to marry (because they are close family members of the opposite gender) and her husband (to whom she is already married). Implied and therefore in no need of explicit mention as *mahrem* in this arrangement are people in the same-sex category, who are categorically ineligible for marriage. Nevertheless, the operation of *mahrem* depends not upon a simple, dichotomous sex segregation of male/female, but upon a complex logic of masculine sexual desire that is mapped through gender expression and age. This gender formation orders nonheterosexual orientations, variant gender performances, and noncisgender embodiments into normative gendered intimacies along the axes of masculinity/femininity and age. *Mahrem* thus includes women as part of the same-sex category, including lesbian women (who remain mostly invisible), as well as adolescent and gay men who are not (yet) subjects but rather (potential) objects of masculine sexual desire.[2]

Mahrem/harem has long been studied from Orientalist perspectives and in terms of power in the negative, repressive mode, with an emphasis on seclusion/segregation and gendered oppression (Ahmed 1982). Less emphasized is the productivity of this gender formation and the nonbinary construction and complexity of the gendered spaces and relationships nestled in it. *Mahrem* is often thought of as seclusion by gender in space and protection from gaze, usually in terms of covered body and closed domestic quarters. What is often understood as a mechanism for creating taboos and gender segregation is better understood as a mechanism of creating gendered intimacies and publics (Sehlikoglu 2016, 2021). Thinking *mahrem* in terms of relational and affective affinities renders visible the production of gendered spaces, sociabilities, subjectivities, and feelings. Far from a rigid and timeless religious/cultural code, mahrem generates a situated, flexible, diffused, and felt sense with which to gauge who is a stranger to whom, who is an intimate of whom, and who can share how much with whom, and where. A gendered compass of intimacy, *mahrem* thus provides not just a static map of the heteropatriarchal relations of marriageability but a larger, more dynamic symbolic orientation around social relations and spaces that operates through a felt sense of gendered intimacy. This intimacy shapes how affective closeness and distance are felt and performed in and through spatialized social relations.

Explicitly demarcating a zone of forbidden intimacy, *mahremiyet* simultaneously constitutes the realm of proper intimacies (Sehlikoglu 2016). It not only distances opposite-sex nonkin as "strangers" (*yabancı*) but also brings people ineligible for marriage closer together. Those who are *mahrem* can be legitimately intimate. They can share space, socialize closely, and see each other (uncovered) in ways that those outside the circle of *mahrem* may not, at least not legitimately. Sociality among *mahrem* individuals is intimate: more is revealed more comfortably. Relational intimacy is routinely cultivated among (same-sex) nonmarriageables, and such homosocial bonds are more amenable to producing affective intimacy. As social ties are thickened in *mahrem* publics, strong homosocial affinities, whether familial, neighborly, or friendly, may compete with or take precedence over heterosexual intimacies of sexual/reproductive relations, such as romance and marriage (Kandiyoti 1987; Olson 1982; Sirman 2005). Sociality among *namahremler* (those who are not *mahrem* to each other), such as between an adult woman and men who are eligible for marriage, is more restricted, and their intimacy is managed through relational and spatial strategies such as affective distance, reserved behavior, modest clothing, and spatial segregation (Göle 1996; Sehlikoglu 2016). Concomitantly, the affinity-creating force of *mahrem* conjures intimate publics of femininity, where those who are potential objects of masculine sexual desire experience (femininity as) comfort (Sehlikoglu 2016, 2021), intimacy (Korkman 2015c), and inside((r)ness) (Peirce 1993).

The widespread and everyday practice of coffee fortune-telling fits squarely in *mahrem* sociabilities. It is part of the domestic habitus of femininity in a society where adult, married women regularly mingle in same-sex groups in the privacy of their homes and where offering coffee is a habitual part of properly hosting a guest. Similarly, commercial cup readers are invited to women's prebridal parties, a (re)invented and commodified version of women-only "henna night" celebrations hybridized with bachelorette party rituals and merchandise. Coffee divination's appropriation in the context of fortune-telling cafés derives from these *mahrem* sociospatial gendered arrangements in which cup readings circulate.

At fortune-telling cafés, the majority of fortune-tellers are women. Café fortune-tellers are predominantly adult, heterosexual, cisgender women, usually married or divorced as opposed to never married. There are fewer younger and single women readers compared to male readers, and female readers are almost never (publicly) acknowledged as queer. A small number of transgender women, whose chances of employment are otherwise highly limited and pigeonholed into sex work, also find employment at fortune-telling businesses. Male fortune-tellers are fewer, younger, and single. While larger cafés often employ male cooks and waiters and are more likely than smaller establishments to have adult male owners, these men often remain outside the cup-reading sociabilities in the café. An overwhelming majority of divination clients are women. There are teenage girls, young adult women, middle-agers, and older women. In contrast to the profusion and wide age range of the female clientele, male customers are rare and tend to be young. Whereas women frequently visit fortune-telling cafés both alone and in groups, men often arrive in the company of women. Men are an infrequent sight in smaller fortune-telling cafés, while larger cafés sporting extra attractions such as an expansive menu, games, or water pipes draw more heterosexual men, who are less likely to get their fortunes read.

Although most clients and customers are women, fortune-telling cafés are not women-only segregated publics. In addition to the less common male customers, there are also male fortune-tellers. A significant number of male café readers perform a nonhegemonic masculinity that is culturally intelligible as feminine and/or queer, as the two may overlap in dominant gender expectations in Turkey. In the field, such gender nonconformity was often articulated in terms other than LGBTIQ identity categories. For example, Serkan, a male reader in his twenties, was described to me by a heterosexual cisgender woman reader in the neighboring café as "different" and "both a man and a woman." Before introducing me to Serkan, she "alerted" me to the situation and added that "we do not have such [queer] things here [in our café] but over there [at the restaurant where Serkan works] they do. You would not think it, given the owner." The owner of the café where Serkan read cups, she added, was a Kurdish immigrant woman, implying that the woman's ethnic identity and immigrant status, stereotypically associated with gender traditionalism, stood in unexpected contrast to her unusual accommodation of Serkan's gender fluidity, in effect further othering Serkan's queerness within the tropes of racial aberration.[3] Such rhetorical distancing did not mean, however, that she was not intimate with Serkan; indeed, she shared habitual reciprocal cup-reading visits with him in the early morning hours when business was slow. While reading Serkan's cup during one of these visits, she informed Serkan that someone dressed in a uniform would give him some money. Hearing this, Serkan cheerfully turned to tell me, "I have a soldier husband. Well, one of many!" Weeks later, during an extended private conversation, Serkan explained to me that he has many jinn (*cinler*), both male and female, who are in love with him, jealous of him, and want to marry him. Rather than resorting to LGBTIQ identity categories, Serkan and those around him communicate his sexual identity in the idiom of the supernatural and by situating him as an object of male desire, desired either by the jinn with whom he communicates or by the "husbands" that appear in his coffee cup. Indeed, while only a few fortune-tellers publicly identify with LGBTIQ categories, queer men and those around them often recognize and express gender and sexual nonnormativity in such occult(ed) ways. In the context of divination publics, nonconforming men are thus mapped onto and rendered legible within the heteropatriarchal logic of sexual desire that determines who is in and out of *mahrem* intimacies.

The *mahrem* relations of divination produce confidants who share what is otherwise hidden and not to be said to outsiders. This relational intimacy among those who are *mahrem* to one another allows intimate topics to circulate among those gathering around coffee cups. "Private life [*özel hayat*]," fortune-tellers answer in unison when asked what kinds of issues are addressed in divination sessions. Divination scenarios are set in realms deemed private and personal, where romantic and sexual relations constitute the main subject. Readers and clients spend a lot of time exploring scenarios of *namahrem* intimacy that are on their way to becoming (hopefully, potentially) *mahrem*. They describe past or prospective suitors, analyze failed and future romantic relationships, and calibrate the prospects of love and marriage. The focus of divination publics is often those intimate relations with strangers (nonkin, opposite-sex *namahremler*) who are eligible to become *mahrem* (intimate romantic/sexual partners). Whereas discussing such matters with those outside the intimacy of *mahrem* (such as with heterosexual nonkin/male strangers) runs the risk of being read as a breach of the *mahrem* boundaries of normative intimacy and modesty and potentially an excuse for further breaches of *mahrem* boundaries, including (unwelcome) sexual advances from the interlocutor, in the intimate publics of divination, the sharing of private matters actually fortifies the boundaries between intimates and strangers. In essence, divination publics provide spaces for sharing intimately within the relative safety promised by the community of the feminized.

Spatializing Intimate Publics

The first and still the largest fortune-telling café in Istanbul, Melekler Kahvesi (Angels Café), is located in a multistory building with several large salons and smaller rooms. The mixed-gender parts of the café are on the entry-level ground floor, consisting of large salons with high, richly decorated ceilings and heavy, elaborate curtains. Sets of chairs are organized around individual tables so as to seat several groups at a time. Customers sitting at each table face those in their company under the indirect, anonymous gaze of other customers. Below this, in the basement, are smaller rooms reserved for women-only groups. These women's quarters are more casual, with lower, undecorated ceilings and homey armchairs and couches facing each other arranged around central coffee tables. In addition to a random selection of artificial flowers and glass ornaments,

FIGURE 4.1. A room reserved for women-only groups at Angels Café.

these rooms are decorated with Atatürk portraits, a common sight in living rooms of secularist households. To prevent complete privacy in these rooms, which might render them hospitable to intimacies not intended by the management, a small window opening on the inner corridor has been cut in the wall of each room, allowing for oversight.

INTIMACY IS A SPATIALIZED accomplishment. While reserving certain parts of the café exclusively for female customers is a rare but direct way of creating *mahrem* spaces, all fortune-telling businesses mobilize spatial strategies to enable and boost the relational and affective intimacies fortune-telling depends upon. To begin with, coffee divination is culturally marked as a feminine, domestic activity, and its presence is itself domesticizing and feminizing of the space in which appears.[4] Divination spaces may also be rendered intimate through queering gestures that do not connote heteronormative femininity, but that nonetheless distance them from heteronormative masculinity. The basement of a restaurant was used by Serkan, a young queer man, as his fortune-telling quarters. Filled with restaurant tables and chairs with the ambitious yet unfulfilled expectation that the upstairs salon would overflow with customers, the windowless basement unit became Serkan's exclusive place in which to afford privacy to fortune-telling customers, partially decorated with a few personal touches. Serkan's presence dominated the space through the use of one table as a stand for dozens of stuffed animals. "I love them," he responded when I inquired about them, grabbing and hugging one of the many teddy bears joyously in a childish gesture. "They are all gifts from my clients," he boasted, parading the close affection of his clientele, who gifted to him what flirting youths might give to each other.

Divination cafés are made further legible and inhabitable as intimate publics through various gendered ways of shaping and socializing in space, such as decorating, partitioning, and, importantly for the design of *mahrem* spaces, spatially regulating interactions among the café inhabitants. Because the creation of *mahrem* intimacies depends upon preventing *namahrem* ones, policing mixed-gender socialization is a common strategy for rendering divination space an intimate public. At Angels Café, the women-only rule, the living room–style decoration, and the windows combine to foster *mahrem* intimacies while simultaneously policing *namahrem* ones.[5] Some other cafés refrain from providing (semi)private spaces they may not be able to supervise in the fear that clients might use them to be sexually intimate, given that the unmarried youths who most frequent the cafés tend to have limited access to spaces without parental or neighborly supervision. Adolescents being affectionate despite these precautions may be given a warning in the form of a direct probing gaze or remark. Some owners explicitly take upon themselves the role of the paternalist patriarch protecting the (honor of the) women in the café (both café workers and clients) and police any infractions of proper intimacy. This might include closely watching those suspect male customers who arrive unattended by a woman and asking them to leave if they are observed gazing at or engaging with women inappropriately.[6] These strategies seek to control the presence of *namahrem*/male strangers whose male gaze and sexual desire may disrupt the comfort and intimacy feminized publics of divination depend upon.

The spatial, relational, and affective intimacies of divination publics are embedded in and enabled by the production of embodied intimacies. In a neighborhood sporting many fortune-telling cafés, a piece of paper announcing "Fortune-Telling Available" is plastered on the street-facing window of a first-floor flat in a residential apartment building. It takes me a minute to realize that this is the window of a waxing salon. I ring the bell and am buzzed into the building, where a modest sign directs me to the first-floor apartment housing the salon. I walk into the waiting room, designed and furnished like a living room with couches and armchairs facing each other around a coffee table. There is a desk with a cash register by the entrance, a reminder that this is a commercial business. The two inner rooms are reserved for waxing. While the drinking of Turkish coffee and the occasional cup reading are an ordinary practice in women's beauty salons, it takes a particularly entrepreneurial owner to double her waxing salon business as a fortune-telling café. "I'm still doing exactly what I've been doing for years now," the owner explains. A straightforward woman in her thirties, Reyhan has long been serving coffee to, reading cups for, and sharing in the troubles of her regular clients. "I just started to charge for it," she remarks casually on the transformation of her business into a waxing/fortune-telling salon. She has decorated the corridor connecting the waiting room to the waxing rooms with three sets of pink, nursery-sized tables and chairs. This furniture suggests a feminine café look, but they are too small to be functional, so she serves coffee and reads cups in the living room–turned–waiting room. Still, this waxing salon/fortune-telling café benefits from its unique combination of the bodily, spatial, and relational intimacies of the practices of waxing, the furniture of living rooms, and the relations of coffee fortune-telling to produce a place fit for *mahrem* publics.

Bodily intimacies of femininity regularly appear in many divination sessions as a way of delineating *mahrem* communities. Wombs and their many orderly and disorderly states (like pregnancies, miscarriages, abortions, births, and cysts) and breasts and their various ailments (like lumps and cancers) regularly make their appearance in coffee residues, instigating discussions about the private parts of female bodies that are otherwise supposed to remain hidden even from the gaze of fellow same-sex members of the *mahrem* community and the many medical, sexual, and reproductive issues revolving around them. The bodily intimacies of femininity are not limited to female reproductive organs but also extend to the many practices meant to produce and sustain normatively feminine bodies.[7] The shaping of the eyebrows, the straightening of the hair, the waxing of the legs, the polishing of the nails—together, these and other forms of backstage labor designed to produce normatively feminine bodies fit for male desire create intimate publics of femininity in beauty salons. Such bodily intimacies reinforce relational and affective intimacies and mobilize similar sociospatial arrangements to conjure the feelings of comfort and closeness that *mahrem* intimacies depend upon.[8]

Spatialized intimacy often extends beyond the female body and the inner space of the fortune-telling café and out into the neighborhoods in which divination businesses are located. As an everyday, noncommercial practice, women's coffee visits serve to forge good neighborly relations (*iyi komşuluk*) (Helms 2010). Specifically, it is because they facilitate closer relations and the circulation of personal information among residents that coffee divinations function as a constitutive medium for producing the neighborhood space as intimate (Mills 2010). Such cultivation through fortune-telling of the social ties that render space intimate is relevant to commercial fortune-telling in multiple ways. Like many other businesses, fortune-telling cafés mushroom in the vicinity of each other. As the workers of neighboring fortune-telling cafés visit one another to have a cup of coffee and a chitchat, they forge good neighborly relations. During those visits, workers from competing businesses regularly exchange readings and information, just as residential neighbors would. Fortune-telling cafés attract neighborly visits, not only from adjacent fortune-tellers but also from (predominantly female and young male) acquaintances, friends, and family members of the café owners and staff who stop by to say hello, help out with chores, have a glass of tea or a cup of coffee, and sometimes get a reading, just as they would were they visiting someone's home.

Divination cafés change the experience of urban space for their clients, who, to get a reading, may find themselves visiting neighborhoods and walking streets where they have not previously felt comfortable. Having walked almost half a mile with the many shopping bags they had just finished filling at the famous weekly Tuesday bazaar close by, two women in their late fifties arrived out of breath at a fortune-telling café in the Asian-side Kadıköy district of Istanbul. They were two among many other women who visited cafés as an extension of their habitual traffic in the urban center, combining their movement to the main commercial district to run errands, pay bills, or do some shopping with a coffee reading. As they dropped their bags and collapsed into their chairs, they explained half-jokingly that they had gotten lost on their way to the café, only to find themselves "among those Satanists," a phrase insultingly used for the youths who hang out around and in the cafés and bars at the other end of the street, less than a hundred meters from the café. "We never come here," they demurred, referring to what has been called "the street of bars," a long strip of cafés and bars featuring alcoholic drinks, live music, and a public culture of youths mingling in mixed-gender groups, drinking and dancing.

The presence of intimate publics of divination shapes the gendered experiences of urban space. The owner of a fortune-telling café in the central Istanbul district of Beyoğlu boasted, quite correctly, that in a society where street harassment is rampant, his business drew women into a back alley of the neighborhood they would never have dared venture down before. "Only working women [*çalışan kadınlar*] visited this street before we opened shop," he said, to suggest that only sex workers, also called "street women" (*sokak kadınları*) in Turkish, frequented the area previously. After the fortune-telling cafés took over, the street was nicknamed "Fortune-Telling Street" (Fal Sokağı), in reference to the many divination cafés it hosted, and began to be frequented by women from various walks of life. The alley is located near İstiklal Caddesi in the prominent district of Beyoğlu. With its patisseries, cafés, bars, and clubs, the area has long served as the center of Istanbul's mixed-gender public life, as well as of LGBTIQ publics.[9]

Indeed, the presence of fortune-telling cafés is itself indicative of the gendered ordering of social space. Fortune-telling cafés appear in (close vicinity of) mixed-gender public spaces of leisure and socializing, such as those that have been historically located in parts of the Beyoğlu and Kadıköy districts. Many divination businesses are almost indistinguishable spatially from the mixed-gender businesses around them, sharing the same neighborhood, street, building, or even the same space. They nonetheless conjure, through their sociabilities and the felt intimacies they are host to, feminized publics that are distinct from the mixed-gender publics they grow in proximity to. The significance of this particular spatialization of intimate publics of divination lies in the history and modernist politics of gendered publics.

FIGURE 4.2. Adnan Işık Sokak in Beyoğlu, also known as Fal Sokağı, Fortune-Telling Street.

At a café, you take a photo with your lips pursed.
At a coffeehouse, you will get an ax on your head for doing that.

At a café, you drink white chocolate mocha [I had to google this for spelling].
At a coffeehouse, you drink tea or treat yourself to an orange powder drink [Oralet].

At a café, you listen to foreign music.
At a coffeehouse, you listen to Turkish classical music [*Türk sanat müziği*].

At a café, you play Monopoly.
At a coffeehouse, you play 101, *batak, yanık* [three local card games].

At a café, you smoke a million kinds of flavored hookahs.
At a coffeehouse, you smoke tobacco [*tömbeki*].

At a café, you spend time with Pelinsu [contemporary female name] and her friends.
At a coffeehouse, you spend time with Tilki Selim and Muzo Dayı [customary male nicknames].

—Cayisallama, *Öğretmen Sözlük*, August 21, 2015

As suggested in the quotation above from a humorous social media website, coffeehouses are marked as traditional, local settings for male homosocial relations, while cafés are marked as modern, Western venues for mixed-gender socializing.[10] This culturally resonant difference between a coffeehouse (*kahvehane*) and a café (*kafe*) is the product of a gendered bifurcation of coffee publics that emerged in the sixteenth-century Ottoman Empire. With the push to modernize in the nineteenth and twentieth centuries, the former, male-only coffeehouses would become objects of a (self-)Orientalizing gaze that deemed them embarrassing traditional institutions of gender segregation to be reformed, while their mixed-gender counterparts—cafés—would hold the promise of rehabilitating and modernizing the men who segregated in coffeehouses as well as the women who were isolated in harems. By tracing the six-century history of the journey of sociabilities around coffee, from the first Ottoman coffeehouses that fashioned coffee consumption into male-only coffeehouses to the mixed-gender European cafés (Ellis 2011) that inspired Habermas's ([1962] 1991) canonical work on the nature of the public sphere, this section highlights how feminized coffee publics emerged for the first time in divination cafés. Distinct from mixed-gender publics in their conjuring of a community of women and young and gay men (and not adult heterosexual men), and distinct from women's domestic gatherings in their emplacement in publicly accessible, commercial, and nonsegregated venues, divination cafés present a novel gendered arrangement of sociability and publicness.

The first documented coffee publics were formed by Sufis who integrated the drink into their religious rituals. As the drink's popularity spread out from Sufi circles, the first coffee stalls emerged in the early sixteenth century around mosques in Mecca (Desmet-Grégoire and Georgeon 1999). With the arrival of coffee in large cities, "some merchants of the bean took an imaginative entrepreneurial step and created an institution for its consumption in a social setting" (Kafadar 2002, 53), and coffeehouses were born. By midcentury, Ottoman courtly elites were enjoying the drink, and coffeehouses had reached the capital of the Ottoman Empire. Breaching conventional social boundaries, these emergent spaces and the new consumption habits they fostered brought men of various religious, ethnic, and social strata together. Bringing together individuals from across social classes and distinctions outside the mosque, coffeehouses created a new kind of public space and sociability (Kömeçoğlu 2005; Özkoçak 2007), hinting at a "secularization of public space" (Kafadar 2002, 52). Coffeehouses fostered "critical communication, be it in the form of rational, aesthetic, emotional, or playful criticism" (Karababa and Ger 2011, 747), through conversations, games, performances, readings, and such, fostering an early-modern public sphere.

As coffee spread to the popular classes and became an object of mass consumption in the sixteenth and seventeenth centuries, it fostered a type of social space for socializing and leisure that quickly became the subject of religious and political criticism. Competing with the mosque as a gathering space for Muslim men, serving as a hub of sins and immoralities like narcotics and gambling, and breeding political conversation critical of state officials and even the sultan himself, coffeehouses were seen as sources of social disorder and were attacked by religious and political authorities. Sunni Islamic authorities issued official religious opinion after opinion to denounce coffee consumption and the illicit activities it accompanied, while Sufi poems represented coffee favorably (Karababa and Ger 2011). From the perspective of the ruling elite, coffeehouses were also perceived as a sign of social disorder because they carried the political, which was yet to be separated from the religious, into the realm of the public, the outside, and the profane.[11] Numerous closures and prohibitions starting in the sixteenth century notwithstanding, repression was neither complete nor successful. Resistance, toleration, accommodation, and routinization characterized the historical development of the relationship between coffeehouses and religious and political authorities (Karababa and Ger 2011; Öztürk 2008).

Coffeehouses were exclusively male publics. In that sense, a coffeehouse was a "man's house" (Desmet-Grégoire and Georgeon 1999). Coffeehouse publics hosted what might today be read as nonheteronormative masculine desires, suggested, for example, by the employment of "beautiful boys" in coffeehouses (Hattox 2014). However, by the eighteenth century, coffee consumption was a well-established feature of domestic life within the household and part of women's sociabilities. Coffee was served in homes, both in *selamlık* quarters where nonkin men visited with the men of the household and in *haremlık* quarters reserved for women and *mahrem* males. The harem quarters of one elite household even hosted a designated alcove in which to prepare coffee (Kallander 2013). As coffee became the offering of choice for displaying hospitality, wealthy households hired servants whose sole responsibility was serving coffee, and judges accepted coffee as a basic household provision that would, should a husband fail to furnish it, grant even a poorer woman legitimate grounds for asking for a divorce (Çağman 1993). A cup of coffee became such an essential daily consumption item that the modern Turkish word for breakfast, *kahvaltı*, is shortened from *kahve altı*, meaning "before coffee." When a prospective groom's family or a matchmaker acting in their name paid a visit to the home of a marriageable girl, they would sip their coffee slowly so as to observe and judge the suitability of the bride-to-be (Abdülaziz Bey 1995). Ottoman women socialized around a cup of coffee not only at home visits but also in women-only spaces such as public baths (Sokołowicz 2019). The latter was famously called a "women's coffeehouse" by Lady Montague, an English observer of eighteenth-century Ottoman society (Fernea 1981).[12] While male public consumption of coffee has attracted fervent interest, and the communications accompanying it have been closely examined for both political (for example, by the Ottoman secret police) and academic reasons (for example, by historians examining the records state officials left behind), feminine and domestic consumption of coffee has attracted less interest.

Publics that congregated around coffee were not neatly distributed into an already existing distinction between male/public and female/domestic, but rather aligned with and realigned space and sociability along an intersectional axis of masculinity and femininity shaped by economic, ethnoracial, and religious differences. While gender segregation was a normative ideal for Ottoman Muslims, it was not always attainable for the ruled classes. Poorer men and women often circulated and worked in public together out of necessity, while wealthy, respectable men and women surrounded themselves with an entourage while out in public (Peirce 1993, 2010). In contrast to the elite, who could afford separate male and female quarters (*selamlık* and *haremlik*) in their homes, for many men, coffeehouses served as a male-only *selamlık* where they could host their guests and socialize with other men. Shifting the conventional terms of analysis, coffeehouses might be said to have functioned as extensions of the domestic space for men of the popular classes, which in turn provided women who could not afford separate *haremlik* quarters with an empty house in which to accept their female guests (Mikhail 2007). The emergence of coffeehouses as publics for men might have allowed women to inhabit their homes as spaces where they could host nonkin women who were *namahrem* to the men of the house. In this sense, the coffeehouse as a masculinized space and the house as a feminized space for same-sex intimacies might have coconstituted each other.

For the modernizing elites of Ottoman Empire for whom the perceived immoderations of gender segregation and the lamented absence of gender mixing was a marker of difference from and inferiority to the West, gender-segregated sociabilities and spaces would come to signify simultaneously a postcolonial lack (of Western modernity) and excess (of Eastern/Islamic religion and tradition) (Kandiyoti 1997). They would find objectionable both harems, which were believed to leave secluded women in the exclusive company of their female peers and thus unprepared to participate in public life and even socialize with their husbands, and male public spaces like coffeehouses, which were believed to be incompatible with modern family life and the conjugal intimacy it required (Öztürk 2005). Longing for mixed-gender socialization and companionate marriages, these modernizers were (younger) men who felt themselves to be limited by the patriarchal controls over women's visibility and mobility exercised by the oldest male head of the extended household, a family structure that limited the autonomy of its younger male members along with that of the females (Kandiyoti 1994; Sirman 2000). The public mixing of genders as well as the ideals of romantic love and marital compatibility were central political issues for the Ottoman reformists and their later political heirs, the Turkish nationalist secularists. Indeed, while nineteenth-century public discussions around coffeehouses compared traditional neighborhood coffeehouses to modern reading houses modeled after European ones, twentieth-century discussions would focus on a desire for coffeehouses to function like "clubs" (*kulüp*) where women could join men (Öztürk 2005).

Public places where men and women mingled drinking coffee emerged in the latter half of the nineteenth century in non-Muslim and Westernized urban quarters like Pera (Beyoğlu) in Istanbul. Adopting the French word for coffee-house, these mixed-gender spaces employing female waitresses were called cafés. The distinction between a *kahvehane* (coffeehouse) and a *kafe* (café) can be literally translated into English only at the expense of losing the culturally meaningful distinction predicated upon the postcolonial gendered tension between modern and traditional that is then mapped onto a distinction between gender-mixed and gender-segregated socialization. The public presence of women as workers and clients marked cafés as modern, distinguishing them from gender-segregated, male-only coffeehouses marked as traditional.

Echoing their Ottoman predecessors, the nationalist (male) state elites of twentieth-century Republican Turkey were proto-feminists who were vocally critical of gender segregation, which they perceived as the remnant of an overly religious, traditional, and backward past, and who advocated greater participation of women in public life, a social reform they held to be a prime symbol of modernization and secularization. Women's public presence was key to the establishment of a secular public sphere in Turkey (Göle 1997). From the classroom to the parliament, the Turkish Republic strategically and symbolically fostered women's public visibility and mixed-gender socialization by instituting a range of policies, such as compulsory coed schooling and women's suffrage, while banning independent (feminist) women's organizations and writing women's activism out of official history (Kılıç 1998). The state replaced sharia family law with Swiss civil law, thereby codifying a modern patriarchal family model with individual male heads of nuclear households (Sirman 2000), and promoted a modernizing ideal of feminine domesticity in the image of rationalized, educated mothers and wives (Navaro-Yaşın 2000). While women's inclusion in the public sphere brought immense political significance to the identity of the new nation as Westernizing/Westernized, it also fostered anxieties over national identity and difference. Anxieties around over-Westernization and national authenticity situated women in public on a tightrope between tradition and modernity, demanding a "modern but modest" public presence (Durakbaşa 2000). Women's inclusion in the publicness of a mixed-gender social life was constitutive and significant, but also instrumental and disciplined.

Gender-mixed public spaces in contemporary Turkey are central to mainstream public sociability and consumption practices, as attested by a widespread and diversified, if decisively urban, presence of cafés.[13] Nonetheless, there was and still is a tension between the aspirations of mixed-gender and heterosexual sociability and closeness and the continuing appeal of gender-segregated socialization and homosocial intimacy (Olson 1982; Sirman 2005). In the 1930s, when the founder of the Turkish Republic, Atatürk himself, was daringly asking the wives of state elites in attendance to dance with him on the empty dance floor of a new social club in Ankara, a coffeehouse owner in Istanbul was admitting that the concrete dance floor he had been required to build on the order of the municipality was never used for mixed-gender dancing (Öztürk 2005). Because the relations of gender-segregated intimacy sit uneasily with the modernist ideals of mixed-gender sociability, women may be found complaining about their husbands spending too much time in coffeehouses and other spaces of male intimacy, and men may be found complaining about their wives idling around coffee cups and other modes of feminine intimacy. Even the socializing habits of mixed-gender groups might inadvertently fall across both male and female groupings, and so their members warn each other apologetically vis-à-vis an internalized modernizing gaze by invoking the gender-segregated confines of homosocial intimacy: "Let's not make it *haremlik-selamlık*" (gender segregated). The discontents of state-led modernization and (an almost postcolonial) secularist nationalism thus operate in the fabric of everyday life through a deeply felt tension in and negotiation over the gendered practices and affects of intimacy and spatialized sociability.

The lifestyle and consumption habits of the middle classes play a significant role in the fostering of the emphasis on heteronormative domesticity and mixed-gender public life, as well as on the attendant transformations of the relations between gender, space, and sociability. Tracing the changing uses of household space from the Ottoman to the modern Turkish era, Ozbay (1999) observes that harem quarters were transformed into backstage living rooms, situated in the inner quarters of the house where the informal, day-to-day activities of the nuclear family took place, while *selamlık* quarters became the front-stage salon, rooms located in the outer section of the apartment where the conjugal couple hosted their mixed-gender guests. It was also in these salons that women held "reception days" called *gün*, which translates literally as "day" and refers to periodic and rotating home gatherings of a group of women scheduled during the daytime when the men of the house are away. These women-only receptions were hosted in the outward-facing section of the house, in the salon rather than the family living room, suggesting that women were "moving into a species of public life" (Ozbay 1999, 5). Among such women's sociabilities nestled in their houses and gender-segregated sociabilities, coffee cup readings constitute regular pastimes. As the distinction between living room and salon began to fade, hinting at a reorganization of the gendered relationships between space, intimacy, and sociability, coffee cup readings moved out of the house to the burgeoning fortune-telling cafés where *mahrem* intimacies of the domestic and feminine spheres and the stranger sociabilities of the mixed-gender urban settings are conjoined in new ways.

The neoliberal and postsecular remakings of middle-class habitus in Turkey today contribute to the transformations of gendered habits of sociability and intimacy, adding to the blurring of the distinction between cafés and coffeehouses. These two places of coffee consumption have long differed, not only in terms of the gendered sociabilities they fostered but often also in terms of the class habitus they signified, connoted by location, decoration, and menu (Göle 2000). Whereas in coffeehouses the main beverage has been brewed black tea alongside Turkish coffee, cafés offered cappuccinos, lattes, and herbal teas, and even skipped more conventional selections like Turkish coffee and black tea. Since the 2000s, however, a new generation of local coffee chains has reappropriated Turkish coffee into the café form. Informed by a millennial taste for reclaiming the traditional, they have stylized it as a trendy café beverage alongside more recently introduced coffee beverages for the consumption of mixed-gender groups, attesting to the novel brokering of the gendered categories of the traditional and the modern that have long set the terms for the coffeehouse/café distinction in particular and for secular middle-class public life in general.[14]

The gendered dynamics of public space that distinguish coffeehouses and cafés have even been subject of direct action by feminists. In 1989, a major daily reported that "feminist groups who have been very active lately raided a coffeehouse and discussed women's rights with the men present."[15] Women entering a coffeehouse and talking to men about women's rights constitutes a newsworthy feminist intervention where coffeehouses mark public space as masculine; even when walking past a coffeehouse, neighborhood women are expected to avoid them. As key sites of the constructions and performances of masculinity in the public sphere, coffeehouses are so naturalized as part of hegemonic masculinity that, when asked if and why they visit coffeehouses, most male respondents were taken aback, replying blankly that all men visit coffeehouses (Arık 2009), a retort analogous to many of my fortune-telling informants who commented that all housewives read coffee cups. Feminist gestures ranging from "raids" in the 1980s when women defiantly entered coffeehouses and interacted with men in front of press cameras to the imprinting of a coffeehouse front window with the names of women murdered by men in the 2010s notwithstanding, the gendered distinction between coffeehouses and cafés persists.

In this context, the fortune-telling café emerges as a novel kind of public space that does not easily map onto the long-standing bifurcation along gendered lines of coffee sociabilities into cafés and coffeehouses and their attendant binary of mixed-gender and gender-segregated spaces. In fortune-telling

FIGURE 4.3. A customer arriving at Women's Coffeehouse (Kadınlar Kahvesi) in Beyoğlu.

cafés, intimate publics organized around the affective and relational affinities of the feminized are hosted in non-gender-segregated urban public spaces that are located in the spatial and cultural vicinity of mixed-gender publics. Indeed, the names of the earliest fortune-telling cafés themselves constitute a reflection of and on their gendered novelty. The first such café, Melekler Kahvesi, subverts the distinction in Turkish between a coffeehouse reserved for men, a *kahvehane* (abbreviated as *kahve*, which also refers to the drink itself), and a café (*kafe*) reserved for mixed-gender socializing. This novel use of the gender-nonspecific portmanteau *kahve* (coffee/coffeehouse) highlights the interesting combination of a public space where mostly women socialize around coffee in a café, including in Melekler Kahvesi's unusual female-only rooms. While the Turkish version of the business's name deploys the word *kahve* along with the feminine and modern/secular-sounding adjective *melekler* (angels), the English translation coined by the owners, Angels Café, switches to the word *café*, which would translate in Turkish as *kafe*, not *kahve*. Even more obvious was another early fortune-telling café that called itself Women's Coffeehouse (Kadınlar Kahvesi), self-reflexively emphasizing the challenge these public spaces posed to the established terms of gendered publicness in Turkey at the start of the twenty-first century.

This chapter has detailed the affective and sociospatial relations of gendered intimacy as they are brokered in postsecular coffee publics. In this inquiry, fortune-telling cafés emerge as novel arrangements that represent a new configuration of femininity and intimacy which draws upon and remakes the Islamicate and modernist secularist formulations of privacy and publicness in a postsecular milieu. Distinct from both gender-segregated domestic sociabilities and gender-mixed public sociabilities, these divination businesses conjure for the first time a new kind of gendered public that is squarely centered around the intimacies of the feminized and is singularly dependent upon public, and not domestic, spaces and sociabilities. Fostering novel public intimacies among women and young and gay men (but not adult heterosexual men), fortune-telling cafés negotiate *mahrem* bonds of intimacy and secularist ideals of publicness under a millennial neoliberal and neoconservative intimization of the broader public sphere. Therefore, they necessarily pose new questions about the personal and political stakes of intimacy and publicness, themes pursued in chapter 5.

5

———————————

————————

————

THE JOYS AND PERILS OF INTIMACY

Elif is a soft-spoken woman in her early twenties. She's just graduated from college and is looking for work, letting people know she is looking, sending résumés around. She's exploring her options for a higher degree. Maybe. She hasn't decided yet. She's also busy managing her romantic life under the gaze of her parents, with whom she lives. She emphasizes that she's very close to her mother and shares with her many personal troubles but also admits that with a fortune-teller she can talk about things she would rather not talk about with her mother. She started frequenting fortune-telling cafés last year when she had a boyfriend with whom she had an unstable relationship. "My mom knew about him," she confirms, and "was understanding at first." After Elif repeatedly broke up and then got back together with the boyfriend with whom she "did not have a future [marriage prospects]," her mother became disapproving.

Elif did not want to hear her insistent recommendations that she cut him off for good. So she decided to keep things to herself, letting her mother think that the relationship was over. This secrecy not only meant that to meet with him she had to lie her way around her mother's supervision but also that she could no longer benefit from her mother's emotional support through the ups and downs of her romantic life. "I knew already that nothing would come of it [the relationship]," she admits. "But I just needed someone who would understand." That's when she began frequenting fortune-telling cafés. She enjoyed a close relationship with a particular fortune-teller, a woman of her mother's generation. Although her troubling romantic relationship is now over, she still enjoys visiting fortune-telling cafés as places where she can find an intimate confidant.

Elif's story reminds me of my high school classmate Sibel. It was the 1990s. Fortune-telling cafés were not around yet. On a pleasant spring afternoon, Sibel invited me and another girlfriend to hang out at her house after school. Her stay-at-home mom welcomed us. We spent time in Sibel's room relaxing and chatting, talking about things that high school girls are supposed to talk about—school, romance, friendships. After a while, Sibel's mom invited us to the balcony to have Turkish coffee. I distinctly remember that I felt complimented to be treated like a real houseguest; Sibel's mother was offering us coffee and conversation the way she would with her peers. She even offered to read our cups. I was excited to be treated like an adult woman. Cup reading felt different from the adolescent ritual my best friend and I shared, where we would do a simple opening with a standard deck of playing cards (*iskambil falı*) for each other to get answers to questions like, "Will he call today?" I don't remember what Sibel's mom told me and my friend. I do clearly remember my surprise upon hearing her comments about a boy who was romantically interested in Sibel. Sibel had a boyfriend with whom, much to our admiration, she held hands and visited cafés. We knew about it, and we also knew not to know it around her mom. So we listened intently but quietly, as did Sibel, while Sibel's mother recounted her daughter's romantic prospects in the cup. A few weeks later, Sibel missed class for many days, and we became worried about the reasons why. My friend talked to her on the phone briefly and reported back to me what Sibel had confided in her: Sibel had been grounded following a beating by her father and older brother, who had caught her getting out of a car with her boyfriend. Her mother had snitched on her; it was an intimate betrayal.

DIVINATION PROVIDES A CULTURALLY intelligible template for intimacy through which the reader and the recipient can readily enter the terrain of the personal and the private through a close, if transient, interaction. Yet, as the chronicle in this chapter reveals, the intimacy of divination is in the process of being transformed under its commodification in fortune-telling cafés in the larger context of the neoliberal intimization of a postsecular public sphere. Fueled by the anxieties of a postsecular moment and the vulnerabilities of heteropatriarchal subordination, secular Muslim women clients like Elif come to fortune-telling cafés to hear the intimate details of their lives as retold by a stranger so that they may avoid the potential costs associated with the revelation of their intimate lives without the shield of confidentiality like Sibel experienced.

The romantic and sexual lives of women and LGBTIQ individuals are disciplined in the family, community, and, increasingly, in the millennial public culture and political realm of Turkey, where the neoliberal media, from daytime shows to television serials, abounds with the brokering of the intimate in previously unseen openness and where an Islamically accented gender-conservative government and the vital feminist and LGBTIQ movements it targets both place the intimate at the heart of the public and the political. In this milieu, intimacy, especially of the public kind, entails both strong appeals and grave risks. Here lies the significance of the novel combination of anonymity and intimacy offered by the proliferating practices of commercial fortune-telling. Meeting the desire to broker the intimate outside their social circle with the provision of the relative safety of a disembedded interaction, fortune-telling cafés provide those for whom public intimacy can prove costly—at times even fatal—a safe space in which to discursivize the intimate in public and yet away from the prying eyes of relatives, friends, neighbors, community members, and the government. The inquiry presented in this chapter into the various constellations of publicness and intimacy entailed in commercial divination requires, therefore, a nuanced feminist reckoning with divination's novel intimate publics of strangers within which the personal is generalized to the point where its consumers feel both recognized and reflected without feeling autobiographically uncovered. In feminized publics of divination, the gendered stakes of recognition and exposure are played out with exceptional lucidity, illuminating the contradictions and challenges of feminist and LGBTIQ politics, particularly in neoliberal and postsecular times of reactionary gender conservatisms.

Key to the transformation of the intimacies of fortune-telling in twenty-first-century Turkey is their move from socially embedded domestic settings to anonymous public venues. When circulating in the enduring social networks of family members, neighbors, and friends, divination is rooted in the already established intimacies of kinship and community. In this context, divination serves as a medium for producing, expressing, and sustaining relational intimacy, as well as for negotiating the prescribed terms of the intimacy accompanying a relationship. Through cup readings, younger siblings can advise their elders without being disrespectful, concerned friends can provide critical commentary on a sensitive topic without coming off as rude, nosy neighbors can speculate on the marriage of the couple next door without sounding intrusive, and curious mothers can inquire about their daughters' romantic lives without explicitly cross-examining them. Divination works along the relational boundaries that define existing relationships between readers and recipients. These boundaries have been set by the conventions of intimacy so as to allow for temporary breaches and produce deeper intimacies.[1] In the context of lasting social ties, the entry that divination provides into otherwise inaccessible terrains of intimacy might serve a range of relational objectives. Divination can be a medium for checking on, advising, comforting, inspiring, encouraging, celebrating, and supporting. It can also serve as a tool for questioning, manipulating, controlling, shaming, and sanctioning. Especially in the context of familial and communal relationships that situate the individual as a gendered member of a social group, revelation carries the risk of exposure. The price to be paid for being exposed under the heteropatriarchal gaze of the family and the neighborhood might be judgment about or intervention into one's life. Depending on participants' social status and vulnerabilities, exposure might trigger disciplining, gossip, exclusion, and even physical violence, particularly in the context of hierarchical kinship ties. This is the dark side of socially embedded intimacies.

The move of coffee divination from the realm of feminine domesticity to the realm of the market and the city recalibrated the relationships between intimacy, sociability, and the public. By removing divination from embedded social networks and joining up with capitalist flows of commodities and services in the market, the commodification of divination created the necessary conditions for the emergence of a new regime of intimacy. Brought together at a fortune-telling business under the terms of a commercial contract that reduced their interaction to the exchange of a fee for a service provided for a standard period of time at the provider's workplace, the reader and the client became strangers conducting an economic transaction in a clearly specified time and place, under no obligation to develop or sustain a social relationship. The commodified intimacy of divination thus allows clients to indulge in the pleasures of sharing their intimate lives under the gaze of a stranger, but in the safety of an anonymous and therefore confidential interaction. Sanctioning intimacy as a commodified experience unbound from social expectations and free for circulation among strangers, commercial divination fosters anonymous intimacies.[2] Öznur, a divorcée in her late thirties with a college degree who began reading cups after a full year of desperate job seeking, explains, "People share very private issues. We are strangers. We're not from their social circles. So there is no chance that what they share might be heard by someone who knows them."[3] The newfound anonymity of commercial fortune-telling renders the closeness of divination intimate/authentic (*samimi*) for those clients who can more genuinely explore their feelings and desires in the absence of the looming threat of social sanctioning.[4] In other words, the "bounded authenticity" (Bernstein 2007, 103) of the intimacy in this commercial interaction is deeply structured by and valued precisely for its disembeddedness, anonymity, and thus confidentiality.

Confidentiality is precious to those who strategize their intimate lives under conditions of relative secrecy while navigating relations of love and domination. For Elif, women fortune-tellers of her mother's generation offer a caring compassion that is felt as genuine, welcomed precisely for its motherliness. But such authentic sharing is possible only because these women are not in fact her mother, as Sibel's story indicates. Like many youth and gender and sexual minorities who depend on "facades" to manage their personal lives without explicitly conflicting with their families and communities (Özyeğin 2009, 2015), Elif's and Sibel's romantic lives were partially but not fully transparent to their mothers. Their mothers initially knew about and supported their flirting, going even so far as to cooperate with the young women in keeping up the facade of premarital modesty vis-à-vis the larger family and community. When Elif's mother withdrew her support for her daughter's romantic relationship because of its lack of marital prospects, Elif turned to the nonfamilial intimacies of commercial divination and kept up a facade of submission to her mother. For Sibel, the familial intimacies that grew through that fateful divination session with her mother years ago proved costly, as facades broke down between Sibel, her mother, and the male members of her family, who intervened violently.

Commodification loosens cup readings from the disciplining heteropatriarchal gaze and lateralizes this social practice, providing a space for those whose intimate lives, particularly romantic and sexual behaviors, are denied legitimacy and autonomy in dominant cultural narratives and are controlled through heteropatriarchal disciplining and violence. Fortune-telling cafés may not be as hospitable as many other kinds of cafés and bars are to the *namahrem* intimacies of flirting and cruising. But they are more amenable to another kind of intimacy among the *mahrem* community of the feminized, one that provides the emotional support necessary for self-sustenance through the ups and downs of navigating *namahrem* intimacies that are unsupported by the hegemonic institutions of intimacy such as family and marriage.

Single, married, and divorced women may explore in fortune-telling cafés issues they may not otherwise safely broach in familial and even friendship contexts (for example, marital dissatisfaction, premarital or extramarital relationships, divorce) with the confidence that the fortune-teller cannot circulate the information in their social circles. The threat of male violence in retribution for perceived breaches of modesty such as premarital or extramarital flirting or planning to leave a relationship or marriage is what makes the sharing of intimate issues in intimate publics that do not offer anonymity so volatile for women. In such a milieu, many café readers are well aware of the gendered asymmetries inherent in their clients' need for confidential intimacy—and of the potential costs of a breach. Echoing many other café readers, Öznur insists, "I would never tell a husband that his wife is cheating on him or that she wants to leave him. He could do anything. You never know. I would never share something like that."

Commercial divination provides not only youths and women but also sometimes LGBTIQ populations with a safer space in which to explore *namahrem* intimacies that would render them vulnerable within and outside the heteronormative spaces of intimacy of family and marriage. A female client in her early thirties was delighted to be offered predictions about her female romantic partner when the young male fortune-teller who read tarot cards alongside coffee residues directed her attention toward a specific card with a queen figure and inquired if it might represent her romantic interest. Indeed, some café fortune-tellers have devised ways of acknowledging their clients' same-sex desires in their prognostications, sometimes simply by taking advantage of the fact that personal pronouns are not gendered in Turkish, thereby leaving the gender of a person of romantic interest ambiguous. Readers can thus strategically avoid potentially uncomfortable revelations while still making space for diversions from heteronormativity.

The anonymous intimacies of divination interactions are tucked into the larger anonymity of urban spaces. A fortune-telling café is, after all, a café, a place to be outside and away from one's family home and neighborhood, a place to be around strangers. Clients are not in the living room of someone's home getting a reading from a neighbor, auntie, or girlfriend. They are in public getting a reading from a stranger away from the prying eyes and ears of the family home or the rest of the neighborhood. Fortune-telling cafés are located in the commercial strips of neighborhoods like Beyoğlu and Kadıköy, where other forms of urban leisure and entertainment businesses are located. Unlike traditional residential neighborhoods where especially younger and female members of the community may be supervised not only by their family members but also by neighbors who might check and report on their mobilities and sociabilities, neighborhoods like Beyoğlu and Kadıköy allow for a type of urban anonymity where different kinds of gendered and sexual intimacies can flourish beyond the heteropatriarchal norm (Sandıkçı 2015). "I was never normal," Bayhan, a male fortune-teller in his midthirties, verbalizes in the most explicit terms he has ever used with me to describe his gender queerness. Referring to the many years he lived and worked in Beyoğlu, Bayhan concludes, "I am not normal. Taksim [Beyoğlu] let that abnormality fully emerge." For the unmarried, youth, and LGBTIQ individuals, the anonymity of certain urban neighborhoods provides an oasis for nonnormative intimacies.

Anonymous spatial intimacies of divination are also increasingly folded into stranger sociabilities conducted in the virtual realm. As commercial fortune-telling is provided more and more often in online businesses, both the reader and the client become further disembedded from in situ social and relational markers. Here, interactions are mediated by texts, images, and sounds that the reader and client choose to share online as they adopt pseudonyms, craft self-presentations, and fill out basic demographic information forms. Customers and fortune-tellers exchange pictures of coffee cups and money with textual or audio recordings of interpretations, chat sessions, and, less often, live video sessions. In the virtual sphere, clients' and readers' social and physical locations are, on the one hand, flexibly inhabited and, on the other hand, hard to escape. Meral is a young lesbian reader who works part-time for a transnational digital fortune-telling website using the online persona of an older straight woman. She had a regular young male client who at some point in their ongoing chat exchanges came out by talking about his romantic interest in a man. He later shared that he lived in a provincial town where he was under a lot of pressure from his family and larger community and feared for his safety. Meral wanted to reach out and support him but did not wish to come out of her online persona herself, so she decided to remain in character but disclose as the supportive mother of an adult gay son. Under this alibi, she offered practical resources such as the contact information of LGBTIQ individuals and organizations that might be of assistance, all located in Istanbul. Meral was disappointed when she did not hear from her client for a while. The virtual care and solidarity she extended to this young man was valuable but not enough to breach his geographical isolation. "He needs to get out of there [the town he lives in with his family] and come here [to Beyoğlu, Istanbul]," she insisted.

Allowing clients to share intimately with strangers in public without being exposed as they could easily be in the family or the neighborhood, in situ and online intimacies of commodified fortune-telling create safer venues where intimacy and authenticity can be coupled with anonymity and confidentiality. In millennial Turkey, these venues indulge the increasing desire to talk about the intimate in public that is incited by the growing intimacy of the political and public culture. The personal and political significance of the anonymous intimacies of divination lie in this broader context in which the questions of who can talk about the intimate publicly, in what ways, and in what venues, and who can afford or choose to be intimate and authentic are highly contested and consequential (Sehlikoğlu 2013; Sehlikoglu 2015).

The Treacherous Imperative of Public Intimacy

Television is a spectacle of the intimate. Zapped through during daylight hours of the week when programming is directed at a presumed audience of stay-at-home women, the screen is filled with ordinary people living ordinary lives, with their so generic yet so personal moments of love and betrayal, care and violence on full display. I feel the pull of this publicly mediated world of domestic femininity during those mornings and early afternoons when I relax at home before heading out to fortune-telling cafés, where business picks up later in the afternoon. A number of *Oprah*-esque programs compete on different channels. Each features a female host interacting with an anonymous offstage audience of ordinary people who voice all manner of generic public opinions, accompanied by a few experts—a doctor, a therapist, a lawyer. Sometimes there is an astrologer, fortune-tellers being, after all, experts in all matters intimate. The object of reflection is the intimate, performed by the few onstage guests who share their extraordinarily ordinary stories of private lives gone awry. They are there to find a way out, a way through. They are there to be seen and heard. They reenact scenes of gendered marginalization. They narrate in self-disclosure as the host primes the audience to be attentive and to feel along with her guests, to offer advice or put-downs. The audience reacts in empathy, pity, anger, or joy. They comment and reason. People regularly break down in tears or stand up to dance in joy. Later in the day, during the primetime television hours following the evening news, the screen is again filled with media genres brokering the intimate: fictional series dramatizing romantic and familial adventures and misadventures glue people to the screens, while the actors' off-screen lives are brought into public view in accompanying paparazzi shows.[5]

There is no escaping intimate publics by moving beyond popular culture. On the news I hear in the background on the evening television as I type my field notes, statesmen refer to reproduction and the family with increasing regularity and detail. They insist that youths should not delay marriage and that women should have more children. Hardly found on the mainstream news but visible to me in the streets and the alternative media, feminist and LGBTIQ voices address issues of sexuality and reproduction more unequivocally than ever in defense of nonnormative intimacies. The various speakers differ in their relation to state power and in their political stances, but they are all brokering the intimate in the political public sphere.

TURKEY OF THE 2000S has seen a proliferation of intimate publics (*mahrem kamusallıklar*) in the larger context of the intimization of the public sphere. This has followed the neoliberalization of the Turkish economy and the concomitant privatization and expansion of the media in the 1980s and 1990s, when the intimate became increasingly discursivized and displayed in a neoliberal "shop window" (Gürbilek 2013). "Taboos are breaking down" (*Tabular yıkılıyor*) was the motto of the post-1980s, which brought forth the innovations of paparazzi, dating, and debate shows, rendering *mahrem* public in previously unseen and unspoken ways. The intimacies of mainstream public culture have expanded exponentially since 2000, with feminized *Oprah*-esque daytime programs, matchmaking programs, and reality shows taking central stage. In the postsecular popular culture of the 2010s, religiously flavored, moralistic, "real-life story" series demonstrated how mundane sins and virtues were punished and rewarded with this-worldly consequences, and Islamic charity shows invited viewers to peek into the dispossessed lives of the deserving poor before and after makeovers, while more secularly flavored versions featured ordinary people living together in a television studio house, filmed in their own home, or walking the halls of a show studio and followed around by cameras in routine, everyday situations like hosting a dinner party or shopping for clothes. The intimate became the centerpiece of public culture.

Watching daytime television in particular has become an exercise in attuning to the intimate publics of femininity. Daytime shows encourage troubled people of diverse social ranks to dissect their dramatic yet everyday misadventures, guiding and assisting them back to gendered normativity though the public scrutiny of their *mahrem*. In these programs, audiences of anonymous strangers are invited to watch (and incited to volunteer themselves as participants) as ordinary people disclose their insides: the insides of their homes, their personal lives, their bodies, their psyches. In the intimate public culture of neoliberalism, individuals are primed to present themselves on the (romantic/economic) market to be appraised, to prove themselves valuable, deserving, and desirable. They make themselves over and compete with each other. They talk explicitly, fight, act in wayward ways, and often do not end up coupled, reformed, or remade. They are on screen to be talked about, compared, judged, apprised, disclosed, refashioned, improved, advertised. They may survive, or win, or neither. Yet the mediatized publics insist on providing pseudo-remedies for the vulnerabilities of gendered marginalization and the destructions of neoliberalization intensified by destabilizations of the postsecular era. In these intimate publics, the unemployed and disabled seek alleviation of their destitution through charity. Missing girls, including young adult women who are deliberately not in contact with their families, are found with the help of the community. The poor and the elderly are married as a supposed remedy for their social isolation and poverty. The intimate is thoroughly exposed to public gaze as the boundaries of *mahrem* and *namahrem* are rendered porous in new ways.

Not only feminized intimate publics but also masculinized realms of the political public sphere are increasingly rendered intimate. From celebrities to ordinary citizens, from religiously conservative politicians to feminist and LGBTIQ activists, everybody seems to be talking about intimate matters or displaying intimate scenarios in public. Whether arguing over social policy or relating personal experience, intimate issues that have not previously been discursivized in public debate gain new visibility on news and political debate shows. At venues ranging in scope from private wedding celebrations to international population conferences, the most vocal mouthpiece of this new politics of intimacy, current president and long-time prime minister, Recep Tayyip Erdoğan, repeatedly prescribes romantic and reproductive decisions in increasing detail: "Do not delay marriage! Do not be too picky in choosing a spouse!"[6] "Have at least three children!" (Çetik, Gültekin, and Kuşdemir 2008). "Abortion is murder!" "I am against cesarian section births."[7] Protesting Erdoğan's habitual comments on sexuality and reproduction, which they frame as illegitimate state intervention into the intimate, feminists chant, "Where, how, with whom? None of your business, Tayyip!" and defiantly declare, "I will have sex and not get married. I will get pregnant and not give birth."[8] Echoing feminist activists, a woman MP from the main opposition party, the Republican People's Party (Cumhuriyet Halk Partisi), Aylin Nazlıaka responded, "Erdoğan should stop playing the vagina watchman."[9] In an effort to publicly shame her, the then deputy prime minister, Bülent Arınç, rhetorically asked,

"How can a woman MP married with children speak of her organ so openly, without feeling any shame?" (Tahaoğlu 2012). The political public sphere is saturated through and through with all things intimate and with incessant debates about the proper and improper forms and displays of the intimate (Acar and Altunok 2013; Korkman 2016).

By the third decade of the twenty-first century, proliferating neoliberal scenes of intimacy have been increasingly shaped by an Islamically accented neoconservative familialism, a recently rearticulated ideology of marital, procreative, and heteronormative intimacy and sexuality that has been fiercely promoted by the state.[10] Far from being a passive endorsement of what citizens traditionally have done and habitually are still doing, neoconservative familialism is in fact a call for citizen subjects to reclaim and revalue heteronormativity and gender conservatism in an era when the intimate is increasingly debated in public and when feminist and LGBTIQ movements are increasingly vocal (Korkman 2015a). In this postsecular moment, a religiously tinted "masculinist restoration project" (Kandiyoti 2013) professing to reconstruct masculinist authority remains in full swing, and the reinstatement of the family is at the center of its efforts to order not only the political realm but also public culture.

In a context where the government promotes pronatalist and promarital policies, such as financial rewards for new mothers and low-rate credit for newlyweds, and even takes on the explicit role of matchmaker, as when the then prime minister Ahmet Davutoğlu announced that citizens "who wish to marry should come to us [the government],"[11] and the feminist and queer opposition decry this across-the-board endorsement of heteronormative family, insisting that "there is life outside the family," marriage-focused matchmaking television shows and related spin-offs become the most popular genre of feminized intimate publics. Aligning neoliberal refashionings of the self with the neoconservative remakings of gender and sexuality in televised intimate publics, marriage shows reassert the family as the main frame of gendered normativity and self-making (Akınerdem 2015). Varieties of desire and violence to be legitimately admitted into heteronormativity are constantly negotiated here: a marriage show host heavily chastises a woman for daring to call in to find a female partner, while another host is protested by feminists for inviting to his show a man who killed two previous wives.[12] New types of family- and marriage-oriented shows are regularly invented to train their female guests and viewers in the arts of being a suitable bride and wife. In *Bride's Home*, newlywed women display their household goods and decor in order to compete over who has the best taste and shopping wit.[13] In *Mother's Heart*, on-staff pseudo-moms and mothers-in-law supervise young women contestants on domestic chores such as cleaning, knitting, and cooking in a bid to win the title of "most eligible bride" (Korkman 2017). The disquiets of gender liberalization are addressed in increasingly neoconservative ways, as women are retrained into heteronormative femininity, ad infinitum.

The neoconservatization of public culture is not autonomous from the political processes of neoconservatization. The limits of what can be said by whom about intimate matters are managed by governmental suppression of feminist and LGBTIQ voices, as exemplified by the bans and attacks on Pride and International Women's Day marches and the criminalization of feminist and queer activists, as well as by state intervention into the media representations of the intimate though financial incentives, fees, and other punishments. While shows that train women in normative femininity are sometimes financially supported by the Ministry of Family and Social Policy and screened on official state channels, others hosting feminized intimate publics are regularly issued monetary fines and temporary broadcasting closure penalties from the national regulatory board for radio and television broadcasting, the RTÜK. Most of these RTÜK decisions refer to infractions of Article 8(f) of Law No. 6112 regulating broadcasting, which stipulates that broadcasting "should not contradict national and spiritual values and the principle of the protection of general morality and the family" (*toplumun millî ve manevî değerlerine, genel ahlaka ve ailenin korunması ilkesine aykırı olamaz*).[14] In fact, a large share of the board's penalties targets daytime feminized publics. In one incident, a daytime *Oprah*-esque show exclusively addressing mother-in-law/daughter-in-law relations was found harmful by RTÜK, since "familial problems were discussed in detail in front of millions of viewers, creating negative feelings about the institution of family and marriage," and the channel was issued monetary fines for "having violated the privacy/intimacy [*mahremiyet*] of the family."[15]

By the late 2010s, the neoconservative push had reached such form and intensity that even marriage shows were deemed threatening to the gender order the government sought to endorse. In 2016, RTÜK convened all marriage program producers in a meeting to discipline them.[16] Months later, a statutory decree (KHK/690) added to Article 8 of Law No. 6112 the stipulation that broadcasting cannot include "programs where individuals are introduced to each other or brought together with the purposes of finding a friend" (*arkadaş bulma amacıyla kişilerin tanıştırıldığı ve/veya buluşturulduğu türden programlar*).[17] "Friendship" (*arkadaşlık*) in Turkish is commonly used as a semidisguised way to describe premarital relations between men and women, and the decree was broadly interpreted as banning marriage programs.[18] Since the decree, marriage shows have often continued to be broadcast under the same names with the same hosts, but they have shifted their focus from premarital matchmaking to neoconservative family reparation. The decree also assigned to RTÜK, in consultation with the Ministry of Family and Social Policy, the mission to financially incentivize family and child-friendly programs deemed to "support the integrity and continuity of the family and the psychic, mental, and moral development of children and youth."[19]

The neoconservative politics of intimacy is executed not only by productive and repressive powers regulating discourse in public culture and the political public sphere, but also by coercive powers directly targeting feminized bodies. In addition to escalating and violent police attacks on feminist and LGBTIQ protestors, the state's repressive apparatus, which has routinely utilized sexual violence, has been operating intimately with new sorts of public visibility. During a 2016 military attack on Kurdish-populated cities, Turkish special military forces scattered the houses they invaded with women's underwear, lipstick, and condoms, and graffitied threats like, "Girls we're here. Where are you?" (Baysal 2016). The soldiers shared photos of these exploits on social media, including graffiti addressing the president that read, "I love you, long man," using one of the president's masculinist nicknames with clear sexual innuendo.[20] In another instance, the state defended sexual violence committed under its auspices aggressively, when, for example, a woman journalist who had reported on child rape in prisons was arrested for the alleged crime of "exposing the privacy/intimacy [*mahremiyet*] of the state."[21] Even the governmentalized apparatus of public medicine has been operating in coercively intimate ways in its eagerness to promote particular sexual and reproductive behaviors. As part of pronatalist paternalism, family doctors have sent text messages to women who have tested positive for pregnancy, inadvertently sharing information with whichever family member was the primary provider of social security and had their phone number on record; in one case, the father of an unmarried woman who attempted to stab his daughter (Saluk 2021).[22] Other, longer-standing examples include public hospitals performing mandatory measuring of trans women's vaginas (Zengin 2016) and nonconsensual virginity tests (Parla 2001). The masculinist politics of intimacy thus depends upon a violent denial of the right to intimacy for LGBTIQ individuals and women, particularly for younger and single women and racially and sexually marked populations such as Kurdish and transgender women.

Despite the contentious and violent disciplinings of intimacy in an intimate public culture and political public sphere, the most desirable commodity to be produced and consumed continues to be the intimate itself, and demand seems to increase with supply. Not only are audiences trained to consume it with growing appetite, but the mass supply of (a commodified and staged) intimacy is felt to risk diminishment of the intimate quality of the very thing that is on display. Producers, hosts, guests, and audiences continuously demand more intimacy and accuse each other of not disclosing enough, or of not disclosing honestly enough, or of lacking genuineness or authenticity. The public display of the intimate never seems to suffice; there is always the suspicion of yet another layer to be revealed. Are we really getting an inside view, or is what we are seeing just a scripted dialogue, a manicured house, an actor from the casting office, a manipulative host? Debates about who is truly open and sincere (*samimi ve içten*, the latter term literally translating as "from the inside") versus who is acting or putting on a show abound in intimate publics. "Stop pretending and be authentic!" guests, contestants, hosts, and audience members demand, as intimacy (*samimiyet*) becomes an ethical imperative for appearing and speaking in public. Politicians accuse each other of not being intimate (*samimi*), while tapes leaking private conversations or sexual liaisons involving statesmen produce unexpected intimacies. The more the intimate is displayed and dissected in public, the more intense is the felt crisis of and paradoxical push for intimacy.

Yet the insistent desire and demand for intimate self-disclosure in public that accompanies the saturation of public debate and culture by the intimate (*mahrem*) is a treacherous imperative. Even beyond the coercive reach of state institutions, the privileges and costs, risks and rewards of being publicly intimate are unevenly distributed along heteropatriarchal lines. Being authentic could endanger one's social standing, relationships, and safety. This holds especially true in the context of rising femicide rates in Turkey in the first two decades of the twenty-first century, which was marked by a brief early period of gender equality reforms that were quickly followed by a rising reactionary gender conservatism, accompanied all along by a vocal feminist and queer movement (Atuk 2020). For women who have invested a fragile trust in intimate publics such as daytime shows despite their deep knowledge that intimacy holds the potential of violence close at hand for the feminized, the cost has sometimes been their very lives (Akınerdem 2020). A woman who married a man she had met on live television was murdered by him three months later.[23] Another woman was shot and seriously wounded by her teenaged son after sharing her experiences of domestic violence on a daytime show (Schleifer 2005). The provocation to discursivize and display the private and the personal brings new desires and new troubles where gendered expectations of propriety, honor, and shame increase not only the risks of romantic and familial intimacy for the feminized, but also the costs of being intimate in public.

It is in this context that divination cafés flourish by offering a safer, more anonymous type of public intimacy while also satisfying the desire for the making of the intimate in public. Products of a long history of shifting relationships between gender, intimacy, sociability, and space, divination cafés reconfigure the logic of intimacy (*mahremiyet*) by reordering the relationships between stranger sociability, privacy, and publicness. By offering the benefits and pleasures of a particular combination of urban anonymity and confidentiality together with feminized intimacy, comfort, and familiarity, they reduce the risks associated with being intimate in public for gender and sexual minorities. In relation to the many forms and layers of intimate publics that surround them, this particularity makes the feminized publics of divination a productive entry point into feminist politics and critiques of public intimacies and intimate publics in their various incarnations and entanglements.

Intimate Publics and Feminist Politics

— We'll release them [sex workers–turned–revolutionary agitators] out into the world. We'll send them to various cities and towns in proportion to the frequency of femicides. We'll make sure that they each have a new career and are able to support themselves. Their task will be to congregate with other women, converse [*muhabbet kurmak*], organize *günler* [rotating daytime female parties hosted at home]. For now . . .
— [Interrupting.] We should think about the television series too.
— How . . .
— [Interrupting again.] What will they talk about?
— We need to talk about [them] watching TV serials and then interpreting them together. Don't we mean to implode the discourses from inside?
— Sooo . . .
— From a communist perspective, [they'll talk about] human relations, what [it] is to give birth and to die [*can vermek*], what love is, what commodity relations are, what struggle is, how to raise kids, what to do in the household.
— Yes, but they shouldn't just propagandize. They should be able to spark debate by asking questions from different perspectives.
— I like the idea of using television serials to do that.
— Yeah . . . besides those, I also think that fortune-telling [*fal*] is a good method. I mean, interpreting, propagandizing through cup readings. After all, fortune-telling is an indirect communication medium.

— Yes, yes. As we talked about before. What if there was a women's coffeehouse where fortunes were told, but with hidden mics on the tables, sending messages via that medium?

— The café business is too eccentric and too institutional. Let's think about this. Women's [television] shows are also important. . . .

— Okay. Looking at all these issues, we should teach them stuff like anthropology, participant observation, and such. Not too in-depth though.

— All right. Moving on. This is what we gather from reading the testimonials [of sex workers]: were these women not in this line of business, they would want to be "normal" women, have a family or some such thing.

— This is why, after completing their training, they should go flood a women's shelter. One calamity is worth more than a thousand words of advice.

—Suphi Nejat Ağırnaslı, *Menkibe: Mevcut,
Menkul ve Müşterek Komünizmde Israr Beyanı*

The above discussion is taken from a self-consciously ironic personal political manifesto (Ağırnaslı 2013, 125–26). In this political fantasy, a mixed-gender group of revolutionaries are discussing their plans to recruit and train former sex workers as underground feminist revolutionary agitators who will deploy women's everyday practices like discussing television shows and reading fortunes in an effort to subvert normative femininity itself. Written with dry wit and dark humor by a young male leftist who was trained as a sociologist and lost his life as a revolutionary fighter during the defense of the autonomous Kurdish region of Kobane, the dialogue provides a rare if comical reflection on the political potential of gendered practices of divination and fortune-telling cafés. Indeed, with rare exceptions such as Kandiyoti's (1987) insightful comparison of the gender-segregated close bonds of women in Turkey with Western feminist consciousness-raising groups, which similarly insulated women sharing the intimacies of femininity, intimate publics of divination are not perceived as significant for feminist politics.

It is most certainly the case that, unless infiltrated by sex workers–turned–revolutionary agitators, fortune-telling cafés are not readily oriented toward politics as such. There is a potentiality to divination publics as proto-political publics, as was the case, for example, with gay clubs or bathhouses, which were not (perceived as) spaces for political identity formation and activism until they become spaces of organized resistance and oppositional action, often in response to police harassment and repression. Nevertheless, divination publics are clearly not counterpublics (Fraser 1990) where subaltern groups gather to regroup and form their voices, only to return to the dominant public sphere to speak back, as feminist and queer political organizations do. They are rather, as Berlant (2008) put it, juxtapolitical publics that lie to the side of the political and are valued by their participants for their very distance from the formal political realm.

Importantly, counterpublics such as feminist groups and juxtapolitical publics such as fortune-telling cafés are not necessarily exclusive of one another but share audiences, spaces, and genres. There are individuals who identify with feminist and LGBTIQ politics and also populate divination publics, and their political discourses and intimate feelings inform the divinations they give or receive. Divination publics also resonate in more direct and unexpected ways with counterpublics, such as occurred in the 2014 urban protests known as the Gezi Uprising, to which feminist and queer politics were central. The counterpublic of the Gezi Uprising was placed in the close vicinity of the birthplace and hub of fortune-telling cafés around Taksim Square in the Beyoğlu district. As a modern urban square, Taksim was a highly contested site of political protest, public access to which has long been obstructed by the state and fought for by oppositional groups. Connected to the square, both Gezi Park and the major shopping thoroughfare of İstiklal Caddesi were subjects of highly contested past, ongoing, and planned redevelopment and commercialization projects that threatened to destroy the lifeworlds of those who inhabited them as subjects on the fringes of economic, ethnoracial, religious, and gendered normativity (Parla and Özgül 2016; Potuoğlu-Cook 2015; Yıldız 2014). It was in this context that some workers and clients used fortune-telling cafés in the area as regrouping grounds during the uprising to escape police violence on the streets and provide for their own needs. Complementarily, the occupied Gezi Park grounds included a makeshift wishing tree to which protestors attached rags and notes, deploying the practice of wish making also common in coffee fortune-telling to express their hopes and desires in the politically oriented counterpublic of Gezi Park.

Despite these connections to the political, the worth of fortune-telling cafés does not inhere in their intersections with or proximity to counterpublics. To the contrary, in a time of intimate politics, the significance of divination publics lies in their very distance from politically oriented publics. As we have seen in this chapter, the political public sphere in Turkey is increasingly dominated by a postsecular, neoliberal politics of intimacy that often employs disciplinary and moralizing modes, while in mainstream public culture, the intimate is increasingly demanded, produced, and regulated in alignment with an Islamically accented neoconservative familialism. In this context, the inquiry explored in this chapter forwards the argument that the intimacies of the political public sphere and public culture offer an inviting yet treacherous terrain for those disadvantaged by heteropatriarchal hierarchies for whom public disclosure may prove dangerous. While part and parcel of the larger trend of the intimization of the public sphere, divination publics offer some relief from the push for public revelation of the intimate and the normativizing and governmentalizing impulses of mainstream public culture and the political public sphere. Rather than orienting their discourses outward for the reformulation of the(ir) clients' intimate (grievances) toward larger public and political spheres, such as a television show or political group might do, divination cafés are oriented inward so as to safeguard the confidentiality of the anonymous intimacies they produce. Here the intimate is not primarily or readily an object of voyeuristic consumption or of disciplining governance, but is instead afforded a degree of privacy where it can remain safely confidential while being nurtured through social relations among the feminized. This is highly significant from a feminist perspective, given that the growing trend of intimate/authentic self-disclosure, which might demand that youths, women, and queer folk shed the practices of keeping up facades, is likely to result in stricter supervision, control, and even violence over and against them.

Having struggled for the recognition that the personal is political, feminists have long bemoaned the artificial separation of public and private and the dismissal of feminized issues from the political public sphere as private. Yet in these times of the mainstreaming of feminist and even LGBTIQ politics and religiously accented reactionary gender conservatisms, feminists have also come to bemoan the rendering of the political as thoroughly intimate that has been fostered by neoconservative masculinist politics and biopolitical governmentalization. Further complicating feminist considerations around publics and intimacies is the fact that the desire to reach and influence the public at large might conflict with the (at times mortal) need to create and sustain safe(r) publics for the feminized.[24] In this context, venues for the articulation and expression of the intimate feelings of gender and sexual minorities below the radar of the political public sphere and mainstream public culture are highly noteworthy. As the earlier examples of masculinist violence following the mother-daughter fortune-telling session or the sharing of domestic violence experiences on a women's daytime show indicate, however, juxtapolitical intimate publics are neither necessarily nor effortlessly safe(r), let alone readily amenable to feminist aspirations. It is perhaps for this reason that intimate publics of femininity are not easily (recognized as) compatible with feminist praxis. For example, feminists in Turkey have long inveighed against the gender-normative discourse of television shows, petitioning them to take on feminist messages and divest themselves of their misogynist baggage, even resorting to demands for the abandonment of some daytime women's shows altogether. In a more mundane moment of feminist politics, concerned volunteers at a domestic violence shelter for women hesitated to replace broken coffee cups for fear that fortune-telling among residents fostered fatalism.

In consideration of these multilayered contradictions and feminist hesitations, part II of this book has approached the intimate publics of femininity that are conjured in fortune-telling cafés as a case in point to insist on a nuanced inquiry into the shifting, complex, and (juxta)political terms of the gendered relationships between affect, intimacy, and publics in a postsecular, neoliberal milieu. Part III continues the inquiry into the affectivity of divination by turning to the labors of fortune-tellers who conjure the intimate publics in which the feminized may attune to their secular anxieties and gendered vulnerabilities, if only at the expense of the growing precarity of their own divination labors.

PART III

FEELING LABOR,

PRECARITY, AND

ENTREPRENEURIALISM

6

FEELING LABORS OF DIVINATION

"How do you read fortunes?" I ask Bayhan, a thirtysomething man who has been reading coffee cups at cafés for over a decade. He pulls another cigarette out of a box of the cheap local brand he smokes and lights it up. After a long exhale, he starts to speak.

> I look into their eyes. I hold their hands. I feel their energy. It's not really about the shapes [of the coffee residues]. But if I said things out of the blue, they'd be scared. Coffee, tarot cards—these are just instruments. Everyone has feelings. Mine are rather intense, highly developed. At times, feelings arise merely by touching someone. I once made a bet with a coworker at the café I used to work at about a female customer. I bet that she had just had a breakup and had run straightaway to the café. She

was getting a reading at the table next to us. We listened in, and I won fifty liras. My friend was surprised. "How do you know?" "It's a feeling," I said. "I get a feeling" [*içime doğuyor*]. Something happens when I see someone. It grows stronger when I touch them. Sometimes without any instruments. I would never consult tarot cards or coffee residues. One day an *abla* [elder sister] arrived. I read her fortune without even opening her cup. She asked me why I didn't look at the residues. "I paid for it. I drank it," she objected. My boss chewed me out. That's how I learned to read cups, for formality's sake. Name a few shapes, rotate it once or twice, create the impression. But it's all about feelings. The goldsmith knows the diamond. He feels its authenticity from its radiance. He is that familiar with it. This is about familiarity with seeing people. Taxi drivers, salespeople—their feelings are strong. They're in constant interaction with others. They have intense feelings. Some occupations are like public relations: they know people, they see them, their feelings grow stronger.

Fortune-tellers feel people. "I feel it" (*hissediyorum*), most café readers insist when asked why they say what they say and how they know what they know. Most find this process of feeling hard to explain in any more detail, but, like Bayhan, some are quick to clarify that coffee residues, cards, and other mediums are mere instruments—excuses, even—there to provide a well-recognized container for the deployment of their feeling capacities. Sight is a key sense and idiom in divination, feeding and substantiating the process of feeling. Readers often preface their comments by saying "I see" (*görüyorum*) or "it seems" (*görünüyor*). One looks at, rather than reads, fortunes in Turkish (*fal bakmak*), an apt description of the perceptive skills of fortune-tellers who see the people they interact with through the lens of a deeper if intuitive attentiveness to who they are. Feelings grow stronger for those in regular contact with strangers, Bayhan asserts, indexing the discerning sensibility developed by fortune-tellers and others who come into regular contact with large numbers of people. Such familiarity with and knowledge of different classes of people whose characteristics, from clothing style to body language, hint at their socially patterned if deeply individuated dreams and troubles operates in fortune-telling not as a reflexive thought process but as a visceral process of feeling.

Fortune-tellers do not just feel people; they also make people feel. Feeling in divination refers not only to the process of skillfully if intuitively seeing people for who they are, but also to the ongoing processes of affective attunement and being moved that characterize the fortune-telling interaction. The sense of touch (*dokunmak*) is central to divination in terms of its wider usage in Turkish, as in English, to denote the state of being touched or affectively moved. Like seeing, touching complements this divinatory sense of feeling, giving substance to the otherwise undefinable process of feeling that allows fortune-tellers to read and move others. For Bayhan, touch is key to feeling others, and he often asks to hold the client's hand before opening the cup. But most café readers do not regularly initiate physical touch with their clients. All readers do, however, attune to their clients, opening themselves to being moved by them. It is this opening to mutual affect that increases their ability to say the right things in the right way, allowing the clients to be moved in their turn. "Feeling labor" refers to this particular modality of feeling people and making them feel.

Part III explores the feeling labors feminized secular Muslim fortune-tellers perform in the service of living precariously. While coffee divinations have long served as a medium of feeling one's way through gendered vulnerabilities, they are increasingly appropriated in the service of managing a compounded neoliberal and postsecular precarity. This chapter examines how, as a product of and a response to the gendered precarities of neoliberalization and the gendered allures of neoliberalism's therapeutic accompaniments, the feeling labors of divination are mobilized so as to survive precarity. These feeling labors not only offer a way for fortune-tellers to make a living; they also provide a service for emotionally sustaining clients through the disappointments of femininity, the frustrations of postsecularism, and the distresses of neoliberalism. Ironically, feeling labors are increasingly put to therapeutic use to address precarities produced by the interlockings of heteropatriarchy, secularism and Islamism, and neoliberalization at the expense of placing the fortune-tellers themselves in highly precarious labor conditions. In an era when the anxieties of economic neoliberalization, rising Islamism, and shifting gender norms are increasingly soothed by the reassurances of enchanted therapeutic remedies, this chapter grapples with the interlocking and gendered relationships between femininity, affect, labor, and precarity as they play out in the postsecular divination economy. Together, chapters 6 and 7 trace the transformation of feeling labors under the therapeutic ethos and self-entrepreneurial idiom of neoliberalism and the commercialization, digitalization, and transnationalization of divination under AKP's particular brand of religiously accented neoliberalism.

Feeling people and making people feel is hard work. Hidden behind the customary disparagement of fortune-tellers as quacks and the routine degrading of coffee fortune-telling as a feminine diversion is the labor that reading fortunes entails. While reading fortunes is often assumed to be an easy and effortless job, attuning affectively to and facilitating the expression of others' feelings not only can be difficult and exhausting; it also takes skill and experience. The feeling labors of divination require skillfulness and effort on both affective and emotional levels. As readers tune into and help thicken floating, yet-to-be personalized affective intensities, they also stimulate and verbalize their clients' culturally legible emotions (Korkman 2015b). Whereas the concept of emotional labor has been used to render visible the modulation of workers' inner states in order to produce a desired emotional result in their clients (Hall 1993; Hochschild 1983; Kang 2003; Lively 2000; Paules 1991; Pierce 1999), and the concept of affective labor has been used to explore the commodified production of affects (Ducey 2007; Hardt 1999; Negri and Hardt 1999; Wissinger 2007), I use the phrase *feeling labor* to emphasize the mutual embeddedness of both emotional and affective processes. The term *feeling* is usefully ambiguous and can thus conjure both of these dimensions (Cvetkovich 2003). It also mirrors fortune-tellers' own understanding of their work as an active process of "feeling" (*hissetmek*). This conceptualization allows for an analysis of the intersubjective and inseparable processes of affective attunement and emotional expression that is highly cognizant of the laboriousness and commodification of these processes but does not reduce their productivity and value to their instrumentalization under neoliberal capitalism.

While the management of emotions at work has been examined by a now well-established emotional labor literature, the production of affect at work has only recently and cursorily been addressed by an emerging literature on affective labor. The concept of feeling labor synthesizes and intervenes in these literatures to outline a holistic approach that neither focuses on one dimension at the expense of the other nor collapses these analytically distinct levels together, but instead takes both emotional and affective dimensions into account in their specificity and their interrelation. Feeling labor retains emotional labor's emphasis on the gendered inequalities that characterize the capitalist commodification of emotional capacities and experiences (Bellas 1999; Hall 1993; Hochschild 1983; Kang 2003; Lively 2000; Paules 1991; Pierce 1999). The conception of emotional labor as the management of the customer's mood through the display of either feigned or successfully self-induced emotions by the worker, as originally suggested by Hochschild (1983) and widely adopted in the field, is insufficient to capture the intersubjective process of feeling labor. Particularly constraining are the underlying assumptions about the individual, which, based on a binary of alienated/authentic selves, blunt the concept's analytical and critical edge (Weeks 2007). With its emphasis on preindividual, precognitive, and yet thoroughly social processes, the concept of affective labor provides an alternative to the atomistic individualist and instrumentalist undertones that often accompany the concept of emotional labor. Informed by scholarship on immaterial labor (Lazzaratto 1996), the concept of feeling labor thus contributes to those nascent affective labor studies that highlight the capitalist production and channeling of flows of affect which work to connect disparate bodies and individuals and create spaces for the flourishing of subjectivities and social relations (Ducey 2007; Freeman 2011, 2015; Hardt 1999, 2007; Negri and Hardt 1999; Wissinger 2007). Yet although feeling labor depends on affective labor characterized by "the creation and manipulation of affects" (Hardt 1999, 96), it is not reducible to such affective labor. Feeling labor operates instead through interpersonal processes of affective attunement that foster emotional incitement and identification and thus blur the very boundaries between self and other as well as between spontaneous versus manufactured feelings.

The feeling labors of divination are directed initially at the creation and maintenance of an affectively intense atmosphere that moves the client strongly and deeply, irrespective of the particular emotional accent into which this affectivity might be translated. Before anything else in the session can unfold, the client needs to get into an excitedly/anxiously expectant mood, ready to be affected. The caffeine consumption closely preceding the reading helps stimulate the body into an alert state, prompting a restless readiness. One reader takes a long pause before opening the cup, inviting clients to bring their full concentration to the table. Another withholds the opening of the cup until late in the session, keeping her eyes on the client and demanding instead the return of her gaze and attention. Some readers open the session by offering a deck of tarot cards for the client to pick from, solemnly placing the chosen cards face down on the table in a specific order only to be turned face up one by one later in the session. Others start off by speaking frantically, as though they have too much to say in the limited time available with the client and cannot afford a pause or distraction, absorbing instead as much as they can by staying alert and feverishly present. Whatever individual styles and gestures they adopt, it takes a confident, charismatic presence and an impressive opening of the session on the part of the reader to summon the affective intensity required to prepare the client to be read.

Creating an effective circuit of feedback requires a customer whose attention is focused on the reader, who is literate in the genre, and who is "open," in the lingo of divination, to be read/affected. "I have been to many fortune-tellers, but no one can read my fortune," remarks a young woman in her twenties as she sips her coffee and waits for her turn with the reader. She is visiting the café with her boyfriend, who is also drinking coffee but explains that he is not interested in getting a reading. "There was only one person who was accurate. I went to her twice, but after that I couldn't locate her," the woman explains with the familiar mixture of nagging doubt and insistent hope that brings many back to fortune-telling cafés. "If you believe her and if you are open, she is very good," the owner of the café offers. Being open refers to the client's ability and willingness to work with the reader to flexibly interpret predictions as personally meaningful and to provide feedback. Such openness might present as brainstorming for possible people in their lives when the reader mentions someone whose name starts with the letter S or T, correcting the reader who has made an almost but not truly accurate dating of the time of one's marital troubles, or selectively responding to those comments that hit the nail on the head while disregarding those that are off base. Readers are wary of customers who are unresponsive and uncooperative, either too timid in offering feedback or too exacting in their questions. "Closed" customers are likely to leave disappointed, as they neither feed into nor feed from the affective intensity of the interaction. In contrast, open customers serve as porous and generous nodes of an affective circuit, helping both themselves and the reader to a good reading.

Throughout the session, reader and client feel each other out within the enchanted intersubjective space of divination via affective attunement. The reader incites agitated anticipation on the part of the client by keeping the suspense and surprise going, increasing the capacity of both the reader and the client to affect and be affected. The reader's initial scanning of the coffee residues at the bottom of the cup, their gaze quietly focused on a seemingly random shape identified in the residues, their unexpected comment or unusual phrasing—all feed the attention and engagement of the client. The clients' looks of concentration, their nervous tapping, their nodding in recognition, their abrupt exclamations and quick questions—all feed the reader. Readers probe the client by offering partial and vague cues and prompts, describing a tall man to be met, depicting an ailing body part, or suggesting travel to a remote destination— all incite the client to feel. Clients provide feedback to the reader to the extent that they are (dis)affected by the interaction, guiding the reader to continue with a particularly moving topic or to pursue other avenues that might provoke more engagement. Some readers encourage specific forms of feedback, such as when they tell clients to jump in with their questions at any time or urge them to take notes on the predictions they want to remember. Others ask clients to save questions for the end or refrain from recording and focus on listening in the moment instead. The client and the reader are continuously aligned and realigned as they feel each other out, producing, sustaining, and revitalizing the affectively intense atmosphere through its highs and lows. It is within this affective circuit that the reader and the client feel each other, feeding the inter-subjective space in which affects circulate before dissolving or gaining traction to be subsequently individuated and articulated as emotions. The reader and the client develop the capacities to summon, experience, and express emotions in the representational realm offered by the cup-reading genre out of an amorphous intensity of flows of affect animating the intersubjective space of divination.

The coffee divination genre offers a template with which fortune-tellers can voice (their clients' potential) emotions, allowing customers to engage with a shadowy sketch of their most intimate selves from a safe distance. Coffee divination starts with the client drinking a cup of finely ground Turkish cof-fee. Consuming the coffee creates an enchanted and personalized connection between the drinker and the coffee grounds, which can then be read as a reflec-tion of the drinker's fortune. Prognostications usually start by sketching the client as a stick figure with a few basic lines, usually marital and employment status, and continue by adding a few contours—a personality trait, a dominant mood descriptor. This initial personalization allows clients to enter the cup, so to speak, and identify as the (hypothetical) person being described by the reader. The main body of divination sessions consists of descriptions of past and present scenarios that address the client's prior and prevailing circum-stances and future scenarios that reflect possibilities, narrated in an emotional style befitting the situation described, ranging from lamentation to celebration. Cup readers encourage their clients to subjectively embody the narrated de-sires and fears, hopes and regrets, and expectations and frustrations by inviting them to situate themselves in these scenarios and experience the emotions that arise from imagining themselves to be the subject of the situations described. Consumers' affective openness and readiness to identify with the scenes are essential to the successful delivery of the service of divination. As clients turn inward and approach their intimate lives through the reader's lens, they partici-pate in the coproduction of the divination service by consuming the reading as personally relevant, meaningful, and moving.

Clients' appetite for and aptness in turning inward in order to process their intimate experiences and emotions in an encounter with a stranger is accentuated in a neoliberal era where the intimate is displayed and managed in public, especially in those intimate publics of femininity where therapeu-tic modalities figure prominently.[1] In this milieu, the feeling labors of divina-tion join a postsecular terrain of therapeutic discourses and interventions that promise to alleviate the unequally distributed burdens of life in all its precarity. For the clients, the intimacy of fortune-telling conjured by the feeling labors of divination provides an enchanted venue in which to process therapeutically the gendered precarities exacerbated by postsecularism and neoliberalization.

The Therapeutic Ethos of Neoliberalism

Readers and clients alike regularly compare fortune-telling to therapy, or at least to what they imagine therapy might be like, given that only a few have had firsthand experience with it. Semra, a fortysomething, married, lower-middle-class woman with two teenage children, explains the therapeutic labor involved in cup reading.

> You know what it is we actually do? Psychological treatment! You sit the client down across the table, facing you. By the time the cup reading is over you have already bonded, and you have a conversation [*muhabbet kurulur*]. "You see, this and that happened, so do this and that, my daughter" [*kızım*, used to address a younger woman]. Based on your life experiences, you advise the client. And they actually leave happy. "You really comforted me. I'm in utter bliss!" [they say]. They arrive desolate and leave with a wide smile. [Fortune-tellers provide] that kind of support. Actually, this is psychological treatment to the tee. Some [clients] explicitly say that instead of going to a doctor and paying a lot of money, they come here and pay a little.

Situated outside officially sanctioned biomedical and psychotherapeutic modalities of care, the amalgam figure of the cup reader–as-therapist provides what is expected of the therapist, but without the stigma, cost, and, importantly, the hierarchical relationship of authority over the client that pertains in formal care modalities. Indeed, one of the most cited reasons clients offer for visiting café fortune-tellers is that it comforts them and raises their spirits and morale—an outcome they have come to expect from a therapy session—without the monetary and social price tag attached to visiting a mental health specialist.

Fortune-tellers' and their clients' eagerness to describe divination as therapy is informed by a familiarity with and desire to speak in the parlance of the larger therapeutic culture accompanying neoliberalism. Neoliberalization of the Turkish economy started in the early 1980s under the tutelage of the International Monetary Fund and the World Bank following a military coup. The 1980s' deregulation, privatization, and liberalization of the economy brought previously unseen opportunities for sudden enrichment and unmatched scenes of conspicuous consumption. But this was only for the lucky few, while the masses were faced with increasing income inequality, inflation, and unemployment. During the 1990s and early 2000s, optimism and hope were increasingly replaced by disappointment and anxious anticipation, as *crisis* became the key word for describing the economic and political climate of repeated economic downturns and unstable governmental coalitions. Following the economic crisis in 2001, the AKP would rise to power, preaching democratization, social justice, and integration into the global economy. Also, in 2001, the first fortune-telling café would open its doors in Istanbul, seeding what would become a robust economy of commodified divinatory services in the next decades.

Following the neoliberal turn of the 1980s, Turkey was increasingly immersed in the global expansion of a therapeutic culture (Rose 1990). Private television channels abounding with therapeutic programming such as *Oprah*-esque talk shows and self-help literatures circulated to teach individuals to confess and reflect upon troubling intimate experiences, perform pathology, and seek well-being in proximity to therapeutic discourses and experts, often at a distance from sociopolitical remedies (Peck 2016; Rimke 2000; Rose 1992). This therapeutic turn was facilitated by a historical conjuncture in which psychiatric expertise and categories become more widely distributed, particularly for intervention in the wake of sociopolitical disasters such as war and earthquake (Açıksöz 2015; Dole 2015, 2020).[2] With a new lingua franca gaining currency in Muslim/new age therapeutic literatures and modalities in the postsecular 2000s, the reach and appeal of this therapeutic culture grew in religiously/ spiritually accented ways. Cup readings were pulled into this neoliberal terrain shaped by the therapeutic ethos of neoliberalism and joined other commodified therapeutic services, from lead pouring and Reiki to talk therapy and psychiatric medicine, some offered by informal practitioners and others by professionalized psy-experts such as therapists and psychiatrists (Illouz 2008; Rose 1998; Tucker 2002). Recalibrating the boundaries of the intimate in public, these new and reinvented therapeutic mediums created novel avenues for crafting and healing neoliberal, (post)secular selves.

Therapeutic culture has an affinity with neoliberalization because neoliberal precarity produces anxious subjects (Beer 2016; Berg, Huijben, and Larsen 2016; Wilson 2017), which the therapeutic culture of neoliberalism then promises to soothe (Foster 2016; Peck 2016; Rose 1990). As a political-economic project that recalibrates society in line with market principles, neoliberalization is administered by the state through liberalization, privatization, deregulation, and the dismantling of social security and services (Harvey 2005), thinning out the systems of support individuals depend upon in times of crisis and vulnerability. At the same time, neoliberalization entails selectively distributing opportunities for individual choice and freedom to the privileged portions of a citizenry trained to be self-responsible, while reserving paternalistic disciplining and criminalization for marginalized populations (Wacquant 2012). In these ways, neoliberal restructuring renders personal fortunes less stable and fates less prone to individual mastery, deepening the level and reach of economic precarity and intensifying the intimate condition of gendered precariousness the feminized already had to contend with. At the same time, neoliberal ideology exalts, and neoliberal technologies of the self propel, the ideal of an enterprising, self-governing, self-fulfilling, self-responsible, autonomous individual (Rose 1992). The neoliberal imperatives of self-sufficiency and self-realization are simultaneously encouraged by the millennial assurances of economic opportunity and frustrated by the structural limitations of the neoliberal economy, fueling anxious anticipation (Beer 2016; Berg, Huijben, and Larsen 2016; Cossman 2013; Foster 2017; Isin 2004; Molé 2010; Scharff 2016). Rather than resolving the contradiction, the therapeutic ethos of neoliberalism seeks to channel the anxieties emanating from the incompatibility of the human condition of insecurity and dependency with a neoliberal ideal of self-sufficiency into therapeutic self-making activities, harnessing the psychic energies instigated by the very wounds of neoliberalization into the cultivation of neoliberal subjects (Foster 2017). In this context, therapeutic modalities that mind or even promise to mend the gap between the ideal of individually secured futures and the reality of intimate misfortunes beyond one's control abound. In particular, enchanted therapeutic modes such as commodified forms of religion and spirituality, especially modes like money magic that preach magical formulas for enrichment, have a structural affinity with millennial neoliberalism, which depends on more and more occulted mechanisms of accumulation and dispossession (Comaroff and Comaroff 1999, 2000a, 2000b).

The feeling labors of divination are put to new tasks and under new pressures when they are reconceived as the commercial therapeutical modes of a postsecular neoliberal era. Fortune-tellers move their clients, both in the sense of making them feel something and in the sense of moving them across the emotional spectrum. Qualitatively different from emotional labor that "requires one to induce or suppress feeling in order to sustain the outward countenance that produces the proper state of mind in others" (Hochschild 1983, 6–7), feeling labor takes clients on an emotional journey. Rather than creating and maintaining a particular mood (of contentment), readers strive to open clients to experience a range of affective intensities and emotional states, to move them, for example, from peaceful tranquility to agitated anticipation and from nagging worry to cautious hope.

But if the feeling labors of divination provide a space both for feeling one's feelings and for feeling better, the increasing value of clients feeling good in commercial fortune-telling sometimes comes at the expense of experiencing a broad array of feelings. Many fortune-tellers find themselves recalibrating their performances on their way from amateur or underground commercial contexts to fortune-telling cafés, learning to balance "the bad news with the good," self-censoring to "never speak of death," and monitoring clients so as "not to devastate an already depressed person." A confident cup reader bluntly declares, "I can relax people, no doubt. But it all depends on me. I could speak in a way that makes the client anxious. Their spirits would definitely not be raised were I to tell them that their past was horrible, their present sucks, and their future will only get worse!" But he is only partially justified in his confidence, since the range of affective/emotional experiences offered in commercial divination is influenced not only by the moral sensibilities of fortune-tellers but also by café managers. While employee training in fortune-telling cafés is nonexistent and managerial oversight and intervention are limited, employers still exercise some control over the labor process through customer feedback and selective hiring and firing practices that exclude readers deemed too intense or too negative.

Bayhan, who has spent the last decade working at fortune-telling cafés and the previous decade working in the underground economies of healing and divination, complains, "Fortune-telling has changed a lot since we started. I now call café divination 'customer fortune-telling.' The reader deceives, says everything is going to be all right. This is customer fortune-telling. . . . I recount whatever I see and feel. But the younger ones, the newer ones, offer whatever is demanded. It's a matter of supply and demand. Whatever the client wants. . . . In short, after a decade, divination is no more." The range of feeling offered by divination is under constant pressure from the contradictory influences of commodification to shrink and rebound. On the one hand, following the imperatives of the service industry, readings are increasingly valued for their capacity to produce what is generically called "customer satisfaction," often reduced to the production of a positive emotional state in the client. On the other hand, as Bayhan's remarks indicate, this instrumentalist imperative to make clients happy threatens divination as a therapeutic industry by turning it into little better than a feel-good-quick service. Paradoxically, the very measures taken to ensure customer satisfaction may ultimately threaten to depreciate the service by rendering readings too tame or too optimistic. A single woman in her early twenties I had accompanied to a fortune-telling café returned to our table after her session with a young male reader with an annoyed expression on her face and quickly advised her friend who was waiting her turn with a closed cup not to waste her money. "It was no fortune-telling," she declared with contempt. "Just pleasantries and advice." She was not alone in her disappointment, as I heard such complaints regularly. If deemed too tame, flat, or instrumentally oriented so as to create only positive feelings, a divination session might be judged unsatisfactory or even declassified as a proper divination service altogether.

In the midst of these contradictory forces, readers meticulously work from a delicate position to read, respond to, and successfully involve their clients such that, even as they are affectively moved and incited to engage with a variety of emotions (sadness, anxiety, fear), they remain safely anchored to the fortune-teller so that by the end of the session they can be led to emotional security and an uplifted mood. Esra, an articulate queer woman in her thirties, eloquently expresses this fragile balance: "It's like opening a wound, and you'd better not open it unless you know how to heal it. . . . One of my clients told me the most beautiful thing. She told me, 'Esra, you make me walk naked in the snow and not get cold.'" The most adept fortune-tellers are the ones who can walk their clients through worry, despair, hope, and faith, and leave them deeply affected but safely unscratched. The clients should be moved, but in close connection to the reader, who remains attuned to their needs and desires, including the common expectation to be comforted in a semitherapeutic encounter.

If divination is like therapy, it nevertheless comes packaged in an enchanted form that remains key to the affective appeal and intensity the interaction commands in a postsecular milieu. Hearing client after client emphasize how they are simply there to pour their heart out and be comforted, Nazan, a fortune-telling café owner in her early sixties, regularly joked that if she could find a legal loophole for this type of business, she would start a "tell me your troubles" service. This was perhaps the same line of reasoning that motivated the young man who sat on the pavement of İstiklal Caddesi, not far from the fortune-telling café street, behind a piece of cardboard that read, "I will listen to your troubles for one lira." Indeed, many online fortune-telling platforms have added a "share your troubles" (dert ortağı) option to their menus of coffee, tarot, palm, and other readings, inviting customers to unburden themselves of those difficulties they cannot otherwise share with those close to them. More often and with more commercial success, however, cup readings are integrated with other enchanted forms of therapeutic care, including globally circulating new age forms such as Reiki and Islamically accented, locally familiar forms such as pouring lead into water and reading its shapes so as to dispel the evil eye.

"Reiki is my gift when you get a lead pouring," explains Derya when I inquire about the services she advertises. Derya owns and works at a small

FIGURE 6.1. A fortune-telling café in Beyoğlu advertising coffee and tarot readings alongside life coaching, Reiki, meditation, holistic healing services, dream interpretation, and various Turkish coffee options, also posted in Russian and English.

fortune-telling café on a tiny but busy street in Kadıköy alongside her only employee, Nazmiye. "It will really comfort you. You'll feel good," affirms Nazmiye, who has just read my coffee cup in her unusual style of pacing the small reading room while talking animatedly and offering hopeful predictions alongside dire warnings about intimate matters of love, family, and work. Lead pouring "will help with all those troubles we talked about," Nazmiye insists. The next day, I return to Derya's café, where the few tables and chairs are so tiny and are packed so tightly that they look more like a symbolic gesture approximating the fortune-telling café format than they do actually functioning furniture. Derya soon walks me into the little back room reserved for readings and treatments. Inviting me to sit in the single chair in the middle of the room, she starts melting the lead in a metal ladle held over the heat from a mini propane tank on a small table, where a deep orange-pink crystal lamp is also glowing. The room is decorated with blue glass evil eye charms (*nazarlık*) of many sizes and shapes and a tiny angel figure on the wall. Tightly packing the small bookshelf are popular fiction, romance, and international and local self-help best sellers. I recognize the famous Sufi text *Sırru'l Esrar* (Secret of secrets), in hard cover with its title in gold letters. As the lead starts to melt, Derya prays—in Turkish, the verb is *reads (okumak)*—over the water. I follow her gaze to the water and watch her lips move. I can barely hear her murmuring prayers. Instructing me to cover up with a blanket she has provided, Derya holds a bowl of water over my head and pours the hot lead into the cool water. I feel simultaneously safe and vulnerable, cozy under the blanket with an unnerving sizzling over my head. Soon it is time for me to see what is uncovered in the water. Derya asks me to shed the blanket and observe what the lead has revealed. She shows me the pieces of now cold, solidified lead swimming in the water. "Eyes. So many eyes," she interprets. "You have so much evil eye [*nazar*] upon you. You should be glad you arrived for the session so you can ward it off before it really gets to you," she comments. "And tongues. Such pointy tongues," she adds, after melting and pouring the lead a second time, showing me the long, thin lines into which the hot lead has coagulated in the cool water. Derya performs another round of melting and pouring, this time showing me all the dusty residue at the bottom of the bowl the crumbling lead has left, a testament to the power of the treatment to neutralize the evil eye. After a quick and final reading of the lead, now poured directly onto the concrete floor of the room, it is time for Reiki.

"Reiki will further cleanse your energy," Derya says, translating the modality of lead pouring into the idiom of Reiki. She asks me to sit with a straight back and feet placed firmly on the ground for my next treatment. "I will now take all the negative energy and replace it with positive energy. You would understand if you studied quantum [physics] even just a little bit," she adds, demanding my familiarity with quantum theory–inspired new age concepts of energy and well-being. After quietly holding her hands on my chest and back for a few minutes, she starts observing. "You are blocked in this area. Do you get back pain?" When I confirm, she says that it is because I have been carrying a lot and holding on and not forgiving, giving a lot but receiving little in relationships. "You have to let go and you have to balance this," she insists. Derya teaches me a trick to protect my energy. "Imagine a zipper in your midsection," she instructs. "Mentally close it up every morning before leaving the house." She also recommends some affirmations to practice regularly. "Every morning when you wake up, say, 'I am precious, and I deserve the best.' Every night before you go to sleep, think about the person you cannot forgive and say to them that you are letting them go free and thank them for all they have taught you." I leave her business with affirmations to repeat, a folded piece of lead to dispose of in the soil or, better yet, the sea, and the prayed-over water poured into a plastic bottle to anoint myself with for most benefit.

A lead-pouring session with a gift of Reiki joins an eclectic market of therapeutic interventions that merge two or more modalities. The lead pouring is informed by an Islamicate universe of the evil eye, which is detected doubly in the form of the eyes and tongues into which the lead molds in the water, and in the form of various alignments of the body and misfortunes of life. As the lead is formed and deformed and the client is covered and uncovered repeatedly, the evil eye is manifested and neutralized with the divining and healing powers of water and prayer, which work to restore the proper boundaries of the intimate that have been disturbed by the evil eye and eliminate the ill effects on the client's well-being. Attached now to lead pouring is Reiki, performed in the new age universe of disturbed energy, which manifests in imbalances and disorders of affectively felt energy and related misalignments of the body, mind, and life. These are treated with energy healing, coaching, and affirmations that redraw the boundaries of the individual so as to restore the client's depleted vitality and cultivate the client as a self-contained and active agent of self-care.

Integrating divination, lead pouring, energy healing, life coaching, and other modalities, Derya is in good company in the fortune-telling scene of the thoroughly postsecular late 2010s, where increasingly therapeutically conceived neoliberal selves are fashioned and mended. Practitioners of divination have long combined fortune-telling with a range of therapeutic practices, from dispelling the evil eye to exorcizing jinn. In the neoliberal era, however, the therapeutic associations and accompaniments of fortune-telling are expanded and reconceived, with a heightened focus on the individual as the locus and agent of therapy and a growing emphasis on feeling good. Long the focal point of feminized practices of fortune-telling, the precarious romantic and familial fortunes of the feminized remain central to this therapeutic milieu.

Precarity as an Intimate Condition

I accompany my newly married friend in her late twenties on a long drive to the poorer outskirts of the city and the house of a fortune-teller. Hacı Ana (Hajji Mother, a respectful title for an older woman who has made the pilgrimage to Mecca) receives us in her living room decorated with a framed photo of the Kaaba and sits us on the floor in front of her seat on the couch. She opens a *yıldızname* to read our fortunes with the help of the stars and the occult science of letters and numbers. Asking for my friend's and her mother's name, as well as her birthday, she makes a brief calculation, converting letters into numbers. With a quick murmur of prayer, she finds the relevant pages in the *yıldızname* and reads my friend's fortune. She predicts that in a few years' time my friend will be a divorcée. My friend becomes deeply upset. "Search for an amulet," the reader advises, suggesting that it must have been placed somewhere around her husband to sabotage their marriage. She conducts a detailed search and finds a suspicious piece of paper with Arabic writing in the office of her husband's business, which is going down fast and causing a great deal of stress that is seeping into their marriage. She takes the evidence of the malevolent spell not back to the original reader, who was both exceptionally expensive and thoroughly distressing, but to another underground reader, who agrees to neutralize it for a modest fee and is more generous in offering comfort.

PRECARIOUSNESS IS AN INTIMATE condition that permeates the familial, domestic, and psychic realms. While thoroughly institutionalized and normalized, heteronormative femininity is far from being a terrain of psychic (or, for that matter, physical) safety for women. It is instead fraught with feelings of insecurity. In fortune-telling, all the conventional life stages of womanhood line up as a series of fears—or as desires turned into fears. As my friend's reading illustrates, the fortunes of married women are filled with husbands sleeping in separate beds and taking long work trips, female figures who stand suspiciously close to distractible husbands, failing businesses that leave husbands frustrated and households anxious, failed attempts to conceive, lost pregnancies, and children who misbehave, stray away, or fail to fulfill their parents' dreams. A sense of powerlessness over those who are cast in the most intimate roles in our lives yet who fail to act their part per romantic and familial fantasies permeates readings. It is this sense of powerlessness that provokes various efforts and interventions, including those of the occult kind, such as future readings available in fortune-telling cafés, or those that dispel malevolent spells, for which one might have to look further.

If married life is characterized by a sense of vulnerability for women, singlehood, too, is troubled, particularly by the unreliable outcome of pursuing a romance that will culminate in marriage. The qualms of a perilous romantic market and single women's fraught efforts to secure stable relationships figure prominently in fortune-telling. "I see Zeynep alone," Bayhan says as he starts reading my fortune.

A man a little taller than you, well-built, brunette, not too dark. A relationship whose terms are not as clear as you would like them to be. He acts like he would like to break up, but when it comes to it, he will not. He confuses you. A hypocrite, a double dealer. You feel like you're wasting your time. You want to know where you stand with him. He knows this but he cannot deliver. He is not in a place to do it. I see a knife that will cut this off. There are many Zeyneps in you. One is still thinking of the past; the others tell you to stop thinking about it. One wants to have children but is not willing to have a relationship simply for a child's sake. One is stuck with this man creating uncertainty. And the last one wants to put all this aside and ponder what she really wants. She is weighing whether she wants an adventurous and exciting partner or a mature and reliable one, and the latter weighs heavier in the balance.

Like a ship on the high seas, Bayhan's reading sails through the conflicting desires and uncertainties of femininity. Following this procession of contradictory longings, Bayhan reassures me with a hopeful future scenario that resolves the dilemmas of the present, if a little too swiftly: "You will meet someone new, someone mature." After exploring work and home fronts, where he predicts failed attempts at change and improvement, Bayhan concludes the session by reminding me that "love will have its turn only after work and home issues have been clarified." Under the stairs in a low-traffic area of the café where Bayhan works is a less advertised menu, listing among other services a treatment for "increasing one's marriage chances" (kısmet açmak), available for those who are not willing to wait and can spare the expense, which is many times the price of a reading. When I inquire, however, Bayhan brushes me off, likely worried about confirming that the café offers a service that is usually provided by hodjas, religiously accented and criminalized practitioners. So I am left to rerun Bayhan's predictions in my head. As a thirtysomething secular urban middle-class woman not sporting a wedding ring, I feel that I have heard many versions of this story before. Time and again, I have been placed in romantic scenes of an unpredictable, unreliable, disappointing relationship, only to be reassured of my chances at story's end of successfully navigating this treacherous marriage market. The fragilities of heteronormative aspirations make young single women the prime customers of fortune-telling cafés where, with the help of the feeling labors of divination, they can feel their way through the shifting terrain of normative femininity, where secularists, Islamists, and feminists stake their conflicting claims in increasingly vocal and intimate terms and where secular middle-class femininity is increasingly felt under the threat of a neoliberal Islamist government.

Precariousness is thoroughly intimate for LGBTIQ individuals in an era when queer futures are shaped by blatant discrimination and homophobia punctuated by fragile moments of political recognition and community building. Denied the support of the complex social infrastructure that upholds normative forms of intimacy and otherized actively and violently, queer intimacies are systematically rendered precarious. After reading my fortune, Bayhan, a thirtysomething queer reader who is speaking with an accent I recognize as Roma, starts narrating his life history for me: "My family, well . . . it was like I didn't belong to that family. I couldn't be a part of that family. I was a twelve- or thirteen-year-old who would roam free. Call me a free, stubborn, unshackled child, or whatever you please. I would travel from city to city with people I didn't know. Like I didn't belong to that family." Without a strong attachment to his family, Bayhan wandered the margins of society.

> I grew up in an abnormal environment. The normal there is my normal now. I would just walk right into Women's Coffeehouse [Kadınlar Kahvesi in Beyoğlu, one of the earliest fortune-telling cafés]. I grew up in places where there was no distinction between men and women. I am not normal. Taksim [Beyoğlu] let that abnormality fully emerge. Istanbul increased the degree of abnormality in me—it was tripled. It is there that I was fully formed [*hamur yoğruldu*]. I would enter the Roma community, the Jewish community, and I wasn't treated as someone abnormal. In Samsun, Ankara, Urfa, Adıyaman, I was treated as normal in very conservative circles. My friends told me that I would be killed in Fatih Çarşamba [the most conservative neighborhood of Istanbul], but I went nonetheless. I attended Naqshbandi meetings in Adıyaman Menzil for a few years. No one questioned why I was this way. . . . Either they get used to me, or they see me as a guest and are curious. There's a normal family woman [*normal aile kadını*] here, and this *abla* loves me. We meet in the middle.

Bayhan drifted through a smattering of disparate peripheral social worlds in search of a place to be (queer): on the ethnoracial margins among the Roma people, on the religious margins among the Jewish community and the Menzil sect of the Naqshbandi Sufi order, on the gendered/sexual margins among the LGBTIQ community in Beyoğlu. It was the latter that offered him a new normal he could grow into. While Bayhan does not employ LGBTIQ terms, he strongly articulates a queerness as he describes his negotiation of a social life for his queer presence in all manner of unlikely places. Clear about where and why he does and does not fit the (hetero) norm, Bayhan is content with himself as he reasserts his independence of the familial and the mainstream. In proud defiance, he insists that he is "a free soul who does not follow the rules." He nonetheless expresses a deep sense of disappointment in his personal fortunes. When faced with a life that has not delivered on its promises, Bayhan vents his sense of frustration as he repeats his sense of having been deprived of something that is his due: "I've been cheated. I've been cheated in every way." When I ask delicately about his romantic life, he cuts my inquiry short: "I am just asexual in my private life." A little later, he adds melancholily, "Life has cheated me. At school, at work, at divination, I've been often deceived. In romance, I've most certainly been cheated. The disappointments have made me asexual. . . . I've been betrayed by people I let in, close friends, lovers. . . . I closed myself off. I decided not to look for someone. That became my choice. I lost hope that I would ever find a partner. I lost hope that someone even exists." When faced with the many disappointments of familial, communal, and romantic life, Bayhan experiences his multidimensional nonnormativity as an axis of vulnerability and expresses more resignation than hope.

As the entanglement of various forms of inequality and exclusion in Bayhan's life history suggests, intimate lives are rendered precarious along the intersectional lines of religion, ethnicity, race, and citizenship. As they are filled up with precarious hope (Parla 2019) through "democratic openings," in the parlance of the Turkey of the early 2000s, only to be frustrated in an era of multiculturalist democratizing gestures that punctuate systemic discrimination, dehumanization, and violence against minorities (Weiss 2016; Yilmaz and Barry 2019), lives are made differentially disposable (Butler 2004). Whether through spectacular bursts of brutality, war, and displacement or mundane undercurrents of everyday microaggressions, unpredictability and instability shape the lives of the minoritized. While these events and nonevents seldom figure explicitly in the language of divination—except perhaps in their individualized and privatized effects—they nevertheless powerfully shape the larger social worlds in which people try to get or keep a job, find a life partner, have children, and just try to live. They summon a tenuous landscape of hope and disillusionment, leaving but a precarious hold on intimate dreams.

The precariousness of the intimate lives of the feminized, whose capacities to shape their own fortunes in romantic and familial realms are structurally constrained under heteropatriarchal imperatives, has long been processed affectively through the feeling labors of divination. The commodification of feeling labors carries into the postsecular neoliberal market of therapeutic services this enchanted engagement with gendered precariousness, a precariousness that is only exacerbated by the unstable labor conditions fortune-telling cafés' working-class employees and middle-class clients find themselves in.

The Precarity of Divination Labor

"Cheated," Bayhan repeats again and again as he recounts expectations that did not materialize and hopes that were not fulfilled. "Cheated at school, at work, at relationships. I was cheated at school. I wanted to attend the conservatory to study opera and ballet. I didn't get a high enough grade in the entry exam. So they advised me to study electronics instead, suggesting that I attend that high school for one year only. I ended up studying for three years there. I didn't go to college. I was disadvantaged in the college entry exams by having graduated from a vocational high school."

Bayhan's educational experiences left him feeling misdirected, led astray from his aspirations. During this time, Bayhan started his work in divination. "I was cheated at divination." He narrates his early misadventures as an adolescent clairvoyant apprenticed to and working with an older hodja:

> I was about thirteen or fourteen. I would locate missing people, missing things, missing kids. Once, at a séance, they hypnotized me to find a stolen car with the help of the three-lettered [jinn]. I described a place in Kayseri that I had never seen before. They found the car, just as I had described. We had agreed on ten billion liras, but they never paid up. . . . This other time was big. It was in the newspapers. You might remember. A famous family's grandson was kidnapped. We found him. You know what happened then? They accused us! That is when I vowed never to find the missing again.

Cheated out of an agreed-upon fee and under threat of criminalization in proximity to his mentor, who was being pressed on all sides by both the police and the mafia, Bayhan had to move on and find a way to make a living via other means. "Fortune-teller, waiter, textile worker, salesperson, promotion, distribution—I did it all. I even sold *simit* [a Turkish sesame bread shaped like a large bagel] as a child, you know. What have I not done? I have not polished shoes."

After cycling through a long list of precarious jobs, Bayhan finally ended up in his midtwenties at a fortune-telling café. "I left behind working at bars and nightclubs and was considering working as a pollster. Then a friend reminded me that my readings come true, thank God, and suggested that I work at a fortune-telling café for a few months. A few months turned into a few years, and I ended up working at cafés for a decade.

"We were used like slaves," Bayhan sums up dramatically, referring to the work conditions at the large famous fortune-telling café where he was first employed. He found himself cheated at fortune-telling cafés, too. "[I worked there] for over a year. The customers paid five or six liras; we got only seventy-five *kuruş* [cents]. We were reading seventy to eighty fortunes a day. I started keeping tabs on how many readings we did because they would keep faulty records to fool us and then keep the money themselves. An older coworker put it this way: 'We're paid less than a beggar. You give beggars one lira.' No lunch provided, nothing."

Bayhan's next stop was an informal cottage industry that had sprung up alongside the fortune-telling cafés as part of a semiunderground divination economy. "I worked at fortune-telling houses [*falevi*] and fortune-telling offices [*falbüro*]. . . . These are apartments with waiting rooms and separate rooms for doing readings. . . . They don't have a signboard. The clients who already know you follow you there. The conditions were good. I worked with an *abla*. It was split fifty-fifty. I got twenty liras per reading."

While the underground businesses usually offered higher remuneration rates and more autonomy and respect, Bayhan and his partner had to stay under the radar and thus had difficulty recruiting new clients. Bayhan worked at four other fortune-telling cafés in Beyoğlu and Kadıköy before eventually finding his way to the small long-standing café in which I met him. "I've been here for a few days now. . . . I'm here to help out until they find someone regular. When a few clients complimented me, they asked me to stay. If customers like me, want me, I might just stay. We'll see if this will be permanent or not. I can't sit still, you know—that's my nature."

The uncertainty of this informal trial period did not stand out as unusual to Bayhan, whose entire working life, including his fortune-telling career, had been structured by flexibility and instability. The familiarity of this set of affairs did not, however, make the financial insecurity any less dire or cut any less close to the bone. "My housing situation is complicated. I'm in between. You know, rotating stays at a few places," he says, euphemistically describing his near homelessness.

Bayhan has been disappointed too many times to continue to hope. "We'll see what happens next." He pauses and then cuts his brief flight of hope short with a keen sense of constraint: "People have offered to shake hands and work together as partners, but I don't want that. . . . I can't be a business owner. I can't run my own business. I know this." Conceding his refusal to aspire, his life narrative draws circles recounting his sense of disappointment.

PRECARIOUS LABOR CONDITIONS have systematically limited Bayhan's fortunes throughout his life. With a family that did not deliver sufficient material and emotional resources, Bayhan has worked odd jobs since childhood. He studied at a vocational school that closed off to him one of the few opportunities for upward mobility available to poorer children—a college education—and distanced him from his gender-nonnormative dreams of training for the opera and ballet. Unable to follow his queer dreams into a conservatory or pursue his middle-class aspirations through college, Bayhan was apprenticed as a teen into the underground divination economy, where he became immediately vulnerable to exploitation and criminalization. As an adult, Bayhan entered the labor market soon after the neoliberal opening and deregulation of the Turkish economy with a vocational high school degree whose recipients could not expect to find stable working-class jobs. Bayhan's ensuing search for a living took him in many directions, yet every job he took was marked by irregularity, insecurity, flexibility, informality, and poverty. Café fortune-telling was no different.

Reading fortunes is precarious work. The exploitative conditions Bayhan equates with slavery, the long and flexible work hours without lunch or restroom breaks, low and irregular incomes, high turnover rates, and the lack of job security and benefits—all are par for the course in fortune-telling cafés. The Café and Bar Workers Association (Kafe-Bar Çalışanları Birliği) reports that these conditions permeate the larger café-bar industry, resulting in what one member called "premature aging" (Kural 2014). While the extended hours and high customer volume dictate a relentless work pace in larger businesses, smaller cafés often mean insufficient work. In these venues, readers may sit idly for hours on end waiting for a customer, only to find their shifts reduced to Friday to Sunday employment when there might be enough customers to support a(nother) reader. Extended trial periods for readers are also common. So are the "unemployed" who "just hang out" at a café, helping out with serving or reading fortunes when needed, having a free drink or hosting a few friends as a perk, lingering until "something better comes along" (*daha iyi bir şey çıkana kadar*). Even when employment is more regular, with explicitly if verbally set terms, it is rarely long term. Like Bayhan, most readers move from café to café. Accumulating regular customers and then changing employers are two of the few strategies readers have at their disposal for improving their incomes.

In turn, café owners play a double game, attempting with one hand to limit employer-initiated mobility by policing the exchange of contact information between fortune-tellers and clients and trying with the other hand to recruit new fortune-teller faces whom they hope will both be attractive to their patrons and bring along their regulars from another café. Adding to the irregularity of employment is the risk of criminalization, which renders café readers vulnerable not only to the employers who hire and fire them informally but also to disgruntled clients whom readers fear might file a legal complaint.

In a global age when the relationship between the state, the market, and the citizen has been recalibrated to "harness the first [the state] to impose the stamp of the second [the market] onto the third [the citizen]" (Wacquant 2012, 71), fortune-tellers are part of the growing segment of workers whose labor conditions are characterized by various forms of labor insecurity: unguaranteed and low incomes, flexible and disposable employment, and even the collapse of the distinction between employment and unemployment (Bourdieu 1998; Hardt and Negri 2004; Standing 2011). However, for those like Bayhan, labor precarity is less a novel condition and more a given that limits life chances. The expectation of labor security has been a historically and geographically limited achievement of (Western white male) organized labor, making precarity more the global norm than the exception (Neilson and Rossiter 2008). In the Global South, informality and insecurity seem to be the rule (Mosoetsa, Stillerman, and Tilly 2016; Munck 2013). In Turkey, where the informal economy supplies over a third of total employment, flexibility and disposability are widespread (Guloglu 2005). Inaugurated in the early 1980s under the tutelage of the International Monetary Fund and the World Bank through deregulation, privatization, and liberalization (Öniş 2004), the neoliberalization of the Turkish economy deepened the disciplining, poverty, and precarity of the working classes (Balkan and Savran 2002; Boratav and Yeldan 2006; Bozkurt-Güngen 2018). The ensuing growing precarity was then addressed, if only partially and unsatisfactorily, through an increasingly familialized, privatized, charity-based, and clientelist distribution of social assistance (Bugra and Candas 2011; Eder 2013; Elveren 2008). In this context, labor precarity is hardly news for gender, sexual, religious, ethnic, and racial minorities, immigrants, and large segments of the working class who have been relegated to informal and irregular employment.

Given the larger constraints of feminized labor, which has not only been low paid and contingent but even unpaid, unrecognized, and structurally excluded from wage labor as such (Federici 2008), labor precarity does not present itself as exceptional, especially to women. Coffee divinations have long been provided as part of women's unpaid reproductive labor in the household and have sporadically served as an informal income-generating activity. Coffee cup reading is considered a natural feminine propensity that "any housewife can do." As such, it enters the labor market as a low-skilled and low-income-generating occupation to be performed by feminized workers. Most readers are women, with few heterosexual and some gay men in the ranks. Male readers are not only rarer but also tend to be younger, better educated, and less likely to depend on their café income to support dependents.

Female labor force participation rates have historically been and currently remain low in Turkey, limited, among other factors, by a patriarchal gender contract that shapes state and social practices which frame women's employment as secondary (Moghadam 2005). After a period of decrease in women's employment rates because of the neoliberal disintegration of agriculture and women's concomitant housewifization (Mies 1998), female labor force participation rates are slowly increasing (Dayıoğlu and Kırdar 2010), aided by the growth of the service industry (İlkkaracan 2012) and the presence of a small but significant segment of highly educated urban women with career aspirations. Poorer women's labor force participation is also triggered by periodic economic crises that leave husbands unemployed and push women into paid work (Başlevent and Onaran 2003). Of women who are in the workforce, over one-third are employed informally (Toksöz 2007), with poorly educated, married, urban women being largely delegated to the informal sector (Çınar 1994; Dedeoğlu 2010; White 2004). Women earn approximately half of what men earn (Kasnakoğlu and Dayıoğlu 1997). They are also more likely to suffer unemployment. Unofficial unemployment rates for 2019, which include marginally attached, discouraged, and underemployed workers, are 25 percent for youth, 28 percent for young women, and 31 percent for women overall, excluding agricultural workers, compared to 21 percent for the general population (DISK-AR 2019). By the end of the 2010s, the ratio of women left unemployed because of the ending of a temporary job increased to one-fourth of all unemployed women, highlighting the spread and impact of precarious employment for women (Yılmaz 2019). Recent initiatives for women's employment colored by neoconservative appeals explicitly direct women into flexible employment and encourage women's low-status, low-paid (care) work in the home, recruiting women in the service of the neoliberal privatization of welfare (Çavdar and Yaşar 2019; Korkman 2015a; Toksöz 2016; Yazici 2012). And in the absence of legal protections, discrimination at work and exclusion from employment opportunities remain unchecked for lesbian, gay, bisexual, and transgender individuals (Öztürk 2011; Yılmaz and Göçmen 2016). In such a climate, urban poor women, unemployed youth, and marginalized LGBTIQ individuals find in café divination an acceptable opportunity despite its precarity.

Labor precarity is further distributed along ethnic, racial, national, and citizenship lines. The majority of café workers have Turkish citizenship, are considered to look Turkish, and speak Turkish with the right urban (Istanbul) accent. Readers like Bayhan who speak with another accent or display other (embodied) signs of ethnoracial minority identity are an exception. Stigmatized, criminalized, and limited to the most marginalized forms of work (Akkan, Deniz, and Ertan 2017), Roma people have long offered fortune-telling on the streets and in parks. They now find themselves mostly excluded from cafés, even as their imagery is appropriated in online businesses where digital fortune-teller avatars don Roma names and clothing. Also excluded are Syrian refugees, who are largely delegated to unemployment, illegality, and temporary, low-paid labor (Baban, İlcan, and Rygiel 2017; Şenses 2016). Female labor migrants from post-Soviet republics who are already largely delegated to informal care work (Akalın 2007; Kaşka 2007; Şenses 2020) can be very rarely found at cafés, offering readings in their native languages. The racialized exclusion

FIGURE 6.2. Screenshot from an online fortune-telling service featuring stylized fortune-teller avatars (*falcıbot*) with appropriated Roma symbolism ("Online Falcıbot-Sanal Kahve Fali," Tellwe, September 16, 2020, https://www.tellwe.com/fal-baktir/falcibot-fali-bak).

of these groups of women from café work is closely tied to their exclusion from respectable femininity and domesticity as nomads, refugees, or immigrants. Heteronormativity and racialization thus deeply and mutually structure the making of feminized labor as precarious (Gutiérrez-Rodríguez 2014).

Labor precarity structures and compounds the broader anxiety felt by the secular and secularist citizens of Turkey's postsecular era. As neoliberal economic restructuring has progressed in Turkey, precarious labor conditions have expanded to include previously shielded sections of the labor force. The spread of labor precarity is an anxiety-producing indignity for members of the downwardly mobile secular middle classes of Turkey in particular (Bora 2013). Their nervousness has intensified under the latest millennial waves of neoliberalization shepherded by the Islamist AKP government. Members of this class now suffer their loss of the prospect of landing a job as a state employee, a career trajectory that had previously provided a path to stable employment for those with a secular education but that has now been ideologically devalued and practically diminished and deregulated (Köroğlu 2010). At the same time that the AKP's populism partially buttresses the destruction brought about through its neoliberal restructuring, it also works to contain ethnoracial opposition through a neoconservative welfare/workfare model operated by state and nongovernmental Islamic charities (Buğra and Adar 2008; Morvaridi 2013; Yörük 2012) whose patriarchal, class, ethnic, racial, and religious considerations do not prioritize the downwardly mobile secular Turks. In such a postsecular neoliberal climate, the secular middle classes increasingly find themselves and their children unable to accomplish upward mobility or even class reproduction. Instead, they struggle to hold onto insecure careers and are frequently under- or unemployed and in debt.

The amplification and wider distribution of labor precarity fuels both the demand and supply ends of café divination as more feminized, secular, working- and lower-middle-class employees are enlisted into fortune-telling and as more feminized, secular, middle-class customers seek divination as a way of living precariously. The precariousness of the intimate lives of those who are feminized and disadvantaged along the axes of gendered, sexual, ethnic, racial, religious, and classed inequalities is exacerbated by the deepening and broadening labor precarity under the early 2000s Turkey's postsecular brand of neoliberalization. These coconstitutive layers of precariousness are then affectively processed through the commodified feeling labors of divination under the sway of the enchanted therapeutic ethos of neoliberalism, ironically entailing the further recruitment of gender and sexual minorities into labor precarity and into the affective terrain of feeling precarious.

Feeling Unsettled

"Your fortune is already set" (*senin falın fallanmış*), cup readers will tell you if you are contentedly coupled, married with children, have a stable career, or are otherwise financially secure—in other words, if you are settled into your life, into a life that resembles something proper.[3] When asked what brings clients to their doors, readers repeatedly narrate acute and chronic scenes of unsettlement. Those with unsettled lives, those who are not yet married or are just divorced, those who are heartbroken, those who are childless, those who are looking for a job or for a better job, those who are waiting to get accepted to college—they are the ones whose fortunes need to be told. Those who do not know exactly what to do with their lives, whose life plans do not hold, who are scandalized by their lost privileges, who have aspirations that exceed the confines of the structural barriers imposed on their life chances, who insist on hoping and wishing, they need divination to help them look for a way through, a way out. Those who feel unsettled, fraught with uncertainty, anticipation, and anxiety—they are divination's prime subjects.

NOT HAVING YOUR FORTUNE already played out and your future already set is to some extent a matter of life stage, as younger people are less likely to have settled into a (heteronormatively adult kind of) life with a job, a romantic partner, and children. And to a large extent, having one's life unsettled is a matter of precariousness. Conceived broadly as vulnerability to the misfortunes of life, precariousness is distributed unevenly along the lines of ethnic, racial, religious, classed, sexual, and gendered privileges, unsettling lives with unequal frequency and intensity. Labor precarity deepened by neoliberalism renders stable and secure work less and less available and the concomitant process of settling into a job, a house, and an intimate relationship less tangible, even for (aspiring) middle classes. A vital feminist and queer movement competing with a religiously tinted project of masculinist restoration confers upon gender normativity a far from stable trajectory.[4] In this context, not only do more people find their lives unsettled; in the face of precariousness, more people feel unsettled, propelling the neoliberal work of self-making assisted by enchanted therapeutic and self-entrepreneurial technologies like divination.

Precariousness is an everyday condition demanding to be felt. It folds into a structure of feeling, a feeling that permeates one's being in the world. It accumulates in the body and the psyche. How you feel precariousness and what you do with it however depends on who and where you are. How neoliberal precarity is felt and how feelings of precariousness get managed are mediated through one's (imaginary relationship to one's) socioeconomic position and its cultural and political articulation in a particular time and place (Althusser 1971; Neilson 2015). Similarly, how gendered vulnerability is felt in its intersections with ethnoracial and classed marginalization and in which direction such feelings of precariousness are channeled depend upon one's (culturally legible, sociopolitically legitimate, and economically accessible) aspirations. The possible ways to affectively engage with precarity are varied. Some, like working-class Russian Muslim immigrant women, embrace their gendered precarity with a sense of perseverance and promise that they sustain through their entrepreneurial, social, and spiritual labors (Rabinovich 2018). Others hang on to a "cruel optimism" (Berlant 2011) where aspirations for normativity are frustrated but attachments are not suspended, in contexts ranging from the post-Reaganite United States to postrevolutionary Egypt (Pettit 2019).

For many secular, fragilely middle-class, straight, and cisgender female divination customers who fear and experience (intergenerational as well as lifetime) downward mobility exacerbated by a neoliberal Islamist government, while managing their intimate lives marked by heteronormative aspirations and a generous dose of gendered fragility intensified by a religiously tinted neoconservative familialism, precariousness feels like an unsettling condition they orient toward and work to keep at bay.[5] They thus come to readers while they work on themselves and on securing a living, while they prepare (their children) for college entry exams, study for more diplomas and certificates, make out job applications, manage careers, launch business ventures, buy and sell houses, find and keep marriage partners, have children and raise them with good prospects, and try to piece together and keep afloat a (hetero)normative middle-class standing about which they feel an increasingly frustrated aspiration or even entitlement. As this becomes a progressively more tenuous goal, they attempt anxiously to gain a sense of control and efficacy by striving and hoping, and by getting readings to help them continue striving and hoping. With these efforts, the feminized secular Muslims of Turkey's divination cafés join the ranks of the anticipating (Molé 2010) or even neurotic subjects of neoliberalism (Cossman 2013; Isin 2004) who are subjectified by the therapeutic technologies that interpellate anxious selves.

In the twenty-first century, Turkey's felt relationship to the future has been shifting. On the one hand, secular and secularist actors in Turkey have been feeling increasingly nervous about their present under a neoliberal Islamist government that has squelched their economic and gendered aspirations. In response, secular and secularist actors in Turkey have maintained nostalgic attachments to a secularist past (Özyürek 2006) and nurtured faith in their futures in a booming economy of fortune-telling businesses. On the other hand, a newly confident hopefulness, exemplified by the broader trend of neo-Ottomanism, which refers to a novel appropriation and valuation of the Ottoman heritage and history, has been thoroughly infusing Turkey's affective landscape, reaching into and well beyond the pious and Islamist segments of the population. In the first decade of the 2000s, the AKP's Turkey was globally touted as a model Muslim democracy and a candidate for impending European Union membership, with a relatively broad ruling coalition that afforded some democratizing reforms to the country and a relative stability in economic growth. This hopeful conjuncture encouraged a new assertiveness in the present and an assured expectation for the future. In this conjuncture, a novel, neoimperial pride in the past stood in contrast to an almost postcolonial sense of shame about the past, a nervous feeling of inferiority in a present that was always already lagging behind (the West), and a tired hope of catching up in the future (with the West), which had combined to produce the temporal landscape of secular Turkish national identity throughout the twentieth century. Indeed, numerological divinations of the Islamist nationalist variety have been summoning a promising Islamist future for the country for some time now, with AKP propaganda emphasizing the years 2023, 2053, and 2071—representing, respectively, the one hundredth anniversary of the foundation of the Turkish Republic, the six hundredth anniversary of the conquest of Constantinople, and the one thousandth anniversary of the Seljuk Turks' decisive military victory in Anatolia—to project a repetition of the glories of Turkish history by way of the continuation of AKP reign. That conjuring trick of prophesying an Islamist future with a simple recitation of numbers places the country and the AKP in a cyclical temporality of glory, rendering the future a fantasy landscape of assured expectation. In the economic terrain, the performative recitation of other kinds of numbers, such as those related to the Turkish economy's global standing and growth, have sought to boost confidence in the country's economic future (Korkman 2015a). But in the vein of assurances about neoliberal ideology that circulate globally, this local brand of futuristic millennialism could not deliver on its promises and fell progressively flatter as the 2010s progressed.

By the end of the 2010s, gone were the hopeful expectations of a millennial moment. A previously eager process of European Union harmonization that had encouraged democratizing reforms, including gender equality policies, seems irrevocably over. In its place stands a neoconservative familialism that has bankrolled neoliberalization on the backs of the feminized, who have with increasing violence been put back in their places through policies ranging from

Turkey's withdrawal from the Istanbul Convention that ordered protections against gendered violence to escalating police attacks on feminist and LGBTIQ activists. The hopeful graduates of an exponentially growing number of universities the AKP resolved to establish in every city across the country were rudely told not to feel entitled to landing a job upon graduation because economic growth rates had stagnated and unemployment had soared. Any hopes of democratization that were instigated by the broad hegemonic coalition initially forged by the AKP have turned increasingly sour as the AKP party/state has under Erdoğan's leadership become more and more authoritarian. A pro-Western, shy Islamism that worked in coalition with liberal political elements has instead made way for an isolationist, aggressively confident inflection of religion into public policy. As all semblance of a multicultural recognition and peace process has been abandoned, once again, in favor of military violence and repression, any formerly held expectations of peace and justice for the Kurdish people and other ethnoracial and religious minorities have been prematurely precluded. In a public sphere where previously banned languages were heard and scantly populated Pride marches turned into mass events, repression and censorship have amped up. A flourishing urban public life with both secular and pious shades has faded as public spaces have become less and less hospitable for leisurely activities in the wake of uprisings, a coup attempt, an extended state of emergency, suicide bombings, police violence and securitization, and, unexpectedly, a global pandemic.

In millennial Turkey, magical promises have been paired with limiting circumstances, aspirations have been repeatedly cultivated and then frustrated, and political, economic, and cultural formations that prescribe and support normative desires and prerogatives have been rearranged in fast succession. In the rapidly changing context of the first two decades of the 2000s, where frustrated secular, middle-class, and gendered aspirations combine with political and economic instability to render previously reasonable life expectations and long-cultivated desires quickly out of reach or out of fashion—even over the relatively short period of a decade and a half that this research has explored—the feeling of being unsettled has intensified. Where unsettlement sets the tone of feeling, divination emerges as a most resonant response. The proliferating practices of fortune-telling have been providing a venue in which those feeling unsettled may attune themselves to their gendered fortunes with all of their instability and possibility.[6] In the intimate publics hosted by fortune-telling businesses, the feeling labors of divination serve as a particularly fitting medium for reassuring and recharging secular Muslim women and LGBTIQ individuals tasked with managing the pressures of neoliberal precarity, gender in flux, and political hegemony in dissolve.

If precariousness often feels unsettling to secular, middle-class women and youths in Turkey, this is not a universal but a historically and geographically specific structure of feeling, one that is filtered through gendered, classed, ethnic, racial, and religious positionality and produced through one's subjective and situated engagement with a social terrain of shifting expectations and possibilities. Bayhan, the thirtysomething queer reader who spent over a decade at fortune-telling cafés, looks and feels worn out as he reflects wistfully, "I have aged beyond my years." He keeps his graying, shoulder-length hair in a tiny ponytail. His teeth are stained from the cigarettes he chain smokes as he drinks coffee and tea. He is dressed in an old, wrinkled T-shirt with jeans and sneakers. His body language matches his clothes: shoulders dropped, leaning back. He is speaking in a low-energy voice. "I've experienced a lot of pain, and I've matured. My hair went white at seventeen. People think I'm forty or fifty years old. They tell me that I sound like an old person," he concludes after a long and intense conversation recounting the various disappointments of his life. Suddenly, he does seem old, sitting squarely in his depression, refusing the healing reflex, holding out for a pause in the rush of life. To Bayhan, precariousness feels like attrition, a wearing out of the body and the soul. It leaves him with prematurely receding hopes and graying hair. Life offers but a series of deceptions: the unrealized promises of a family, a stable job, a long-term partner, and a permanent home; a string of frustrated efforts that did not amount to a sense of safety and belonging. Too wise to believe in the promise that he can improve things through personal effort, too tired to strive to make his life amount to something resembling a middle-class, heteronormative Turkish life, Bayhan judges his life to have already been lived out. I feel deeply sad listening to him. Tempted to dispel my sadness by relieving his, I long to give him some consolation. But unlike me or many of his middle-class clients, he is not subjectified by the bits of therapeutic discourse I mumble. His dour acquiescence and stubborn resignation are refusals of the quick therapeutic fix. They are demands for something deeper. Sitting with this affect and in this impasse is an opportunity to ponder what propels (and gets buried under) the mainstream therapeutic impulses to fix (Cvetkovich 2012).[7]

Standing in contrast to the unsettled quest to feel better and the constant striving for better futures that most of his customers and colleagues orient their readings toward, Bayhan's depression renders the nervously aspiring souls around him visible as just one of many possible responses to labor precarity and a broader condition of precariousness. For someone like Bayhan who has a keen and likely realistic sense of his own immobility and limitation as a secular working-class queer Roma man and who is not subjectified by promises of improving one's lot by working on oneself as a self-entrepreneurial project, the response to precarity is not an energetic pushing against but a sluggish wearing out; more of a lateral agency (Berlant 2007) that smells like cigarettes and looks like premature aging. Bayhan's precariousness, structured as much by neoliberal labor precarity as by the compounded effects of ethnoracial, classed, and gendered and sexualized vulnerabilities, refuses the postsecular neoliberal therapeutic invitation to funnel this condition into an animated anxiety and striving activity.

Unlike Bayhan and some of his fellow working-class colleagues who brook a stale, dense depression, however, a majority of secular, middle class, Turkish café readers and their clients feel precariousness as an unsettlement where a combination of anxious anticipation sits uneasily with a tenacious hope and turn to divination therapy to help raise their spirits vis-à-vis the wearing out that Bayhan has settled into. Indeed, increasing numbers of fortune-tellers who share the aspirational horizon of the middle classes yet find themselves engaging in divination work through a combination of downward mobility and ambitious business acumen are embodying the dominant therapeutic ethos of neoliberalism so as to manage their own and their clients' feelings of unsettlement. As we have seen throughout this chapter, in contrast to Bayhan, who is not enticed by the booming new age therapeutic entrepreneurialism that motivates some of his colleagues to specialize in such new services as "life coaching"—an endeavor he dubs "a classy way of being a son of a bitch"—this new generation of fortune-tellers increasingly mobilizes the commercialized feeling labors of divination to cultivate themselves and their clients as neoliberal (post)secular subjects who can acclimate to their newfound compounded precariousness. Their feeling labors play a central role in containing the gendered contradictions of a postsecular neoliberal capitalism. The acclimatization they proffer and participate in through the feeling labors of divination is affected through an anxious activity that wraps itself in the enchanted idiom of self-entrepreneurship, the subject of chapter 7.

7

ENTREPRENEURIAL FORTUNES

"My life choice might be a little surprising. I'm actually an economist with a BA from a good university in Istanbul," starts Ada, who offers coffee and tarot readings in her fortune-telling office alongside a range of services, including lead pouring, Reiki, and life coaching.

Ada grew up in a secular Muslim lower-middle-class family. "My father was some kind of a civil servant," she states flatly. "My mother was a housewife," she adds with indifference. Ada's parents did not embody her aspirational horizons. But with their support, she earned an economics degree from an august public college in Istanbul. Upon graduating, she launched a successful career as a corporate manager "at four different big firms, one in cosmetics, two in the water business, and one in logistics . . . as a city manager, regional manager, and sales manager." While success came through conventional means, in her life narrative she spoke of her career in the same breath as she indexed a lack of choice and self-realization: "This was a choice I made given the rules of the world I lived in, given my family."

Ada made all the grades that were supposed to deliver a good life: a valued college education, an accomplished career, marriage, motherhood. She had it all, at least, all that an urban, secular, college-educated, middle-class Turkish woman should expect. Yet she was unsettled. Her marriage fell apart while her child was still young. Her career was anything but fulfilling for her. "I wasn't satisfied. Waking up in the morning, dressing up, working, but not really being useful to anyone. I noticed something [that irked me]: be it in a corporate firm or a family firm, someone who may not be as educated or aware as you are pats you on the back. 'You're doing great. You're so successful,' they say. And you feel wonderful. But all you're doing is making money for them." Ada insists that she "just resigned overnight," emphasizing how she more or less impulsively left her corporate career behind. The reasons, she contends, were moral and spiritual. "For me, fatigue is about my conscience, my heart, my soul. If they're not tired, I'm not tired. I was very tired in corporate life."

If moral critique and soul searching drove Ada out of the corporate world, so did labor precarity, from which even managerial positions like hers were not shielded. "Ten, fifteen years of working like this, moving from one company to the next. This was my fate. I thought it all a waste. But once I found this new occupation, that didn't concern me anymore. Whenever I would transfer to a new company, I would wonder how long I was going to last. I don't have to worry about that anymore. I've been in this office for four years."

Until she found a sense of stability running her own divination business, in every position she held, Ada had an acute sense of tentativeness. Combined with the feelings of exhaustion and alienation her career elicited, Ada felt that her work life was thoroughly taxing, despite decent financial returns.

After resigning for the last time, Ada combined some entrepreneurial know-how with her business management acumen to create a new type of business that could successfully compete with fortune-telling cafés in her neighborhood. Housed on the high-traffic, entry-level floor of a centrally located apartment building, Ada's business is located in an apartment where she can give coffee, tarot, and astrological readings in the comfort and intimacy of a feminized business space that looks like a cross between a private apartment and an office and that is populated heavily but not exclusively by women. Here, Ada offers a full, thoroughly postsecular range of therapeutic services, including lead pouring, Reiki, spiritual therapy, detox, Emotional Freedom Technique (EFT), Neuro-Linguistic Programming (NLP), and life coaching. She also offers workshops in some of these specializations, granting participants certificates with which they can start their own practices. She takes great entrepreneurial pride in the business she created. "Given my background, I wanted to start an official/legal [*resmi*] business. This is official. I'm billing clients for fortune-telling. Yes, fortune-telling! We are registered for 'spiritual and astrological services and fortune-telling.' This is what my tax certificate says."

Taking advantage of recent tax regulations that allow the registration of economic activity under the banner of "fortune-telling, astrology, and spiritualist services," Ada has been able to create an official business to manage, something she knows well. Ada manages a team of several women, including sales, administration, and her business's media presence personnel. She takes customer relations seriously. Scrolling through her list of several thousand registered clients, she explains, "I enter them all into my computer and send them messages on holidays, the way corporations do. I remember their birthdays." Ada's business also has a high-quality online presence via a webpage advertising her services, where offerings with traditional and Islamic resonance such as coffee readings and lead pouring are omitted and new age services with a semi-professional aura are described in detail. Here, Ada also sells jewelry that has "spiritual and energy value" while also being appropriate for corporate settings, a combination she hungered for in her previous life as a manager.

Ada's biggest asset is the class habitus and associated economic and personal orientations she shares with her clients: they work at similar occupations, shop at the same malls, hope their children will attend the same schools, and employ similar techniques to mend and manage their businesses and their selves.

> I understand my friends who are living corporate lives so well. I thought a lot about why they come to me, what makes me different, why I have such a good client portfolio. I think I have the right temperament. This is different from my soul. I love people. I'm welcoming. I'm a great confidant. This is my personality. But I also come from a good background. I'm from a good family. I have good morals. I can prepare a CV for someone. I have a printer, a computer here. I can prepare a marketing system. If it's an industry I'm familiar with, I can advise them myself. I also connect clients up with people who know people—in the United States even. Either I resolve the business issue for them, or I connect them up with someone who can. With this setup, people consult with me. I also believe I have strong foresight.

Her strong foresight mentioned almost as an afterthought, the amalgam of affective and business services Ada provides makes her a forerunner in the postsecular neoliberal divination economy, where entrepreneurial conduct of business and the self is increasingly in supply and demand.

THIS CHAPTER DETAILS how fortune-telling is reconceived by feminized secular Muslim readers like Ada in the idiom of entrepreneurship, which envelops not only the economic enterprise of commercial divination but also the personal enterprise of fashioning the self through divination and associated therapeutic practices. Tracking the increasingly (self-) entrepreneurial, digital, and transnational routes commodified fortune-tellings are circulated in, this chapter chronicles the becomings of the feeling labors of divination in a context where the economic and spiritual activity of fortune-telling serves as a medium of working (on the self) in response to the unsettlements of postsecular neoliberal precarity and gendered precariousness. As evident in Ada's work, the personal and business realms fuse together in this entrepreneurial milieu: work and life goals and processes become indistinguishable, and navigating the economic and intimate conditions of precarity becomes an individuated and enchanted journey.

Under neoliberalization, entrepreneurship has emerged as a highly desirable subject position, gaining value beyond its mere economic utility to become a moral and personal orientation to life writ large. As an ideal, entrepreneurship draws Ada's aspirational horizons. Unlike her father's generation, after the erosion of public employee salaries and the narrowing of public employment opportunities brought about by neoliberal economic restructuring, secular Muslims like Ada could not depend on a government job to secure middle-class status. But then again, in an era when the figure of the self-propelled, neoliberal entrepreneurial subject (*girişimci*, entrepreneur) was constructed in opposition to the degraded figure of the passive, dependent civil servant (*memur*) and a rule-bound, bureaucratic conduct (*memur zihniyeti*, civil servant mentality) became the despised other of risk-taking, innovative, entrepreneurial conduct (*girişimcilik*), Ada would not want such a government-secured job. Having grown up with an orientation toward a secular, modern femininity with claims to public life beyond the confines of familial roles and in times of a rising feminist movement that encouraged women's self-realization outside the family, staying at home as a wife and mother like her mother had was another social position Ada could not be content with. Indeed, even when she took several years off after marriage to raise her only child, Ada thought of herself as self-searching, with a strong desire to "find" herself.

Entrepreneurship is increasingly the answer to labor precarity. Armed with one of the most prized degrees for urban middle-class children of her generation (an economics degree designed to cultivate the very qualities of an entrepreneur), Ada was set on the right path to the most prestigious jobs a lower-middle-class kid could hope for: a managerial position in the private sector, maybe in banking, finance, or communications, all sectors that had blossomed with the liberalization of the Turkish economy. For Ada, the path delivered on its promise. In the 1990s, Ada was one of growing numbers of college-educated women to find formal, relatively well-paid work in the expanding service and financial sectors, if only to be (and to constantly anticipate being) laid off. Throughout the first decade of the 2000s, crisis after crisis left many periodically unemployed, forcing workers to ready themselves preemptively or even to make the next move and leave in the hopes of hedging against a future when times were sure to get tough for their company of employment. It was in this context that, turning to entrepreneurship, Ada joined the growing ranks of self-employed women whose numbers increased to one-tenth of all employed women in the 2010s (Yılmaz 2019). Ada is now a proud entrepreneur who not only makes a solid living from her exceptionally successful business but also works with a degree of flexibility that, as a single mother, allows her to care for her teenage daughter while enjoying the sense of authenticity and self-direction so critical to meaning making in her work and her life.

Long coded as male and associated with the masculine values of independence and dominance, the entrepreneur is reenvisioned in the female under neoliberalism (Ahl 2002; Connell 1995). In Turkey, as elsewhere, women's small-scale entrepreneurship is touted as a fix for the many destructions brought about by neoliberal economic restructuring. An assortment of NGOs promote women's entrepreneurship by cultivating women as self-sufficient, self-governing, neoliberal subjects and at the same time recruiting them as altruistic contributors to and caretakers of their families (Altan-Olcay 2014). But in bundling together the contradictory ideals of a neoliberal, individualistic self and a feminized, other-directed self, such civil society programs are unable to resolve the contradictions they purport to remedy. In the Global South, co-opting feminist discourses of women's empowerment and eagerly hailing women as neoliberal subjects, women's employment, microfinance, and entrepreneurship initiatives promise economic and social gains to women and their families, while in practice often leaving poor women indebted and burdening them with the duty of holding together the social fabric through their reproductive and productive labors under the assault of global capital (Al-Dajani et al. 2014; Cornwall 2018; Karim 2011;

Roy 2010). Nonetheless, the discourses and practices of entrepreneurship continue to provide ideological justification for and practical responses to neoliberal economic policies, gaining renewed traction on the ground as a feminized and individualized self is placed at the center of the entrepreneurial enterprise.

Entrepreneurship is increasingly a project of the self. Under neoliberalism, the individual self is reenvisioned as one's own capital to invest by mobilizing a whole host of individual capacities and activities for profitability and self-fulfillment (Foucault 2008; Rose 1992). Ada is not only an entrepreneur opening a new business; she is also a self-entrepreneur who invests in herself and who coaches others in their self-entrepreneurial ventures. Ada brings her business skills into her new line of work, not only by managing her business professionally but also by offering career and business advice to her divination customers. The intuitions of a fortune-teller and the prudence of a professional woman come together seamlessly for Ada in her advice to a client. She concludes that her "area of expertise is people, it's sales; and sales is everything in life."

The hegemony of neoliberalism recasts every aspect of human existence in the idiom of the economical (Brown 2015). The collapsing of the distinction between the economic and the personal allows the self to be reconceived as an entrepreneurial project. When Ada attunes to her clients and assists them through her feeling labors, her work is closely informed by her familiarity both with the logics of the corporate world of business and finance and with the logics of self-fashioning in which her clients are steeped. Ada's business management education, her business savvy born of experience, and her familiarity with Islamicate and new age modalities put in service of self-entrepreneurship all cultivate her business. But it is her ability to seamlessly combine practical work and business support (everything from preparing résumés to formulating winning tenders) with intimate spiritual care (lead pouring to dispel the evil eye and card reading for tips on the next business opportunity) that produces such a potent business model.

As self-entrepreneurship becomes the prescribed response to the demands for flexibility and adjustability of a precarious labor market, women are interpellated and positioned as ideal neoliberal subjects prized for their capacity for self-management and self-transformation (McRobbie 2009; Ringrose and Walkerdine 2008; Scharff 2016; Weber 2009). The feminized mandate of self-remaking, long expected of women who have to reinvent and correct their bodies and souls to be valued, is extended to all (heterosexual male) workers (Sender 2006). In this context, Ada, alongside an increasing number of café readers and workers from other niches, are continuously investing in themselves so as to maximize their work opportunities as well as the sense of meaning in their lives. Densely embedded in new age and psychologized discourses of self-improvement and self-realization, the books, courses, and workshops in Reiki, life coaching, astrology, spiritual therapy, and other fields offer these eager female consumers postsecular venues for neoliberal self-entrepreneurship.

Enchantments of Self-Entrepreneurship

For Ada, whose sense of insecurity accompanying her corporate employment was coupled with a nagging sense of meaninglessness, self-entrepreneurship was an enchanted quest. In search of the sense of purpose and significance her career could not deliver elsewhere, Ada worked hard during her years as a corporate manager to develop herself by hungrily reading books and spending her weekends at spiritually/psychologically oriented self-development workshops and trainings that proliferated in the postsecular milieu of millennial Turkey. Unrelated to her sales career, these endeavors soothed her unsettled soul and imbued in her an alternate sense of meaning and satisfaction that helped to sustain her through an unsatisfying job. "I trained in Reiki while I was working because I had to find a way to love my life over the weekends. I learned NLP. I also studied EFT. For some ten or twelve years I had these trainings over the weekend. Now I have quite a number of diplomas."

Ada's weekends dedicated to learning and practicing new age and self-help technologies gave her the sense of fulfillment and nourishment she was starved for at work. She enjoyed the process and felt inspired, dedicating her time outside work to her quest for personal and spiritual development.

Although her spiritual development journey took considerable time, effort, and money and would eventually prove profitable, culminating in a gainful divination career, Ada did not describe her sustained labors of self-investment and her later decision to leave her managerial career in financial or instrumental terms. To Ada, they were moral, emotional, and spiritual decisions: she felt moved by her "conscience," her "heart," and her "soul." If proud of her many certificates, which she framed and displayed in her office, she also felt ordained by a dream in which the thirteenth-century Sufi master Jalal al-Din Rumi called her Ada, a newly popular female first name meaning "island," thereby bestowing upon her a new taken name. Ada's new work of divination was as much an escape from her estranging and precarious previous career as a deeply felt and spiritually articulated inner calling.

ADA IS A MEMBER of a transnational class of "spiritual entrepreneurs" who use spiritual discourses and new age mediums to retool and reenergize themselves as workers, gaining a new sense of meaning and agency by attuning to the very neoliberal precarity that renders them in need of retooling and re-energizing in the first place (Gregory 2012). Ada may be a professional busi-nesswoman managing an innovative business, but she also feels strongly that this is her personal spiritual path. Combining ideals of secular femininity with an eclectic religious/spiritual sensibility and practice, Ada's thoroughly postsecular business gives her a sense of ethical and mystical direction that si-multaneously sustains her spirit and her pocketbook. Framed as a spiritual self-entrepreneurial activity, the commodified feeling labors of divination allow Ada to integrate the business of work (caring for her clients) and the business of life (caring for herself and her daughter). She not only finds personal ful-fillment in her work and works nonstop to develop her capacities for finding work and fulfillment by training in new modalities; she also supports her clients through the emotional and practical ups and downs of their lives and careers, offering business wisdom and spiritual healing to help them improve themselves at work and in life. In so doing, feminized secular practitioners like Ada propel themselves and others forward in the ever-incomplete efforts that make up self-entrepreneurialism, using enchanted mediums for reinvesting in and reinventing themselves and their labor capacity so as to live with labor pre-carity and the broader sense of insecurity that attends gendered vulnerabilities and postsecular anxieties.

Postsecular spiritual self-entrepreneurship is enabled and energized by therapeutic modalities fit for an age of anxious precarity.[1] Fueled by the con-tradictions of neoliberalism, which preaches self-sufficiency and refuses to acknowledge the reality of deepening dependency and precarity, the "enter-prising self" (Rose 1992) is by its very nature an anxious self. The available answer for such constitutional anxiety is the therapeutic and spiritual cultiva-tion and care of the self. Applied via the consumption of services and educa-tion in self-help, divination, energy healing, and other therapeutic specialties, the remedy requires repeated applications to soothe and energize postsecular neoliberal self-entrepreneurs, who again and again find themselves drained and worried.

Self-entrepreneurship is a continuous and laborious process, but is (supposed to be) experienced as unalienated labor that restores meaningfulness to life and work while at the same time yielding financial returns. Importantly, it promises a path to semiprofessionalization for fortune-tellers. While many seek informal and affordable ways to develop themselves professionally through mentorship from fellow readers or by reading new age best sellers from pirated copies sold on street corners, quite a few readers like Ada attend (when they can spare the expense and make the time) official classes and proudly frame and display the certificates they receive from them. Crucially, unlike Ada, many find that their self-entrepreneurial efforts bring few if any returns, at least in the short run. Yet the activity itself keeps precarious working- and lower-middle-class self-entrepreneurs busy hoping and investing. Similarly, in the hopes of sustaining themselves through insecurities and alienation from their prior or current corporate and business careers, through the anxieties of secularism in decline and secular femininity under threat, and through the perils and fragility of their romantic and familial relationships, secular feminized divination clients visit businesses like Ada's to consume feeling labors in the form of readings and other spiritual and self-help therapies and to obtain training in these modalities. Feeling labors directed toward self-entrepreneurship thus allow Ada and similar readers to experience their labor as settling and nourishing to both their clients and themselves.

The neoliberal cultivation of entrepreneurial selves is facilitated by feminized forms of affective labor (Freeman 2015; Ouelette and Wilson 2011). Cup readings, which have long helped the feminized navigate their intimate vulnerabilities and process their feelings of precariousness, are in this context recruited in the service of neoliberal self-making. In the process, the neoliberal ideals of the individual are cultivated, and feminized labor is recruited into the labor market, not despite but through a range of affective investments facilitated through religious/spiritual discourses, in realms ranging from the divination economies of secular Muslim fortune-telling women to the pious economies of devout Muslim women (Isik 2014).

(G)localizing and enchanting the ideas and practices of self-entrepreneurship is their entanglement with broader spiritual and religious discourses, which are recruited in the service of the moral elevation of entrepreneurship as a mode of profit-oriented economic activity. To authenticate and sacralize the processes of self-enterprising, aspiring spiritual self-entrepreneurs of the neoliberal era across the globe harness locally resonant religious discourses (Freeman 2015; Gooptu 2013). Informed by the growth of popular religious and new age sensibilities in postsecular neoliberal Turkey, Ada and many other spiritual (self-)entrepreneurs draw on Islamic and new age idioms as they fashion their identities and services. They legitimize their expertise by reciting dreams in which saints appear in stereotypical robes and white beards to endow them with authority. They translate new age and psychologized discourses of the self into established local idioms, such as framing disturbed energy flows as effects of the evil eye. If secular Muslims participating in the divination economy are busy hybridizing new age and Muslim discourses and practices with the aim of enchanting self-entrepreneurial ideas and activities, their pious Muslim peers craft similarly therapeutic personas and services so as to attract a devout customer base, framing their offerings in familiar popular religious idioms such as gratitude (*şükür*) and peace (*huzur*).[2]

While individual practitioners and their clients navigate neoliberal precarity through these religious/spiritual ideas and modalities, the Islamically accented AKP government also borrows from resonant Muslim vocabularies such as blessings (*bereket*) to sacralize its neoliberal economic policies and to hail citizens in their now dually conceived economic and spiritual capacities to act both profitably and piously. Government officials claim that, just as the pious government is blessed, so are its pious citizens. As recompense for their devout behavior in the intimate and work/business realms—(male) profit-seeking economic activities performed in public piously and (female) familial labors such as having children or taking care of the disabled and the elderly at home dutifully—citizens can expect heavenly economic rewards. "The economy is blessed," they declare to celebrate economic growth rates. "Children are blessings," they insist to encourage women to have more babies (Korkman 2015a).[3]

These governmental policies resonate in a neoliberal era when the global best seller *The Secret* (Byrne 2006) preaches and a transnational network of prosperity churches teaches (Hasu 2006; Hunt 2000; Maxwell 1998) that the right kind of "individual will" and "energy" exuded into the universe will magically attract financial and spiritual well-being and that God blesses the faithful with wealth. It was Karl Marx (1977) who first brought back the notion of the occult at the heart of the modern world through the concept of commodity fetishism, which he used to account for the magical nature of the capitalist mode of production and consumption (Taussig 1980). By highlighting the ways in which classed societies are doomed to rely on mystification, the concept of fetish has enabled the critique of the modernist premise that reason will supersede religion and superstition. In this vein, Jean Comaroff and John Comaroff (1999, 2000a, 2000b) have claimed that what fuels the global rise in the occult is a faith in the millennial and messianic promises of neoliberalism facing the realities of the structural marginalization produced by neoliberalization. In this world made millennial through a peculiarly materialist spirituality, navigating neoliberal precarity is an enchanted endeavor. Under the ideas and practices of spiritual self-entrepreneurship, the tensions between financial and moral, business and personal, and communal and individual considerations are occulted by design. Working as enterprising dually signifies personal fulfillment in this world and the fulfillment of one's purpose in the otherworld. It doubly instantiates one's contribution both to societal well-being and to the religious/spiritual order of things. As the economic and personal activity of entrepreneurship is endowed with new moral weight, Turkey's millennial fortune-tellers shed their earlier modesty about their work to speak proudly and assertively in an entrepreneurial language.

Entrepreneurs of Divination, Old and New

No doubt it took an entrepreneur, in the narrower literal sense of the word as one who manages and assumes the risks of a business, to start and operate a fortune-telling café in early 2000s Turkey. Fortune-telling café owners had not only to display considerable initiative in pursuing this new business niche; they also had to take on substantive financial and legal risks. But even by 2010, when fortune-telling cafés were mushrooming one after the other, only a minority of their owners (and an even smaller number of their workers) spoke the entrepreneurial lingo that was soon to become the norm. With the exception of a few male owners of the earliest and largest fortune-telling cafés, when asked how it was that they began adding fortune-telling to their businesses, most café owners drew from a stock list of market-related justifications: "We had to outdo the competition." "I wasn't making enough money to keep the café open." "This was the only way anyone would climb all those stairs." These owners, many of whom were women, offered up the stories of their business battles in modest, almost apologetic tones, emphasizing compelling but impersonal and external factors, such as constraint, necessity, and obligation (*mecburiyet*). They stood in stark contrast to the divination entrepreneurs of the second decade of the twenty-first century, who would eagerly emphasize their initiative in operating a fortune-telling business, rejoicing not only in entrepreneurial pride but also in a curious kind of self-celebratory enthusiasm that hailed work as a personal and spiritual experience.

The most touted entrepreneur of divination of the 2010s, Sertaç Taşdelen, is the founding partner and CEO of Binnaz Abla (Elder Sister Binnaz), a popular online platform and mobile application that allows clients to obtain written, audio-recorded, phone, or live video readings from fortune-tellers of their choosing.

A poster child of entrepreneurship in a postsecular neoliberal era, Taşdelen is highly literate in spiritual self-entrepreneurship discourses. Commenting on the success of his new business, Taşdelen declares, "This is not about creating a start-up. It's the endless journey of self discovery" (Hariri 2014). Following the quick growth of his business into a transnational corporation that employs

FIGURE 7.1. Screenshot from the digital fortune-telling website Binnaz Abla that reads, "Real Fortune-Tellers. Choose your interpreter, send your fortune" ("Gerçek Falcılar: Yorumcunu Seç Falını Gönder," Binnaz Abla, September 16, 2020, https://www.binnaz.com/tr).

hundreds of workers as fortune-tellers, translators, tech support personnel, and a management team, Taşdelen receives generous media coverage and invitations to entrepreneurship workshops and awards ceremonies. "Interviewing him was like talking to a life coach," a journalist enthusiastically attests. "He enshrined in my mind this message: You can do it! Why not? . . . He has an irresistible energy, and I think this is the secret of his success" (Tavşanoğlu 2013). "No success is coincidental. May Sertaç's story inspire you as much as it inspired me," cheers one blogger, herself a self-titled "lifestyle CEO" and an escapee from a corporate career (Mutlu 2017). In one of the many entrepreneurship workshops he speaks at in high schools and universities around the country, Taşdelen defines his notion of "success as happiness," which he explains is "an inner state, a choice."[4]

ENTREPRENEURSHIP IS A NEWLY dominant discourse, its moralization and valuation of economic activity novel in the context of fortune-telling cafés. It is certainly the case that the fortune-telling café business was from its very beginnings an entrepreneurial venture, in the sense that it depended upon inventing and operating an innovative business model. From its early days, the first and largest fortune-telling café, the Angels Café (Melekler Kahvesi), and a few other large businesses modeled after it were exceptional in exuding an entrepreneurial assertiveness backed by a complex and formal business administration model. A forerunner in this niche, the Angels Café diversified its products to include a range of fortune-telling services, drinks, snacks, games, and more. It designed, printed, and patented its own divination card deck and coffee cups and opened a sister publication house that released several personal development books. It operated a membership system that encouraged and rewarded repeat customers. It actively fostered coverage of its services and business model in the local and international media, where its all-male group of owners proudly and joyfully celebrated their entrepreneurial agency in creating a new kind of business.

But during the first decade of the twenty-first century, entrepreneurial discourses were rather uncommon and self-entrepreneurial ones downright unfamiliar in the fortune-telling economy. Unlike a handful of larger businesses, most cafés were microenterprises, opened with little monetary investment, maintained for a period of time through intense self-exploitation, offering a living for a few people at best, and surviving only for a time through the ebbs and flows of the crisis-prone Turkish economy. Their owners insisted that they simply "had to" resort to this line of business when faced with competition and need. "Every other café in the neighborhood was offering readings," they contended, shifting responsibility for their switch to a generalized category of other business owners. "We just had to," they explained, noting that their financial survival was at stake. Similarly, employees in these years also situated their decision to read fortunes in a narrative of constraint and struggle, describing their otherwise limited work options, histories of unemployment, and other people's insistence that they "give it a try." Many remained content with practicing coffee fortune-telling, often construed as a feminized nonskill, sometimes adding tarot cards to the mix. Individual will and initiative were de-emphasized and work/business was narrated in the externalized idiom of economic necessity.

In the almost two decades that have passed since the opening of the first fortune-telling café in Istanbul in 2001, the discourses and practices of self-entrepreneurship have thoroughly enveloped café fortune-tellers and their employers.[5] In the mid-to-late 2010s, more and more owners and workers, including smaller businesses and women, were speaking not only with entrepreneurial assertiveness but also in a fully elaborated self-entrepreneurial idiom. In the divination sector, this development was encouraged in the beginning by a loose imposition of laws criminalizing commercial fortune-telling and later by new routes of formalization.[6] Under pressure from the increasing saturation of the postsecular divination economy and under the influence of a neoliberal understanding of the self, workers and owners started to advertise their increasingly diversified services more aggressively and assertively. These new entrepreneurs take pride not only in their own agency for having been able to commodify and expand their fortune-telling and related services and for having created new and more successful forms of divination/spiritual/therapeutic businesses; they also delight in describing their work as delivering opportunities for personal fulfillment, moral agency, spiritual meaning, and even societal improvement. In this new idiom, individual choice and agency become both the path to and the marker of business success and moral personhood, endowing work/business with new, personalized, enchanted meaning and even a promise of social benefit.

As the CEO of the international digital fortune-telling venue Binnaz Abla, Taşdelen is the archetype of the spiritual self-entrepreneur of this new postsecular neoliberal era and is celebrated in the Turkish media as the ideal model of the successful, desirable, and moral entrepreneur. In an oft-repeated narrative of corporate drudgery versus entrepreneurial self-realization, Taşdelen's past career as a management consultant at a multinational corporation in Dubai and Singapore preceded by a business administration degree from a prestigious private university in Turkey is narrated as a safe bet he courageously left behind for the radically unpredictable endeavor of managing his own business. Journalists use dramatic, awe-inspiring terms like "resigning overnight," even though Taşdelen himself has stated explicitly more than once that he left his employment only after thorough planning and consideration, once the income from his new venture exceeded his salary at the time. Taşdelen's move from being a high-level corporate employee providing management advice to others to being the manager of his own corporation is described as a successful bid to "escape the prison of the corporate world to the freedom [of] entrepreneurship" (Hariri 2014). Taşdelen on one occasion describes this change in a resonant religious/spiritual metaphor as nothing less than being "born again" (Hariri 2014). Taşdelen's educational and work experiences and his social and cultural capital pale under the bright light of his persona, his energy, and, most copiously, his affect in narrating his business success. His economic activities are signified as affectively intense, personally meaningful, and spiritually significant.

According to media accounts, flexibility, inspiration, creativity, and self-realization characterize Taşdelen's new career as the CEO of Binnaz Abla. "I can live and work anywhere with an internet connection," Taşdelen joyfully comments on his current working life spread across several global cities, including Istanbul, New York, and Singapore, and his touristic travels around the world (Mutlu 2017). Owning an online business with no physical offices, Taşdelen is freed from work locations and schedules. Although he is busy performing management tasks similar to those that occupied him in his earlier career, the degree and kind of flexibility he now enjoys, as well as his sense of self-realization, imbues his new business management tasks with an altogether different meaning and feeling. When asked about his dreams, Taşdelen mentions his aim of making Binnaz Abla a global brand alongside his bucket list of space travel, DJing at the Burning Man festival, and climbing Mount Everest, attesting to how the spirit of self-entrepreneurship seemingly mends the fissures between the realms of business and personal, work and play, and alienation and authenticity.

Through the prism of self-entrepreneurship, profit-oriented work/business activities and lives and selves crafted in the enterprising mode combine to become a moral and political good that promises to alleviate the ethical burdens and social consequences of structural inequality without any recourse whatsoever to collective political solutions. "My life is much more meaningful, with fewer physical possession[s], simpler and much happier," concludes Taşdelen of his post–corporate employment entrepreneurial life, which he describes as though it were an ascetic quest (Hariri 2014). Complementing his almost saintly aura, Taşdelen supports the education of disabled children with Binnaz Abla profits as part of a corporate social responsibility program, is the founding director of the nonprofit online donation platform İyilik Paylaş (Share Good Deeds), which matches NGOs and foundations with donors at no charge, and can be seen mountain climbing for charity. With these endeavors, Taşdelen's (self-)entrepreneurship becomes a quest not only for self-realization and profit but also for societal improvement. Taşdelen articulates the corporate social responsibility program with a similarly virtuous philosopher-king aspiration: "Binnazabla.com is a super, even supernatural, family working hard toward big goals. Our long-term goal is to provide innovative solutions to entrenched social problems, to create projects, and effect systematic change . . . to overcome prejudices so as to help 'human beings,' the first and smallest link in the economic chain" (Çepik 2011). Self-entrepreneurship meets social entrepreneurship, extending the neoliberal economic logic from the individual through the family/company to the whole social realm. By promising not only personal but also social transformation, the self-entrepreneur-cum-philosopher-king empties out the political.

Paralleling this almost magical and decisively masculine entrepreneurial story, however, are the labors of Taşdelen's mother. Taşdelen's interviews detail the lengths his mother went to in supporting him early in his career through regular visits, hosting lavish homemade dinners for his corporate colleagues and friends replete with Turkish coffee and even reading their cups. Taşdelen had the idea for his online venture when his colleagues reminisced about these readings in his mother's absence abroad. Taşdelen sent pictures of their coffee cups to his mother back in Turkey, who then sent back a written reading. With the help of a business partner offering technical infrastructure for the website, Taşdelen created his business. He named the website after his mother, Binnaz Gündoğan, and, in his words, "gifted" it to her on her birthday. A retired pharmacist, Gündoğan then became Taşdelen's first and only worker during the online divination business's trial period. Contributing to his business even now by writing and interviewing for the affiliated blog, Gündoğan's skills and labor appear to have been central to the success of the enterprise that carries her name. Yet she is often framed in the media as a proud mother, not as an entrepreneur or professional. Her determination and many labors are relegated to the background so as to foreground the individual agency of her son, who, by dint of his familiarity with corporate management, appropriated, digitized, and put into transnational circulation the feminized practice of coffee reading.

Taşdelen's popularity owes to the way he and those who portray him downplay his business acumen alongside the feminized labors of his mother to sprinkle his business story with the postsecular neoliberal magic of self-entrepreneurship. The appeal of this magical rendering of Taşdelen's business and persona testifies to the grasp of the discourses of spiritual self-entrepreneurialism in which finding one's calling at work and in life is miraculously rewarded with individual fulfillment and financial well-being at the same time that it also promises to heal the wounds neoliberal capitalism inflicts on society. In a milieu where various actors ranging from the government and big business owners to small-scale divination entrepreneurs and even working-class café readers preach the tackling of precariousness in an enchanted realm of personal and economic activity, Taşdelen shines brightly in the media spotlight. These self-entrepreneurial discourses attract not only managers and business owners like Taşdelen who are busy digitizing and transnationalizing the fortune-telling sector but also their workers, whose labor is rendered at once more self-entrepreneurial and more precarious by the business innovations of divination entrepreneurs like Taşdelen.

Digital, Flexible, and Self-Entrepreneurial: Remaking Feeling Labors

"The advantage [of digital fortune-telling] is that you can do it anywhere that has internet, sitting comfortably in front of a computer," Meral, a reader in her late twenties, notes on the flexibility of digital labor. If Meral agrees with Taşdelen in appreciating the freedom from a fixed workplace and hours that online fortune-telling grants, she is also quick to note the costs and the limits to the freedom promised. "Is it reliable? No, there are no guarantees," she acknowledges. "But it does give you the feeling of being the boss." She also admits "the truth that there are rules, and there is a big difference between what the customer pays and what you receive."[7] She later reads flatly from her screen, "First, thank you so much for your interest in me and our website. Let us now see what your cup shows. . . . I conclude the reading here, but you can always reach me." She then turns to me to ask in a conversational tone, "You know what this is? My first and last words. The website makes us say them." Meral explains that she is required to record a minimum of five minutes of audio per client, but, she says, "I abide by my own standard. I spend seven minutes or more. Seven is my lucky number." With her deep knowledge of the precarity, exploitation, and labor discipline that characterizes digital fortune-telling, Meral is keenly aware that feeling like she's the boss does not make her the boss, even as she enjoys and exerts every bit of autonomy she can muster at work. While for business owners like Taşdelen self-entrepreneurship through divination may literally mean being one's own boss—and by extension may connote individual, moral, and spiritual autonomy—for digital divination workers like Meral, self-entrepreneurship means precarity with a prized yet limited sense of self-direction.

The child of an urban housewife who had once been a rural farmworker and a factory worker who had once been a shopkeeper, Meral grew up in a secular Muslim working-class family in small city with a strong belief that "education would give [her] wings." Unable to afford the private classes for the national university placement exam that her middle-class peers took for granted, she began working full time at a factory, taking the exam repeatedly over the course of several years. Smart and persistent, she was finally placed in the humanities program of a public university in a large city with government tuition support. Her college experience "really encouraged and supported living openly with [her] sexual identity" but did not make her employable. After college, "like any other unemployed university graduate," she returned to her natal home, where she helped her mother raise her niece. Looking for a way out, Meral took the university exam again and enrolled in another program that offered a full year of intensive English language classes, considered essential for a job that might lead to a middle-class life. While her English education did not (immediately) produce a job, during her studies, she ended up developing a romantic relationship with an American citizen and followed her to the United States on a tourist visa. The visa allowed her to stay up to six months a year in the United States, so Meral moved back and forth between the two countries, working at odd jobs in Turkey to save for her return to the United States. When the relationship ended after a few years, Meral resourcefully found her way into a graduate program and a student visa, which allowed her to stay in the United States continuously for the duration of her enrollment, if with significantly limited legal employment options.

As a working-class immigrant, relocating first to a larger city from a provincial one and then to the United States from Turkey, Meral had gone from gig to gig, working in direct sales, giving private lessons, doing housesitting, babysitting, cleaning, and laundry, and "never turning down a job" (*iş ayırmam*). Already mixing and matching a number of precarious informal jobs to make ends meet, Meral added digital divination to the patchwork to get by as an international student. She had for some time been reading her friends' fortunes "for pleasure." Having grown up around her mother, grandmother, in-laws, and neighbors, all of whom gathered in regular rotating women's gatherings (*gün*) to read cups, she was well familiar with the ins and outs of fortune-telling. "I guess I, too, have the power to interpret things," she contended.

Meral's options might be limited, but her aspirational horizons are not. She has her own entrepreneurial dreams for a new model of divination business. "You know what I think about, Zeynep? How I could put divination in conversation with Freudian psychology. I've thought about this a lot, but I would need professional help to make it into something real. How can I bring fortune-telling and science, Freudian psychology, together? See, I'm getting goose bumps! I feel that if I could achieve this, it would be immensely popular in a place like the United States. Maybe even [good enough for] a private clinic in Istanbul. This is what I have in mind."

Meral has a creative idea and the right entrepreneurial affect, one that gives her goose bumps with the anticipation of it coming true. But to pursue her entrepreneurial divination dreams successfully, Meral knows that she will need more than the much-touted entrepreneurial inspiration. Without business management expertise and experience and, more important, the social capital with which to connect her emergent business with the right people who can publicize and expand it, Meral's (self-)entrepreneurial affects and efforts would most likely continue to feel like, but not result in, her becoming the boss.

A PRODUCT OF LABOR PRECARITY, digital divination further institutionalizes and deepens its workers' precarious labor conditions. While entrepreneurs of online fortune-telling like Taşdelen are celebrated for creating businesses with the moral and social potential to remedy the destructions of neoliberalization, online fortune-telling businesses operate with a flexible labor model in which workers are highly disposable. In a labor market where unemployment and underemployment rates are high, especially for women like Meral who constitute the majority of fortune-tellers, online divination businesses supply and swap out workers with both ease and aplomb. In substituting and disposing of workers so seamlessly, they entrench the insecure employment practices that have shaped café fortune-telling.

Hired with a no-strings-attached contract, online fortune-tellers are putatively free to work and earn as much or as little as they can. Meral estimates that over the previous month when school was out of session and she did not have other employment, she read over 250 fortunes. Calculating solely the time spent recording audio readings, she conservatively estimates that she worked for approximately forty hours, earning two-thirds the Turkish monthly minimum wage in the equivalent of a full-time work week in Turkey. "I could work full time and make more than a physician," she optimistically estimates. Yet, Meral admits, digital divination is work with "no guarantees." Not only is there no job security or benefits, but work pace and volume are both variable and monitored and controlled in ways that diminish worker autonomy. Customers who come to the website looking for a reading have the option of asking for a reading from a particular reader or from any available reader. If personally requested, a reader must respond within four hours during the daytime and eight hours during the nighttime. If anonymous, the request goes to a pool where any fortune-teller can pick it up. A fortune-teller can only queue up to four standing fortune-telling requests and cannot accept more until finishing their queue and clearing out their message box by responding to outstanding customer messages. If a reader is repeatedly delayed, their queue capacity is reduced. These regulations limit workers' control over the tempo and volume of work and push them to complete orders swiftly while remaining online as much as possible to avoid underemployment.

Underlining her agency, Meral emphasizes her range of choices in this setup: "You manage it. You decide whether you want to read fortunes or not. You can go online or offline. . . . You just make yourself available. I sit down whenever I have time." She explains how she opens the reader interface of the website and waits for reading requests to come in, records audio or typewritten readings to send to clients, replies to client messages, and views customer reviews.[8] While Meral waits for customers, she completes her academic work, chats with friends, or watches something on the computer. She doesn't complain about the extended time and space such work seeps into and tries to work as much as possible. But life has a way of getting in the way, and she finds it a challenge to sustain the high tempo that would allow her to live off the money she makes from online divination. Indeed, the precarity of the work means that making a living from her digital employment is quite challenging. Even depending on it to supplement her other income is unreliable. Workers thus need to continuously recalibrate how best to allocate their time and energies across their various flexible work options with one or more employers, working whenever and for as long as work becomes available, wholly in the absence of any guarantees.

In an implicit comparison to industrial work where discipline is external to the disaffected, alienated worker, digital work is often touted as a realm of freedom and self-realization. But labor precarity and the self-entrepreneurial responses to it promote a highly individualized and internalized regime of labor discipline. Already transformed under the pressures of the market via their move from the domestic economy to cafés, the feeling labors of divination are further disciplined in digital businesses through standardization and quantification. Labor discipline at cafés consists of cutting lunch breaks short on busy days, taking cell phones away from particularly chatty readers, interrupting long readings when waiting clients are present, and other methods used by café owners to extract labor more efficiently. The larger mandate of customer satisfaction is operationalized through the owner's appraisal of client demand for a reader, supported by limited and voluntary customer feedback. Online divination allows duration to be measured to the second for audio and chat sessions and to the last word for written ones, contents to be prescribed with required fixed statements, and work processes to be controlled via elaborate limits and deadlines around work volume and pace. Unlike the occasional verbal comment offered by or recruited from select clients at cafés, divination websites thoroughly measure customer satisfaction via standardized, numeric, and qualitative measures, in addition to quantitative comments. They evaluate, manage, retain or fire, and pay workers through the regular and quantified use of performance scales. Every client Meral reads for gets to assign her a score (maximum of five) and provide a written review. These points are used to calculate Meral's average for the last 250 readings and to assign her a customer satisfaction rating, converted to a scale of one hundred points. Customer satisfaction is visualized with stars assigned to readers, with three-star readers being allocated a satisfaction rating of 98.5 percent and above, two-star readers 94.5 percent and above, and one-star readers 92.5 percent and above. The price of the reading and the payment the reader receives are three-tiered and are linked directly to their star rating. If ratings drop below the one-star threshold, the reader risks losing employment, making customer satisfaction highly consequential. The process of providing feeling labor as a commodified service is now not only more closely supervised and controlled by management but also more self-reflexively scrutinized and regulated for workers.

In such a highly flexible and meticulously (self-)managed labor regime, the digitization of fortune-telling reinvents the feeling labors of divination. Online customer feedback is crucial in digital divination, not only because of its financial and employment consequences but also because unmediated feedback and two-way interaction are no longer available. By writing or recording readings in the absence of the physical presence of a client based on limited and fixed cues from a customer form, the affective attunement between reader and client otherwise animated by the embodied proximity of two persons is transformed into a process where the readers are alone with their projections of a client while also being overcrowded by an increasingly present management that minutely regulates their delivery of a reading. Readers are now required to speculatively conjure an imaginary client to whom they may address their reading in a way that is moving enough for them to be able to produce a reading likely to please the actual client, while also bearing in mind the directions and limits set by management for their reading. Deprived of the real-time presence and feedback of the client, readers are burdened by the de facto and unalterable feedback that is provided after the reading is consumed and that remains on the reader's profile for future clients to read.[9] This new medium through which feeling labors are delivered changes the way readers connect to their clients and voice their desires and fears, replacing the more intuitive and embedded forms of affective attunement with more regimented forms of customer feedback and more self-reflexive efforts of alignment.

As readers manage the reverberations of living with a constant stream of reviews and evaluations indexing and intensifying their precarity, online fortune-telling recruits the feeling labors of workers both in the service of customers and as a self-directed care and recuperation endeavor. Online fortune-tellers join the growing segments of a precarious labor force around the globe whose psychic lives are colored by anxiety, insecurity, and self-doubt (Scharff 2016). "Free to work anxiously" like their colleagues in other digital on-demand platforms, online readers like Meral simultaneously celebrate the so-called freedom of digital labor and admit to the vulnerabilities flexible employment subjects them to (Malin and Chandler 2017). Despite her confident personality, Meral was quickly worn out by the ongoing stream of customer reviews and the incessant computation of performance metrics the website imposed.

> I read cups for a few months, and my scores started to drop. People started to not like my readings. It's because I was affected by the reviews. The reviews are visible on my page. I was constantly reading them, always checking. Someone would say that they had wasted their money, and I would worry about why they had written that. I was affected. So naturally my scores were dropping. There's pressure from the website to keep your scores above 95 percent, at the very least at 92 percent. If you can't, it means you're not competitive enough.

Performance metrics affect readers' fortunes as well as their moods, increasing their need to work on themselves in order to restore their profitability and spirits and be able to continue to perform the feeling labors of divination for their clients. Quantification in the context of self-entrepreneurship incites workers to self-monitor in an attempt to control the uncontrollability of their precarious labor processes, managing and producing further anxiety in the process (Moore and Robinson 2015). Willed to perform by anxiety, readers work on themselves affectively to keep their spirits up and continue to reinvest and labor in the face of demoralizing customer feedback, dropping performance scores, and threatened livelihoods. The rhythms and pressures of online work leave workers oscillating between panic and depression as they feel the precarity of digital labor (Berardi 2009). Redirecting their feeling labors, readers increasingly need to attune to their own anxiety, an anxiety which, if they are to remain profitable, should move them enough to motivate their self-investment but not so much as to become overwhelming, thereby thwarting their self-reflexive efforts to improve their performance.

The technologically mediated and thoroughly regimented neoliberal labor management that online divination workers are subjected to places continuous demands of self-entrepreneurship on digital fortune-teller workers. To become and remain profitable, readers must continuously invent and reinvent themselves. Meral recalls how the online job application form includes "information presenting yourself: why I want to read fortunes, how I started reading fortunes, why I'm good at it," asking prospective workers not only to explain how they are qualified but also how their sense of self and personal motivations align with their work. "You write a piece introducing yourself pretty much like a personal statement for a college application," summarizes Meral. After a few trial readings are reviewed by the website management team, selected readers are invited to create an online profile, requiring them to assess, fashion, and brand a most profitable version of themselves. For Meral, this meant highlighting the reading and healing skills of multiple generations of women in her family, taking on a nickname, and choosing a stand-in profile picture that presented her as a middle-aged heteronormative woman. "They call me *abla*," she shares, denoting her clients' use of the honorific reserved to address women who are senior to oneself. "They want to get interpretations and advice from someone older and more experienced."

With the tools and the inducement provided by the management, online readers intensify the self-entrepreneurial work of continuously observing and developing their affective labor capacities throughout their employment. When digital readers receive negative reviews or experience a decrease in demand, they may revise their images and portfolio of services in a way that will attract new clients and better reviews. After Meral's performance scores dropped almost below the required minimum, the website manager emailed her to suggest that she start offering tarot readings. Meral had not touched a tarot deck before, so she requested some time to learn it. Her study happened in an unexpected manner.

> It was summer. I was doing cup readings online. I had a crush on a girl. I knew she was straight, but I still felt there was something there. I was really wondering what would happen with her. I thought maybe I should get a reading myself. I picked a tarot reader with a 99 percent rating and sent her a request from my own reader page, disclosing that I was a reader, too. I did not tell her that I am lesbian, of course. In return, she sent me back a request for a cup reading. She has a business degree. After she got divorced and her business dwindled, she found her way to fortune-telling and became one of the top readers on the website. She offered to teach me how to read tarot cards. We Skyped, and she showed me the card spreads and shared with me a few recorded readings. That's how I started reading tarot cards.

The unexpected intimacy between coworkers born of mutual readings helped Meral manage both the emotional vulnerability she felt as a queer woman and the vulnerability of her precarious labor status. Finding a supportive and inspiring reader/friend who was willing to mobilize her feeling labors of divination to mentor a fellow worker helped Meral practically, in that she diversified her services, and emotionally, in that she restored her spirits. The relationship served to bolster her self-entrepreneurial efforts, enabling her to remain gainfully employed. While the feeling labors of divination are directed by the profit-maximizing imperatives of online businesses into a thoroughly self-entrepreneurial form that presupposes competitive and individualistic workers, this does not exhaust their potential for producing other kinds of relations to the self and others. As Meral's unexpected intimacy with and support from a fellow reader demonstrates, workers who are structurally organized to compete against one another and against themselves may also forge relations of solidarity and mutuality in response to their feelings of uncertainty, inadequacy, and insecurity, providing noncommercially feeling labors to help each other stay afloat financially and affectively in the digitized divination economy.

Transnational Futures

Tarık, a small-framed man in his late fifties, has been working as a Turkish-to-Arabic translator at a fortune-telling café for several years now. Born in the southern province of Hatay bordering Syria, he learned Arabic growing up and as a young man joined the then prominent wave of labor migration from Turkey to the Arabian Gulf states. Becoming fluent in Gulf Arabic, Tarık worked for almost three decades as a cook in Bahrain, Dubai, Libya, Oman, Saudi Arabia, and Qatar. In addition to translating, he invites in and welcomes customers in Arabic and Turkish and does some chores around the café. He shakes his shoulders carelessly as he describes his ambivalent circumstances: "I don't believe in this type of thing [fortune-telling and related practices] at all, but what can you do [*ne yapacaksın*]?" Already retired with social security, he seems not to mind that he is informally employed with no benefits. Yet combined with his meager retirement wages, his monthly minimum-wage income from the café is not enough to support his household of a wife and three children. "I would go further into debt every month were it just the salary," he sums up. Tarık depends on tips from fortune-telling clients. Tourists from the Gulf countries "have the money," Tarık insists. Variable rates apply to local and foreign customers, with wealthy-looking Arab tourists charged many times more than the locals. This encourages Tarık to expect relatively high tips, too, but there is no explicit requirement or rate for tips. "Some give generously, others nothing. Whatever their heart pleases [*gönlünden ne koparsa*]," Tarık says modestly, borrowing a phrase from street beggars.

THE NEWLY TRANSNATIONALIZED fortune-telling economy now enlists a new class of precarious workers into their ranks: translators. Digital divination businesses that recruit workers and clients from across the globe and that hire translators to mediate between Turkish-speaking readers and foreign clients are not the only sector to go translational and transnational. In situ divination economies are also transnationalizing. While Taşdelen's Binnaz Abla provides services in different currencies and languages, including English and Arabic, fortune-telling cafés in Istanbul also post signs and offer readings regularly in English, occasionally in Russian, Bulgarian, and other languages spoken by labor immigrants in Turkey, and, from the 2010s, increasingly in Arabic. While readings in English translation have long been provided to the occasional foreign tourists who made their way to a fortune-telling café with the help of a guidebook or travel show, divination in Arabic has grown exponentially in cafés over the last decade.

As the number of tourists from Arab countries, particularly the Arabian Gulf, has increased to a quarter of all international visitors to Turkey and the number of refugees from Syria to over three million, most fortune-telling cafés in the divination hub of Taksim, Istanbul, have begun to advertise divination services in Arabic.[10] Their Arabic signs and designated personnel inviting customers in and translating in Arabic welcome this growing segment of tourists whose presence in Turkey has been cultivated through the transnational circulation of cultural products such as television dramas, as well as through state-sponsored regional broadcasting in which Turkish coffee features prominently as a symbol of the familiarity and benign nature of Turkish influence in the region (Al-Ghazzi and Kraidy 2013; Anaz and Ozcan 2016). Together, neo-Ottomanism, which refers to a postsecular reformulation of Turkish national identity and foreign policy in line with the AKP's reignited neoimperialist ambitions that emphasizes a shared Islamic moral universe and a pluralistic Ottoman heritage in the Muslim Middle East and Africa, and Ottomania, which refers to a neoliberal popular taste for appreciating and consuming the Ottoman past, set the broader terrain for this latest transnational wave of the Turkey-based divination economy (Ergin and Karakaya 2017; Yavuz 1998).

Translating for fortune-tellers is precarious work, but some translators are more precarious than others. Tarık, whose skills include Arabic linguistic and cultural literacy, is lucky to have had regular employment long enough to earn social security and retirement benefits and to hold Turkish citizenship. Together, his national belonging and transnational work history secure him a monthly salary. Not all translators are able to mitigate the effects of their precarious employment relatively well, like Tarık. Hassan is a young Arab man with the look of a teenager and thick brown hair framing his acne-marked face. A refugee from Syria who arrived five year ago, he speaks enough Turkish to translate readings into Arabic but does not get much business. "I don't believe what the Turkish readers say. All lies. I'm not doing that anymore," he says, cutting my inquiry into his career as a translator short. He has a Syrian acquaintance who reads his cup as a friendly gesture. Hassan trusts him. He used to work at the beer houses in the neighborhood and has been helping out at the café for almost a year now. He waits downstairs at the door of the apartment building where the café is located to invite and accompany clients up. He hangs out at the café waiting for things to do, but there's not much business, with a Moldovan immigrant woman cooking and cleaning at the café and only a few customers coming in. He hopes to learn from one of the café owners, a tattoo artist who tells me half-jokingly to take Hassan with me to the United States. "I already looked into that," Hassan responds impatiently. "It has to be either via marriage or a sponsoring company. It's really hard." Later he walks me out. Before bidding me goodbye, he cannot help but half-reprimand me. "What are you doing here? Go back to the United States." He doesn't need to tell me that he feels stuck in Turkey. Many of the country's refugees and migrants hope to make it to a more desirable destination in the Global North.

Hassan's (im)mobility and precarious employment are located in a larger context in which Turkey became a migrant-receiving country not long after the neoliberalization of the economy in the 1980s. Since the 1990s, labor migrants from the collapsed eastern bloc countries and poorer Asian and African countries and war refugees and political asylum seekers from Middle Eastern countries, to whom the doors of the European Union have become increasingly closed, turn to Turkey. Finding entry, yet irregularized through restrictions around work permits, most migrants end up in the informal economy, concentrating overwhelmingly in feminized sectors such as care work, where they are underpaid and insecurely employed (Toksöz and Ulutaş 2012).

In a world of labor and intimacy shaped by transnational movements of migrants, workers, tourists, and lovers, mobility and flexibility pose uneven opportunities and limitations for individuals differentially located along the axes of class, gender, sexuality, religion, race, ethnicity, and citizenship (Constable 2009; Mills 2003). For a once middle-class and now wealthy male entrepreneur like Taşdelen who furthered his business management career at a multinational corporation by relocating from country to country before launching his own transnational online divination business managed from several countries, transnationality of flexible digital labor brings a number of embedded freedoms: the freedom to take formal, well-compensated work and experience life in different world cities across the globe, peppered by touristic travel around the world and visits from a mother who brings to him, wherever he may be, a taste of home cooking and even of fortune-telling. For a working-class queer woman like Meral, transnational divination offers a tool with which to piece together a livelihood amid visa restrictions, financial constraints, and precarious labor conditions, while maximizing mobility and the ability to live, love, and learn.

The relative unboundedness of transnational, and in particular digital, labor from national and industrial time and space is on the one hand habitually coupled with the hyperregulation, criminalization, and devaluation of immigrant labor (Robinson and Santos 2014). This labor's unboundedness is on the other hand tied to the very cultural and language skills that are acquired through immigration and to the constitution of a "transnational cybertariat" in the transnational workspaces digital labor conjures (Alarcón-Medina 2018). Fluently able to navigate the multiple linguistic and aspirational universes their clients are immersed in, employees like Meral who are highly educated yet barred from the formal labor market, insecurely mobile yet ever available for precarious work, are exceptionally qualified for digital transnational labor. Similarly, a translator like Tarık, who grew up in a bilingual borderland and was sucked into transnational labor migration to the Arab Gulf only to find himself reintegrated into the new divination economy formed around other kinds of transnational flows from the same region, is able to find work thanks to his linguistic skills and cultural familiarity. Finally there is Hassan, marginally employed and thoroughly constrained in his chances of economic and geographical mobility under the xenophobia, racism, and neoimperialism that limit the life chances and movement of refugees.

This chapter has documented how, under the transnationalization and digitization of divination, feminized secular Muslim workers of the postsecular fortune-telling economy labor under deepening precarity and in increasingly self-entrepreneurial ways. On the heels of gendered, postsecular, and economic vulnerability, spiritual self-entrepreneurial discourses and practices envelop readers and their clients, making new demands on their labor and their selves. The feeling labors of divination are transformed in the process, increasingly directed toward investing in and regulating workers' own affective capacities and processes. New therapeutically conceived and entrepreneurially inspired modes of conducting the business of divination contribute to its digitization and transnationalization, enlist novel kinds of workers into the fortune-telling economy, and enmesh the (self-)entrepreneurial fortunes of readers and owners of divination businesses with the fragilely transnational lives of ex-migrant and refugee laborers. Along with chapter 6, which details the affectivity of divination as a labor of living precariously, this chapter suggests that reading the transformation of the feminized postsecular feeling labors of fortune-telling is akin to divining the futures of working peoples under neoliberal capitalism, who are pushed to feel their own and others' way through unevenly distributed and compounded precarities by means of therapeutically tinted self-entrepreneurship in an increasingly digitally mediated transnational economy.

Coda
FEMINIST DIVINATIONS

This book has explored the gendered feeling labors of divination as a way to attune to the exacerbated precariousness secular Muslim women and LGBTIQ individuals endure as a result of the coimbricated formations of heteropatriarchy, neoliberalism, (post)secularism, and Islamist authoritarianism. By zooming in on the affects, sociabilities, and labors through which feminized subjects navigate these larger formations, we see how, even as the metanarratives promising a linear development of secularization, a democratized public sphere, increased economic opportunity, and more progressive gender policies fail to deliver, gender and sexual minorities manage to keep their spirits renewed and their livelihoods reinvented. As a means available to them for navigating their feelings of unsettlement in response to their regularly raised and then frustrated hopes, fortune-telling enables women and LGBTIQ individuals in Turkey to feel their way through their precarious livelihoods, secular Muslim identities, and alternative publics. Inspired by the resilience and subtlety of these gendered practices of divination, this book ultimately proposes feeling as a feminist analytic of attunement that can highlight minoritized and feminized ways of living and understanding the world.

The lens of feeling employed here joins calls for "affecting feminism" in order to critically scrutinize the analytical and political potentials of feminist engagements with emotion, affect, and feeling (Pedwell and Whitehead 2012). One does not need to believe in divination to get one's fortune told or even to read fortunes, for that matter; one needs only to engage in it: "Don't believe in fortune-telling, but don't do without it either." The feeling labor entailed in reading one's fortune and getting one's fortune told—opening oneself to feeling and being felt—is the process through which believable projections are generated, even if only provisionally, until they are proven right or wrong. Paradoxically, feminist insight derived from Muslim Egyptian women's piously religious practices, which asserts that belief does not necessarily precede practice but is instead inculcated through it (Mahmood 2001, 2005), also holds true for the popular forms of fortune-telling practiced by nonpious secular Muslim women in Turkey. The feminist redemption of pious Muslim women and the rethinking of feminist agency associated with thinking beyond the categorical distinctions of religious/secular and pious/nonpious challenges commonsense assumptions that pious women live by faith and secular women by reason. If, as can be seen in the feminized publics of divination in Turkey, belief and doubt are not mutually exclusive but rather coconstitutive, if they neither precede nor preclude practice but are in fact entailed by it, then the assumed opposition of pious as unquestioning and secular as skeptical cannot hold. This line of thinking prompts both a revaluation of the otherized pious subject of feminism and a reexamination of the hegemonic secular subject. Reckoning with the discovery that the secular facade of gendered agency conceals within it a complexity and dynamism of belief, doubt, and practice for secular and religious women alike might even inspire a rethinking of the ways feminism's subjects and affects have been imagined.

What might feminism(s) feel like if envisioned via the inherently contradictory dialectic of faith and skepticism that underlies the feeling labors of divination? Feminist and queer scholars have engaged with hope and its coconstitutive companion of hopelessness (Coleman and Ferreday 2010; Duggan and Muñoz 2009) to insist on a nonnaive hope that may be used to fuel the quest of collectively envisioning feminist and queer desirable futures, even if only strategically and in fleetingly stable fashion. By embracing the tongue-in-cheek belief of divination's practitioners, a belief held not through the exclusion of doubt but through an active engagement with it, this book (re)invests in the possibility of collectively conjuring feminist feelings through a practice of feminist divination that reworks the age-old saying about fortune-telling: "Don't believe in feminism, but don't do without it either."

Feminists around the world are having to reckon with the perilous fortunes of feminism in the new millennium (Fraser 2013): their unholy alliances with neoliberalism and neoimperialism; the mainstreaming and co-optation of their premises; masculinist pushback; and the discontents unleashed by racial and sexual differences among feminists themselves. Could such a practice of feminist divination inspire the precise mix of belief and doubt, faith and skepticism, necessary for conjuring feminist scenarios in which we might feel our way through the tangle of fears, hopes, and desires we harbor about our many-dimensioned gendered precariousness? Could feminist divinations practiced in the intimate company of fellow feminists help us find and offer the care we need to sustain us in this reckoning work?

The feminist visioning work that can be facilitated by feminist divinations doesn't require that we rush to extremes: on one hand, prescriptive and normative formulations which demand that we abandon our differently positioned and articulated feelings and skepticisms in the name of a collective political leap of faith; on the other, pessimistic and ineffectual formulations which demand that we abandon our collective faith in politics in the name of our differently positioned and articulated feelings and skepticisms. What it does require is a vulnerable openness to affecting and being affected by one another in the presence of what Clare Hemmings (2012) calls "affective dissonance." Whereas Hemmings deploys "affective dissonance" to scrutinize the feminist political potential of the felt discrepancy between "one's sense of self and the possibilities for its expression and validation" (2012, 154), a dissonance valuable because of its potential to produce feminist feelings, I extend the term here to include the sense of unsettlement driven by the felt mismatch between the myriad forms of gendered predicaments that may bring us into feminism in the first place and the failure of currently existing or dominating feminist political repertoires to do justice to them. Feeling labors of divination might inspire us in our quest to live with such feminist affective dissonance. After all, an apt fortune-teller knows to persist through many failed predictions and accept them as part of the process of attuning to a client, just as an open client continues to invest in the affective circuit of a fortune-telling session through the inevitable misrecognitions fortune-telling generates. It is this kind of intersubjective feeling labor that can foster feminist affective solidarities. In times of transnational unsettlement driven by the ruins of neoliberalism and neoimperialism—rising authoritarianism, revitalized xenophobia, multiplying racisms, religiously tinted reactionary gendered conservatisms, and scorching feminist (self-)critiques—this book insists on the urgent need for a politically inflected feeling labor serviceable enough to grow the feminist feelings necessary for attuning with each other to conjure livable collective futures.

Notes

1 By the term *secularism* (*laiklik*), I refer to, in the Turkish case, a historically state-sponsored modernist nationalist ideology and social engineering project, as well as a basis for social and political identity. By *secular*, I refer to a sociocultural construct that is historically contingent, contested, and dependent upon its other, the religious.

2 I use the participle *feminized*, as opposed to *women's*, *female*, or *feminine*, to emphasize that feminization is an active, accumulated, and ongoing relation of power and subjectification.

3 In the context of this research, I use the term *secular Muslim* to refer to those for whom religion does not constitute a central or significant reference point for living and narrating their lives, even as they identify as Muslims and/or believers, and for whom secularity operates as a marker of a particular (socioeconomic class) habitus and lifestyle. I deploy the term *secularist* to refer to those who are aligned with secularist politics in Turkey, which might mean voting for the secularist Republican People's Party (Cumhuriyet Halk Partisi), following secularist news media, and/or harboring strong secularist attachments to nationalist symbols.

4 All the readers I talked to but one, an Armenian Christian man, identified as Muslim. Of those identifying as Muslim, only one man asserted himself as an atheist, while others negotiated versions of nonpious and secular Muslim identities.

5 Here, by *feminized* I mean those women, LGBTIQ individuals, and young men who gather together in the intimacy of fortune-telling by virtue of their feminization within the heteropatriarchal hierarchies of gender, sexuality, and age. See also note 8.

6 Cup readers, whether amateurs or workers, tend to emphasize the worldly functions of their practice and de-emphasize its religious dimensions, which can be read as a secularizing gesture.

7 I deploy the term *neoliberalization* to refer to political and economic restructuring processes such as liberalization, deregulation, and privatization, and the term *neoliberalism* to refer to the ideological and governmentalizing rationales that legitimize

neoliberal economic transformations and that prescribe the institutional and individual techniques of (self-)governance facilitating these transformations.

8   Here I use *precarious(ness)* in multiple ways: first, to connote a labor condition that is generalized, intensified, and normalized under neoliberalism; second and more broadly, to convey the larger (existential) sense of insecurity and vulnerability of (intimate) life that is unevenly and intersectionally distributed across populations along the axes of gender and sexuality as well as race/ethnicity, religious and secular identity, and class; and third, as a structure of feeling. I frequently deploy the phrase *labor precarity* in reference to the first sense of the term. For a discussion of the different ways in which precarity and precariousness are defined in the literature, see Puar (2012).

9   I use the adjective *young* to refer to men who populate fortune-telling cafés as clients and workers. These are men primarily in their teens or twenties, and less often in their thirties, who are single, do not have children, and who struggle to make a living. In this work, *young* therefore refers less to a category of biological age and more to a social construct informed by the relational power differentials intrinsic to heteropatriarchal domination. Here, the term *young men* refers to males who are not (yet) admitted to heteronormative adult masculinity as associated with breadwinner status, marriage, fatherhood, and so on. Based on this definition, I use *young and gay men* repeatedly as a single phrase to describe heterosexual and gay young men together to emphasize their affinity in terms of their exclusion from masculine privileges tied to hegemonic adult masculinity and their feminization in relations of heteropatriarchal subjection.

10   See Gürsel (2009, 2012) for a highly perceptive take on coffee divination as a means by which Turkish people negotiate and process the uncertainties and ambiguities produced by Turkey's decades-long bid for European Union membership. Also see Seremetakis (2009) for an insightful discussion of cup readings and associated practices such as evil eye treatments and dream interpretations and related involuntary bodily gestures somatic registrations of and the means for reading the effects of broader social transformations on the individual.

11   The research took me to many locations hosting commercial fortune-tellers, including websites, offices, restaurants, bars, and even campgrounds, as well as the houses of fortune-tellers who worked from home. But my main site remained fortune-telling cafés. I spent many months at the first fortune-telling café I gained entry to, and I acquainted myself with the rhythms and patterns of daily life at a divination business and the practices of divination itself. Following this extended entry, I expanded my research to other businesses where fortune-tellers worked, which my initial interlocutors had introduced me to, and later to other fortune-telling cafés I sampled because of their size or location to reflect the diversity of divination businesses available. I returned to these individual fortune-telling cafés several times over days or weeks to acquaint myself with the owners and the readers, observe the interactions between owners, readers, and clients, and immerse myself in the sociabilities that the cafés hosted.

While I talked to many clients and owners of fortune-telling businesses, the main interlocutors of this research were the readers. Although I interviewed and regularly interacted with a number of café owners, some of whom doubled as readers, my relationships with owners were often limited to obtaining their permission as gatekeepers to conduct research at their café. Similarly, while I regularly engaged in casual conversations with café clients, barring a few exceptions where I conducted interviews, these were usually one-off, passing interactions typical among clients at a café. Similarly, because of the built-in anonymity café divinations offered, with few exceptions, I observed the fortune-telling sessions of others only from a distance. At the cafés, I belonged to the circle of readers, with whom I had tea, ate, and hung out waiting for customers. From them I heard about the intimate troubles that brought clients to the café and the challenging demands owners placed on their labor. My sociabilities and loyalties lay with the readers, and I familiarized myself with the world of divination businesses from their standpoint.

12 Here I am inspired by Ann Cvetkovich, who discusses her "mixed feelings about a feminist politics of affect" (1992, 1), so as to distinguish between her scholarly and political investments in the feminist reclaiming of affect as significant and the overly optimistic and co-opted promise that articulations of feminized affect in the political and public realms are necessarily transformative.

13 See also Korkman (2021) for an extended discussion of subversion via mimicry of the gendered conventions of Turkish secularism and the attendant destabilization of the coconstitutive binaries of secular/religious and male/female.

14 See chapter 6 for an in-depth discussion of the distinctions and relations between the terms *affect*, *emotion*, and *feeling* in relation to my conceptualization of divination labor.

1. CRIMES OF DIVINATION

1 Law No. 677, "The Abolition of Dervish Lodges, Cloisters, Shrines, and Related Titles," enacted by the Turkish parliament on November 30, 1925.

2 "Savcılık fal kafelerin peşine düştü!," *Haber 3*, December 8, 2005, https://www .haber3.com/guncel/savcilik-fal-kafelerin-pesine-dustu-haberi-40922. All transla-tions in this book are my own.

3 Fortune-telling cafés had already gained nationwide visibility in the media, but until December 2005 were typically covered in a lighthearted tone as human interest stories.

4 Within Turkish criminal law, prosecutors have the right and the duty to investigate any crimes against the public committed within their jurisdiction, even when there is no grievance or no injured party, or when the injured party does not resort to criminal prosecution. Despite his track record as a zealous guardian of the secular nation, Türkaslan had not understood the infraction against secularist laws these fortune-telling cafés posed until the issue was brought to his attention by İsa Güven, the chair of the Ankara Association of Coffeehouses. Arguing that the emergent fad of fortune-telling in cafés amounted to unjust competition that threatened the economic livelihood of coffeehouses, Güven demanded that the municipality inter-vene to protect the interests of the constituency he represented as guild organization chair by limiting these cafés' services to those legally specified within municipal

regulations. Güven's demands were thus based on the principles of fair competition and the infraction of municipal regulations, not on criminal law. It was Türkaslan who translated Güven's administrative and economic complaint into the framework of a criminal threat against the public.

5 While neither Turkey nor its predecessor, the Ottoman Empire, were ever formally colonized, the Ottoman Empire of the twentieth century faced an imminent threat of colonization. This threat infused modern Turkishness with a sense of inferiority and vulnerability vis-à-vis the West and rendered the making of Turkish national identity an almost postcolonial project.

6 While the highest religious authority/highest judge, held by the office of the Sheikh-ul-Islam (*şeyhülislam*), was authorized to issue religious opinions that could either legitimize the sultan's policies or denounce them as contrary to the prevailing religious orthodoxy, all members of the ulema class were state servants appointed and deposed by the head of state, the sultan (Berkes [1964] 1998).

7 For academic studies on Zati as a geomancer (*remmal*) and poet, see Fleischer (2001) and Kim (2017).

8 For the new Turkish state to establish itself as a secular republic, it had to control religion with both repressive and productive measures, from the cleansing of undesired religious elements to the production of national religious dogma (Parla and Davison 2008).

9 This law was one of the "revolution laws," special-status laws that cannot be revoked on the basis of infraction of constitutional rights. This special status indicates the perceived vulnerability of the republic's secularizing reforms, the tension between its democratic aspirations and its authoritarian tendencies, and a preference for the second in the case of a conflict between democracy and authoritarian secularism. Revolution laws include the exile of the caliphate, the secularization and nationalization of education, the establishment of the Diyanet, the adoption of the Latin alphabet and numbers, the introduction of surnames to replace various types of banned personal titles, the introduction of European hats to replace various types of banned traditional headwear, the banning of religious apparel, the secularization of the marriage contract, and the abolition of religious orders.

2. THE GENDERED POLITICS OF SECULARISM

1 The competition between secular and religious authority persisted over the use of the word *hodja* itself, a title used by religious scholars in the Ottoman Empire that now conjures up a variety of secular and religious meanings, including preacher and teacher in contemporary Turkish. The secularist distinction between the scholarly and the religious rendered everyday uses of the term contentious. Secularist teachers corrected students who addressed them as "hodja" (*hoca*) instead of "teacher" (*öğretmen*) by admonishing that "the hodja is in the mosque." But the "ignorant" kind of hodja Atatürk had associated with the traditional class of religious practitioners of his era and had deemed a corrupting influence on the nation (Atatürk 1989, 148) belonged neither to the mosque nor anywhere else in the new nation, except as a figure of othering and criminalization.

2   The gendered difference of reason and superstition through which claims to secularity are advanced is not fixed upon a stable binary of sex/gender difference that can be taken for granted, but is constructed actively and intersectionally in and through the making of different kinds of masculinities and femininities and the relationships among them, as detailed in this chapter.

3   See also chapter 3 for the constitutive relation between assertions of secular identity and negotiations of partial relief from the gendered expectations of modesty.

4   An Islamicate formation of intimacy (Göle 1996; Sehlikoglu 2016), *mahrem* denotes those who are closely related and thus forbidden to each other in marriage. See part II for an extended discussion.

5   *Ablam* literally means "my older sister," a polite form of address for an older woman.

6   While male *cinci* hodjas are the preferred figures of secularist targeting, women may also provide healing and divinatory services associated with hodjas.

7   During our interview, Ayşe did not comment further on her husband or domestic violence.

8   *Tabir* originally refers to the Sufi art of the interpretation of dreams (Mittermaier 2010; Sviri 1999), a popular practice that was also prevalent in the Ottoman period. Based upon the Islamic understanding that some dreams carry divine messages such as warnings or portents, *tabir* is based upon knowledge of the hidden meanings of specific dream objects and scenes. Numerous booklets outlining these meanings, called *tabirname*, have been in circulation since the fourteenth century (Balaban 2014). Both the word *tabir* and its modern Turkish equivalent, *yorum* (interpretation), are commonly used by fortune-tellers as they describe their practice and extend the method of dream interpretation to reading the random shapes assumed by coffee grounds. This coffee-reading method has been increasingly codified and standardized over the last decades, especially with the emergence of a new market in fortune-telling books and websites in which coffee residue shapes and interpretations may be established, widely circulated, and made instantly available.

9   Perhaps understandably, tarot readers often complain about the increasing popularity and availability of tarot cards and guidebooks and speak nostalgically of the days when one needed to spend considerable time, energy, and money to get access to the cards and their instructions.

10 See chapter 6 for a close examination of the processes of feeling in divination.

11 See chapter 7 for a longer discussion of the eclectic deployment of new age and Sufi discourses and techniques by commercial fortune-tellers.

12 "Ünlü yoga hocasına şok suçlama," *Hürriyet*, July 14, 2014, accessed December 4, 2019, http://www.hurriyet.com.tr/unlu-yoga-hocasina-sok-suclama-26824099.

13 "Amacımız," Yoga Academy, accessed December 5, 2019, http://www.yogaakademi.com.

14 "İçişleri 'yoga' fetvası istedi," *Milliyet*, October 25, 2013, https://www.milliyet.com.tr/gundem/icisleri-yoga-fetvasi-istedi-1782003.

15 "Anasayfa," Uğur Koşar, accessed December 5, 2019, https://www.ugurkosar.com.

16 "'Uğur Koşar' Kimdir?," Uğur Koşar, accessed December 5, 2019, https://www.ugurkosar.com/d/4/ugur-kosar-kimdir.html.

17 Gül Senocak, "Uğur Koşar yorumlar," comment on Uğur Koşar, accessed December 5, 2019, https://www.ugurkosar.com/danisanlarimizin-yorumlari#679.

18 Eda C., "Uğur Koşar yorumlar," comment on Uğur Koşar, accessed December 5, 2019, https://www.ugurkosar.com/danisanlarimizin-yorumlari?Pagenum=2&#413.

19 Özge Şişmanoğlu, "Uğur Koşar yorumlar," comment on Uğur Koşar, accessed December 5, 2019, https://www.ugurkosar.com/danisanlarimizin-yorumlari#682.

20 "Uğur Koşar," Kitapyurdu, accessed December 5, 2019, https://www.kitapyurdu .com/index.php?route=product/manufacturer_products&manufacturer_id =50638&limit=100.

21 "Neo-kadercinin başucu kitapları," Milliyet, May 15, 2007, https://www.milliyet .tr/kultur-sanat/neo-kadercinin-basucu-kitaplari-966173.

22 "Rekortmene fotoşok . . . Uğur Koşar'a boşanma davası," Hürriyet, October 8, 2016, accessed December 4, 2019, http://www.hurriyet.com.tr/rekortmene-fotosok -40243543\.

23 Haberler.com, "Uğur Koşar, 'Beni Aldattı' Diyen Eşiyle Canlı Yayında Yüzleşti," Dailymotion, video, 3:35, October 13, 2016, https://www.dailymotion.com/video/x4x9p5d. See chapter 5 for a discussion of the intimate publics convened in daytime shows and their relation to the intimacies conjured by divinatory and associated practices.

24 "'Cinci Hoca'ya canlı yayında gözaltı," Milliyet, February 18, 2009, https://www .milliyet.com.tr/pembenar/cinci-hoca-ya-canli-yayinda-gozalti-1061079.

3. FEELING POSTSECULAR

1 Atatürk, "Arkadaşlar kahve fincanında ki şekilde ne görüyorsunuz lütfen yorum yapar mısınız, bir ben mi görüyorum?," Facebook, April 15, 2015, https://www .facebook.com/UluOnderimMustafaKemal/photos/a.10151478877812740 .1073741825.42566217739/10153039138907740/?type=1&theater.

2 While the hegemony of secularism has been decisively unsettled by the growing political potency of Islamism and the increasing public presence of Islamic discourses and practices in twenty-first-century Turkey, such denormativization denotes less a radical historical break and more a culmination of the contradictions endemic to Turkish secularism from its very beginnings. Since the early twentieth century, Turkey has radically transformed important facets of institutional and social life such as family law and education and has forcibly exiled undesired religious practices and practitioners from the public sphere in the name of secularization, all the while also heavily investing in a state-controlled version of Islam and mobilizing Islamic discourses for popular legitimacy. Even at the height of its secular reforms in the 1920s and 1930s, the secularist Turkish state thoroughly institutionalized a state Islam and drew upon Islamicate idioms such as the gazi (Islamic warrior) title, which Atatürk himself proudly carried (Ahmad 1993). Following the end of the single-party rule of the secularist Republican People's Party in 1950 and the coming to power of populist governments that were more hospitable to Islamic discourses and public presences (even as they avoided challenging the state's secularist tenets), religion has been mobilized with increasing visibility and fervor. Religion was further rallied in the

post-1980 military coup era with the official reinstatement of Islam as an antidote to widespread leftist mobilization and the resultant popular rise of Islamist political parties in the 1990s (Hale and Ozbudun 2009). While Islamist movements in Turkey are plural and complex, with multiple and competing lineages and trajectories, and are produced at the conjuncture of various local and transnational shifts and flows, it suffices here to emphasize that the Islam-friendly populist governmental gestures of the post-1950s included policies that both tempered the secularist reforms of the early Republican era and provided heightened tolerance and public visibility for a host of exiled religious figures, including fortune-tellers.

3   While the provision of commercial divination via broadcasting would later be banned, fortune-tellers worked to stay one step ahead of the disciplining apparatus of the state by relocating their services to yet-to-be-regulated venues.

4   Although, as forms, "Turkish" coffee and coffee cup readings are certainly not limited to Turkey but are commonly found in the Balkans, the Middle East, and beyond, they are nevertheless consumed in Turkey within a national tradition that evokes a sense of "we-ness" crucial for the imagination of national community, now layered with a reinherited Ottoman past that evokes a sense of continuity and community for the Turkish heirs of the Ottoman Empire. It was in this context that Turkish coffee was branded as a local tradition by social actors ranging from neighborhood fortune-telling cafés to national café chains, providing novel, "tasteful" ways of drinking Turkish coffee and having one's cup read (Korkman 2015c).

5   See part III for a close examination of the double status of divinations as both a symptom and a remedy for neoliberal precarity, intensified by the declining political and economic prospects of secularists in the Turkey of the early twenty-first century.

6   I have observed many veiled women and women who subscribed to more conventional Sunni forms of Islamic piety such as daily prayers as clients and providers of commercial cup readings and other kinds of divinations at home-based divination businesses, but given the ethnographic focus of my research in fortune-telling cafés and my own situated position within a secular and mostly secularist family and social network that shaped my access to underground fortune-telling sites, veiled and/or pious woman were underrepresented in this research.

7   See part II for an extensive discussion of cafés in the context of the gendered politics of the public sphere and secularism in Turkey. See also Deeb and Harb (2013) for a rich analysis of Lebanese negotiations of piety and gendered morality in the context of cafés.

8   "Turkish Deputy Prime Minister Says Women Should Not Laugh Out Loud," *Guardian*, July 29, 2014, https://www.theguardian.com/world/2014/jul/29/turkish-minister-women-laugh-loud-bulent-arinc.

9   According to Article 82 of Law No. 6111, businesses are required to obtain (and previously to display in their place of business) a tax registration certificate listing their business's earnings and consequent tax base, updated yearly.

10 This is not to say that fortune-tellers who present as pious Muslims are not taking advantage of legalization opportunities. They are, however, more likely to be working from home offices and online venues and were thus less likely to be subjects of

this ethnographic research. In one example, in 2014, Leman Hasar, a fortune-telling woman in her early thirties, was featured in newspapers as a criminal subject for having committed the crime of "fraud by the abuse of religious beliefs and feelings" ("Yaptığım işten dolayı devlete vergi ödüyorum," *Milliyet*, January 20, 2014, https://www.milliyet.com.tr/gundem/yaptigim-isten-dolayi-devlete-vergi-oduyorum-1824616). Accompanying a photo featuring Hasar sporting a confident smile and dressed in an elaborate white-and-pink sateen veil and dress, possibly her wedding gown, was a summary of her client's legal complaint. Her Istanbul-based client, a twentysomething single woman, had located Adana-based Hasar's phone number on her website, titled Medyum Sevda, and had wired her a payment for fortune-telling, approximately twice the amount she would pay at a café. According to the complaint, Hasar read her fortune the same day and explained that because of a malicious spell, her boyfriend would marry someone else. Their exchanges initiated repeated services of fortune-telling and spell dispelling, for which the client eventually paid over twenty times the initial fee. Unable to rekindle her relationship with her boyfriend and with Hasar demanding further payment, the client pressed charges. In her defense, Hasar presented her tax license that read "fortune-telling, astrology, and spiritualist services" as evidence. "What I am doing is completely legal. I even have a tax license for it. This person located me from my website and called me. She agreed to pay for a reading. I tried to help her. With her request and within my legal rights, I read her fortune. I [always] issue a receipt for the fees I receive and I pay my taxes." Hasar was eventually judged not guilty. The judge's decision was explained as being "due to insufficient evidence," but Hasar's unusual evidence of a tax license may very well have played a role.

11 See the Turkish Ministry of Industry and Trade law, BIK-TPE: 2002/2.

12 Two other amendments to Law No. 677 allowed for the restoration and opening to visitation of the Sufi shrines closed in 1925, in 1950, upon the permission of the Council of Ministers (Law No. 5566/1), and forty years later in 1990, upon the permission of the Ministry of Culture (Law No. 3612/5). Coming in the 1950s as part of many governmental gestures toward remeasuring Turkey's relationship with Islam and tempering earlier secularization, such as a return from Turkish to Arabic call to prayer and rekindling political relationships with select religious orders, the 1950 amendment allowed for the reopening of shrines that belong to "notable Turkish figures" as well as those with "high art value," encouraging the restoration primarily of those shrines housing the graves of the political figures of mainstream Turkish and Ottoman history, the pashas and sultans, but not those of religious figures. The shrines to be opened would be designated by the Ministry of Education and approved by the Council of Ministers. The 1990 amendment, arriving in a later neoliberal moment of expansion of religious discourses and practices into an expanding public sphere as well as everyday and consumption spaces, transferred the capacity to readmit certain places of worship into public visibility to the exclusive purview of the Ministry of Culture, thereby culturalizing religious orders and practices. By throwing the modernist relations between tradition, religion, and secularism into question, this latter culturalization of religion and tradition reflects

a larger epistemological shift that profoundly shapes the dynamics of a postsecular condition in Turkey.

13 See the Court of Cassation decision, Yargıtay E: 1955/9, K: 1955/17, T: 6/7/1955.

14 A closer analysis of the applications of Law No. 677 and TCK 158 in this context would require a systematic study of the court cases over time, which is beyond the scope of this research. Here, I draw on the wording of the law, relevant Supreme Court decisions, and media reports of related individual court cases.

15 "Diyanet'ten 'fal' hutbesi," *Hürriyet*, January 31, 2002, https://www.hurriyet.com.tr /gundem/diyanetten-fal-hutbesi-51756.

4. FEELING PUBLICS OF FEMININITY

1 Frequently attending studies of sociospatial formations of gendered intimacy in Islamicate contexts is the assumption that the private is female and apolitical, while the public is male and political and thus separate from the private. This assumption is misleading in the Turkish context of today (Göle 1996) and was misleading in the Ottoman context of the past (Peirce 1993). In the imperial cosmology, *harem* designated not only the domestic and the female quarters but also the sacred and the forbidden, including the holy cities of Islam and the domestic quarters of the sultan himself. Because it is premised on the logic of *mahrem*, harem was not ordered by a simple segregation of the sexes; men who were already married to or who were not marriageable to women in harem were part of harem, as were preadolescent boys and in some cases the liminal figures of eunuchs (Lad 2010). What is more, from the corridors of imperial harem to the street corners and cul-de-sacs of neighborhoods, harem extended out into and was surrounded by liminal spaces. Importantly, from the palace down to the houses of lower officials, this domestic space was the very place of the political. Set outside the public and political spheres in European political thought, family and domestic life was also a legitimate terrain of Islamic law. In contrast to the dichotomies of public/commonwealth/male versus private/domestic/female, Peirce (1993) claims that Ottomans understood and ordered space according to the dichotomies of elite/sacred/inside versus mass/profane/outside and that political power resided in the first part of the dichotomy. In particular, the distinction of in(side)/out(side), or *iç(eri)/dış(arı)*, was more indicative of the structures of power and authority than the dichotomy of public/private.

2 Historically, this social ordering of gender and sexuality has interacted with hierarchies of power, social standing, age, and notions of social modesty to produce different formations of *mahrem* (see Andrews and Kalpakli 2005; Babayan and Najmabadi 2008; El-Rouayheb 2005; Najmabadi 2005; Peirce 2009; Ze'evi 2006).

3 Here I take a cue from Roderick Ferguson (2004) in highlighting the centrality of pushing otherized peoples out of gendered and sexual normativity in the making and maintainence of racial formations.

4 Nadia Seremetakis (2009) similarly categorizes the cup-reading practices of Greek women as properly belonging to the private and feminine spaces.

5 Among the more idiosyncratic strategies that signify fortune-telling cafés as hospitable to feminized intimate publics is the offering of free food to women on March 8, International Women's Day, a significant if not entirely intentional gesture which the Angels Café's owner explained as a pious remembrance of his beloved mother, who had passed away on that very day.

6 Such policing is not exclusive to fortune-telling cafés but is present in other public businesses hosting mixed-gender socializing such as teahouses, cafés, bars, and clubs where men not accompanied by women may be explicitly prevented entry. Such policing rules are often announced with signs reading *Damsız Girilmez* (No Entry without an Adult Woman) or *Aile Salonu* (Family Salon, with the word *family* referring to the wife and close/*mahrem* opposite-sex relatives of a man).

7 Indeed, while most businesses do not combine divinatory and beauty salon services, fortune-telling cafés have curious similarities to women's hair and waxing salons, many of which admit solely female clients in Turkey. The affinity between fortune-telling cafés and these beauty salons finds its expression in a transfer of colloquialism from hair or waxing salon to fortune-telling café, where a customer may be greeted with the peculiar expression a hairdresser or waxing client expects to hear, "What will it be? [*Ne olacaktı?*]" Like fortune-telling cafés, men with what is culturally intelligible as a feminine gender expression regularly serve the female clientele of women's hair salons, not only by providing the particular salon service being paid for but also by lending an ear to their clients' private troubles and partaking in intimate conversations, thanks to their unthreatening gender performance.

8 See Liebelt (2016) for a thoughtful discussion of intimacy (*mahremiyet/samimiyet*) in beauty salons in Istanbul, with attention to the ways in which commodified bodily intimacies are configured in salons run and frequented by secular and pious women of different socioeconomic classes in similar and divergent ways.

9 After the targeted demolition and gradual transformation of Beyoğlu by the government following the Gezi Protests of 2013, many of these sociabilities and the businesses hosting them, including fortune-telling cafés, migrated to the district of Kadıköy and especially to Moda neighborhood, which already hosted a comparable if relatively smaller and less diverse social life.

10 Cayisallama, "Kahvehane ile kafe arasındaki farklar," *Öğretmen Sözlük*, August 21, 2015, https://ogretmensozluk.net/kahvehane-ile-kafe-arasindaki-farklar_4592.

11 For a more in-depth review of the bifurcation of this-worldly (secular) and heavenly (religious) powers into two distinct and competing spheres through the process of secularization during the late Ottoman period of modernization, see chapter 1.

12 Women's gender-segregated consumption of coffee in a commercial venue outside the house had parallels to men's gender-segregated consumption of coffee in coffeehouses in its facilitation of sociabilities outside the domestic realm. While women's early coffee consumption outside the domestic space and the intimacies it fostered may also be compared to contemporary feminized coffee publics like those nestled in fortune-telling cafés, the former was accessed exclusively by women (and their young male children), categorically excluded postpubescent men, and was not in physical and cultural proximity of mixed-gender publics.

13 Shopping malls have also been described as democratized public spaces for women (Durakbaşa and Cindoğlu 2002) and as spaces for empowering femininities and queer visibilities (Özbay 2015).

14 See chapter 3 for a more in-depth discussion of the commodification of reinvented traditions in this context.

15 "Feministler Bu Kez Kahve Bastı," *Milliyet*, November 26, 1989, 3.

5. THE JOYS AND PERILS OF INTIMACY

1 See Seremetakis (2009) for a discussion of cup reading and related beliefs and practices such as the use of the evil eye as a means for negotiating what she calls voluntary and involuntary social intimacies in Greece.

2 The dynamics of intimacy and (dis)embeddedness are fluid. Even in fortune-telling cafés, the disembedded intimacies of commercial divination are not always distinct from the embedded intimacies of existing relationships, especially relations among friends and, more rarely, among cross-generational family members who get readings together.

At a home-based fortune-telling party, I sit, hanging out with a group of women in the living room, each of us waiting for our turn with the commercial fortune-teller who is doing cup readings in the privacy of the kitchen table. Most of the women here already know each other as former work colleagues. We are well-educated, middle-class women in our late twenties and thirties. Some of us have left careers to raise children, but most are still employed, which makes a Sunday afternoon the best time to gather. Our host's husband departs with their toddler to leave the house men- and child-free for the party. The hostess serves tea and coffee and adds guests' baked goods to the table, which she has already filled with many offerings. We snack and chat, listening to those returning from the kitchen recount how their reading has gone. One woman shares that the fortune-teller knew everything about her, even that she is on the verge of a divorce. As we listen with curiosity, another woman whispers that the reader even saw in the cup of her divorcing friend the "other man" she had shared a kiss with. I worry that the divulging of this sensitive piece of information might hurt its owner should it circulate beyond this circle of friends, rendering her vulnerable, for example, to retribution in her marital relationship or to an unfavorable outcome in a custody battle. Even within commercial contexts, the intimate sharing that comes with fortune-telling might render women vulnerable to gossiping, shaming, control, and retaliation.

3 While readers often describe this newfound intimacy in the familiar vocabularies of kinship, neighborliness, and friendship to emphasize its authenticity and render it legitimate, the fact is that they cannot effectively gossip about their clients. In a society where kinship provides a very strong template for giving meaning to sociability and intimacy in most spheres of social life beyond the familial, the affinities of divination intimacy are regularly expressed in the language of or compared directly to kinship. While it is common for clients to describe readers as motherly or sisterly and for readers to insist that "we are like family here" to communicate the closeness

that makes it possible for them to address intimate issues comfortably, the fact remains that they are not family. Öznur explains the complexities to me: "Sometimes daughters come first, and then bring along their mothers. The whole family comes. They come together." But she then adds, "They each trust that I will not relate one family member's words to the other."

4 Akınerdem (2019) similarly discusses the uses of anonymity in intimate publics of women's marriage-themed social media groups, where women negotiate *mahremiyet* by intimately sharing personal details while anonymizing their identities, especially when they stray from the norm.

5 For an insightful analysis of the fantasies of family and the transgressions and violences surrounding the familial norm in reality shows and television serials in the Turkish media, see Sirman (2019).

6 "Evlilik konusunda çok seçici olmayın," *Milliyet*, July 19, 2014, https://www.milliyet .com.tr/evlilik-konusunda-cok-secici/siyaset/detay/1913996/default.htm.

7 "Erdoğan: Sezaryene karşıyım, kürtaj cinayettir," *T24*, May 25, 2012, https://t24 .com.tr/haber/erdogan-sezaryene-karsiyim-kurtaj-cinayettir,204821.

8 "Nerede, nasıl, kimle Tayyip bunlardan sanane!," *KaosGL*, November 11, 2013. https://kaosgl.org/haber/lsquonerede-nasil-kimle-tayyip-bunlardan-sananersquo. Feminist and LGBTIQ activists regularly and strategically address Erdoğan by his first name, Tayyip, as they would someone intimate, such as a family member or close friend. This gesture critiques by mimicking what they deem to be the inappropriate intimacy Erdoğan seeks with (particularly women) citizens by talking about intimate issues such as reproduction. For a closer analysis of the role of language in challenging Erdoğan's intimately gendered rule, see Korkman and Açıksöz (2014).

9 "CHP'li Nazlıaka: Başbakan vajina bekçiliğini bıraksın!," *T24*, May 26, 2012, https://t24.com.tr/haber/chpli-nazliaka-basbakan-vajina-bekciligini-biraksin,204868.

10 The masculinist pushback against perceived relaxation of conventional norms of gendered propriety was in the making long before the twenty-first century. It was in 1990, while presiding over a special commission to protect the Turkish family, that Family and Social Policy minister Cemil Çiçek declared flirting, prostitution, and feminism to be perversions, triggering a feminist protest (see Koçali 2002).

11 "Davutoğlu: Aileniz eş bulamazsa bize başvuracaksınız," *Al Jazeera*, October 22, 2015, http://www.aljazeera.com.tr/haber/davutoglu-aileniz-es-bulamazsa-bize -basvuracaksiniz.

12 Aytuğ (2010); "Women Organizations Protest Seda Sayan," *Bianet*, September 5, 2014, https://bianet.org/english/women/158320-women-organizations-protest -seda-sayan.

13 Similarly, in bride blogs, women share intimately about married life, consulting, advising, and judging each other per their proximity or distance from the fantasy of a happy marriage (Akınerdem 2019).

14 "Radyo ve Televizyon Kuruluş ve Yayın Hizmetleri Hakkında Kanun," Mevzuat Bilgi Systemi, February 15, 2011, https://www.mevzuat.gov.tr/MevzuatMetin/1.5.6112.pdf.

15 "Seda Sayan'ın programına rekor ceza," *Cumhuriyet*, March 24, 2014, https://www .cumhuriyet.com.tr/haber/seda-sayanin-programina-rekor-ceza-53687.

16 "RTÜK'te 'Evlilik Programları Hakkında İstişare Toplantısı' Yapıldı," RTÜK, February 17, 2016, https://www.rtuk.gov.tr/17-02-2016-rtukte-evlilik-programlari-hakkinda-istisare-toplantisi-yapildi/2767.

17 "KHK/690: Olağanüstü Hal Kapsamında Bazı Düzenlemelerin Yapılması Hakkında Kanun Hükmünde Kararname," *Resmi Gazete*, April 29, 2017, https://www.resmigazete.gov.tr/eskiler/2017/04/20170429-M1-2.htm.

18 "İki Yeni KHK Yayımlandı, Evlilik Programları Yasaklandı," *Bianet*, April 29, 2017, https://bianet.org/bianet/siyaset/186039-iki-yeni-khk-yayimlandi-evlilik-programlari-yasaklandi.

19 "KHK/690."

20 "Erdoğan'ı duygulandıran 'özel' fotoğraf: Seni seviyoruz uzun adam," *Diken*, February 2, 2016, https://www.diken.com.tr/erdogani-duygulandiran-fotograf-seni-seviyoruz-uzun-adam/.

21 "Pozantı'nın hem sanığı hem de tanığı!," *DIHA*, November 6, 2014, Accessed November 7, 2014, http://www.diclehaber.com/tr/news/content/view/428748?from=578230118.

22 "Aile hekiminden bekar genç kız babasına şok cep mesajı: Tebrikler kızınız hamile," *Hürriyet*, June 25, 2012, https://www.hurriyet.com.tr/gundem/aile-hekiminden-bekar-genc-kiz-babasina-sok-cep-mesaji-tebrikler-kiziniz-hamile-20837705.

23 "Televizyon programında evlendiği eşini öldüren adama ağırlaştırılmış müebbet," *T24*, December 16, 2015, https://t24.com.tr/haber/televizyon-programinda-evlendigi-esini-olduren-adama-agirlastirilmis-muebbet,320553.

24 For example, following the 2015 rape and murder of twenty-year-old Özgecan Aslan by the driver of the shared taxi she was riding in, a feminist campaign invited women to share their experiences of sexual harassment. In addition to other campaign actions, including large-scale commemorations of those who have been murdered, organized protests, and demands for legal justice and reform, women were encouraged to share testimonies on social media, particularly on Twitter, with the hashtag #sendeanlat (#youtelltoo). While the campaign was highly successful and empowering, having made the quotidian threat and experience of sexual violence that accompanies women's mobility in public space an object of politicized public debate, it also created new vulnerabilities. The question of who should be allowed to read, write, and comment on testimony to sexual violence on social media proved a politically sticky problem. Some women, threatened by the presence of insensitive and hostile men commenting in response to their testimonies, felt their experiences invalidated by such voyeurism and demanded more boundaries. Others felt that the openness of the platform was key to its political function. "Sosyal medyada 'Sen de anlat' kampanyası," BBC News Türkçe, February 15, 2015, https://www.bbc.com/turkce/haberler/2015/02/150212_sen_de_anlat.

6. FEELING LABORS OF DIVINATION

1 See chapter 5 for an analysis of the intimate publics in which divinations circulate.

2 Television serials in which psychological therapy scenes and gendered dramas of familial and romantic life feature prominently would arrive with much popularity

at the end of the second decade of the twenty-first century, attesting to the growing hold of therapeutic culture in Turkey and the centrality of gendered precariousness to its growing allure. See the television shows *Doğdugun Ev Kaderindir* (2019), *Masumlar Apartmanı* (2020), and *Kırmızı Oda* (2021).

3 For a thoughtful analysis of the fantasy and desire for a proper, well-lived life among lower- and middle-class married women of Istanbul, see Tekçe (2019).

4 Such unsettlement can also be thought of in terms of the structural anxieties of detraditionalization and individualization that have rendered personal life an object of intense self-reflection and self-making (Bauman 2000; Beck and Beck-Gernsheim 1995; Giddens 1991, 1992), although this phenomenon is far from neutral in terms of gender, sexuality, class, ethnicity, and race.

5 Here I am inspired by Purnima Mankekar (2015), who deploys "unsettling" as an analytic to destabilize an ostensibly coherent (in this case, Indian) notion of gendered national identity as she describes the disconcerting affective states her informants experience while they negotiate the shifting notions of Indianness.

6 Anthropologists have approached ritual as setting out a liminal space in which the established social position of the recipient is in limbo (Turner 1977). As a quasi-ritual that brackets the recipient into an enchanted space of feeling and reflection, coffee cup reading can also be thought of in terms of liminality. But rather than transitioning the recipient out of liminality, readings attract and hold individuals who are unsettled in liminality, whether they are single as a matter of life stage, unemployed as a result of labor precarity, or disoriented in an era of swift societal change. Importantly, their liminal position may carry the expectation of, but does not (anymore) securely promise, a stable social position as the next step.

7 Cvetkovich (2012) explores in depth depression's potential for reflecting on what is problematic or stuck yet is not in need of (biomedical) therapeutic interventions; stuck not simply or necessarily at the individual, psychological level, but also at the social and existential level.

7. ENTREPRENEURIAL FORTUNES

1 See chapter 6 for a closer discussion of the therapeutic ethos of neoliberalism as a response to neoliberally exacerbated precariousness.

2 See chapters 2 and 3 for a closer analysis of such (g)localization.

3 The AKP government similarly relies on religiously inflected homophobia and misogyny to discipline those who stray from the prescribed path, for example, when the president supported a top cleric who declared nonmarital sex and homosexuality to be evil or when he commented that feminists fail to understand how women are not equal to men, but are different by nature/creation (*fitrat*). "Turkish President Backs Up Cleric Who Said Homosexuality Brings Disease," April 28, 2020, NBC News, https://www.nbcnews.com/feature/nbc-out/turkish-president-backs-cleric-who-said -homosexuality-brings-disease-n1194206; "Erdoğan: Kadın-erkek eşitliği fıtrata ters," BBC News Türkçe, November 24, 2014, https://www.bbc.com/turkce/haberler/2014 /11/141124_kadininfitrati_erdogan.

4 "Bir Beyaz Yakalının Masa Başından Milyonerliğe Yolculuğu," *Demirören Haber Ajansı*, December 23, 2016, https://www.haberler.com/guncel/bir-beyaz-yakalinin-masa-basindan-milyonerlige-9091824-haberi/.

5 While the new discursive terrain of (self-)entrepreneurship and the subjectivities it hails are novel constructions in a moral universe where taking individual initiative has been de-emphasized and compliance with external factors overemphasized, as a novelty, self-entrepreneurship does not necessarily stand in contradiction to or as extraneous to the subjects who speak in its lingua franca. Instead, readers and owners speak in multiple idioms, and newer discourses are unevenly translated into and creatively articulated alongside more long-standing ones, as discussed in the previous section.

6 See chapter 3 for a detailed discussion of new legalization routes.

7 Like readers in cafés, online readers work for someone who profits from their labor and who passes on to the worker only a fraction of what the customer pays, after costs and profits have been retained. Like fortune-telling café owners, digital businesses protect this intercessory position by prohibiting readers from sharing personal and contact information with their clients.

8 On their end, customers use the website or its mobile applications to buy promotional packages they then cash in for readings. They choose a divination method, browse through readers' profiles and reviews, choose someone, fill in a short form with their name, age, marital status, occupation, and any questions they have for the reader, send in photos of their cup if asking for a coffee cup reading, send a follow-up message to the reader, and offer a score and comments in their review of the reader.

9 Included as a standard part of the service purchased, online messaging between the reader and the customer after the reading provides space to perform some alignment between the client and the reader. It is, however, separated temporally from the initial reading and restricted to a limited number of textual exchanges.

10 "Istanbul'da Arap turistin payı 8 yılda %10'dan %25'e çıktı," Turizm Güncel, June 6, 2019, https://www.turizmguncel.com/haber/Istanbulda-arap-turistin-payi-8-yilda-10dan-25e-cikti.

References

Abbas, Sadia. 2013. "The Echo Chamber of Freedom: The Muslim Woman and the Pretext of Agency." *boundary 2* 40 (1): 155–89.

Abdülaziz Bey. 1995. *Osmanli Adet, Merasim ve Tabirleri.* 2 vols. Istanbul: Tarih Vakfı Yurt Yayınları.

Abu-Lughod, Lila. 1986. *Veiled Sentiments: Honor and Poetry in a Bedouin Society.* Berkeley: University of California Press.

Abu-Lughod, Lila. 2002. "Do Muslim Women Really Need Saving? Anthropological Reflections on Cultural Relativism and Its Others." *American Anthropologist* 104 (3): 783–90.

Acar, Feride, and Gülbanu Altunok. 2013. "The 'Politics of Intimate' at the Intersection of Neo-liberalism and Neo-conservatism in Contemporary Turkey." *Women's Studies International Forum* 41:14–23. https://doi.org/10.1016/j.wsif.2012.10.001.

Açıksöz, Salih Can. 2015. "Ghosts Within: A Genealogy of War Trauma in Turkey." *Journal of the Ottoman and Turkish Studies Association* 2 (2): 259–80.

Açıksöz, Salih Can. 2019. *Sacrificial Limbs: Masculinity, Disability, and Political Violence in Turkey.* Berkeley: University of California Press.

Ağırnaslı, Suphi Nejat. 2013. *Menkibe: Mevcut, Menkul ve Müşterek Komünizmde Israr Beyanı.* Tortu Yayın Sanat Kollektifi. https://kolektiftortu.files.wordpress.com/2014/11/menkc4b1be-pdf.pdf.

Ahl, Helene Jonson. 2002. "The Construction of the Female Entrepreneur as the Other." In *Casting the Other: Maintaining Gender Inequalities in the Workplace,* edited by Barbara Czarniawska and Heather Hopfl, 64–71. Abingdon, UK: Routledge.

Ahmad, Attiya. 2017. *Everyday Conversions: Islam, Domestic Work, and South Asian Migrant Women in Kuwait.* Durham, NC: Duke University Press.

Ahmad, Feroz. 1993. *The Making of Modern Turkey.* New York: Routledge.

Ahmed, Leila. 1982. "Western Ethnocentrism and Perceptions of the Harem." *Feminist Studies* 8 (3): 521–34. https://doi.org/10.2307/3177710.

Ahmed, Sara. 2004. "Affective Economies." *Social Text* 22 (2): 117–39. https://doi.org/10.1215/01642472-22-2_79-117.

Ahmed, Sara. 2014. *The Cultural Politics of Emotion*. Edinburgh: Edinburg University Press.

Akalın, Ayşe. 2007. "Hired as a Caregiver, Demanded as a Housewife: Becoming a Migrant Domestic Worker in Turkey." *European Journal of Women's Studies* 14 (3): 209–25. https://doi.org/10.1177/1350506807079011.

Akınerdem, Feyza. 2019. "Fantasy and Judgement: Brides' Intimate Talk on Facebook." *European Journal of Turkish Studies*, no. 28, 1–15. https://doi.org/10.4000/ejts.6262.

Akınerdem, Feyza. 2020. "Women's Fragile Trust: Safety, Familiarity, and Secrecy in the Marriage Show." In *Television in Turkey: Local Production, Transnational Expansion and Political Aspirations*, edited by Yeşim Kaptan and Ece Algan, 103–23. New York: Palgrave Macmillan.

Akınerdem, Zeyneb Feyza. 2015. "Marriage Safe and Sound: Subjectivity, Embodiment and Movement in the Production Space of Television in Turkey." PhD diss., City University London.

Akkan, Başak, Mehmet Baki Deniz, and Mehmet Ertan. 2017. "The Romanization of Poverty: Spatial Stigmatization of Roma Neighborhoods in Turkey." *Romani Studies* 27 (1): 73–93. https://doi.org/10.3828/rs.2017.4.

Alarcón-Medina, Rafael. 2018. "Informational Returnees: Deportation, Digital Media, and the Making of a Transnational Cybertariat in the Mexican Call Center Industry." *Dialectical Anthropology* 42 (3): 293–308. https://doi.org/10.1007/s10624-018-9518-5.

Al-Dajani, Haya, Zografia Bika, Lorna Collins, and Janine Swail. 2014. "Gender and Family Business: New Theoretical Directions." *International Journal of Gender and Entrepreneurship* 6 (3): 218–30. https://doi.org/10.1108/IJGE-11-2013-0069.

Al-Ghazzi, Omar, and Marwan M. Kraidy. 2013. "Turkey, the Middle East and the Media | Neo-Ottoman Cool 2: Turkish Nation Branding and Arabic-Language Transnational Broadcasting." *International Journal of Communication* 7 (October): 20.

Altan-Olcay, Özlem. 2014. "Entrepreneurial Subjectivities and Gendered Complexities: Neoliberal Citizenship in Turkey." *Feminist Economics* 20 (4): 235–59. https://doi.org/10.1080/13545701.2014.950978.

Althusser, Louis. 1971. "Ideology and Ideological State Apparatuses (Notes towards an Investigation)." In *Lenin and Philosophy and Other Essays*, translated by Ben Brewster, 85–126. New York: New York University Press.

Anaz, Necati, and Ceyhun Can Ozcan. 2016. "Geography of Turkish Soap Operas: Tourism, Soft Power, and Alternative Narratives." In *Alternative Tourism in Turkey: Role, Potential Development and Sustainability*, edited by Istvan Egresi, 247–58. Cham: Springer.

Andrews, Walter G., and Mehmet Kalpakli. 2005. *The Age of Beloveds: Love and the Beloved in Early-Modern Ottoman and European Culture and Society*. Durham, NC: Duke University Press.

Arık, Hülya. 2009. "Kahvehanede Erkek Olmak: Kamusal Alanda Erkek Egemenliğin Antropolojisi." In *Cins Cins Mekan*, edited by Ayten Alkan, 168–201. Istanbul: Varlık.

Asad, Talal. 1993. *Genealogies of Religion: Discipline and Reasons of Power in Christianity and Islam*. Baltimore, MD: Johns Hopkins University Press.

Asad, Talal. 2003. *Formations of the Secular: Christianity, Islam, Modernity*. Stanford, CA: Stanford University Press.

Atatürk, Mustafa Kemal. 1989. *Atatürk'ün Söylev ve Demeçleri*, edited by Nimet Arsan. 3 vols. Ankara: Atatürk Kültür, Dil ve Tarih Yüksek Kurumu.

Atuk, Sumru. 2020. "Femicide and the Speaking State: Woman Killing and Woman (Re)making in Turkey." *Journal of Middle East Women's Studies* 16 (3): 283–306.

Aydın, Mehmet. 1995. "Fal." In *Türkiye Diyanet Vakfı İslam Ansiklopedisi*, vol. 12, 134–38. Istanbul: Türkiye Diyanet Vakfı Yayınları.

Aydüz, Salim. 2006. "Osmanlı Devleti'nde Müneccimbaşılık Müessesesi." *Belleten* 70 (257): 167–264.

Aytuğ, Yüksel. 2010. "Evlilik programında kadın, kadına talip." *Haber7com*, February 10. https://www.haber7.com/medya/haber/480733-evlilik-programinda-kadin-kadina -talip.

Baban, Feyzi, Suzan Ilcan, and Kim Rygiel. 2017. "Syrian Refugees in Turkey: Pathways to Precarity, Differential Inclusion, and Negotiated Citizenship Rights." *Journal of Ethnic and Migration Studies* 43 (1): 41–57. https://doi.org/10.1080/1369183X.2016.1192996.

Babayan, Kathryn, and Afsaneh Najmabadi, eds. 2008. *Islamicate Sexualities: Translations across Temporal Geographies of Desire*. Cambridge, MA: Harvard University Press.

Bakiner, Onur. 2018. "A Key to Turkish Politics? The Center-Periphery Framework Revisited." *Turkish Studies* 19 (4): 503–22.

Balaban, Adem. 2014. "Türkçe Yazma Tabirnameler / Turkish Manuscript Interpretation of Dreams." *Dil ve Edebiyat Eğitimi Dergisi* 2 (9): 112.

Balkan, Neşecan, and Sungur Savran, eds. 2002. *The Ravages of Neo-liberalism: Economy, Society and Gender in Turkey*. Hauppauge, NY: Nova Science.

Başlevent, Cem, and Özlem Onaran. 2003. "Are Married Women in Turkey More Likely to Become Added or Discouraged Workers?" *Labour* 17 (3): 439–58.

Bauman, Zygmunt. 2000. *Liquid Modernity*. Cambridge: Polity.

Baysal, Nurcan. 2016. "Cizre'deki evlerin içinden: 'Kızlar biz geldik siz yoktunuz' yazıları, yerlerde sergilenen kadın çamaşırları!.." *T24*, March 6. https://t24.com.tr/yazarlar /nurcan-baysal/cizrenin-gorunmeyenleri,14049.

Beck, Ulrich, and Elisabeth Beck-Gernsheim. 1995. *The Normal Chaos of Love*. Cambridge: Polity.

Beer, David. 2016. "Is Neoliberalism Making You Anxious? Metrics and the Production of Uncertainty." *British Politics and Policy at LSE* (blog), May 24. https://blogs.lse.ac .uk/politicsandpolicy/55395-2/.

Bellas, Marcia L. 1999. "Emotional Labor in Academia: The Case of Professors." *Annals of the American Academy of Political and Social Science* 561: 96–110. https://doi.org/10 .1177/000271629956100107.

Berardi, Franco "Bifo." 2009. *The Soul at Work: From Alienation to Autonomy*. Translated by Francesca Cadel and Giuseppina Mecchia. Los Angeles: Semiotext(e).

Berg, Lawrence D., Edward H. Huijbens, and Henrik Gutzon Larsen. 2016. "Producing Anxiety in the Neoliberal University." *Canadian Geographer / Le Géographe Canadien* 60 (2): 168–80. https://doi.org/10.1111/cag.12261.

Berkes, Niyazi. (1964) 1998. *The Development of Secularism in Turkey*. London: C. Hurst.

Berkey, Jonathan P. 2003. *The Formation of Islam: Religion and Society in the Near East, 600–1800*. Cambridge: Cambridge University Press.

Berlant, Lauren. 2007. "Slow Death (Sovereignty, Obesity, Lateral Agency)." *Critical Inquiry* 33 (4): 754–80. https://doi.org/10.1086/521568.

Berlant, Lauren. 2008. *The Female Complaint: Unfinished Business of Sentimentality in American Culture*. Durham, NC: Duke University Press. https://doi.org/10.1215/9780822389163.

Berlant, Lauren. 2011. *Cruel Optimism*. Durham, NC: Duke University Press.

Bernstein, Elizabeth. 2007. *Temporarily Yours: Intimacy, Authenticity, and the Commerce of Sex*. Chicago: University of Chicago Press.

Bilal, Melissa. 2019. "Lullabies and the Memory of Pain: Armenian Women's Remembrance of the Past in Turkey." *Dialectical Anthropology* 43 (2): 185–206.

Biner, Zerrin Özlem. 2019. *States of Dispossession: Violence and Precarious Coexistence in Southeast Turkey*. Philadelphia: University of Pennsylvania Press.

Bora, Tanil. 2013. "Notes on the White Turks Debate." In *Turkey between Nationalism and Globalization*, edited by Riva Castoryano, 99–116. London: Routledge.

Boratav, Korkut, and Erinc Yeldan. 2006. "Turkey, 1980–2000: Financial Liberalization, Macroeconomic (In)Stability, and Patterns of Distribution." In *External Liberalization in Asia, Post-socialist Europe, and Brazil*, edited by Lance Taylor, 417–55. https://doi.org/10.1093/acprof:oso/9780195189322.003.0014.

Boris, Eileen, and Rhacel Salazar Parrenas. 2010. *Intimate Labors: Cultures, Technologies, and the Politics of Care*. Stanford, CA: Stanford University Press.

Bourdieu, Pierre. 1998. *Acts of Resistance: Against the Tyranny of the Market*. Translated by Richard Nice. New York: New Press.

Bozkurt, Eren. 2017. "Adana'da 'falcı' operasyonu." *Anadolu Ajansı*, May 24. https://www.aa.com.tr/tr/turkiye/adanada-falci-operasyonu/824950.

Bozkurt-Güngen, Sümercan. 2018. "Labour and Authoritarian Neoliberalism: Changes and Continuities under the AKP Governments in Turkey." *South European Society and Politics* 23 (2): 219–38. https://doi.org/10.1080/13608746.2018.1471834.

Braidotti, Rosi. 2008. "In Spite of the Times: The Post-secular Turn in Feminism." *Theory, Culture & Society* 25 (6): 1–24. https://doi.org/10.1177/0263276408095542.

Brown, Wendy. 2015. *Undoing the Demos: Neoliberalism's Stealth Revolution*. Brooklyn, NY: Zone.

Buğra, Ayşe, and Sinem Adar. 2008. "Social Policy Change in Countries without Mature Welfare States: The Case of Turkey." *New Perspectives on Turkey* 38 (spring): 83–106. https://doi.org/10.1017/S0896634600004933.

Bugra, Ayşe, and Aysen Candas. 2011. "Change and Continuity under an Eclectic Social Security Regime: The Case of Turkey." *Middle Eastern Studies* 47 (3): 515–28. https://doi.org/10.1080/00263206.2011.565145.

Burak Adli, Feyza. 2020. "Trajectories of Modern Sufism: An Ethnohistorical Study of the Rifai Order and Social Change in Turkey." PhD diss., Boston University.

Butler, Judith. 2004. *Precarious Life: The Power of Mourning and Violence*. London: Verso.

Butler, Judith. 2011. *Gender Trouble: Feminism and the Subversion of Identity*. London: Routledge. https://doi.org/10.4324/9780203824979.

Byrne, Rhonda. 2006. *The Secret*. New York: Atria/Beyond Words.

Byrne, Rhonda. 2007. *The Secret: Sır*. Translated by Can Üstünuçar. Istanbul: Mia Basım Yayın.

Cady, Linell E., and Elizabeth Shakman Hurd, eds. 2010. *Comparative Secularisms in a Global Age*. New York: Palgrave Macmillan.

Çağman, Filiz. 1993. "Family Life and Laws." In *Woman in Anatolia: 9000 Years of the Anatolian Woman*, edited by Günsel Renda, 202-95. Istanbul: Turkish Republic Ministry of Culture.

Çavdar, Gamze, and Yavuz Yaşar. 2019. *Women in Turkey: Silent Consensus in the Age of Neoliberalism and Islamic Conservatism*. Abingdon, UK: Routledge.

Çelebi, İlyas. 1995. "İslam'da Fal." In *Türkiye Diyanet Vakfı İslam Ansiklopedisi*, vol. 12, 138–39. Istanbul: Türkiye Diyanet Vakfı Yayınları.

Çepik, Reyhan. 2011. "Hobiydi e-ticaret platformu oldu: Binnazabla.com." *Vadideki Reyhan*, November 16. Accessed January 3, 2018. http://www.vadidekireyhan.com /hobiydi-e-ticaret-platformu-oldu-binnazabla-com/.

Çetik, Arzu, Turan Gültekin, and Yavuz Kuşdemir. 2008. "Erdoğan: En az üç çocuk doğurun." *Hürriyet*, March 3. https://www.hurriyet.com.tr/gundem/erdogan-en-az-uc -cocuk-dogurun-8401981.

Chatterjee, Partha. 1986. *Nationalist Thought and the Colonial World: A Derivative Discourse?* London: Zed.

Chatterjee, Partha. 1993. *The Nation and Its Fragments: Colonial and Postcolonial Histories*. Princeton, NJ: Princeton University Press.

Chatterjee, Partha. 1999. *The Partha Chatterjee Omnibus: Nationalist Thought and the Colonial World, The Nation and Its Fragments, A Possible India*. New Delhi: Oxford University Press.

Çınar, Alev. 2005. *Modernity, Islam, and Secularism in Turkey*. Minneapolis: University of Minnesota Press.

Çınar, Mine E. 1994. "Unskilled Urban Migrant Women and Disguised Employment: Home-Working Women in Istanbul, Turkey." *World Development* 22 (3): 369–80.

Clough, Patricia Ticineto, and Jean Halley. 2007. *The Affective Turn: Theorizing the Social*. Durham, NC: Duke University Press.

Coleman, Rebecca, and Debra Ferreday. 2010. "Introduction: Hope and Feminist Theory." *Journal for Cultural Research* 14 (4): 313–21.

Comaroff, Jean, and John L. Comaroff. 1999. "Occult Economies and the Violence of Abstraction: Notes from the South African Postcolony." *American Ethnologist* 26 (2): 279–303.

Comaroff, Jean, and John L. Comaroff. 2000a. "Millennial Capitalism: First Thoughts on a Second Coming." *Public Culture* 12 (2): 291–343. https://doi.org/10.1215 /08992363-12-2-291.

Comaroff, Jean, and John Comaroff. 2000b. "Privatizing the Millennium: New Protestant Ethics and the Spirits of Capitalism in Africa, and Elsewhere." *Africa Spectrum* 35 (3): 293–312.

Connell, R. W. 1995. *Masculinities*. Berkeley: University of California Press.

Connolly, William E. 1999. *Why I Am Not a Secularist*. Minneapolis: University of Minnesota Press.

Constable, Nicole. 2009. "The Commodification of Intimacy: Marriage, Sex, and Reproductive Labor." *Annual Review of Anthropology* 38 (1): 49–64. https://doi.org/10.1146 /annurev.anthro.37.081407.085133.

Cornwall, Andrea. 2018. "Beyond 'Empowerment Lite': Women's Empowerment, Neoliberal Development and Global Justice." *Cadernos Pagu* 52 (November). https://doi.org/10.1590/18094449201800520002.

Cossman, Brenda. 2013. "Anxiety Governance." *Law and Social Inquiry* 38 (4): 892–919. https://doi.org/10.1111/lsi.12027.

Cruz, Jon. 1999. *Culture on the Margins: The Black Spiritual and the Rise of American Cultural Interpretation*. Princeton, NJ: Princeton University Press.

Cvetkovich, Ann. 1992. *Mixed Feelings: Feminism, Mass Culture, and Victorian Sensationalism*. New Brunswick, NJ: Rutgers University Press.

Cvetkovich, Ann. 2003. *An Archive of Feelings: Trauma, Sexuality, and Lesbian Public Cultures*. Durham, NC: Duke University Press. https://doi.org/10.1215/9780822384434.

Cvetkovich, Ann. 2012. *Depression: A Public Feeling*. Durham, NC: Duke University Press.

Dalla Costa, Mariarosa, and Selma James. 1972. *The Power of Women and the Subversion of the Community*. Bristol: Falling Wall.

Dayıoğlu, Meltem, and Murat Kırdar. 2010. "Determinants of and Trends in Labor Force Participation of Women in Turkey." Working Paper Number 5, SPO and World Bank Welfare and Social Policy Analytical Work Program. Ankara.

Dedeoğlu, Saniye. 2010. "Visible Hands–Invisible Women: Garment Production in Turkey." *Feminist Economics* 16 (4): 1–32.

Dedeoglu, Saniye, and Adem Yavuz Elveren. 2012. *Gender and Society in Turkey: The Impact of Neoliberal Policies, Political Islam and EU Accession*. London: I. B. Tauris.

Deeb, Lara. 2006. *An Enchanted Modern*. Princeton, NJ: Princeton University Press.

Deeb, Lara, and Mona Harb. 2013. *Leisurely Islam: Negotiating Morality and Geography in Shi'i South Beirut*. Princeton, NJ: Princeton University Press.

de Lauretis, Teresa. 1999. "Popular Culture, Public and Private Fantasies: Femininity and Fetishism in David Cronenberg's 'M. Butterfly.'" *Signs* 24 (2): 303–34. https://doi.org/10.1086/495342.

Deringil, Selim. 1993. "The Invention of Tradition as Public Image in the Late Ottoman Empire, 1808 to 1908." *Comparative Studies in Society and History* 35 (1): 3–29.

Desmet-Grégoire, Hélène, and François Georgeon, eds. 1999. *Doğu'da kahve ve kahvehaneler*. Translated by Meltem Atik and Esra Özdoğan. Istanbul: Yapı Kredi Kültür Sanat Yayıncılık Ticaret ve Sanayi YKY.

DISK-AR. 2019. "İşsizlik ve İstihdam: Işsizlikte Vahim Tablo Sürüyor: 1 Yılda 1 Milyon 334 Bin Işsiz Istihdamda 704 Bin Kayip." Istanbul: Türkiye Devrimci İşçi Sendikaları Konfederasyonu Araştırma Dairesi (DISK-AR). http://disk.org.tr/2019/06/disk-ar-haziran-2019-issizlik-ve-istihdam-raporu-1-yilda-1-milyon-334-bin-issiz/.

Dole, Christopher. 2006. "Mass Media and the Repulsive Allure of Religious Healing: The Cinci Hoca in Turkish Modernity." *International Journal of Middle East Studies* 38 (1): 31–54. https://doi.org/10.1017/S0020743806412241.

Dole, Christopher. 2012. *Healing Secular Life: Loss and Devotion in Modern Turkey*. Philadelphia: University of Pennsylvania Press.

Dole, Christopher. 2015. "The House That Saddam Built: Protest and Psychiatry in Post-disaster Turkey." *Journal of the Ottoman and Turkish Studies Association* 2 (2): 281.

Dole, Christopher. 2020. "Experiments in Scale: Humanitarian Psychiatry in Post-disaster Turkey." *Medical Anthropology* 39 (5): 1–15.

Dressler, Markus, and Arvind Mandair. 2011. *Secularism and Religion-Making*. Oxford: Oxford University Press.

Ducey, Ariel. 2007. "More Than a Job: Meaning, Affect, and Training Health Care Workers." In *The Affective Turn: Theorizing the Social*, edited by Patricia Ticineto Clough and Jean Halley, 187–208. Durham, NC: Duke University Press. https://doi.org/10.1215/9780822389606-009.

Duggan, Lisa, and José Esteban Muñoz. 2009. "Hope and Hopelessness: A Dialogue." *Women and Performance: A Journal of Feminist Theory* 19 (2): 275–83.

Durakbaşa, Ayşe. 2000. "Kemalism as Identity Politics in Turkey." In *Deconstructing Images of the Turkish Woman*, edited by Zehra Arat, 139–50. New York: Palgrave.

Durakbaşa, Ayşe, and Dilek Cindoğlu. 2002. "Encounters at the Counter: Gender and the Shopping Experience." In *Fragments of Culture: The Everyday of Modern Turkey*, edited by Deniz Kandioti and Ayşe Saktanber, 73–89. New Brunswick, NJ: Rutgers University Press.

Ecevit, Yıldız. 2003. "Women's Labor and Social Security." In *Bridging the Gender Gap in Turkey: A Milestone towards Faster Socio-economic Development and Poverty Reduction*, 73–106. Poverty Reduction and Economic Management Unit Europe and Central Asia Region.

Eder, Mine. 2013. "Deepening Neoliberalisation and a Changing Welfare Regime in Turkey: Mutations of a Populist, 'Sub-optimal' Democracy." In *Turkey's Democratization Process*, edited by Carmen Rodriguez, Antonio Avalos, Hakan Yilmaz, and Ana I. Planet, 195–220. Abingdon, UK: Routledge.

Ehrenreich, Barbara, and Arlie Russell Hochschild. 2002. *Global Woman: Nannies, Maids, and Sex Workers in the New Economy*. New York: Henry Holt.

Ellis, Markman. 2011. *The Coffee-House: A Cultural History*. London: Weidenfeld and Nicolson.

El-Rouayheb, Khaled. 2005. *Before Homosexuality in the Arab-Islamic World, 1500–1800*. Chicago: University of Chicago Press.

Elveren, Adem Y. 2008. "Social Security Reform in Turkey: A Critical Perspective." *Review of Radical Political Economics* 40 (2): 212–32. https://doi.org/10.1177/0486613407310561.

Engin, Ceylan, Hazal Hürman, and Kimber Harvey. 2020. "Marriage and Family in Turkey: Trends and Attitudes." In *International Handbook on the Demography of Marriage and the Family*, edited by D. Nicole Faris and Alex J. J. Bourque, 105–19. Cham: Springer.

Erdem, Y. Hakan. 2010. "Magic, Theft, and Arson: The Life and Death of an Enslaved African Woman in Ottoman Izmit." In *Race and Slavery in the Middle East: Histories of Trans-Saharan Africans in Nineteenth-Century Egypt, Sudan, and the Ottoman Mediterranean*, edited by Terence Walz and Kenneth M. Cuno, 125–46. Cairo: American University in Cairo Press.

Ergin, Murat, and Yağmur Karakaya. 2017. "Between Neo-Ottomanism and Ottomania: Navigating State-Led and Popular Cultural Representations of the Past." *New Perspectives on Turkey* 56:33–59. https://doi.org/10.1017/npt.2017.4.

Ergun, Mahinur, dir. 1997. *Sıdıka* (TV series). Istanbul: Show TV.

Federici, Silvia. 1975. *Wages against Housework*. Bristol: Falling Wall.

Federici, Silvia. 2004. *Caliban and the Witch: Women, the Body and Primitive Accumulation*. New York: Autonomedia.

Federici, Silvia. 2008. "Precarious Labor: A Feminist Viewpoint." *In the Middle of a Whirlwind* (blog), June 6. https://inthemiddleofthewhirlwind.wordpress.com /precarious-labor-a-feminist-viewpoint/.

Ferguson, Roderick A. 2004. *Aberrations in Black: Toward a Queer of Color Critique*. Minneapolis: University of Minnesota Press.

Fernea, Elizabeth Warnock. 1981. "An Early Ethnographer of Middle Eastern Women: Lady Mary Wortley Montagu (1689–1762)." *Journal of Near Eastern Studies* 40 (4): 329–38. https://doi.org/10.1086/372902.

Fiske, John. 2011. *Reading the Popular*. London: Routledge.

Fleischer, Cornell. 2001. "Seer to the Sultan: Haydar-i Remmal and Sultan Süleyman." In *Cultural Horizons: A Festschrift in Honor of Talat S. Halman*, vol. 1, edited by Ehud Toledano and Jayne L. Warner, 290–99. Syracuse, NY: Syracuse University Press.

Fleischer, Cornell H. 2010. "Ancient Wisdom and New Sciences: Prophecies in the Ottoman Court in the Fifteenth and Early Sixteenth Centuries." In *Falnama: The Book of Omens*, edited by Massumeh Farhad and Serpil Bağcı, 231–43. London: Thames and Hudson.

Foster, Roger. 2016. "The Therapeutic Spirit of Neoliberalism." *Political Theory* 44 (1): 82–105.

Foster, Roger. 2017. "Social Character: Erich Fromm and the Ideological Glue of Neoliberalism." *Critical Horizons* 18 (1): 1–18. https://doi.org/10.1080/14409917.2017.1275166.

Foucault, Michel. 2008. *The Birth of Biopolitics: Lectures at the College de France 1978–1979*. Translated by Graham Burchell. New York: Palgrave Macmillan.

Fraser, Nancy. 1990. "Rethinking the Public Sphere: A Contribution to the Critique of Actually Existing Democracy." *Social Text*, nos. 25–26, 56–80. https://doi.org/10.2307 /466240.

Fraser, Nancy. 2013. *Fortunes of Feminism: From State-Managed Capitalism to Neoliberal Crisis*. London: Verso.

Freeman, Carla. 2011. "Neoliberalism: Embodying and Affecting Neoliberalism." In *A Companion to the Anthropology of the Body and Embodiment*, 353–69. Hoboken, NJ: John Wiley.

Freeman, Carla. 2015. *Entrepreneurial Selves: Neoliberal Respectability and the Making of a Caribbean Middle Class*. Durham, NC: Duke University Press.

Gellner, Ernest. 1981. *Muslim Society*. Cambridge: Cambridge University Press.

Giddens, Anthony. 1991. *Modernity and Self-Identity: Self and Society in the Late Modern Age*. Stanford, CA: Stanford University Press.

Giddens, Anthony. 1992. *The Transformation of Intimacy: Sexuality, Love and Eroticism in Modern Societies*. Cambridge: Polity.

Gill, Denise. 2017. *Melancholic Modalities: Affect, Islam, and Turkish Classical Musicians*. New York: Oxford University Press.

Gill, Rosalind, and Andy Pratt. 2008. "In the Social Factory? Immaterial Labour, Precariousness and Cultural Work." *Theory, Culture and Society* 25 (7–8): 1–30.

Gökarıksel, Banu. 2012. "The Intimate Politics of Secularism and the Headscarf: The Mall, the Neighborhood, and the Public Square in Istanbul." *Gender, Place and Culture* 19 (1): 1–20.

Gökarıksel, Banu, and Anna Secor. 2015. "Post-secular Geographies and the Problem of Pluralism: Religion and Everyday Life in Istanbul, Turkey." *Political Geography* 46 (May): 21–30. https://doi.org/10.1016/j.polgeo.2014.10.006.

Göle, Nilüfer. 1996. *The Forbidden Modern: Civilization and Veiling.* Ann Arbor: University of Michigan Press.

Göle, Nilüfer. 1997. "The Gendered Nature of the Public Sphere." *Public Culture* 10 (1): 61–81. https://doi.org/10.1215/08992363-10-1-61.

Göle, Nilüfer. 2000. *Melez Desenler.* Istanbul: Metis Yayınları.

Göle, Nilüfer. 2002. "Islam in Public: New Visibilities and New Imaginaries." *Public Culture* 14 (1): 173–90. https://doi.org/10.1215/08992363-14-1-173.

Göle, Nilüfer. 2012. "Post-secular Turkey." *New Perspectives Quarterly* 29 (1): 7–11. https://doi.org/10.1111/j.1540-5842.2012.01290.x.

Gooptu, Nandini. 2013. "New Spiritualism and the Micro Politics of Self-Making in India's Enterprise Culture." In *Enterprise Culture in Neoliberal India: Studies in Youth, Class, Work and Media,* edited by Nandini Gooptu, 73–90. London: Routledge.

Gorski, Philip, David Kyuman Kim, John Torpey, and Jonathan VanAntwerpen. 2012. *The Post-secular in Question: Religion in Contemporary Society.* New York: New York University Press.

Gregory, Karen. 2012. "Negotiating Precarity: Tarot as Spiritual Entrepreneurialism." *WSQ: Women's Studies Quarterly* 40 (3): 264–80. https://doi.org/10.1353/wsq.2013.0025.

Güler, Ezgi. 2020. "A Divided Sisterhood: Support Networks of Trans Sex Workers in Urban Turkey." *Annals of the American Academy of Political and Social Science* 689 (1): 149–67.

Guloglu, Tuncay. 2005. "The Reality of Informal Employment in Turkey." Visiting Fellows Working Papers. Ithaca, NY: School of Industrial and Labor Relations, Cornell University. https://hdl.handle.net/1813/89751.

Gürbilek, Nurdan. 2013. *The New Cultural Climate in Turkey: Living in a Shop Window.* London: Zed.

Gürpınar, Hüseyin Rahmi. (1913) 2015. *Gulyabani.* Istanbul: İthaki Yayınları.

Gürpınar, Hüseyin Rahmi. (1924) 2018. *Efsuncu Baba.* Istanbul: İş Bankası Kültür Yayınları.

Gürpınar, Hüseyin Rahmi. (1964) 2010. *Dirilen İskelet.* Istanbul: Everest Yayınları.

Gürsel, Zeynep. 2012. "Following Coffee Futures: Reflections on Speculative Traditions and Visual Politics." In *Sensible Politics: The Visual Culture of Nongovernmental Activism,* edited by Ben Lenzner, 372–93. New York: Zone.

Gürsel, Zeynep Devrim. 2009. *Neyse Halim Ciksin Falim (Coffee Futures).* Distributed by Documentary Educational Resources.

Gutiérrez-Rodríguez, Encarnación. 2014. "The Precarity of Feminisation." *International Journal of Politics, Culture, and Society* 27 (2): 191–202. https://doi.org/10.1007/s10767-013-9154-7.

Habermas, Jürgen. (1962) 1991. *The Structural Transformation of the Public Sphere.* Translated by Thomas Burger and Frederick Lawrence. Cambridge, MA: MIT Press.

Habermas, Jürgen. 2008. "Notes on Post-secular Society." *New Perspectives Quarterly* 25 (4): 17–29. https://doi.org/10.1111/j.1540-5842.2008.01017.x.

Hale, William, and Ergun Ozbudun. 2009. *Islamism, Democracy, and Liberalism in Turkey: The Case of the AKP*. Abingdon, UK: Routledge.

Hall, Elaine J. 1993. "Smiling, Deferring, and Flirting: Doing Gender by Giving 'Good Service.'" *Work and Occupations* 20 (4): 452–71. https://doi.org/10.1177 /0730888493020004003.

Hall, Stuart, ed. 1997. *Representation: Cultural Representations and Signifying Practices*. London: Sage.

Hall, Stuart. 2001. "Encoding/Decoding." In *Media and Cultural Studies: Keyworks*, edited by M. G. Durham and D. M. Kellner, 163–73. Minneapolis: University of Minnesota Press.

Hardt, Michael. 1999. "Affective Labor." *boundary 2* 26 (2): 89–100.

Hardt, Michael. 2007. "Foreword: What Affects Are Good For." In *The Affective Turn: Theorizing the Social*, edited by Patricia Ticineto Clough and Jean Halley. Durham, NC: Duke University Press.

Hardt, Michael, and Antonio Negri. 2004. *Multitude: War and Democracy in the Age of Empire*. New York: Penguin.

Hariri, Noha. 2014. "A Different Online Service: Fortune Telling!" Arabnet, July 10. https://www.arabnet.me/english/editorials/technology/apps/a-different-online -service-fortune-telling.

Harvey, David. 2005. *A Brief History of Neoliberalism*. Oxford: Oxford University Press.

Hasu, Päivi. 2006. "World Bank and Heavenly Bank in Poverty and Prosperity: The Case of Tanzanian Faith Gospel." *Review of African Political Economy* 33 (110): 679–92.

Hattox, Ralph S. 2014. *Coffee and Coffeehouses: The Origins of a Social Beverage in the Medieval Near East*. Seattle: University of Washington Press.

Hebdige, Dick. 1995. "Subculture: The Meaning of Style." *Critical Quarterly* 37 (2): 120–24. https://doi.org/10.1111/j.1467-8705.1995.tb01063.x.

Helms, Elissa. 2010. "The Gender of Coffee: Women and Reconciliation Initiatives in Post-war Bosnia and Herzegovina." *Focaal: Tijdschrift Voor Antropologie* 57:17–32. https://doi.org/10.3167/fcl.2010.570102.

Hemmings, Clare. 2012. "Affective Solidarity: Feminist Reflexivity and Political Trans-formation." *Feminist Theory* 13 (2): 147–61.

Hochschild, Arlie. 1983. *The Managed Heart: Commercialization of Human Feeling*. Berkeley: University of California Press.

Hunt, Stephen. 2000. "'Winning Ways': Globalisation and the Impact of the Health and Wealth Gospel." *Journal of Contemporary Religion* 15 (3): 331–47. https://doi.org/10 .1080/713676038.

İlkkaracan, İpek. 2012. "Why So Few Women in the Labor Market in Turkey?" *Feminist Economics* 18 (1): 1–37.

Illouz, Eva. 2008. *Saving the Modern Soul: Therapy, Emotions, and the Culture of Self-Help*. Berkeley: University of California Press.

Isik, Damla. 2008. "On Sabır and Agency: The Politics of Pious Practice in Konya's Carpet Weaving Industry." *International Feminist Journal of Politics* 10 (4): 518–41.

Isik, Damla. 2014. "'Just Like Prophet Mohammad Preached': Labor, Piety, and Charity in Contemporary Turkey." *Feminist Economics* 20 (4): 212–34. https://doi.org/10.1080/13545701.2013.825376.

Isin, Engin F. 2004. "The Neurotic Citizen." *Citizenship Studies* 8 (3): 217–35. https://doi.org/10.1080/1362102042000256970.

Jamal, Amina. 2015. "Piety, Transgression and the Feminist Debate on Muslim Women: Transnationalizing the Victim-Subject of Honor-Related Violence." *Signs: Journal of Women in Culture and Society* 41 (1): 55–79.

Kadioğlu, Ayşe. 1996. "The Paradox of Turkish Nationalism and the Construction of Official Identity." *Middle Eastern Studies* 32 (2): 177–93. https://doi.org/10.1080/00263209608701110.

Kado, Medyum. 2016. "Medyum Memiş-Medyum Keto Olayı-Medyum Kado." YouTube video, 3:03, uploaded September 17. https://www.youtube.com/watch?v=8pliLvUIU5Q.

Kafadar, Cemal. 1989. "Self and Others: The Diary of a Dervish in Seventeenth Century Istanbul and First-Person Narratives in Ottoman Literature." *Studia Islamica*, no. 69, 121–50. https://doi.org/10.2307/1596070.

Kafadar, Cemal. 1993. "Women in Seljuk and Ottoman Society up to the Mid 19th Century." In *Woman in Anatolia: 9000 Years of the Anatolian Woman*, edited by Günsel Renda, 192–201. Istanbul: Turkish Republic Ministry of Culture.

Kafadar, Cemal. 1994. *Asiye Hatun: Rüya Mektupları*. İstanbul: Oğlak Yayınları.

Kafadar, Cemal. 2002. "A History of Coffee." Thirteenth Congress of the International Economic History Association (IEHA), July 22–26, Buenos Aires, Argentina. https://sites.duke.edu/rethinkingglobalcities/files/2014/09/64Kafadar16-coffeehistory.pdf.

Kallander, Amy Aisen. 2013. *Women, Gender, and the Palace Households in Ottoman Tunisia*. Austin: University of Texas Press.

Kandiyoti, Deniz. 1987. "Emancipated but Unliberated? Reflections on the Turkish Case." *Feminist Studies* 13 (2): 317–38. https://doi.org/10.2307/3177804.

Kandiyoti, Deniz. 1991. "End of Empire: Islam, Nationalism and Women in Turkey." In *Women, Islam and the State*, edited by Deniz Kandiyoti, 22–47. London: Palgrave Macmillan UK. https://doi.org/10.1007/978-1-349-21178-4_2.

Kandiyoti, Deniz. 1994. "The Paradoxes of Masculinity: Some Thoughts on Segregated Societies." In *Dislocating Masculinity: Comparative Ethnographies*, edited by Andrea Cornwall and Nancy Lindisfarne, 197–213. London: Routledge. https://doi.org/10.4324/9780203393437_chapter_12.

Kandiyoti, Deniz. 1997. "Gendering the Modern: On Missing Dimensions in the Study of Turkish Modernity." In *Rethinking Modernity and National Identity in Turkey*, edited by Sibel Bozdoğan, Sibel Bozdogan, and Reşat Kasaba, 113–32. Seattle: University of Washington Press.

Kandiyoti, Deniz. 2002. "Introduction: Reading the Fragments," In *Fragments of Culture: The Everyday of Modern Turkey*, edited by Deniz Kandiyoti and Ayşe Saktanber, 1–24. New Brunswick, NJ: Rutgers University Press.

Kandiyoti, Deniz. 2012. "The Travails of the Secular: Puzzle and Paradox in Turkey." *Economy and Society* 41 (4): 513–31. https://doi.org/10.1080/03085147.2012.718631.

Kandiyoti, Deniz. 2013. "Fear and Fury: Women and Post-revolutionary Violence." *OpenDemocracy*, January 10. https://www.opendemocracy.net/en/5050/fear-and-fury -women-and-post-revolutionary-violence/.

Kandiyoti, Deniz, and Ayşe Saktanber, eds. 2002. *Fragments of Culture: The Everyday of Modern Turkey*. New Brunswick, NJ: Rutgers University Press.

Kang, Miliann. 2003. "The Managed Hand: The Commercialization of Bodies and Emotions in Korean Immigrant-Owned Nail Salons." *Gender and Society* 17 (6): 820–39.

Kanna, Ahmed. 2010. "Flexible Citizenship in Dubai: Neoliberal Subjectivity in the Emerging 'City-Corporation.'" *Cultural Anthropology* 25 (1): 100–129. https://doi.org /10.1111/j.1548-1360.2009.01053.x.

Kaplan, Sam. 2006. *The Pedagogical State: Education and the Politics of National Culture in Post-1980 Turkey*. Stanford, CA: Stanford University Press.

Karababa, Eminegül, and Güliz Ger. 2011. "Early Modern Ottoman Coffeehouse Culture and the Formation of the Consumer Subject." *Journal of Consumer Research* 37 (5): 737–60. https://doi.org/10.1086/656422.

Karim, Lamia. 2011. *Microfinance and Its Discontents*. Minneapolis: University of Minnesota Press.

Karpat, Kemal H. 1960. "Social Themes in Contemporary Turkish Literature: Part II." *Middle East Journal* 14 (2): 153–68.

Kaşka, Selmin. 2007. "Ev içi hizmetlerin küreselleşmesi ve Türkiye'deki göçmen kadınlar." In *Türkiye'de Yabancı İşçiler Uluslarası Göç, İşgücü ve Nüfus Hareketleri*, edited by F. Aylan Arı, 225–40. Istanbul: Derin Yayınları.

Kasnakoğlu, Zeynep, and Meltem Dayıoğlu. 1997. "Female Labor Force Participation and Earnings Differentials between Genders in Turkey." In *Economic Dimensions of Gender Inequality*, 95–117, edited by Janet Rives and Mahmood Yousefi. London: Praeger.

Keddie, Nikki R. 2003. "Secularism and Its Discontents." *Daedalus* 132 (3): 14–30.

Kılavuz, Ahmet Saim. 1993. "Cin" in *Türkiye Diyanet Vakfı İslam Ansiklopedisi*, vol. 8, 8–10. İstanbul: Türkiye Diyanet Vakfı Yayınları.

Kılıç, Zulal. 1998. "Cumhuriyet Türkiye'sinde Kadın Hareketine Genel Bir Bakış." In *75. Yilda Kadinlar ve Erkekler*, edited by Ayşe Berktay Hacımirzaoğlu, 347–60. Istanbul: Tarih Vakfı Yayınları.

Kim, Sooyong. 2017. *The Last of an Age: The Making and Unmaking of a Sixteenth-Century Ottoman Poet*. London: Routledge.

Koçali, Filiz. 2002. "Çiçek: Feminizm Sapıklık, Flört Fahişeliktir." *Bianet*, November 18. https://m.bianet.org/bianet/siyaset/14696-cicek-feminizm-sapiklik-flort -fahiseliktir.

Kocamaner, Hikmet. 2019. "Regulating the Family through Religion: Secularism, Islam, and the Politics of the Family in Contemporary Turkey." *American Ethnologist* 46 (4): 495–508.

Kömeçoğlu, Uğur. 2005. "The Publicness and Sociabilities of the Ottoman Coffeehouse." *Javnost: The Public* 12 (2): 5–22. https://doi.org/10.1080/13183222.2005.11008885.

Kontovas, Nicholas. 2012. "Lubunca: The Historical Development of Istanbul's Queer Slang and a Social-Functional Approach to Diachronic Processes in Language." PhD diss., Indiana University.

Korkman, Zeynep Kurtulus. 2015a. "Blessing Neoliberalism: Economy, Family, and the Occult in Millennial Turkey." *Journal of the Ottoman and Turkish Studies Association* 2 (2): 335–57. https://doi.org/10.2979/jottturstuass.2.2.06.

Korkman, Zeynep Kurtulus. 2015b. "Feeling Labor: Commercial Divination and Commodified Intimacy in Turkey." *Gender and Society* 29 (2): 195–218. https://doi.org/10.1177/0891243214566269.

Korkman, Zeynep Kurtulus. 2015c. "Fortunes for Sale: Cultural Politics and Commodification of Culture in Millennial Turkey." *European Journal of Cultural Studies* 18 (3): 319–38.

Korkman, Zeynep Kurtuluş. 2016. "Politics of Intimacy in Turkey: A Distraction from 'Real' Politics?" *Journal of Middle East Women's Studies* 12 (1): 112–21. https://doi.org/10.1215/15525864-3422611.

Korkman, Zeynep. 2017. "Yeni Türkiye'nin gelinler alemi." *Çatlak Zemin* (blog), September 25. https://catlakzemin.com/yeni-turkiyenin-gelinler-alemi/.

Korkman, Zeynep Kurtulus. 2021. "Trans-secular Interventions: Destabilizing the (Cis) Gender Politics of Secularism." In *Religion, Secularism, and Political Belonging*, edited by Leerom Medovoi and Elizabeth Bentley, 283–304. Durham, NC: Duke University Press.

Korkman, Zeynep Kurtuluş, and Salih Can Açıksöz. 2014. "Erdoğan's Masculinity and the Language of the Gezi Resistance." *JadMag Pedagogy Publications* 1(4): 37–39.

Köroğlu, Özlem Taner. 2010. "Türkiye'de Personel Yönetiminden İnsan Kaynaklarına Geçişte Esneklik ve Memur Statüsü." *Türk İdare Dergisi* 469:139–64.

Koşar, Emel. 2008. *Hüseyin Rahmi Gürpınar'ın Romanlarında Bâtıl İnançlar*. Istanbul: Piya Art Yayıncılık.

Koşar, Uğur. 2013. *Allah De Ötesini Bırak*. Istanbul: Destek Yayınları.

Kural, Beyza. 2014. "Biranızı Getiren Garson Kaç Saattir Çalışıyor?" *Bianet*, September 15. http://bianet.org/bianet/yasam/158515-biranizi-getiren-garson-kac-saattir-calisiyor.

Kuru, Ahmet. 2007. "Passive and Assertive Secularism: Historical Conditions, Ideological Struggles, and State Policies toward Religion." *World Politics* 59 (4): 568–94. https://doi.org/10.1353/wp.2008.0005.

Lad, Jateen. 2010. "Panoptic Bodies: Black Eunuchs as Guardians of the Topkapi Harem." In *Harem Histories: Envisioning Places and Living Spaces*, edited by Marilyn Booth, 136–76. Durham, NC: Duke University Press. https://doi.org/10.1215/9780822393467-009.

Lazzarato, Maurizio. 1996. "Immaterial Labor." In *Radical Thought in Italy: A Potential Politics*, edited by Paolo Virno and Michael Hardt, translated by Paul Colilli and Ed Emery, 133–47. Minnesota: University of Minnesota Press.

Liebelt, Claudia. 2016. "Grooming Istanbul: Intimate Encounters and Concerns in Turkish Beauty Salons." *Journal of Middle East Women's Studies* 12 (2): 181–202.

Lively, Kathryn J. 2000. "Reciprocal Emotion Management: Working Together to Maintain Stratification in Private Law Firms." *Work and Occupations* 27 (1): 32–63. https://doi.org/10.1177/0730888400027001003.

Lloyd, Genevieve. 2004. *The Man of Reason: "Male" and "Female" in Western Philosophy.* London: Routledge.

Mahmood, Saba. 2001. "Feminist Theory, Embodiment, and the Docile Agent: Some Reflections on the Egyptian Islamic Revival." *Cultural Anthropology* 16 (2): 202–36.

Mahmood, Saba. 2005. *Politics of Piety: The Islamic Revival and the Feminist Subject.* Princeton, NJ: Princeton University Press.

Makdisi, Ussama. 2002. "Ottoman Orientalism." *American Historical Review* 107 (3): 768–96. https://doi.org/10.1086/ahr/107.3.768.

Malin, Brenton J., and Curry Chandler. 2017. "Free to Work Anxiously: Splintering Precarity among Drivers for Uber and Lyft." *Communication, Culture and Critique* 10 (2): 382–400. https://doi.org/10.1111/cccr.12157.

Mankekar, Purnima. 2015. *Unsettling India: Affect, Temporality, Transnationality.* Durham, NC: Duke University Press. https://doi.org/10.1215/9780822375838.

Mardin, Şerif. 1973. "Center-Periphery Relations: A Key to Turkish Politics?" *Daedalus* 102 (1): 169–90.

Mardin, Şerif. 1990. "Türk Siyasasını Açıklayabilecek Bir Anahtar: Merkez-Çevre İlişkileri." In *Türkiye'de Toplum ve Siyaset: Makaleler 1*, edited by Mümtaz'er Türköne and Tuncay Önder, 197–201. Istanbul: İletişim Yayınları.

Marx, Karl. 1977. *Capital*, vol. 1. New York: Vintage.

Massumi, Brian. 2002. *Parables for the Virtual: Movement, Affect, Sensation.* Durham, NC: Duke University Press.

Maxwell, David. 1998. "'Delivered from the Spirit of Poverty?': Pentecostalism, Prosperity and Modernity in Zimbabwe." *Journal of Religion in Africa* 28 (3): 350–73. https://doi.org/10.2307/1581574.

McClintock, Anne. 1995. *Imperial Leather: Race, Gender, and Sexuality in the Colonial Contest.* Oxon: Routledge.

McLennan, Gregor. 2007. "Towards Post-secular Sociology?" *Sociology* 41 (5): 857–70. https://doi.org/10.1177/0038038507080441.

McRobbie, Angela. 2009. *The Aftermath of Feminism: Gender, Culture and Social Change.* London: Sage.

Mernissi, Fatema. 2001. *Scheherazade Goes West: Different Cultures, Different Harems.* New York: Simon and Schuster.

Mies, Maria. 1998. *Patriarchy and Accumulation on a World Scale: Women in the International Division of Labour.* London: Zed.

Mikhail, Alan. 2007. "The Heart's Desire: Gender, Urban Space and the Ottoman Coffeehouse." In *Ottoman Tulips, Ottoman Coffee: Leisure and Lifestyle in the Eighteenth Century*, edited by Dana Sajdi, 133–70. London: I. B. Tauris.

Mills, Amy. 2010. *Streets of Memory: Landscape, Tolerance, and National Identity in Istanbul.* Athens: University of Georgia Press.

Mills, Mary Beth. 2003. "Gender and Inequality in the Global Labor Force." *Annual Review of Anthropology* 32 (1): 41–62. https://doi.org/10.1146/annurev.anthro.32.061002.093107.

Mittermaier, Amira. 2010. *Dreams That Matter: Egyptian Landscapes of the Imagination.* Berkeley: University of California Press.

Moallem, Minoo. 2018. *Persian Carpets: The Nation as a Transnational Commodity*. New York: Routledge.

Moghadam, Valentine M. 2005. "Women's Economic Participation in the Middle East: What Difference Has the Neoliberal Policy Turn Made?" *Journal of Middle East Women's Studies* 1 (1): 110–46.

Molé, Noelle J. 2010. "Precarious Subjects: Anticipating Neoliberalism in Northern Italy's Workplace." *American Anthropologist* 112 (1): 38–53. https://doi.org/10.1111/j.1548-1433.2009.01195.x.

Moore, Phoebe, and Andrew Robinson. 2015. "The Quantified Self: What Counts in the Neoliberal Workplace." *New Media and Society*, September. https://doi.org/10.1177/1461444815604328.

Morvaridi, Behrooz. 2013. "The Politics of Philanthropy and Welfare Governance: The Case of Turkey." *European Journal of Development Research* 25 (2): 305–21.

Mosoetsa, Sarah, Joel Stillerman, and Chris Tilly. 2016. "Precarious Labor, South and North: An Introduction." *International Labor and Working-Class History* 89: 5–19. https://doi.org/10.1017/S0147547916000028.

Muehlebach, Andrea. 2011. "On Affective Labor in Post-Fordist Italy." *Cultural Anthropology* 26 (1): 59–82.

Munck, Ronaldo. 2013. "The Precariat: A View from the South." *Third World Quarterly* 34 (5): 747–62. https://doi.org/10.1080/01436597.2013.800751.

Muñoz, José Esteban. 1999. *Disidentifications: Queers of Color and the Performance of Politics*. Minneapolis: University of Minnesota Press.

Mutlu, Yeşim. 2017. "En Şekerli Falcınız Binnaz Abla!" *Milliyet*, February 22. Accessed January 3, 2018. http://www.milliyet.com.tr/en-sekerli-falciniz-binnaz-abla--pembenar-yazardetay-yasam-2401206/.

Mutluer, Nil. 2019. "The Intersectionality of Gender, Sexuality, and Religion: Novelties and Continuities during the AKP Era." *Southeast European and Black Sea Studies* 19 (1): 99–118.

Najmabadi, Afsaneh. 2005. *Women with Mustaches and Men without Beards: Gender and Sexual Anxieties of Iranian Modernity*. Berkeley: University of California Press.

Navaro, Yael. 2017. "Diversifying Affect." *Cultural Anthropology* 32 (2): 209–14.

Navaro-Yashin, Yael. 2002. *Faces of the State: Secularism and Public Life in Turkey*. Princeton, NJ: Princeton University Press.

Navaro-Yashin, Yael. 2012. *The Make-Believe Space: Affective Geography in a Postwar Polity*. Durham, NC: Duke University Press.

Navaro-Yaşın, Yael. 2000. "Evde Taylorizm: Türkiye Cumhuriyeti'nin İlk Yıllarında Evişinin Rasyonelleşmesi (1928–40)." *Toplum ve Bilim* 84:51–74.

Negri, Antonio, and Michael Hardt. 1999. "Value and Affect." *boundary 2* 26 (2): 77–88.

Neilson, Brett, and Ned Rossiter. 2008. "Precarity as a Political Concept, or, Fordism as Exception." *Theory, Culture and Society* 25 (7–8): 51–72. https://doi.org/10.1177/0263276408097796.

Neilson, David. 2015. "Class, Precarity, and Anxiety under Neoliberal Global Capitalism: From Denial to Resistance." *Theory and Psychology* 25 (2): 184–201. https://doi.org/10.1177/0959354315580607.

Olson, Emelie A. 1982. "Duofocal Family Structure and an Alternative Model of Husband-Wife Relationship." In *Sex Roles, Family and Community in Turkey*, edited by Çiğdem Kağıtçıbaşı, 33–72. Bloomington: Indiana University Turkish Studies Press.

Öncü, Ayşe. 2005. "Becoming 'Secular Muslims': Yaşar Nuri Öztürk as a Super-Subject on Turkish Television." *In Religion, Media, and the Public Sphere*, edited by Birgit Meyer and Annelies Moors, 227–50. Bloomington: Indiana University Press.

Ong, Aihwa. 2006. *Neoliberalism as Exception: Mutations in Citizenship and Sovereignty*. Durham, NC: Duke University Press.

Ong, Aihwa. 2010. *Spirits of Resistance and Capitalist Discipline: Factory Women in Malaysia*. Albany: State University of New York Press.

Öniş, Ziya. 2004. "Turgut Özal and His Economic Legacy: Turkish Neo-liberalism in Critical Perspective." *Middle Eastern Studies* 40 (4): 113–34.

Ouellette, Laurie, and Julie Wilson. 2011. "Women's Work: Affective Labour and Convergence Culture." *Cultural Studies* 25 (4–5): 548–65. https://doi.org/10.1080/09502386.2011.600546.

Özbay, Cenk. 2010. "Nocturnal Queers: Rent Boys' Masculinity in Istanbul." *Sexualities* 13 (5): 645–63.

Özbay, Cenk. 2015. "'Men Are Less Manly, Women Are More Feminine': The Shopping Mall as a Site for Gender Crisis in Istanbul." In *Gender and Sexuality in Muslim Cultures*, edited by Gul Ozyegin, 73–94. Farnham, UK: Ashgate.

Özbay, Cenk. 2017. *Queering Sexualities in Turkey: Gay Men, Male Prostitutes and the City*. New York: I. B. Tauris.

Ozbay, Ferhunde. 1999. "Gendered Space: A New Look at Turkish Modernisation." *Gender and History* 11 (3): 555–68. https://doi.org/10.1111/1468-0424.00163.

Özkoçak, Selma Akyazici. 2007. "Coffeehouses: Rethinking the Public and Private in Early Modern Istanbul." *Journal of Urban History* 33 (6): 965–86. https://doi.org/10.1177/0096144207304018.

Öztürk, Mustafa Bilgehan. 2011. "Sexual Orientation Discrimination: Exploring the Experiences of Lesbian, Gay and Bisexual Employees in Turkey." *Human Relations* 64 (8): 1099–1118.

Öztürk, Serdar. 2005. *Cumhuriyet Türkiyesinde Kahvehane ve Iktidar, 1930–1945*. Istanbul: Kırmızı Yayınları.

Öztürk, Serdar. 2008. "The Struggle over Turkish Village Coffeehouses (1923–45)." *Middle Eastern Studies* 44 (3): 435–54. https://doi.org/10.1080/00263200802021590.

Ozyegin, Gul. 2000. *Untidy Gender: Domestic Service in Turkey*. Philadelphia: Temple University Press.

Özyeğin, Gül. 2009. "Virginal Facades: Sexual Freedom and Guilt among Young Turkish Women." *European Journal of Women's Studies* 16 (2): 103–23.

Özyeğin, Gül. 2015. *New Desires, New Selves: Sex, Love, and Piety among Turkish Youth*. New York: New York University Press.

Özyürek, Esra. 2006. *Nostalgia for the Modern: State Secularism and Everyday Politics in Turkey*. Durham, NC: Duke University Press.

Papacharissi, Zizi. 2015. *Affective Publics: Sentiment, Technology, and Politics*. Oxford: Oxford University Press.

Parla, Ayse. 2001. "The 'Honor' of the State: Virginity Examinations in Turkey." *Feminist Studies* 27 (1): 65–88. https://doi.org/10.2307/3178449.

Parla, Ayşe. 2019. *Precarious Hope: Migration and the Limits of Belonging in Turkey*. Stanford, CA: Stanford University Press.

Parla, Ayşe, and Ceren Özgül. 2016. "Property, Dispossession, and Citizenship in Turkey; or, the History of the Gezi Uprising Starts in the Surp Hagop Armenian Cemetery." *Public Culture* 28 (3): 617–53. https://doi.org/10.1215/08992363-3511574.

Parla, Taha, and Andrew Davison. 2008. "Secularism and Laicism in Turkey." In *Secularisms*, edited by Janet R. Jakobsen and Ann Pellegrini, 58–75. Durham, NC: Duke University Press.

Parmaksız, Umut. 2018. "Making Sense of the Post-secular." *European Journal of Social Theory* 21 (1): 98–116.

Paules, Greta Foff. 1991. *Dishing It Out: Power and Resistance among Waitresses in a New Jersey Restaurant*. Philadelphia: Temple University Press.

Peck, Janice. 2016. *Age of Oprah: Cultural Icon for the Neoliberal Era*. Abingdon, UK: Routledge.

Pedwell, Carolyn, and Anne Whitehead. 2012. "Affecting Feminism: Questions of Feeling in Feminist Theory." *Feminist Theory*, 13 (2): 115–29.

Peirce, Leslie P. 1993. *The Imperial Harem: Women and Sovereignty in the Ottoman Empire*. New York: Oxford University Press.

Peirce, Leslie. 2009. "Writing Histories of Sexuality in the Middle East." *American Historical Review* 114 (5): 1325–39.

Peirce, Leslie P. 2010. "Domesticating Sexuality: Harem Culture in Ottoman Imperial Law." In *Harem Histories: Envisioning Places and Living Spaces*, edited by Marilyn Booth, 104–35. Durham, NC: Duke University Press.

Pettit, Harry. 2019. "The Cruelty of Hope: Emotional Cultures of Precarity in Neoliberal Cairo." *Environment and Planning D: Society and Space* 37 (4): 722–39. https://doi.org/10.1177/0263775818825264.

Pierce, Jennifer L. 1999. "Emotional Labor among Paralegals." *Annals of the American Academy of Political and Social Science* 561 (1): 127–42. https://www.jstor.org/stable/1049286.

Potuoğlu-Cook, Öykü. 2006. "Beyond the Glitter: Belly Dance and Neoliberal Gentrification in Istanbul." *Cultural Anthropology* 21 (4): 633–60. https://doi.org/10.1525/can.2006.21.4.633.

Potuoğlu-Cook, Öykü. 2015. "Hope with Qualms: A Feminist Analysis of the 2013 Gezi Protests." *Feminist Review* 109 (1): 96–123. https://doi.org/10.1057/fr.2014.56.

Puar, Jasbir. 2007. *Terrorist Assemblages: Homonationalism in Queer Times*. Durham, NC: Duke University Press.

Puar, Jasbir. 2012. "Precarity Talk: A Virtual Roundtable with Lauren Berlant, Judith Butler, Bojana Cvejić, Isabell Lorey, Jasbir Puar, and Ana Vujanović." *TDR/The Drama Review* 56 (4): 163–77. https://doi.org/10.1162/DRAM_a_00221.

Quataert, Donald. 2005. *The Ottoman Empire, 1700–1922*. Cambridge: Cambridge University Press.

Rabinovich, Tatiana. 2018. "Laboring on the Margins: Muslim Women, Precarity, and Potentiality in Russia." PhD diss., University of Arizona.

Radway, Janice A. 1983. "Women Read the Romance: The Interaction of Text and Context." *Feminist Studies* 9 (1): 53–78. https://doi.org/10.2307/3177683.

Razack, Sherene. 2008. *Casting Out: The Eviction of Muslims from Western Law and Politics*. Toronto: University of Toronto Press.

Rimke, Heidi Marie. 2000. "Governing Citizens through Self-Help Literature." *Cultural Studies* 14 (1): 61–78. https://doi.org/10.1080/095023800334986.

Ringrose, Jessica, and Valerie Walkerdine. 2008. "Regulating the Abject: The TV Makeover as Site of Neo-liberal Reinvention toward Bourgeois Femininity." *Feminist Media Studies* 8 (3): 227–46.

Robinson, William, and Xuan Santos. 2014. "Global Capitalism, Immigrant Labor, and the Struggle for Justice." *Class, Race and Corporate Power* 2 (3). https://doi.org/10.25148/CRCP.2.3.16092122.

Rosati, Massimo. 2016. *The Making of a Post-secular Society: A Durkheimian Approach to Memory, Pluralism and Religion in Turkey*. London: Routledge.

Rose, Nikolas S. 1990. *Governing the Soul: The Shaping of the Private Self*. Abingdon, UK: Routledge.

Rose, Nikolas. 1992. "Governing the Enterprising Self." In *The Values of the Enterprise Culture: The Moral Debate*, edited by Paul Heelas and Paul Morris, 141–64. Abingdon, UK: Routledge.

Rose, Nikolas. 1998. *Inventing Our Selves: Psychology, Power, and Personhood*. Cambridge: Cambridge University Press.

Roy, Ananya. 2010. *Poverty Capital: Microfinance and the Making of Development*. Abingdon, UK: Routledge.

Saktanber, Ayşe. 2002. *Living Islam: Women, Religion and the Politicization of Culture in Turkey*. London: I. B. Tauris.

Saluk, Seda. 2021. "Monitoring Pregnancies: The Politics and Ethics of Reproductive Health Surveillance in Turkey." In *The Politics of the Female Body in Contemporary Turkey: Reproduction, Maternity, Sexuality*, edited by Hilal Alkan, Ayşe Dayı, Sezin Topcu, and Betül Yarar, 127–47. London: I. B. Taurus.

Sandıkcı, Özlem. 2015. "Strolling through Istanbul's Beyoğlu: In-Between Difference and Containment." *Space and Culture* 18 (2): 198–211. https://doi.org/10.1177/1206331213501129.

Sarıoğlu, Esra. 2016. "New Imaginaries of Gender in Turkey's Service Economy: Women Workers and Identity Making on the Sales Floor." *Women's Studies International Forum* 54:39–47.

Savci, Evren. 2021. *Queer in Translation: Sexual Politics under Neoliberal Islam*. Durham, NC: Duke University Press.

Scharff, Christina. 2016. "Gender and Neoliberalism: Young Women as Ideal Neoliberal Subjects." In *Handbook of Neoliberalism*, edited by Simon Springer, Kean Birch, and Julie MacLeavy, 217–26. Abingdon, UK: Routledge.

Schick, İrvin Cemil. 2010. "The Harem as Gendered Space and the Spatial Reproduction of Gender." In *Harem Histories: Envisioning Places and Living Spaces*, edited by Marilyn Booth, 69–84. Durham, NC: Duke University Press. https://doi.org/10.1215/9780822393467-005.

Schimmel, Annemarie. 1992. *Islam: An Introduction*. Albany: State University of New York Press.

Schleifer, Yigal. 2005. "On Turkish TV, Women Face Life and Death." *Women's eNews*, May 24. https://womensenews.org/2005/05/turkish-tv-women-face-life-and-death/.

Scott, David, and Charles Hirschkind, eds. 2006. *Powers of the Secular Modern: Talal Asad and His Interlocutors*. Stanford, CA: Stanford University Press.

Sehlikoğlu, Sertaç. 2013. "Kissing the Mahrem in Ankara." Hot Spots, *Fieldsights*, October 31. https://culanth.org/fieldsights/kissing-the-mahrem-in-ankara.

Sehlikoğlu, Sertaç. 2015. "Intimate Publics, Public Intimacies: Natural Limits, Creation and the Culture of Mahremiyet in Turkey." *Cambridge Journal of Anthropology* 33 (2): 77–89. https://doi.org/10.3167/ca.2015.330207.

Sehlikoğlu, Sertaç. 2016. "Exercising in Comfort: Islamicate Culture of *Mahremiyet* in Everyday Istanbul." *Journal of Middle East Women's Studies* 12 (2): 143–65. https://doi.org/10.1215/15525864-3507606.

Sehlikoğlu, Sertaç. 2021. *Working out Desire: Women, Sport, and Self-Making in Istanbul*. Syracuse Press: Syracuse, New York.

Şen, A. Tunç. 2017. "Practicing Astral Magic in Sixteenth-Century Ottoman Istanbul: A Treatise on Talismans Attributed to Ibn Kemāl (d. 1534)." *Magic, Ritual, and Witchcraft* 12 (1): 66–88.

Sender, Katherine. 2006. "Queens for a Day: Queer Eye for the Straight Guy and the Neoliberal Project." *Critical Studies in Media Communication* 23 (2): 131–51.

Şenödeyici, Özer, and Halil Sercan Koşik. 2015. "En Muteber Kaynaktan Gaybı Öğrenmek: Bir Kuran Falı Manzumesi." *Littera Turca Journal of Turkish Language and Literature* 1 (1): 71–96.

Şenses, Nazlı. 2016. "Rethinking Migration in the Context of Precarity: The Case of Turkey." *Critical Sociology* 42 (7–8): 975–87. https://doi.org/10.1177/0896920515606503.

Şenses, Nazlı. 2020. "Rethinking Migration in the Context of Precarity: The Case of Turkey." In *Women, Migration and Asylum in Turkey: Developing Gender-Sensitivity in Migration Research, Policy and Practice*, edited by Lucy Williams, Emel Coşkun, and Selmin Kaşka, 975–87. Migration, Diasporas and Citizenship. Cham: Palgrave Macmillan.

Seremetakis, Nadia C. 2009. "Divination, Media, and the Networked Body of Modernity." *American Ethnologist* 36 (2): 337–50.

Sezer, Sennur. 1998. *Osmanlı'da Fal ve Falnameler*. Istanbul: Milliyet Yayınları.

Shively, Kim. 2008. "Taming Islam: Studying Religion in Secular Turkey." *Anthropological Quarterly* 81 (3): 683–711. https://doi.org/10.1353/anq.0.0017.

Shultz, Susanne. 2006. "Dissolved Boundaries and 'Affective Labor': On the Disappearance of Reproductive Labor and Feminist Critique in *Empire*." Translated by Frederic Peters. *Capitalism, Nature, Socialism* 17 (1): 77–82.

Sirman, Nükhet. 2000. "Gender Construction and Nationalist Discourse: Dethroning the Father in the Early Turkish Novel." In *Gender and Identity Construction: Women of Central Asia, the Caucasus and Turkey*, edited by Feride Acar and Ayse Güneş-Ayata, 162–76. Leiden: Brill.

Sirman, Nükhet. 2005. "The Making of Familial Citizenship in Turkey." In *Citizenship in a Global World: European Questions and Turkish Experiences*, edited by E. Fuat Keyman and Ahmet İçduygu, 147–72. London: Routledge.

Sirman, Nükhet. 2019. "Mediated Fantasies of the Family on Turkish Television." *European Journal of Turkish Studies*, no. 28, 1–14. https://doi.org/10.4000/ejts.6329.

Sokołowicz, Małgorzata. 2019. "A Taste of Empire: Eighteenth-Century Eastern and Western European Women's Journeys into Ottoman Culinary Spaces." *Early Modern Women* 14 (1): 152–63. https://doi.org/10.1353/emw.2019.0061.

Standing, Guy. 2011. *The Precariat: The New Dangerous Class*. London: Bloomsbury Academic.

Steedman, Carolyn. 1987. *Landscape for a Good Woman: A Story of Two Lives*. New Brunswick, NJ: Rutgers University Press.

Stewart, Kathleen. 2007. *Ordinary Affects*. Durham, NC: Duke University Press.

Stewart, Kathleen. 2011. "Atmospheric Attunements." *Environment and Planning D: Society and Space* 29 (3): 445–53.

Stokes, Martin. 2010. *The Republic of Love: Cultural Intimacy in Turkish Popular Music*. Chicago: University of Chicago Press.

Sviri, Sara. 1999. "Dreaming Analyzed and Recorded." In *Dream Cultures: Explorations in the Comparative History of Dreaming*, edited by David Shulman and Guy G. Stroumsa, 252–73. New York: Oxford University Press.

Tahaoğlu, Çiçek. 2012. "Arınç'ın 'Vajina Monologu'na Suç Duyurusu." *Bianet*, December 20. https://bianet.org/kadin/siyaset/142959-arinc-in-vajina-monologu-na-suc-duyurusu.

Takeyama, Akiko. 2010. "Intimacy for Sale: Masculinity, Entrepreneurship, and Commodity Self in Japan's Neoliberal Situation." *Japanese Studies* 30 (2): 231–46. https://doi.org/10.1080/10371397.2010.497579.

Tan, Turhan M. (1938) 1990. *Osmanlı Rasputini Cinci Hoca*. Istanbul: İnkilap ve Ata.

Taussig, Michael. 1980. *The Devil and Commodity Fetishism in South America*. Chapel Hill: University of North Carolina Press.

Taussig, Michael. 2003. "Viscerality, Faith, and Skepticism: Another Theory of Magic." In *Magic and Modernity: Interfaces of Revelation and Concealment*, edited by Birgit Meyer and Peter Pels, 272–306. Stanford, CA: Stanford University Press.

Tavşanoğlu, Serkan. 2013. "Evrenden Torpili Var! Sertaç Taşdelen." MAG, May 7. https://www.magdergi.com/roportajlar/evrenden-torpili-var-sertac-tasdelen/.

Tedü, Suavi, dir. 1953. *Cinci Hoca*. Istanbul: Halk Film.

Tekçe, Belgin. 2019. "Fantasy and Propriety in Familial Lives." *European Journal of Turkish Studies*, no. 28, 1–17. https://doi.org/10.4000/ejts.6226.

Thompson, Elizabeth. 2003. "Public and Private in Middle Eastern Women's History." *Journal of Women's History* 15 (1): 52–69. https://doi.org/10.1353/jowh.2003.0037.

Toksöz, Gülay. 2007. *Women's Employment Situation in Turkey*. Ankara: International Labor Office.

Toksöz, Gülay. 2016. "Transition from 'Woman' to 'Family': An Analysis of AKP Era Employment Policies from a Gender Perspective." *Journal für Entwicklungspolitik* 32 (1/2): 64–83.

Toksöz, Gülay, and Çağla Ulutaş. 2012. "Is Migration Feminized? A Gender and Ethnicity Based Review of the Literature on Irregular Migration to Turkey." In *Turkey Migration and the EU: Potential, Challenges and Opportunities*, edited by Seçil Paçacı Elitok and Thomas Straubhaar. Hamburg: Hamburg University Press.

Tucker, James. 2002. "New Age Religion and the Cult of the Self." *Society* 39 (2): 46–51. https://doi.org/10.1007/BF02717528.

Tunalı, İnsan, Murat G. Kırdar, and Meltem Dayıoğlu. 2017. "Female Labor Force Participation in Turkey: A Synthetic Cohort Analysis, 1988–2013." TUBITAK. Project No. 112K517.

Türk Dil Kurumu. 2019. "Mahrem," "Mahremiyet." Güncel Türkçe Sözlük. Accessed September 12. https://sozluk.gov.tr/.

Turner, Victor. 1977. "Variations on a Theme of Liminality." In *Secular Ritual*, edited by Sally Falk Moore and Barbara G. Myerhoff, 36–52. Assen: Gorcum.

Vasilaki, Rosa. 2016. "The Politics of Post-secular Feminism." *Theory, Culture and Society* 33 (2): 103–23. https://doi.org/10.1177/0263276415590235.

Wacquant, Loïc. 2012. "Three Steps to a Historical Anthropology of Actually Existing Neoliberalism." *Social Anthropology* 20 (1): 66–79. https://doi.org/10.1111/j.1469-8676.2011.00189.x.

Warner, Michael. 2005. *Publics and Counterpublics*. New York: Zone.

Warner, Michael, Jonathan VanAntwerpen, and Craig Calhoun, eds. 2010. *Varieties of Secularism in a Secular Age*. Cambridge, MA: Harvard University Press.

Weber, Brenda R. 2009. *Makeover TV: Selfhood, Citizenship, and Celebrity*. Durham, NC: Duke University Press.

Weeks, Kathi. 2007. "Life within and against Work: Affective Labor, Feminist Critique, and Post-Fordist Politics." *Ephemera* 7 (1): 233–49.

Weiss, Matthew. 2016. "From Constructive Engagement to Renewed Estrangement? Securitization and Turkey's Deteriorating Relations with Its Kurdish Minority." *Turkish Studies* 17 (4): 567–98. https://doi.org/10.1080/14683849.2016.1228456.

White, Jenny B. 2004. *Money Makes Us Relatives: Women's Labor in Urban Turkey*. New York: Routledge.

White, Jenny. 2014. *Muslim Nationalism and the New Turks*. Princeton, NJ: Princeton University Press.

Williams, Raymond. 1977. *Marxism and Literature*. Oxford: Oxford University Press.

Wilson, Julie. 2017. *Neoliberalism*. New York: Routledge.

Wissinger, Elizabeth. 2007. "Always on Display: Affective Production in the Modeling Industry." In *The Affective Turn: Theorizing the Social*, edited by Patricia Ticineto Clough and Jean Halley, 231–60. Durham, NC: Duke University Press. https://doi.org/10.1215/9780822389606-011.

Yavuz, M. Hakan. 1998. "Turkish Identity and Foreign Policy in Flux: The Rise of Neo-Ottomanism." *Critique: Critical Middle Eastern Studies* 7 (12): 19–41. https://doi.org/10.1080/10669929808720119.

Yazici, Berna. 2012. "The Return to the Family: Welfare, State, and Politics of the Family in Turkey." *Anthropological Quarterly* 85 (1): 103–40.

Yıldırım, Umut. 2019. "Space, Loss and Resistance: A Haunted Pool-Map in South-Eastern Turkey." *Anthropological Theory* 19 (4): 440–69.

Yıldız, Emrah. 2014. "Cruising Politics: Sexuality, Solidarity and Modularity after Gezi." In *The Making of a Protest Movement in Turkey: #occupygezi*, edited by Umut Özkırımlı, 103–20. London: Palgrave Pivot. https://doi.org/10.1057/9781137413789_8.

Yılmaz, Demet Özmen. 2019. "Female Labor in the Neoliberal Era: The Case of Turkey." In *Economic and Business Issues in Retrospect and Prospect*, edited by Marcel Mečiar, Kerem Gökten, and Ahmet Arif Eren, 203–11. London: IJOPEC.

Yilmaz, Ihsan, and James Barry. 2020. "The AKP's De-securitization and Re-securitization of a Minority Community: The Alevi Opening and Closing." *Turkish Studies* 21 (2): 231–53. https://doi.org/10.1080/14683849.2019.1601564.

Yılmaz, Volkan, and İpek Göçmen. 2016. "Denied Citizens of Turkey: Experiences of Discrimination among LGBT Individuals in Employment, Housing and Health Care." *Gender, Work and Organization* 23 (5): 470–88. https://doi.org/10.1111/gwao.12122.

Yörük, Erdem. 2012. "Welfare Provision as Political Containment: The Politics of Social Assistance and the Kurdish Conflict in Turkey." *Politics and Society* 40 (4): 517–47. https://doi.org/10.1177/0032329212461130.

Ze'evi, Dror. 2006. *Producing Desire: Changing Sexual Discourse in the Ottoman Middle East, 1500–1900*. Berkeley: University of California Press.

Zengin, Asli. 2016. "Violent Intimacies: Tactile State Power, Sex/Gender Transgression, and the Politics of Touch in Contemporary Turkey." *Journal of Middle East Women's Studies* 12 (2): 225–45. https://doi.org/10.1215/15525864-3507650.

Zengin, Aslı. 2020. *İktidarın Mahremiyeti: Istanbul'da Hayat Kadınları, Seks İşçiliği ve Şiddet*. Istanbul: Metis Yayınları.

Zeydanlıoğlu, Welat. 2008. "The White Turkish Man's Burden: Orientalism, Kemalism and the Kurds in Turkey." In *Neo-colonial Mentalities in Contemporary Europe? Language and Discourse in the Construction of Identities*, edited by Guido Rings and Anne Ife, 155–74. Newcastle, UK: Cambridge Scholars.

Zürcher, Erik J. 2004. *Turkey: A Modern History*. London: I. B. Tauris.

Index

Note: An italicized *f* following a page number indicates a figure.

Atatürk (continued)

and, 56–57; on the defense, 95–96; fortune-telling café decorations and, 124; hodjas and, 56, 228n1; on Islam, 58; overviews, 52; mixed-gender dancing and, 134; on-line coffee grounds image and, 25, 87–90, 88f; on Ottoman Empire, 54; personal titles and, 230n2; secular nationalism and, 55–56; tradition/religion/superstition and, 52–56, 230n2; ulema and, 55. *See also* Turkish Republic

atheism, 225n4

authentic (*hakiki*), 92

author: ethnographic research overviews, 12, 17–21, 28, 30–31, 226n11, 227n11, 231n6; feelings and, 16–17; as fortune-teller, 20; identities of, 1, 18, 19–20, 231n6; readings of, 1–2, 16–17, 19–20, 111–12, 116–18, 173–75, 176–78

authoritarianism, Islamist. democracy and, 228n9; Islamism and, 190; overviews, 2, 3, 10, 221, 223; secularism and, 12, 23, 26, 52; secularism/religion and, 228n8. *See also* AKP (Adalet ve Kalkınma Partisi) (Justice and Development Party); heteronormative order (patriarchy) (gender norms) (conservatism/conformity); laws

authority, masculine, 61

authority, medical, 70–73, 83, 146

authority, spiritual, 102–3

authority of fortune-tellers, 79, 168

authority to practice (*el almadım*), 76–77, 78

autonomy, 211–12

Ayşe (married woman, early forties, reader), 72, 75, 229n7

baba (Bektaşi sheikh), 57

Bayhan (thirtysomething secular working-class, queer Roma man), 145, 161–63, 171, 176–82, 185, 191–92

"beautiful boys," 131

beauty, 94, 95

beauty salons, 234n7, 234n 8

Bektaşi (religious order), 41, 43

Berkes, Niyazi, 41

Berlant, Laurent, 115

Beyoğlu, Istanbul, 3, 127, 132, 136f, 144–45, 173f, 178, 234n9

Binnaz Abla website, 7f, 203, 204f, 206–7, 208, 229

Birol Gündoğdu (Turkish publisher), 83

Black people. *See* Arab and Black people; ethnoracial hierarchies and racialization

blessings (*bereket*), 202

bodily gestures, involuntary, 226n10

book clubs, 26

book fortune-telling (*kitap falı*), 47

brides, 113, 131, 149–50, 236n13. *See also* marriage

büyücü (sorcerer), 57

Café and Bar Workers Association (Kafe-Bar Çalışanları Birliği), 182

caliphate, 228n9

caliphs, 55, 57

calligraphy, 92

capitalism. *See* colonialism and imperialism; neoliberalism (capitalism) and neoliberalization

cards and beans, 106

care and healing. *See* therapeutic spirit of neoliberalism (healing and care)

Cayisallama (*Öğretmen Sözlük*), 129

çelebi (leader of a Mevlevi order), 57

Çelebi, Evliya, 46–47

censorship, 171, 190

Chatterjee, Partha, 54

chief timekeeper (*başmuvakkitlik*), 58

children, having. Ada and, 196; AKP and, 202; author's readings and, 16–17, 19; careers and, 235n2; customers and, 177; economic rewards and, 202; Erdoğan and, 148–49, 236n8; feeling unsettled and, 187; overviews, 10, 12; political fantasy and, 153; precarity and, 176, 179; television and, 147, 148, 149–51. *See also* education; families

Chinese characters, 102f, 103

Çiçek, Cemil, 236n10

Çiğdem (single, middle-aged female fortune-teller), 79, 97

cin (clever person), 75. *See also* jinn (*cinler*)

cinci hoca, 59, 64, 65f, 229n6. *See also* Cinci Hodjas; hodjas and *hodja* bashing

Cinci Hoca (movie), 62–63, 63f

Cinci Hodjas, 62, 229n6

cinler. See jinn (*cinler*)

citizenship, 179, 185, 217, 218

"civilization" (*medeniyet*), 53

civil servant mentality (*memur zihniyeti*) (rule-bound, bureaucratic conduct), 196

class, socioeconomic. Abdülaziz Bey on, 48–49, 50–51; customers and, 70; feeling unsettled and, 238n4; feelings and, 162; heteronormative domesticity and, 134; intimacy and, 234n8; lower, 238n3; lower-middle, 186, 201; mystification and, 202; Ottoman Empire and, 46–48, 130, 131–32; precarity and, 187, 226n8; public space and, 130; secularity and, 225n3; secularization and, 22–23; ulema and, 42–43, 55, 228n6; working or lower, 12, 42, 66, 183, 188, 192, 208, 217–18 (*see also* Bayhan; Meral). *See also* elitism; masculine/feminine distinction; middle class; middle-class fortune-tellers and customers

closed customers, 166

closing cup (*kapatmak*), 6, 117, 172

coffee consumption, 92–93, 135, 167, 217, 231n4, 234n12

coffee readings (*kahve falı*). *See* readings

coffeehouses (*kahvehane*), 129–32, 134–37, 136f, 137, 227n14. *See also* Ankara Association of Coffeehouses

emotion; enchantment; feeling labors; feeling postsecular; intimacy (*mahremiyet*); precarity (vulnerability); romantic love and sexual desire; therapeutic spirit of neoliberalism

feeling unsettled, 187–92, 199, 223, 238n4, 238n5, 238n6. *See also* Ada

"female complaint" literary genre, 115

femicides, 153

femininity and feminization: affective labor, unpaid and devalued and, 28–29, 34, 183–84; affective labors and, 28–32; Atatürk and, 58; author and, 17, 111–12; criminalization and, 58; defined, 225n2, 225n3, 225n4, 225n5; feeling labor and, 163–64; fortune-tellers and, 6–7, 8; gender normativity and, 8; heteronormative gender order and, 115; historical context and, 23; intimate publics and, 15, 25–27; labor migrants and, 186; labor participation and, 184; labor precarity and, 14; national modernist secularism and, 33; neoliberalism and, 34; nonhegemonic masculinity and, 121; Ottoman Empire and, 45; overviews, 12–14, 23, 32–34, 40, 221; secular Muslims and, 103; self-entrepreneurialism and, 32, 196; shopping malls and, 235n13; subjectification and, 32; subjects and, 113, 115; superstition and, 55; young and gay men and, 226n9. *See also* affect; children; domestic spaces and domesticity; emotion; feeling labors; feeling publics of femininity; feeling (*hissetmek*); feminist voices (feminism/activism, scholarship); gendering; irrational femininity; LGBTIQ; marriage; modesty; publics, feminized

feminist analytics: affective labor and, 28, 30, 31–32; feeling and, 2; pseudofeminist discourse and, 3; heteronormative gender order, 34; hope and, 222; Middle Eastern, 28; neoliberalism and, 34; public feelings and, 33–34; publics and, 25; US, 28

feminist divinations, 221–24

feminist politics, 147, 153–57

feminist voices (feminism/activism, scholarship): AKA and, 10; author and, 17; Çiçek and, 236n10; colonial assumptions and, 27; Erdoğan and, 236n8, 238n3; heteronormative family and, 149; intimate publics and, 147; marriage and children and, 149; on Middle East, 33; neoconservative politics and, 10, 150, 156; neoliberalism and, 222; overviews, 152, 221–23; political publics and, 155; "politics of affect" and, 227n12; precarious futures and, 187–88; secularism and, 12; suppression of, 150; television and, 149, 153, 157; Turkish Republic and, 133; US, 28; violence against, 189–90; Western consciousness-raising groups and, 154. *See also* author

Ferguson, Roderick, 233n3

fiqh (Islamic jurisprudence), 83

flirting, 236n10

folk religion, 54. *See also* superstition

fortune-tellers, fortune-telling, and divination: diversity of, 226n11; incomes and, 182, 184, 209, 211, 213, 216, 239n7; male practitioners, 76, 121, 184 (*See also* astrology and astrologers; *hodjas* and *hodja* bashing; self-entrepreneurialism); overviews, 5–9, 31, 221–23. *See also* crimes and criminalization; feeling (*hissetmek*); femininity and feminization; feminist divinations; gendered fortunes; genealogies (historical contexts); precarity; readings; secular Muslims; therapeutic neoliberalism

fortune-telling book (*falname*), 47

fortune-telling cafés (*falkafe*): author's research and, 226n11; beauty salons compared, 234n7; images, 4f, 123f; media and, 227n3; morality and, 231n7; overviews, 3, 5–6, 38; politics and, 154–57; spaces described, 121–24, 123f; working conditions and, 181. *See also* Café and Bar Workers Association; coffeehouses (*kahvehane*); crimes and criminalization; feeling publics of femininity; publics; spaces

fortune-telling café owners: author's research and, 227n11; criminalized, 37–38, 39, 67f; feeling publics of femininity and, 118; fortune-tellers and, 183; Fortune-Telling Street and, 127; heteronormative gender order and, 125; Kurdish immigrant woman, 121–22; labor precarity and, 212–13; legality and, 73–74; oversight and intervention and, 73–74, 171–72; paternalism and, 125; self-entrepreneurialism and, 203, 205, 239n5; therapy and, 172. *see also* Derya

fortune-telling houses (*falevi*), 181

fortune-telling offices (*falbüro*), 181

Fortune-Telling Street (Adnan Işık Sokak or Fal Sokağı), 127, 128f

"fraud by the abuse of religious beliefs and feelings" (*dini inanç ve duygularının istismarı suretiyle dolandırıcılık*), 104

Freudian psychology, 210

"friendship" (*arkadaşlık*), 150

fully formed (*hamur yoğruldu*), 178

gaipten haber vermek (giving information about the unknown), 57

gazi (Islamic warrior), 230n2

gendered fortunes, 15–32, 190–92, 221–23. *See also* feeling (*hissetmek*); fortune-tellers, fortune-telling, and divination; Islam ("religion"); publics, gendered; secularism (*laiklik*) and secularization; spaces; 21st century overviews; Western modernity

gendering, 2–3, 107. *See also* ethnoracial hierarchies and racialization; femininity and feminization; gendered fortunes; male/female binary; masculinity; precarity

genealogies (historical contexts): author's research and, 18; criminalization and, 37–45; gender and, 23; housewifization and, 29; intimate publics and, 127–37; nationalism and tradition and, 47–51, 53; neoliberalism and, 168–69; overviews, 15, 21, 23, 39–40, 57–58; secular and religious, 40–45;

Index 271

online fortune-tellers and platforms: commodification and, 239n8; customers and, 239n8, 239n9; customer satisfaction ratings and, 212–13, 239n9; displacement from social relations and, 8; dream interpretation and, 229n8; feelings and, 15; income and, 239n7; intimacy and, 89–90; intimate publics and, 145; labor precarity and, 32, 211–16; overviews, 3; pious Muslims and, 231n10; political public sphere *versus*, 11; politics and, 7f; secular Muslim identity and, 18. *See also* anonymity; self-entrepreneurialism; transnational futures

Önsü, Vedia Bülent Çorak, 97

openness, 166, 167, 221–22, 223

Orientalist perspectives, 119

Osmanlı Rasputin'i Cinci Hoca (Tan), 62, 63

othering: ethnoracial hierarchies and, 51, 57; feelings and, 34; gendering and racializing and, 233n3; *hodjas* and, 228n1; knowing and, 34; nationalism and tradition and, 51; queer precarity and, 178; secularism and, 39; secularization and, 58; of the superstitious, 38

Ottoman Empire: coffee houses and, 129–33; colonialism and, 228n5; commodification and, 92; criminalization and, 39, 40–51; cultural elites and, 44; European imperialism and, 43–44; fortune-tellers and, 45–48; *hodjas* and, 228n1; hope and, 189; millennial Turkey and, 228n5; nationalism and coffee consumption and, 231n4; overviews, 58; public (male)/private (female) and, 228n1; reason *versus* superstition and, 61; religion and, 228n6; secularism/religion and, 41–45, 234n11; television and, 92; tradition and religion and, 49–50; Westernization and, 43–44, 52, 54; women and, 43. *See also* neo-Ottomanism; religious orders; sheikhs

Ottomania, 92, 217

Ottoman women, non-Muslim, 50

"ours" (*bize ait*), 92

Öznur (college-educated, divorced thirtysomething woman), 70, 77–78, 236n3

pandemic, global, 190

patriarchy. *See* authoritarianism, Islamist; heteronormative order (patriarchy) (gender norms) (conservatism/conformity); reason, masculine secular; savior narratives

peace (*huzur*), 201

Pera (Beyoğlu), 132

personal titles, 228n9, 230n2

philosophy, 79, 81

phone-in fortune-telling, 105

piety: Ada and, 102; AKP and, 91, 189; Gökalp on, 53–54; hodjas and, 64–65; jinn and, 75; Koşar and, 84; public spaces and, 190; Semra and, 95, 96, 98–99; sociopolitcal processes and, 105; Turkish Republic and, 55–56; Yeşim and, 98–99; yoga

and, 82. *See also* modesty; pious Muslims; rituals, ceremonies, and worship; veil

pious Muslims: colonial, pseudofeminism and, 3; feeling postsecular and, 25; feminism and, 222; hodjas and, 86; legalization and, 231n10; Manaf and, 82–83; neoliberalism and, 201–2; Ottoman, 43, 55, 92, 189; overviews, 12; scholarship and, 23–24; secularism and, 106–7; therapeutic self-entrepreneurialism and, 202. *See also* modesty; pious Muslims; rituals, ceremonies, and worship; veil

pious/nonpious, 225n4, 231n6. *See also* piety; pious Muslims; secular Muslims

political uprisings of 2013, 12

politics of secularism: *hodjas* and, 59, 61, 68–86; jinn and feelings and, 74–80; media and, 59–68; overviews, 229n2; (post)secularism and, 80–86. *See also* secularism (*laiklik*) and secularization

pop psychology, 79–80

popularist governmental gestures, 231n2

pouring lead (*kurşun dökmek*). *See* lead pouring (*kurşun dökmek*)

Praise Allah and Let Go of the Rest (Koşar), 83

prayer beads (*tespih*), 48

prayers, 176, 231n6, 232n12

praying for the patient's health (*okuyup üflemek*), 70

preadolescent boys, 233n1

precarity (vulnerability): affect and, 175, 186, 188, 191; author's reading and, 174; customer, 8, 12; defined, 226n8; examples of, 175–80; feeling labors and, 167–68, 175–80; intimacy and, 175–80, 226n8; neoliberalism and, 20, 30; overviews, 2, 9–10, 12, 29, 30, 157, 163–64, 188, 91, 221, 222–23; queer futures and, 178, 187; self-entrepreneurship and, 201; therapeutic culture and, 30, 31, 163, 167–68, 179–80, 186–88, 238n2. *See also* families; feeling unsettled; hope; intimacy; labor precarity; LGBTIQ; marginalization; sexual harassment; therapeutic spirit of neoliberalism

premarital relations, 150–51

premonition (*önsezi*), 79

Presidency of Religious Affairs (Diyanet İşleri Başkanlığı), 5–6, 18, 55–56, 75, 82, 105–6, 228n9

privacy. *See* intimacy (*mahremiyet*)

private life (*özel hayat*), 122

private spaces, 61, 233n4. *See also* public (male)/private (female)

private (feminine) sphere, 34. *See also* harem (*mahrem* spaces) and *haremlik/selamlık* quarters; housewives and housewifization

prognostication, 46

prostitution, 236n10

public, national, 96

public baths, 130

public (masculine) sphere: amendments to Law No. 677 and, 232n12; Atatürk and, 56; criminalization and, 47; femininities and intimacies and,

14; gendering and, 33; hodja narratives and, 61; Ottoman, 45–46; overviews, 28, 34. *See also hodjas* and *hodja* bashing; secular public sphere

public (male)/private (female), 119, 133, 233n1. *See also* harem (*mahrem* spaces) and *haremlik/selamlık* quarters

publics, gendered: femininity and, 15; feminized, 25–27, 32–33; intimacy and, 25–28, 137; mixed gender and, 133–34, 234n6, 234n12; overviews, 25–28, 131; politics and, 233n1; social relations and, 26. *See also* feeling publics of femininity; intimate publics; public (male)/private (female); spaces

publics, safer & anonymous, 10, 11–12, 15, 27. *See also* intimate publics; labor precarity; online fortunetellers and platforms; spaces; television

publics of femininity. *See* feeling labors

queering gestures, 124

queer voices (individual, activist, scholarly): female readers, 121–22; hodja-bashing and, 69; hope and, 222; intimate publics and, 25; keeping up facades and, 156; marriage and children and, 149; overviews, 3, 10; precarious futures and, 178, 187–88; pseudonyms and, 19; public feelings and, 33–34; readings and, 8; scholarly studies, 32; secularism and, 12; shopping malls and, 235n13; television and, 27

racialization. *See* ethnoracial hierarchies and racialization

Radio and Television Supreme Council (Radyo ve Televizyon Üst Kurulu (RTÜK), 105, 106, 150, 151

Radyo Astroloji (Astrology radio), 91

rational/superstitious distinctions, 85

readingsAtatürk in coffee grounds, 25, 87–90, 88f; author's, 1–2, 16–17, 111–12, 116–18, 173–75, 176–77; described, 6, 8, 165–67; in domestic spaces, 235n2; gendered fortunes and, 6, 8; Greek women and, 233n4; intimacy and, 235n1; irrationality and, 100–1; Islam and, 106; overviews, 3–9; secularism/religion and, 93–94. *See also* Bayhan *and other readers*; crimes and criminalization; feeling labors; schema of interpretation (*tabir*); stars, reading fortunes from (*yıldız falı bakma*) and other divinations

reason, masculine secular. *See also* irrational femininity: Abdülaziz Bey and, 50, 51; Atatürk and, 52; Atatürk in coffee grounds and, 89; feeling postsecular and, 25; feelings and, 34, 79; feeling *versus*, 21, 79; hodjas and, 60–63, 66, 67–68; Islam and, 106; nationalism and, 56–57; overviews, 21, 22, 40; secularism/religion and, 14, 23, 40, 52–53; 73, 101, 106, 222, 229n2; sex/gender and, 229n2; superstition and, 52–54, 70, 202, 229n2; television shows and, 146

receiving electricity (*elektrik almak*), 79

reception days (*gün*), 134

refugees, 217–18

regional differences, 42–43

Reiki, 79, 102f, 169, 172, 173f, 174–75, 194, 199

religion. *See* Islam ("religion"); spirituality and spiritualist services; superstition; tradition

religion, folk, 54

religious authority, 54

religious orders, 41–43, 55, 56, 57, 228n9, 232n12

Republican People's Party (Cumhuriyet Halk Partisi), 89, 104, 148–49, 225n3, 230n2

Reyhan (thirtysomething female reader and waxing salon owner), 125

rituals, ceremonies, and worship: Ada and, 102; coffee publics and, 130; Ottoman, 41–42, 43; readings compared, 238n6; secular Muslim women and, 98–99; Semra and, 94–95; spaces and, 41–42; Yeşim and, 96. *See also* piety

romantic love and sexual desire: author's readings and, 20–21, 176–78; Bayhan and, 179; commodification and, 143–44; feeling labors and, 10–11; Gürpınar and, 62; heteroromantic fantasies, 6, 115; neoliberalism and, 148; Ottoman Empire and, 132; overviews, 141–42; precarity and, 152, 175, 176, 179–80, 201; private and personal realms and, 122; readings of same-sex desires and, 144, 145; romance novels and, 32; television and, 146, 237n2; therapeutic milieu and, 175. *See also* adultery; Elif; intimacy; Meral; *namahremler* (those who are not *mahrem* to each other); sexuality; Sibel

Roma people, 8–9, 48–49, 50, 185, 185f. *See also* Bayhan

Rum (Ottoman Greek Orthodox), 48

Rumi, Jalal al-Din (Sufi master), 102, 102f, 199

Russian Muslim immigrants, 185–86, 188

Rüyanız Hayrolsun (May your dreams be auspicious) (TV show), 91

samimiyet (intimacy), 152, 234n8

Samsun, 178

Sargut, Cemalnur, 97

"Satanists," 127

savior narratives, 69, 74, 81, 85–86

secrecy/privacy (*gizlilik*), 119

secularism (*laiklik*) and seculareization: authoritarianism and, 12, 23, 26, 52; class, religion and race and, 21–25; contemporary Islamism and, 5–6; defined, 225n1; feelings and, 32, 34; feeling unsettled and, 188; femininity and, 34; fortune-tellers and, 225n1; fortune-telling cafés and, 2; gendered, 15, 21–25, 227n12; historical context and, 21; hodja-bashing and, 74; "housewife" *versus* "hodja" and, 67–68; Islam and, 230n2; Istanbul and, 7f; labor precarity and, 228n9; masculine authority and, 61; notions of publicness (*kamusallık*) of, 11; othering and, 58; overviews, 3, 5–6, 15–16, 21, 40, 80, 225n1; politics and, 24–25; readers and, 225n6; religion (Islam) compared, 23; spaces and, 11; tradition and, 82.

secularism (continued)
  See also Atatürk (Mustafa Kemal) and Kemalism;
  crimes and criminalization; education; feeling
  postsecular; heteronormative order (patriarchy)
  (gender norms) (conservatism/conformity); pious/
  nonpious; politics of secularism; reason, masculine
  secular; secularism/religion; secular Muslims
secularism/religion: affect and, 25, 38, 94, 201; authoritarianism and, 228n8; coffee readings and, 89,
  93–94; criminalization and, 22, 33, 39–58, 60, 103;
  decriminalization and, 103, 154; education and, 98;
  feminism and, 222; gendered, 227n13; genealogies
  and, 22, 33, 39–58, 60; healing and, 83; heteronormative gender order and, 23–24; *hodjas* and, 64,
  106–7, 228n1; laws and, 228n9, 230n2, 232n12;
  Ottoman Empire and, 234n11; overviews, 21–25,
  39–41, 107; pious Muslims and, 106–7; politics
  and, 232n12; reason and, 14, 23, 40, 52–53, 73, 101,
  106, 222, 229n2; separation of church and state and,
  40–41; sexual desire and, 81–82; Turkish Republic
  and, 54–55, 228n8; women's piety and public
  presence and, 154. *See also* "Don't believe . . . but
  don't do without it either"; enchantment; feeling
  postsecular; laicism (*laiklik*) and laicization; laws;
  new ageism; pious/nonpious; savior narratives;
  secular Muslims; Western modernity
secularist defined, 225n3
secular Muslims: author as, 20; author's research and,
  222n4; defined, 225n3; feminism and, 222; fortune-
  telling cafés (*falkafe*) and, 27; fragilely middle-class,
  straight, and cisgender female, 188; Muslim identities and, 96–97; overviews, 2, 15, 23–24, 31, 86,
  225n4; pious Egyptian women compared, 222; precarity and, 9, 221; readers, 15; religion and, 90–107;
  secularism and, 25, 93; social media and, 18; spaces
  and, 27; supernatural and, 23–24, 90. *See also* Ada;
  Derya; "Don't believe . . . but don't do without it
  either"; feeling postsecular; globalization; pious/
  nonpious; secularism (laiklik) and secularization;
  secularism (*laiklik*) and secularization; secularism/
  religion; Semra; Yeşim
segregation, 11, 25–26, 28, 129, 234n12. Ottoman class
  and, 131–32. *See also* harem (*mahrem* spaces) and
  haremlik/selamlık quarters
self-development, 199
self-entrepreneurialism: Ada and, 193–196; affect and,
  206, 210–11, 213, 214, 215–16, 219–20; digital feeling
  labors and, 109–216; enchantment and, 192, 196,
  199–203, 206, 208; feeling labors and, 192; feeling
  precarious and, 201; feminized, 32, 196; gendered,
  197; labor precarity and, 109–216; lingo and, 203–9,
  239n5; Meral and, 209–12; neoliberalism and,
  170; overviews, 9, 15, 29, 31–32, 157, 192, 197–98,
  207–08, 219–20; self-realization and, 198–99; social
  responsibility and, 207–8; spirituality and, 200;
  therapeutic services and, 191, 192, 194, 199, 200,

201.202, 206, 219, 220; transnational futures and,
  216–20; 2000s *vs.* 2010s, 203–9. *See also* Ada (fortysomething, divorced, secular, middle-class woman);
  online fortune-tellers and platforms
selfhood, postsecular neoliberal, 15. *See also* neoliberalism (capitalism) and neoliberalization;
  self-entrepreneurialism
self-making, 30, 238n4. *See also* self-entrepreneurialism
self-realization (*kendini gerçekleştirmek*), 31, 83, 198–99
Semra (female married secular Muslim fortune teller),
  73–75, 94–95, 97–99, 168
sensing (*duymak*), 79
Seremetakis, Nadia C., 226n10, 233n4, 235n1
Serkan (non-gender conforming male reader in
  twenties), 121
sexual harassment/violence, 151, 237n24. *See also*
  Manaf, Akif
sexuality: AKP and, 238n3; Bayhan and, 179; commodification and, 143–44; economy and, 81; *mahrem*
  and, 119, 122; Meral and, 209; secularism/religion
  and, 81–82. *See also* adultery; *hodjas* and *hodja*
  bashing; premarital relations; romantic love and
  sexual desire; sexual harassment/violence. *See also*
  adultery; *hodjas* and *hodja* bashing; premarital
  relations; romantic love and sexual desire; sexual
  harassment/violence
sex workers, 153, 154
şeyh (sheikh), 57–58
seyit (*sayyid*, a descendant of the Prophet), 57
Sezer, Şennur, 45
"share your troubles" (*dert ortağı*), 172
sharia family law, 133
sheikhs, 43, 56, 57
Sheikh Said, 57
Sheikh-ul-Islam Ebu Suud, 47
Sheikh-ul-Islam Sheikh-ul-Islam (*şeyhülislam*), 228n6
Shi'ism, 41
shopping malls, 235n13
Sibel (author's high school classmate), 140, 141
Sinan (unmarried male reader), 68–69
singlehood, 176–77
sixth sense (*altıncı his*), 79
Sıdıka (televised comedy), 59–61, 66
Sırru'l Esrar (Secret of secrets) (Sufi text), 174
smoking, 95
social assistance, 183
socially constructed categories, 40
social media, 236n13, 237n24. *See also* online fortune-
  tellers and platforms; television
sorcerer (*büyücü*), 57
South Asian migrant women's conversion to Islam, 29
spaces: Ada's, 194; author's research and, 17–18, 226n11;
  discursive, 32; feeling labors and, 171; feeling publics
  of femininity and, 117–18; feelings and, 10; fortune-
  telling, 4*f*, 102*f*; fortune-telling café decorations,
  174; intimacy and, 15, 26–28, 116–37, 233n1, 235n2;

.

www.ingramcontent.com/pod-product-compliance
Lightning Source LLC
Chambersburg PA
CBHW071733270326
41928CB00013B/2665